A TEXTBOOK ON MUSLIM PERSONAL LAW

Second Edition

A TEXTBOOK ON MUSLIM PERSONAL LAW
2nd Edition

David Pearl

CROOM HELM
London • Sydney • Wolfeboro, New Hampshire

© 1987 David Pearl
Croom Helm Ltd, Provident House, Burrell Row,
Beckenham, Kent, BR3 1AT
Croom Helm Australia, 44-50 Waterloo Road,
North Ryde, 2113, New South Wales

British Library Cataloguing in Publication Data
Pearl, David
  A textbook on Muslim personal law. —
  2nd ed.
  1. Persons (Islamic law)
  I. Title   II. A textbook on Muslim Law
  342.61   [LAW]
  ISBN 0-7099-4089-0

Croom Helm, 27 South Main Street,
Wolfeboro, New Hampshire 03894-2069, USA

Library of Congress Cataloging-in-Publication Data
Pearl, David.
  A textbook on Muslim personal law.

  Rev. ed. of: A textbook on Muslim law. 1979.
  Bibliography: p.
  Includes index.
  1. Domestic relations (Islamic law) I. Pearl, David.
Textbook on Muslim law. II. Title.
LAW   340.5'9   86-24039
ISBN 0-7099-4089-0

Printed and bound in Great Britain by Mackays of Chatham Ltd, Kent

Contents

Preface

1. Historical Introduction   1

2. The Indian Subcontinent   20

2.1	English Law in India	21
2.1.1	The Formulas	29
2.2	Muslim Law and Customary Law	33
2.3	Muslim Law and the General Law	37

3. Marriage: Form and Capacity   41

3.1	The Nikah	41
3.1.1	Formal Requirements	41
3.1.2	Capacity	42
3.2	Classification	46
3.3	Batil Marriages	48
3.3.1	Blood Relatives (Nasab)	48
3.3.2	Relationship by Affinity (Musahara)	48
3.3.3	Relationship by Fosterage (Rada'a)	49
3.3.4	Illicit Sexual Impropriety	49
3.3.5	Remarriage to a Triply Divorced Wife	50
3.3.6	Polyandry	50
3.3.7	Differences of Religion	50
3.4	Fasid Marriages	53
3.4.1	Marriage Without Witnesses	53
3.4.2	The 'Idda	53
3.4.3	Polygamy	54

3.4.4	Unlawful Conjunction (Jam')	54
3.4.5	Kafa'a (Equality)	55
3.4.6	Conclusion	56

4. Marriage: Legal Effects   58

4.1	Sexual Relations	58
4.2	The Right of Control and Guidance	59
4.3	The Dower (Mahr)	60
4.3.1	Definitions	60
4.3.2	Specified Mahr	61
4.3.3	The Prompt and the Deferred Specified Dower	63
4.3.4	The Unspecified Dower	64
4.3.5	Reduction of Dower	64
4.3.6	Enforcement of Dower	65
4.3.6.1	The Deferred Dower	65
4.3.6.2	The Prompt Dower	67
4.4	Maintenance (Nafaqa)	68
4.4.1	Maintenance after Divorce	71
4.5	Property	75
4.6	Shi'i Law	75

5. Polygamy   77

6. Parent and Child   85

6.1	Legitimacy	85
6.1.1	Legitimacy by Birth (al-Walad l'il Firash)	85
6.1.2	Acknowledgement (Iqrar)	90
6.1.3	Adoption	91
6.2	Custody (Hadana)	92
6.3	Guardianship	97

Contents

| 6.3.1 | Property | 97 |
| 6.3.2 | Guardianship of Person (Jabr) | 98 |

7. Dissolution of Marriage — 100

7.1	The Rights of the Husband (the Talaq)	100
7.1.1	The Various Forms of Talaq	100
7.1.1.1	Talaq as-sunna (ahsan form)	100
7.1.1.2	Talaq as-sunna (hasan)	101
7.1.1.3	Talaq al-bid'a	101
7.1.2	Effect of Talaq	102
7.1.3	Formalities	102
7.1.4	Shi'i Law	104
7.1.4.1	Other forms of repudiation	104
7.1.5	Reform in the Muslim World	106
7.1.5.1	Reform in South Asia	109

| 7.2 | The Rights of the Wife | 120 |

7.3	Divorce by Consent of Both Parties	121
7.3.1	South Asia	122
7.3.2	Pakistan Developments	123

7.4	Divorce by Judicial Authority (Faskh)	130
7.4.1	Modern Reforms	131
7.4.1.1	Reforms in South Asia	134

8. The Laws of Inheritance — 138

| 8.1 | Administration of the Estate | 138 |

8.2	Testate Succession	142
8.2.1	Void and Ultra Vires Bequests	143
8.2.1.1	Sunni and Shi'i law	145

| 8.3 | Death Sickness | 146 |

8.4	Compulsory Succession	148
8.4.1	The Qur'anic Heirs	149
8.4.1.1	The Husband	150

Contents

8.4.1.2	The Wife	150
8.4.1.3	The Father	151
8.4.1.4	The True Grandfather	152
8.4.1.5	The Mother	152
8.4.1.6	The True Grandmother	156
8.4.1.7	The Daughter	156
8.4.1.8	The Son's Daughter	157
8.4.1.9	The Germane Sister; The Consanguine Sister	161
8.4.1.10	Uterine Brothers; Uterine Sisters	163
8.4.2	The Rules of Exclusion	166
8.4.3	The Agnatic Link	166
8.4.3.1	The Order	167
8.4.3.2	The Degree	167
8.4.4	Distant Kinsfolk and Associated Problems	167
8.5	Competence to Inherit	168
8.5.1	Religious Differences	169
8.5.2	Homicide	169
8.5.3	Illegitimacy	170
8.5.4	A Child en Ventre sa Mere	170
8.5.5	The Repudiated Wife	170
8.5.6	An Illustrative Case	171
8.6	Shi'i Law of Compulsory Succession	174
8.7	Reforms in the Islamic Law of Inheritance	178
8.7.1	Rigidity	179
8.7.2	The Wife's Share	179
8.7.3	Daughter and Son's Daughter	179
8.7.4	Representation	179
8.7.4.1	Pakistan	182
8.7.5	Fragmentation	187

9. Gift and Waqf 189

9.1	Gift	189
9.1.1	Revocation	192
9.1.2	Musha'	193
9.1.3	Hiba bi'l-iwad	193
9.1.4	Hiba bi'sharti'l-iwad	194

9.2	Waqf	194
9.2.1	Classical Law	194
9.2.2	India and Pakistan	198
9.2.2.1	An illustrative case	202
9.2.3	Waqf in East Africa	204
9.2.4	Modern Reforms	205

10. Conflict of Laws 207

10.1	Introduction	207
10.2	Interpersonal Conflicts within One Class	208
10.2.1	Traditional Law: Apostacy	209
10.2.2	Traditional Law: Conversion	211
10.2.3	Case Law and Statutes: Apostacy	212
10.2.4	Case Law and Statutes: Conversion	213
10.3	International Conflict of Laws	214
10.3.1	The Talaq	216
10.4	English Statutes and Cases	223
10.4.1	The UK Legislation	223
10.4.2	The Cases	225
10.4.3	Talaq Pronounced in England	227
10.4.3.1	Transnational talaq	227
10.4.3.2	Exemptions from Recognition	230
10.4.3.3	Financial Relief after overseas divorce	232
10.4.4	Conclusion	232

11. Conclusion 234

11.1	The Ottoman Reforms	234
11.2	Twentieth Century Reforms and the Codes	235
11.3	Early Family Law Reforms	236
11.4	Later Reforms	237
11.5	Islamicisation	238

Contents

11.5.1	Pakistan	239
11.6	Conclusion	244

Appendix I
		246
1.1	Jurisdictions outside South Asia	246
1.2	India, Pakistan, Bangladesh	247

Appendix II
		254
1.1	Indian Subcontinent	254
1.2	England	257
1.3	Elsewhere	258

Appendix III
		260
1.1	Preparatory Reading	260
1.2	Introduction to Civil Law	261
1.3	Textbooks on Family Law – General	261
1.4	Law Reform	261
1.5	History and Jurisprudence	262
1.6	Reception of English Law in India	262
1.7	Marriage and Divorce	263
1.7.1	Particular Countries	264
1.8	International and Internal Conflict of Laws	264
1.9	Inheritance	265
1.10	Waqfs	265

Appendix IV: Index and Glossary   266

Preface

The second edition of this book is published some seven years after the appearance of the first edition in 1979. The first edition was written as an attempt to provide the English reader with a simple and short guide to the major aspects of Islamic law. The emphasis was placed on domestic relations and inheritance law in India, Pakistan and Bangladesh. The emphasis remains the same for this second edition. It is in the family law area that Islamic law plays a major role and it is in South Asia where the bulk of the Muslim community who have settled in the UK have their roots.

I am grateful to those who reviewed the first edition and I have taken account of all these comments when preparing this new edition. As before, it is hoped that these pages will be of some value to those who wish to know about the background to the laws of Islam: whether it be as students, as lawyers with cases to argue before the courts, or as laymen and laywomen who are simply interested in increasing their knowledge. I have decided to leave out of this edition the collection of legislative documents which appeared in the first edition. This decision was prompted by considerations of space, but in any event there is an excellent collection of material edited by Professor Tahir Mahmood, and there is also the book written by Keith Hodkinson which provides the source material for South Asia (See Appendix III).

At the time of writing this preface, the UK Family Law Bill (1986) is still the subject of legislative discussion, having completed its stages in the House of Lords and gone through the formal first reading in the House of Commons. Part II of the Bill deals with the recognition of divorces, annulments and judicial separations obtained "overseas". The Bill repeals the Recognition of Foreign Divorces and Legal Separations Act 1971 and the Domicile and Matrimonial Proceedings Act 1973 in so far as it deals with this area of the law. In their place, is re-enacted the bases for the recognition of foreign divorces, including non-judicial divorces. A distinction, developed by case law, is now clearly made between the divorce obtained by proceedings (for example, the Pakistan talaq), and the divorce obtained otherwise than by means of proceedings (for example the talaq pronounced in India or Kashmir). In the former case, the talaq will be recognised in the UK if it is effective in Pakistan and at the relevant date either party was habitually resident, domiciled, or a national of that country. In the latter case, the so-called "bare" talaq from India or Kashmir will be recognised in the UK if it is effective by the law of the country where it was obtained (a new provision here) and if at the relevant date each party was domiciled in that country (or if only one is domiciled in that country, then the other is domiciled in another country where

Preface

the talaq is recognised). Recognition of a "bare" talaq is subject to the important proviso that no recognition will be afforded if one of the parties was habitually resident in the UK throughout the period of one year immediately preceeding the pronouncement. (Under the earlier legislation, both parties had to be resident here for one year to prevent recognition). Domicile is construed with reference either to the law in the UK where the issue arises or the law of the particular foreign country. There are discretionary grounds available to a judge to refuse recognition; the only new one being where there is no official document certifying that the divorce is effective under the law of the country where the divorce was obtained. In the case of "bare" talaq, lack of documentation may prove to be a major stumbling block to recognition. The law relating to the so-called transnational talaq will undoubtedly remain the same.

The cases discussed in this book have been taken from the major collections of Indian and Pakistan law reports; namely All India Reporter (AIR), Indian Law Reports (ILR), Pakistan Law Reports (PLD), and Law Reports Indian Appeals (LR IA). These Reports are available in Law Libraries in Oxford, Cambridge and London. Some of the less well known collections of cases, for example the Supreme Court Monthly Reports (SCMR) are not readily available outside the subcontinent, although Harvard Law School, as always, has a near perfect collection.

I have prepared this edition of the book on the University of Cambridge IBM Mainframe Computer (the Phoenix). I should like to thank the staff at the Computer Centre for helping me to grasp the complexities of the system. Even the Islamic laws of inheritance can appear as simplicity itself when set against the "logic" of the computer! Many bugs remained, and I must express a considerable debt to Yeshe Zangmo of the Research Centre for International Law who took over the final stages of the preparation, and who succeeded in extinguishing those bugs I had overlooked. My wife Gillian has been forced to live amongst piles of computer paper well beyond any call of duty. To her, I also say thank you.

The first edition of this book was dedicated to a decade of students who helped to create the book. This second edition is in turn dedicated to another group of students who have been no less patient.

DAVID PEARL.
Cambridge.

1. Historical Introduction

Joseph Schacht commenced his major work *An Introduction to Islamic Law* published in 1964 in the following manner: "The sacred law of Islam (Shari'a) is an all-embracing body of religious duties, the totality of Allah's commands that regulate the life of every Muslim in all its aspects." We can hardly improve on this statement. In the sacred law of Islam, the legal subject matter is but a part of the religious and ethical framework of life. This has been true from the very beginning of Islam; from the Qur'an itself. The essential feature of the Qur'an, the Holy Book of Islam revealed in the early seventh century to Mohammed, is that it is not a code of law. Only some eighty verses refer to legal topics and even in these verses there are both gaps as well as doubts as to whether the legal injunction is obligatory or permissive, as indeed whether it is subject to public or to private sanctions. Thus it is appropriate to describe Islamic law as consisting of the Qur'anic legislation which was subsequently interpreted by succeeding generations and which included much of the customary law of the Arabs. Indeed, the very nature of the Qur'an is such that it could not possibly be a comprehensive code of law. Legal precepts were revealed to Mohammed to meet certain contingencies of his experience as leader, in a pragmatic and empirical fashion. For instance, the fact that increasing numbers of Muslim males fell in battle acted as a catalyst to the verses which enjoined kindness to orphans and at the same time retained the practice of polygamy.[1] Another illustration is Sura XXXIII, verse 37, which abolished the pre-Islamic custom of adoption whereby an adopted child could be assimilated in law into another family. It may well be that the revelation of this verse was designed to settle the controversy which arose from the marriage of Mohammed to the divorced wife of his own adopted son, Zayd. A third illustration is Sura XXIV, verse 4, which lays down the penalty of 80 lashes for the offence of falsely accusing a woman of unchastity.[2] It is thought by some that this verse may well have been revealed after imputations of adultery against Mohammed's wife, 'A'isha.

These three examples should not in any way be seen as a challenge to the divinity of the Qur'an. Indeed, the reverse is intended; for the Qur'an is a contemporary document which reflects the life and aspirations of Mohammed

---

[1] Qur'an, Sura (Chapter) IV, verse 3.
[2] Qadhf.

and his followers in their efforts to create a new community from the desert wastes of Arabia. The legislation contained in the Qur'an, therefore, is piecemeal, superseding some, but certainly nothing near a majority, of the pre-Islamic customary laws of the Arabian communities.

It would be as well to outline in this general historical introduction the most important of the reforms introduced in the Qur'anic verses. First, and certainly of paramount importance, the Qur'an detailed fundamental changes in the laws of inheritance. By and large, the customary law in the pre-Islamic period was patrilineal. The right to inherit property belonged exclusively to the male agnatic relations of the deceased. All females were excluded from the scheme of succession, in part because they were non-combatants in the tribal disputes. The tribal unit was established so firmly that the nearest male agnate succeeded to the property to the exclusion of any other agnatic relation alive at the death of the deceased. Thus, the sons and their issue excluded the father; in the absence of lineal descendants, the father excluded the brothers and their issue; the brothers and their issue, so it is generally assumed, excluded the paternal grandfather; and finally the paternal grandfather excluded the uncles and the issue of the uncles.

The Muslim struggle against adversaries, which depleted the male members of the community leaving many scores of widows and orphans, inevitably interfered with the customary transfer of property on death. It was paramount to introduce generally a more extensive distributive system around the wider family circle, and, in particular, to involve female inheritance. Thus, the most far-reaching reform in the Qur'an in the legal field is contained in the verses which provided a series of fixed fractional inheritance rights to certain relatives of the deceased who, in the pre-Islamic customary law, may not have received any part of the estate.[3] The result of this revelationary material is to translate the old tribal bond of pre-Islamic Arabia into an extended-family bond of the Muslim community, politically allied by religion and legally allied by inheritance. However the new "sharers" did not supersede the old agnatic system; rather the Qur'an introduced the morality of Islam into the customary practices of the Arabs.

The second major reform of the Qur'an is in family law generally, and the status of women in particular. One of Mohammed's major aims was to alleviate the deprived role of the Arabian woman, and thus much of the legal material to be found in the Qur'anic verses concerns the very real attempt to enhance the legal position of the woman. In customary law, the woman was

---

[3] Qur'an, Sura IV, verses 7-14.

Historical Introduction

treated as an "object of sale"; she was fully exploited by her father, and she could be sold in marriage to the highest bidder. The husband was entitled to terminate the contract of marriage on any occasion and for any whim. Qur'anic legislation completely transformed this position. From an object of sale, the revelation directing the husband to pay a dower (mahr) to the wife, involved the wife as a contracting party in her own right.[4] The absolute right of repudiation (the talaq) is at least controlled by the introduction of the 'idda (waiting period) of three menstrual cycles during which time the husband is given the opportunity to reconsider his decision. The right of polygamy is restricted to four concurrent wives, and the husband is obliged to treat these wives equally.[5]

Beyond the prophetic revelation, Mohammed was concerned with the organisation of his religious community (the Umma). To adopt one phrase of Professor Coulson[6] he was the "judge-supreme" responsible for the interpretation of the revelations in the Qur'an to meet the particular problems as and when they arose. For instance, in one case which is known to us as Sa'ad's case, Mohammed worked out the exact relationship between the Qur'anic "sharers" and the pre-Islamic agnatic heirs. Sa'ad, so we are told, was one of the followers of Mohammed who fell in battle. On his death, Sa'ad's brother appropriated the whole of the estate. His widow sought assistance from Mohammed. The early commentators of the Qur'an tell us that Mohammed directed that Sa'ad's widow should take 1/8 from the estate (the sum which is prescribed in the Qur'an); the two daughters should take 2/3 (likewise as prescribed in the Qur'an) and then, that the residue, 5/24, should go to the brother as the agnate. This case, therefore, lays down the important rule that in a competition between the Qur'anic heirs and the "old" agnatic relations, the Qur'anic heirs have first claim on the estate. Other examples of this type of decision-making in the field of inheritance relate, first, to Mohammed's restriction of the power to make bequests to 1/3 of the estate, and, second, to his refusal to permit the making of a bequest in favour of any heir.

This type of synthesis of the Qur'anic revelations with the pre-Islamic custom is almost certainly as far as one can go in the description of the early historical developments of the law without entering into controversial territory. The major question, and perhaps one which requires some sort of explanation

---

[4] Qur'an, Sura IV, verse 19.
[5] Qur'an, Sura IV, verse 3.
[6] N.J.Coulson, *A History of Islamic Law* (Edinburgh, 1964) (paperback edition, 1978 at p. 28).

Historical Introduction

at the outset, but to which we shall return, is: how much of the law now in existence and which is called Islamic law (the Shari'a) can be historically attributed to the words and deeds of Mohammed. The classical formulation of the sources of Islam was worked out some two centuries after Mohammed's death and, as we shall describe, this formulation attributes to Mohammed himself the collection of what are referred to as authentic Hadith (traditions) which, after the Qur'an, is the second of the classical sources of law. The Hadith is seen to be the evidence of what is known as Sunna (practice of the community). Literally, Sunna means the "trodden path" and it is often used to express the customary law prevalent in Arabia before the advent of Islam. After the revelation, the "trodden path" continued to be the accepted law for the Muslim community; but only in so far as it had not been abrogated by Mohammed. The classical theory states that on the advent of Islam the concept of Sunna became, for the Muslim, the model or the normative behaviour of the Prophet. Thus, the Western orientalist Goldhizer refers to the classical concept of Sunna as "all that could be shown to have been the practices of the Prophet and his earliest followers". Hadith describe the "report" or evidence of the Prophet's behaviour. It is self-evident that, for the classical jurist as for the religious Muslim today, Sunna and Hadith are consubstantial in that they refer to the same substantive law. The Sunna is related by traditions known as Hadith. Orientalists do not see the picture exactly this way. The controversy surrounding the legal innovation of Mohammed can best be described by the following question: is it correct to refer to the Hadith as the second source of Islamic law, remembering that the Hadith were collected and compiled some two centuries after Mohammed's death, or rather are the collections an attempt to attribute to the Prophet either, first, the origin for the Sunna which had developed since his death or, second, to undermine the Sunna which had developed in order, for political reasons, to return to what was thought to be the "pristine purity" of the Qur'an? Western orientalists since Goldhizer have doubted the authenticity of large tracts of the Hadith material in their attribution to the Prophet. Particularly, J. Schacht in his seminal work, *Origins of Muhammedan Jurisprudence*, reaches the conclusion that the Sunna, by and large, is anterior to the Hadith rather than being either the reverse or consubstantial.

Be this as it may, Hadith material is in two parts – the text and the transmissional chain (isnad) which provides the names of the narrators supporting the text.[7] The classical theory is that the authenticity of the Hadith

---

[7] For a good intoduction to the material, see A.Rahman I.Doi *Introduction to the Hadith* (Sevenoaks, 1981).

Historical Introduction

is dependent upon the strength of the isnad. The text itself is not subject to critical analysis. It must be stressed, however, that even if one accepts as essentially valid the view of Schacht, this does not in any way at all contradict the ideal vision of an apostolic behaviour. As a source of law, this "behaviour" is second only to the Qur'an. Whether the mass of material reflects the seventh century of Mohammed or a later period of the jurists and administrators is, of course, at the essence of the controversy – but it is rather beside the point. No one doubts that the Hadith collections became the vital source for all decisions in the Muslim world.

It is self-evident that it is necessary to keep firmly in one's mind the vital distinction between the "classical" formulation of the sources of Islamic law on the one hand, and the actual or "material" sources of the law on the other. The Hadith collections are the second of the classical sources after the Qur'an, although the Sunna of Mohammed – his decisions and his actions – represents the beginning of the "material" sources. This Sunna, in part a theoretical idealism, although it cannot be doubted that it includes actual practice, was continued by Mohammed's successors – the four Caliphs: namely Abu Bakr, 'Umar, 'Uthman and 'Ali. The Caliphs continued to solve in an *ad hoc* manner the cases which came before them. The solutions were based on interpretations of the Qur'an from where they drew their source. Two examples can be given.[8] Both examples appear in later Hadith collections, and thus it can be postulated that they both express a decision of a later age turned into a norm by the classical exposition of that other age. It would be consistent with the development of the law, however, to accept both decisions as examples of a gradual filling in of the gaps of the Qur'anic legislation.

The first example is known as the Himariyya or Donkey Case. In this case, a woman died leaving a husband, a mother, two uterine brothers and two full brothers. In the normal Qur'anic distribution, the husband would be entitled to 1/2 of the estate, the mother to 1/6 and the uterine brothers, as Qur'anic heirs, would take 1/3. The full brothers, the agnatic heirs, represented the old pre-Qur'anic inheritors. The Qur'anic heirs, in this situation, exhaust the estate. The full brothers appealed to 'Umar against this decision on the grounds that, as they had the same mother as the deceased – indeed as they possessed the very same quality of relationship which was the exclusive basis of the uterine brothers' right of inheritance, they should be entitled to participate in the inheritance. 'Umar accepted this argument and permitted the full brothers the right to share equally with the uterine brothers in 1/3 of the estate. As the full

---

[8] cf. Coulson, op.cit. pp 24, 25.

brothers claimed to be entitled by virtue of their uterine relationship, this decision represented a victory for the Qur'anic sharers and a defeat for the old agnatic relationship. Indeed, the full brothers are reputed to have told 'Umar, "Assume that our father does not count, consider him a donkey" (a himar).

The second example of this process of decision-making is taken from the caliphate of 'Ali and is known as the Minbariyya (Pulpit Case). 'Ali was faced with the problem of the distribution of an estate between a wife, a father, a mother and two daughters. The Qur'anic distribution would have produced a situation where the estate was exhausted before all the heirs had been fully satisfied. The two daughters obtained 2/3, the father and the mother 1/6 each and the wife 1/8. In solving the difficulty, 'Ali adopted the principle of proportional abatement; thus the wife's share was reduced from 1/8 to 1/9 and the shares of the other relations were abated in proportion.

These two decisions exemplify the piecemeal character of the Caliphs' judgments. They were content to solve problems as and when they arose. In essence, they were filling in the gaps to the Qur'anic legislation. In doing this, the Caliphs were providing the clothes for the bare skin of the revelation. For instance, drinking of wine is prohibited in the Qur'an; but no penalty is laid down. Abu Bakr fixed the penalty at 40 lashes but 'Umar and later 'Ali extended this punishment to 80 lashes. This result was arrived at by analogy with the offence of false accusation of unchastity (qadhf)[9] where the Qur'an had fixed the penalty at 80 lashes. This filling in of gaps continued at least until the founding of the Umayyad dynasty in 661 AD, when it can be said that the formative period came to an end.

In the second period, that is from 661 AD until the end of the Umayyad dynasty in 750 AD, the essential factor contributing to the development of the law was undoubtedly the extension of Muslim rule to the non-Arab territories, and in particular the growth of trading contacts with Byzantium and Persia. Inevitably, Byzantine and Persian legal concepts infiltrated into the Muslim legal philosophy. A few well known examples will suffice for present purposes.

First, one can point to the development of the civil and political status of the non-Muslim communities. Certain non-Muslim citizens of the Muslim state are permitted to reside on Muslim soil in return for the payment of the jizya (the poll tax) and the kharaj (the land tax). They are known as the Dhimmi

---

[9] Qur'an, Sura XXIV, verse 4.

Historical Introduction

communities.[10] The status of Dhimmi was evolved from a fictional contract (the Dhimma) and it is right to point out the similarities with concepts both in Roman and in Jewish law. The details of the Dhimmi/Muslim relationship were laid down by the Umayyad administration showing their major preoccupation; an organised empire with systematic tax laws, law courts and a disciplined administration. Muslim practice recognises the existence of non-Muslims, and allows them to be governed by their own laws. In this basic administrative decision, Muslim law tacitly accepts within its own territory the principle known as "personality of laws". In doing this, the principles of the ancient Hebrews, the Greeks and the Romans are continued.

Similarly, the Umayyads adopted the Byzantine market inspector (the *Agoronomus*), assimilated him to Islamic practice, and granted him a new extended responsibility. He was called the Muhtasib, and he was responsible not only for market affairs but also for safeguarding the standards of religious morality (the hisba).[11]

The Ummayads were also responsible for the introduction of the position of the Qadi. The Qadi served as a judicial officer of state, usually appointed by the Governor of the area in question. Quite naturally, as state appointees, the Qadis often met hostile opposition from the learned men ('Ulema) of the community. The 'Ulema as a body, adopted the attitude that the Qadis, especially when appointed from amongst their own ranks, tended to

---

[10] The Dhimmis are ahl al-Kitab (people of the book). Jews and Christians fall into this category. Magians are referred to in the same verse (Qur'an, Sura XXII, verse 17) although it is controversial whether they should be correctly thought of as Dhimmis. 'Ali is reported as saying that the Magians were once in possession of a scripture, but that they had lost this work. Most Muslim opinion would accept the Magians into the status of Dhimmi. The actual historical experience of the Muslims is different from the Qur'anic formulation. When the Muslims landed in India, for example, they discovered that the Hindus were so numerous that it would have been physically impossible to carry out the injunctions of Islam. Hindus therefore were quickly assimilated into the status of Dhimmi.

One must also contrast the status of Dhimmi with the institution of Musta'min. The Dhimmi is a citizen of the Islamic state, whereas the Musta'min is a foreigner who is granted protection for a period of upto one year whilst he remains in the Islamic state. If he breaks the pledge, the protection ends and he becomes a Harbi (a person from the land of War). See B.Lewis, *The Jews of Islam*. (Princeton, 1984).

[11] Qur'an Sura III, verses 104, 110. For an interesting account of the "public morality committees" in Saudi Arabia today, representing as it does a modern version of the hisba, see A.Layish "'Ulema and Politics in Saudi Arabia." in *Islam and Politics in the Modern Middle East* (London, 1984) ed. M.Heper and R.Israeli p. 29 at p. 35.

Historical Introduction

compromise themselves. It is the case that some Qadis were open to influence, especially in the early period. However, it is far from the truth to say that all Qadis behaved in such a manner. Indeed, the reverse is the case. The decisions of the Qadis on the cases which came before them contributed towards a strong local influence around certain towns. This comes down the centuries as an early vital expression of the Muslim legal process. Quite naturally, in such a diverse empire as that of the Umayyad, the development of the law by the Qadis' courts showed marked peculiarities from area to area. One can surmise that the Governors did indeed interfere from time to time but, as a general rule, Qadis were free to interpret and develop the Islamic law in their own way.

At this early stage, a division can be noticed already between the practice of the Qadis in Kufa as opposed to the practice in Medina. Broadly, the practice in Medina represented the stricter interpretation of Qur'anic injunctions whereas Kufa, with its cosmopolitan outlook, provided a venue for a wider legal fusion of ideas which resulted for example in a set of marriage laws which was substantially more tolerant towards the rights of women. Such differences represent the early stages of diversity in the growth of Islamic law. Indeed, these differences are the first signs of the separation of the schools of Islamic law. All Qadis exercised a discretion (ra'y) in the administration of the law. In strict theory, the ra'y was subject to the overriding authority of the Umayyad dynasty – but such authority was rarely exercised.

It has been shown that there were three major "material" sources of the Islamic law: first, pre-Islamic custom, second, other legal systems, and, third, the interpretations by the Qadis through their undoubted exercise of ra'y. These three sources of law provided a diversity in practice which was accepted, at the time, by all as being in consonance with the requirements of Islam.

From 720 AD, a schism is apparent in the administration of the law. The religious leaders sided increasingly with those who were to become the leaders of the Abbasid regime. The Umayyad dynasty came under the combined attack of the theologians and the frustrated politicians. Indeed, criticism of the Umayyads was present even amongst the ranks of the Qadis; the later Umayyad governors relied more and more heavily on the theologians as Qadis. It was natural that the theologians were less prepared to adopt their own independent judgment (ra'y) if it in any way conflicted with the injunctions of the Qur'an. Joseph Schacht aptly states the position when he writes of the later Umayyad Qadis that "they impregnated the sphere of law with religious and ethical ideas, subjected it to Islamic norms, and incorporated it into the body

Historical Introduction

of duties incumbent on every Muslim."[12] Schacht goes on to comment that the consequence of this impregnation was that the "popular and administrative practice of the late Umayyad period was transformed into the religious law of Islam". Thus for Schacht the beginning of Islamic law proper is dated between 720 and 750 AD – some one hundred years after the Prophetic period. Naturally, such a view is heretical for the religious Muslim scholar. His thesis, however, has been accepted by modern orientalists as essentially sound. Certainly, the classical formulation of the sources of law was a post-720 AD development; thus the controversy, important as it is, centres around the relevance of the early material which we have described, on the Islamic law as it existed in 750 AD.

There are some general points which do not arouse controversy. We know, for example, that the majority of the theologians refrained from accepting political appointments. Rather, they established schools of discussion and learning and, gradually, they developed a system of responsa to questions which were put to them on Islamic ethics and practice. These jurist-theologians were certainly the founders of the early schools of law. In a very loose sense, "schools" were established in a number of centres, the most important being Kufa, Medina, Basra, Mecca and Damascus. The major area of difficulty surrounds the activity of these jurist-theologians.[13] Their aim was to "break out" of the rigid administrative machinery established by the Umayyads. Schacht argues that the theologians accepted the existence of an "actual custom" of the local community, that they were instigators not so much for their views of the actual custom but for the creation of a normative Sunna, or "law as it ought to be". According to Schacht, it was in this way that the early theorists, through their own concept of ra'y, developed a normative value for the Sunna. It must be remarked that the ra'y of the jurist differed from the empirical decision-making of the Qadi. The ra'y for the jurist was a composite concept based upon the consensus of opinion of a number of scholars, all of whom had worked out solutions to particular theoretical problems. This type of consensus is referred to as ijma', a concept to which it will be necessary to return. Another quite useful way to explain the Sunna/Hadith paradigm is that Sunna contains within it two ideas bound together, namely continuity and normativeness. These two ideas were fused into a whole by the development of the traditions (Hadith).

---

[12] J.Schacht, *An Introduction to Islamic Law*, (Oxford, 1964) (paperback reprint, 1982) at p. 27.

[13] See G.Makdisi, *The Rise of Colleges: Institutions of Learning in Islam and the West*, (Edinburgh, 1981).

Historical Introduction

At first, the tradition was projected back to certain early specialists of the region. For instance, in Kufa, the early traditions were ascribed to Ibrahim Nakha'i. Later, in order perhaps to provide the continuity with more authority, the Kufa school ascribed the doctrine to the companions of Ibn Mas'ud (a companion of the Prophet). Somewhat later, the authority is derived from Ibn Mas'ud himself. It was natural for this development (taqlid) to reach ultimately and inevitably the source of all inspiration, the Prophet himself. Thus, some years before the systematised Hadith (reports) had been accepted as a basis for the law, the Iraqis certainly had become used to the idea of Sunna as representing the normative behaviour of the Prophet, as well as the living practice of the community. As the schools became institutionalised, the normative Sunna was stressed more to the exclusion of the practice of the law. The opposition of the schools to the late Umayyads, as well as the sponsorship by the early Abbasid Caliphs, stimulated this trend. It was only natural for the Abbasids, who were eager to show themselves as the true expression of Islamic piety, to encourage any philosophy which tried to cut through the Umayyad administration in order to return to the purity of the source of Islam. Thus the early Abbasid regime sponsored the views of the jurists; and more of their rank were appointed as Qadis than hitherto. Abu Yusuf is an outstanding example. Such appointments naturally stimulated the movement toward the integration between practice and theory.

In order to illustrate how these early scholars developed the law, it would be useful to say a word about the type of legal reasoning employed by them. The chief characteristic of the time was the use of analogy (qiyas). For instance, the characteristics of mahr (dower) given by the husband to the wife on marriage were not sufficiently detailed in the Qur'an, so it was necessary to develop the principles of the law on this subject, in particular to decide upon a minimum acceptable sum. In Kufa, this sum was fixed at 10 dirhams; perhaps because this was also the minimum value of goods which rendered a thief liable to the compulsory punishment of amputation of the hand. A parallel is here drawn between the loss of virginity and the amputation of the hand. In Medina, where 3 dirhams was the value the goods had to amount to before the thief was subjected to the penalty of amputation, a similar analogical deduction led to the minimum dower being fixed at 3 dirhams.

Around 770 AD, the doctrinaire adherents of what we have referred to as the "normativeness of Sunna" began to make themselves more influential than the older group of scholars who, as we have seen, were prepared to accept the contemporaneity of the Sunna. It was at this stage that the Hadith (reports) came into their own, with those of the doctrinaire viewpoint who wished it, using the Hadith material as a way to circumvent the practice of the Qadi. It

Historical Introduction

will be apparent that this conflict of legal theory was won, and won decisively, by the doctrinaire. Living traditions and independent reasoning (ra'y) give way to systematic thought and consistent doctrine. As pupil follows master, this tendency becomes more marked. Practical solutions, with their almost vulgar analogical reasoning, are replaced by an increasing reliance on the traditions of the Prophet and his companions. But even within this new consistency, differences of opinion are not uncommon. If there is a division of opinion in one geographical area, such as Kufa, it is natural for there to be vast conflicts of legal thought between one centre of law and another. In Medina for instance, slaves had a right of ownership reflecting the Arab tradition, but in Kufa, possibly through Roman influences, slaves – being owned themselves – could not own. There are many other examples: for example, in the field of inheritance the Kufans recognised the rights of distant kindred to succeed to an estate in the absence both of Qur'anic sharers and the traditional agnatic relatives. This was not accepted in Medina.

The ancient schools of law built up around themselves an ijma' – a consensus – on a number of points which often differed in principles and certainly differed in detail from other schools. As we have indicated on more than one occasion, the biggest controversy at this time was between the ahl al-ra'y, those who believed in the value of individual reasoning, and the ahl al-Hadith, those who, contrariwise, believed in the authority of the Hadith to the exclusion of all independent reasoning. This conflict is certainly reflected in early writers such as Malik, Abu Laila and so on, but the man who successfully integrated the two points of view was Shafi'i. He was born in 767 AD and he died in 820 AD. He was an adherent of the Medina school.

It is simplest, within the context of this short historical introduction, to describe Shafi'i's concept of law by reference to a number of general statements. First, and certainly by far most importantly, Shafi'i accepted the principal contention of the traditionalists. Thus, for Shafi'i, as for the traditionalist, a Hadith could not be overridden by a contrary practice (Sunna) of the community. Put another way, Shafi'i's thesis, in essence, was based on the acceptance of the normative value of Sunna and the rejection of its continuity. Second, it is true that Shafi'i accepted the paradox that Sunna as he understood it could not even be superseded by the Qur'an, for the Hadith, divinely inspired as it was, could not *contradict* an express revelation in the Qur'an. Thus what may appear to be a contradiction of a Hadith by the Qur'an was far from the case for a further Hadith must surely exist in conformity with the revelation. Further, the Hadith was to be tested only by the chain of authority (isnad) and no other reasoning could be applied to test its veracity. Fourth, Shafi'i rejected ijma' as the consensus of the scholars and reconstructed it as the consensus of the Muslim community. Finally, and in summary, Shafi'i rejected all forms of ra'y, only allowing independent reasoning in the form of qiyas (analogical deduction). Even here, however, qiyas was restricted in that it could only be of value in applying Qur'an, Sunna or ijma' to problems which had not been expressly answered. Shafi'i's work, as accepted by the jurists, brought to an end the use of ra'y by the early schools.

The corpus of the law introduced by the ra'y, however, had become part of the Sunna of the community. Shafi'i's interpretation meant the end of the *dual aspect* of Sunna, but the substantive law which had been integrated into the Shari'a was not rejected. Some people indeed believe that Hadith were created in order to provide authority for the rules of law which had come into existence as a result of this ra'y. Of those who believe in this development, the major exponent, of course, is Joseph Schacht. In essence, Schacht's argument is that Shafi'i was the first man to use traditions of the Prophet as absolute authority. Before him, as for his contemporaries, traditions existed but they were interpreted in the light of the "living tradition". Schacht argues that the classical collections, collected by al-Bukhari, Muslim, Abu Dawud, at-Tirmidhi, an-Nasa'i, and Ibn Maja, all in the third century of Islam, carry within their corpus many traditions which cannot be authentic. The pioneering orientalist, Goldhizer, had long before doubted the "prophetic" end product of the isnad (the chain) and he had suggested that most of the traditions belonged to the first century of Islam rather than to the period of Mohammed. Schacht goes further, and states that a great deal of the Hadith material in the classical collections was put into circulation only *after* Shafi'i's time. Indeed, Schacht is not prepared to date any tradition further back than the latter period of the Umayyad caliphate. It is his view that traditionalists started to circulate Hadith in order to overcome the administrative secularism and pragmatism of the Umayyad Qadis as well as the "living traditions" of the early schools of law. Another leading Western Islamicist, Professor Noel Coulson, whilst accepting the broad sweep of Schacht's analysis, criticises Schacht's theory in a number of areas.[14] He believes that the immediate concerns of the Muslim community during the revelationary period involved Mohammed in the task of making *ad hoc* decisions. These decisions were necessarily publicised by word of mouth; thus early traditions came into existence based on authentic statements and determinations of the Prophet. This early work of Mohammed is, by and large, acknowledged by Schacht; thus Coulson would argue that the acceptance of

---

[14]   N.J.Coulson, *A History of Islamic Law* op.cit. in particular in ch.5.

Historical Introduction

Schacht's thesis assumes a void in the picture of the development of law in early Muslim society. Coulson agrees with Schacht that the isnad is unreliable, but that, nevertheless, the character of the classical Hadith collections contains substantive law which is undeniably traceable to Mohammed's time. Coulson would say also that to prove the invalidity of one chain does not thereby prove the fraudulence of the entire corpus of the Hadith. As he says: "Where the rule [in the Hadith] fits naturally into the circumstances of the Prophet's community at Medina, then [the Hadith] should be tentatively accepted as authentic until reason for the contrary is shown."[15]

It is of course beyond doubt that Shafi'i's vision was an important contributory factor towards the further development of the schools of law. After Shafi'i, scholars devoted their time to sifting the "reliable" Hadith from those deemed to be "unreliable". Thus it is not inconceivable that in this process previously forgotten Hadith were brought to light.

The essential point is simply this: even if the historical criticisms of Schacht (moderated or not by Coulson) are accepted, the concept of Sunna as Shafi'i had expounded it was accepted by the scholars and the resultant compilations of Hadith became the primary code of Islamic jurisprudence. The study of Hadith literature profoundly influenced the next ten centuries of Muslim life. In essence, the previous use of ra'y (independent reasoning) came to an end; the only permitted human reasoning (qiyas) was so framed by Shafi'i as to be dependent entirely on the discipline of the Qur'an and the Sunna. The law was bound to cease its accelerating pace – and to become enshrined in Shafi'i's classical mould.

It is desirable, at this stage, to summarise the situation as it existed after Shafi'i's death in 820 AD, by way of tracing, albeit in outline, the doctrine of *Usul al-fiqh* (the sources of law). There are four sources of law – Qur'an, Sunna, ijma' and qiyas. It has been shown that these sources were developed by two centuries of experience. Classical Islamic theology, however, denies this historical approach. It is important, therefore, to remember that the classical exposition of the sources of the law of Islam carries within itself the fundamental belief that the Qur'an, Sunna, ijma' and qiyas – as a theory of the Shari'a – were laid down from the beginning of the Muslim exegesis.

The most important contribution that ijma' made was its overpowering idea of the agreement (consensus) of the Umma (community) as represented by the scholars that the classical sources of the law – and of the contents of the law at that time – were the authoritative Islam. "The Umma could not

---

[15] ibid.p.70.

Historical Introduction

agree on an error" was enshrined in a retrospective sense; but from that moment on, ijma' becomes exclusionary. Having agreed – or more correctly having agreed to differ – on the nass (the text), a consensus developed that all essential questions had been discussed and settled. Thus from that time on, no one would have the necessary qualifications for independent reasoning in the law. The position which is taken from then on is taqlid (imitation) and a person who is bound to practice taqlid is the muqallid (the imitator).

Thus, the theory of the law denies the right of ra'y. Of course, the actual historical experience of the Qadis, and even of the ancient schools, had been different. The use of human reasoning had played a part in the development of Islamic law, and the jurists of the ninth century appear to have recognised this point in albeit an indirect fashion when they acknowledge the existence of a number of subsidiary sources of law, primarily three in number: ijtihad, istihsan and istislah.

Ijtihad, meaning "an effort", is not strictly a source of law at all; but rather a method by which the Mujtahid (the person who exercises ijtihad) recognises and makes known the legal meaning of the Qur'anic rule or the Sunna. Put another way, ijtihad can be seen to be a method by which the will of Allah is discovered. After the Mujtahid exercises his ijtihad, the consensus of opinion will either reject or accept the theory. If it is accepted by ijma', it becomes an incorporated part of the Shari'a. As it has been already shown, ijma', as a doctrine, carries within it the idea of "no contradiction". Thus from about 900 AD, the exercise of ijtihad has exhausted itself, and from that date the door of independent reasoning is closed. Indeed, some historians refer to the early tenth century as the date of the closing of the door of ijtihad.

The other two subsidiary sources, istihsan and istislah, are but examples of particular forms of ra'y. Thus, when the early jurists, especially those of Kufa, exercised independent reasoning (ra'y) because of the appropriateness of the decision, then the technical term which we ought to employ is istihsan (derived from the word hasan which means to deem or to make something good).[16] One example will be sufficient to illustrate the use of istihsan, from

---

[16] For an important article on istihsan, see John Makdisi "Legal logic and equity in Islamic law." 1985 AJCL vol XXXIII p.63. Makdisi argues that istihsan is the determination of a solution to a legal case based on either (1) a direct provision in the Qur'an, Sunna, or consensus, or (2) reasoning by analogy from one of these three sources. Makdisi says: "[Istihsan] may be motivated by an interest in promoting the public good, taking into consideration need, necessity, interest, convenience and ease, but it must be justified by a provision in the [Qur'an], sunna or consensus, or by a cause ('illa) found through a study of these texts from these sources."

Historical Introduction

the law relating to hire. The consideration which is required for the hire of an object or a person is considered normally in Islamic law necessarily to involve non-fungible objects such as gold or silver. Sunna, however, always allowed the hire of a wet nurse in return for her food and clothing. Early jurists, faced both with the concept of hire as well as the exceptional situation relating to the hire of a wet nurse, exercised istihsan, the juristic preference, and thus permitted the hire of a wet nurse in return for her food and clothing.

Istislah, stemming from the word salih, "in the general interest", is used to express the occasions when the judge or the 'Ulema exercised ra'y out of consideration of the public interest. One example will suffice from the Medinan attitude to the law of sale. The Islamic concept of bay' (sale) is based on the belief that one contract cannot hinge upon the performance of a separate extraneous agreement. Such a contract is batil (void). By strict qiyas, therefore, a contract between A and B whereby A buys leather on condition that B makes the leather into a pair of shoes is void. Well before Shafi'i's work, such a contract was seen by the jurists to be of particular benefit; thus by istislah the Medinans permitted the contract in question.

It has been illustrated that istislah and istihsan were two unorthodox uses of qiyas. Shafi'i obviously disapproved of the procedures. For instance, of the Iraqi school at Kufa he said, "They are accustomed to say 'The qiyas would be but we practice istihsan.'" These methods were grave infringements upon the consistent doctrine of usul al-fiqh as enunciated by Shafi'i. Both istihsan and istislah permitted the use of discretion and personal reasoning, even within certain ascertainable limits; thus they were both unacceptable.

It has been illustrated already that Shafi'i's theories on law were approved by those immediately after him; so it was inevitable that regardless of the adjustments and rationalisations of the previous practice which were bound to take place, the use of istihsan and istislah would quickly be terminated. This is indeed what happened; but we now touch upon one of the most important aspects of the early development of the law. The legal material which had been introduced by the jurisprudential techniques was not abrogated. It all remained within the corpus of Islamic law to be justified by the schools in one of two ways. First, later scholars "traced back" concepts introduced by istihsan to a Hadith. Second, by the doctrine of ijma', the ra'y of the scholars and Qadis in all the schools was accepted as part of the Shari'a for all time. And, further, the prohibition of any further ra'y denied the right of the Mujtahid to change the law which had been accepted by the consensus.

We must now turn our attention to the subsequent history of the schools after Shafi'i. We have seen that centres of learning had sprung up whose purpose was to discuss law on a theoretical plane. These groups, often simply

Historical Introduction

because of the impact of geographical distance, developed both their own peculiar laws and methods of reasoning. Later, due to the influence of Malik, Hanifa, Abu Yusuf, Shaybani and the others, the schools continued to grow apart.

Shafi'i's aim had been centred on his vision of the unity of Islam in both theory and practice. Did he succeed? In one respect, it is possible to answer this question in the affirmative. The classical theory is impregnated by Shafi'i's doctrine, and the only major difference (although admittedly this difference is of some consequence) is that the classical system gives prominence to ijma' and reverts to the pre-Shafi'i idea when ijma' referred to the consensus of the scholars rather than the consensus of the Umma (community). In another respect he failed. New schools arose as a direct result of Shafi'i's work. Law introduced by ra'y, now given the weight of acceptance through ijma' and almost certainly having acquired Hadith as justification, continued as orthodox doctrine within the corpus of Islam. The unorthodox background was conveniently forgotten.

There are four Sunni schools surviving today: Hanafi, Maliki, Shafi'i, and Hanbali. A number of other schools, at one time or another, had been accepted as orthodox interpretations of the Shari'a, but they have not survived. Dawad ibn Khalaf was the founder of a literal school, called the Zahiri. This school has now become extinct. The diversity of the Shari'a between the four schools was accepted by the classical jurisprudence under the umbrella of ijma'.

The Hanafi school was officially adopted by the Abbasid dynasty. It spread to Afghanistan, and to the Indian subcontinent. Emigrants from India spread the school to East Africa and to Malaysia. The Ottoman Empire recognised the Hanafi interpretation; thus Hanafi law is today followed in Turkey, Iraq, Syria, the Balkan countries, Cyprus, Jordan, Sudan, Israel, Egypt and Libya. The Maliki school grew out of the school in Medina. It spread to Egypt, Sudan, Eritrea, Somaliland, Libya, Tunisia, Algeria, Morocco, Central and West Africa and northern Nigeria. It is also practised in the eastern coastal territories of Arabia, bordering on the Gulf. The Shafi'i school, beginning in Cairo where Shafi'i lived for the last five years of his life, spread to South Arabia, the Indian coastline, and then via the Arab trade routes to East Africa and South-East Asia. Shafi'i Muslims predominate in Malaysia, Singapore, Indonesia, the Philippines and Sri Lanka. The fourth surviving school, Hanbali, affirms the traditionalist approach. Before Iran became sectarian, the Hanbali school of thought had many adherents there. Often on the edge of extinction, it was revived by the puritanical movements of the eighteenth and early twentieth centuries. Hanbali law is today followed in Saudi Arabia – but nowhere else.

Historical Introduction

It is true to say that whilst in the Hanafi and Maliki schools, practice came first, and theory only later; in Hanbali and Shafi'i law, by contrast, the theory of law preceded the practice of the law. From this fact, it might be thought that one would be correct to deduce that the content of the Hanbali and Shafi'i law would be closer to each other than the content between Hanafi and Maliki. Broadly, this is indeed correct. Stemming from this, the law developed by istihsan and istislah had become part of Hanafi and Maliki law. The later schools had no such wealth of historical material. Ijma', however, acted as a unifying force which tended from then on to draw the substantive law of the four schools closer together.

So far, we have considered only the Sunni system of Islamic law. Outside the Sunni law, however, there developed sectarian schools. It is necessary in the context of this introduction to say a few words on this phenomenon. A large group within the Muslim community in the world today does not profess adherence to any of the four schools of Sunni Islam; rather this group belongs to one of the branches of Shi'i law; namely the Ithna 'Ashari, or the Isma'ili; or possibly also the Zaydi. This third group, the Zaydis, technically *sui generis*, are mostly to be found in the Yemen. Their legal system represents a fusion of Sunni and Shi'i beliefs. They are not numerically strong. The Ithna 'Ashari group, representing the majority of Shi'i Muslims, are to be found in Iran, Iraq, and in India. The Isma'ilis – themselves divided – are present in Central Asia, Iran and the Gulf.

The Shi'i movement is rooted firmly in political schism. During the reign of the fourth Caliphate of 'Ali, a civil war resulted in victory to Mu'awiya who inaugurated the Umayyad dynasty. However, a group refused to accept the inevitable and gave their support to 'Ali and to his issue. 'Ali had married Fatima, the daughter of Mohammed. The followers of 'Ali (the Shi'at 'Ali) believe in the concept that the successors of Mohammed inherit the title of Imam by divine right. To this extent, they deny the right of the first three Caliphs to the caliphate.

After the death of the fourth Imam, Zayn al-Abidin, one of his sons (Zayd) was accepted as Imam by a group of followers who came to be called Zaydis. They differ from the other Shi'i groups in that they recognise that succession to the Imamate depends on election rather than on the divine right. The majority, at this period of schism, followed Muhamad al-Baqir and, after him, Ja'far al-Sadiq. When Sadiq died, another split occurred. Most adherents supported Musa al-Kazim and the six Imams after him. The twelfth leader was the last, and believers say that it is this Imam who will return to herald the Messianic age. Sadiq's elder brother, Isma'il, led the other faction; and his supporters came to be called Isma'ilis or Seveners. Thus, Shi'is are divided amongst themselves. Their laws will be discussed when we turn to the discussion of the substantive law.

It is necessary, however, before we draw our introductory remarks to a conclusion to return to the administration of the law as we have so far described it. The Qadis assumed jurisdiction in only a *small* area of the law. Jurisdiction in other courts beyond that of the Qadi emerged for a number of interconnected reasons. First, and perhaps of fundamental importance, the Shari'a law as applied by the Qadis was, as we have seen, concerned essentially with the relationship between God and man. This relationship expresses itself in the sphere of family law and succession. It is relevant in other areas, such as public law, but only to a minor extent. The lack of interest of the Shari'a in public matters necessitated the development of secular courts. The Sahib ar-radd often assumed criminal jurisdiction; the mazalim (those in charge of complaints) came to control questions relating to land. In both these spheres of human enterprise, the importance of the subject-matter for the government, as well as the marked initial lack of interest by the Qadis, was responsible for the development of separate governmental courts. Mazalim jurisdiction, in particular, developed in Abbasid times. Indeed it has been observed by Coulson, amongst others, that the distinction between the jurisdiction of the mazalim and the Shari'a came very close to the notion of a division between secular and religious courts. Thus, centuries before any reception of European law, the Muslim community was used to the separation of powers between the religious courts, which dealt with personal matters, and the secular mazalim jurisdiction, which, though still within the corpus of Muslim law, was responsible for criminal law and land law.[17]

There is a second reason for the growth of secular jurisdiction; namely the highly formalised and complex evidential rules prevalent in the Qadis' courts. These rules are based on oath-taking (yamun). The Qadi, in the first instance, questions the defendant (the mudda'a 'allayhi). If the defendant admits the claim, then judgment is made in favour of the plaintiff (mudda'i). If the defendant denies the claim, then the Qadi demands from the plaintiff the production of evidence. The plaintiff is thus required to produce two male adult witnesses, both of whom must be Muslim, who are prepared to testify orally to their knowledge of the truth of the claim. There was bound to develop within this framework the 'shahada' or 'fixed witness' always available to give testimony and whose price depended on his alleged worth. No substitution was permitted to the oral testimony and circumstantial

---

[17] Coulson op.cit. p.129.

Historical Introduction

evidence was excluded. If the plaintiff failed to produce the necessary witnesses, the defendant was ordered to take the oath on the Qur'an. If properly sworn, judgment was given in the defendant's favour. The oath was offered to the defendant three times. On the third refusal, judgment was given to the plaintiff.

This brief description of the rules of evidence suffices to show that the highly regulated procedure was based firmly upon the idealised assumption that a Muslim would not, indeed could not, give false testimony under oath. The rules were so designed as to emphasise the relationship of man with God; the Qur'anic oath was the bond between the two. Balancing of evidence, as it would be understood in modern legal systems, played no part at all.

As the Muslim community extended their contacts with the Byzantine and Persian empires, so legal contacts were extended also. Contracts were written and broken – and the Qadis' courts could not cater for this. Also, the stress laid on the testimony of two adult male Muslims as to their religious and moral probity ('adala) necessarily ensured that many hardened criminals – those who were unaffected by false oath-taking – were unjustly released. The Qadis themselves realised the difficulty. In time, but too late to prevent the flow of work from the court, they came to accept that written documents were necessary to prove private legal transactions. A new science (shurut) developed as a highly sophisticated system of formularies.

Further, the Islamic law of criminal justice emphasised to a considerable extent discretion in punishment (ta'zir). Thus the Governor was permitted (within his own policy necessities) to provide a framework for his criminal law beyond the narrow confines of the Qur'anic hudud (compulsory) punishments. This discretionary area in criminal law is perhaps only an example of the wider concept of siyasa shar'iyya (administrative decisions). As a basic theory of constitutional law, siyasa shar'iyya recognised the sovereign as head of the Islamic state who was empowered to "complete" the Shari'a. He was assumed to be a man of 'adala – fit for the office. Both the Umayyad and Abbasid empires were thus responsible for wide-ranging legislative activities.

Thus we can conclude our introductory chapter in the crystalisation of the classical system of law at a period not later than the thirteenth century, noticing the dual feature of the administration of justice between the mazalim and the Shari'a. Later, we shall have occasion to discuss the emergence of the Muslim legal system from this self-imposed discipline. Our attention, however, must, for the present, be on the Indian subcontinent.

2. The Indian Subcontinent

This book is primarily concerned with the personal law of the Muslim community from South Asia. The community is a large and influential group, dominant in Pakistan and Bangladesh and a very large minority in India. Pakistan is an Islamic state in its inspiration, and recent developments in that country reflect this ideology. After an early flirtation with socialism, Bangladesh too emphasises its Muslim roots. However, it is important to remember that Islam is not indigenous to South Asia, and the peoples from the region are somewhat removed from the heart of Islam. The purpose of this chapter is to explain the influence and impact which English common law and British legislative initiatives had, in their different ways, during the period when the region was controlled by the British. First though, it is necessary to provide a few background comments to the introduction of Islam and Islamic law into South Asia.

Islamic law was introduced into the Indian subcontinent in the early eighth century, when Muhammad b. Qazim conquered Sind. By the thirteenth century, the Shari'a had become established. Although academic opinion differs on the extent of the application of the Shari'a during this early period, as indeed during the Moghul dynastic era, it is probable that the law was applied in a strict manner. However, the concept of siyasa justified significant variations. Thus Aurangzeb applied Shari'a to a far greater extent than Akhbar. The Muslim law as it is applied today in India, Pakistan and Bangladesh is unique. This chapter will trace the three major factors which contribute to this position; first, the impact of the English law, second, the importance of customary law, and, third, the reforms introduced into the general laws by direct legislation. It needs to be said at the outset that the British involvement in India was bound to have a crucial effect on the application of Muslim law, notwithstanding the various attempts to allow the indigenous communities to control their lives by their own customs. It was bound to have this effect for a number of interconnected reasons. First, the judges, appointed by the British, at first were appointed direct from Britain. Even when local judges were appointed, they were British-educated. The Islamic rules of evidence, necessarily, in time came to be ignored by the judges and by the practitioners (similarly trained in Britain) who appeared before them. The second reason for this inevitable influence was the introduction into India of the English doctrine of precedent, of a hierarchical court structure, and subsequently, of law reporting. Thus decisions which may well have been contrary to Islamic law

The Indian Subcontinent

would be followed by lower courts. Linked to this fact, of course, was the involvement of the Judicial Committee of the Privy Council in the appellate structure. Opinions of the Committee had wide-ranging effects on the application of Muslim law in Indian Courts. Moreover, as we shall see later, the doctrine of "justice and right" or "justice, equity and good conscience" often came to imply English law. This formula was laid down by numerous Statutes and Regulations.[1] Legislation of course was very important, and we shall discuss how it affected the application of the Muslim law. Finally, the texts used by the courts, especially the Hadeya, were not authoritative. The Hadeya had been translated into English from a Persian translation of the original Arabic which itself had been completed as late as the twelfth century. The other major commentary – the Fatawa Alamgiri – is equally as unsatisfactory for it simply represents a collection of *responsa* composed on the orders of Aurangzeb, who had his own peculiar interpretation of the Islamic law. More important than all these matters, however, was the policy decision which was finally taken that although the indigenous laws were to be fully respected, the laws themselves would be administered in the unified civil courts of the land rather than in the religious courts. It is to this development that we must first turn.

2.1 English Law in India

The story[2] begins in 1661 when the island of Bombay on the west coast of the subcontinent was ceded to Charles II as part of a marriage treaty with Portugal. For the first few years of the administration (from 1661 to 1668), in theory at least, the island was under the direct rule of English law, a Charter of 1661 having empowered "the Governor and Council in Bombay to judge all persons under them in all causes whether Civil or Criminal, according to the laws of this Kingdom, and to execute judgement accordingly". The possibility of administering justice to the indigenous population other than those who were servants of the East India Company was not contemplated by the Charter itself. It is probable, however, that whenever the Governor and Council were called upon to adjudicate a civil dispute involving Portuguese or other non-English inhabitants, they allowed the Portuguese civil law to govern the

---

[1] See below. See Lord Hobhouse in *Waghela Rajsanji v. Sheikh Masludin* 1886/7 14 LR IA 89.

[2] The major research in this area has been undertaken by C.Fawcett *The First Century of British Justice in India* (Oxford, 1934). Much of the material in the following pages represents a summary of Fawcett's work.

dispute.

In the period from 1661 to 1668, as far as is known, the martial law and the Portuguese civil law were the governing laws, although it should be mentioned that it has been judicially held in *The Advocate-General v. Richmond* [1845] that the cession of 1661 abrogated the application of Portuguese law and the Portuguese courts.[3]

In 1668 the island was leased by the British Crown to the East India Company. In the charter of that year, the company was required to enact laws "consonant to reason and not repugnant or contrary to" and "as near as may be agreeable to English Law". The courts were directed to be "like unto those that are established and used in this Our Realm of England". Under this authority, the company drafted laws for the administration of justice in the island of Bombay. The laws provided for the establishment of a Court of Judicature both for the determination of criminal and civil matters and also for the establishment of juries. It is interesting to notice that:

> All Tryalls in the said Court were to be by Jurys of twelve men where if the matter in variance shall be between English and English there the Jury shall be all English, when the matters in variance are between English and other Nations, or between Stranger and Stranger, then the Jury be one half English and the other half of the Inhabitants of the Island that are not English.

The judges who were appointed were directed to administer justice to all persons "according to the principles of common right". In addition, in the first regulations the judges were directed to behave themselves "duly and truly towards all according to justice and good conscience". Two important points have to be made concerning the company's laws. First, they do not directly impose English law as the sole governing law. Second, the provision relating to the six non-English jurymen in appropriate cases shows that the jurisdiction of the court extended to non-English inhabitants of Bombay. The court was not in fact established until 1672, some four years after the charter, and the evidence available of the administration of the law for these four years illustrates that neither the company's laws nor the laws of England proper were necessarily binding on the Council in Bombay. To quote one case, for instance, the Council in Bombay ordered a prostitute to be "shaved and sat on an ass", which was a penalty commonly imposed by the Muslim Qadis' courts at that time. In 1672, however, one Wilcox, who was a clerk in the Prerogative Office, was appointed judge and the court was established. From

---

[3] 1845 Perry's Oriental Cases 566.

then on, the company's laws (on the whole) were followed. In the absence of any provision in the company's laws, the judge resorted to the laws of England. It was also at this stage that the caste courts (Panchayats) were recognised. These courts assumed jurisdiction over persons who were members of the indigenous population and who had agreed to submit the dispute to the arbitration of the Panchayat. In the absence of such an agreement between the parties, the Court of Judicature had jurisdiction. The Court of Judicature functioned satisfactorily until 1683; but, in that year, a rebellion succeeded in closing the court for a year. After the surrender, another famous name in the development of jurisprudence in India, Dr St John, a doctor of civil law from Leiden, was appointed to be judge of a newly created Admiralty Court. According to the Charter of the Admiralty Court, the judge was to handle all mercantile and maritime cases whatsoever, "according to the rules of equity and good conscience and according to the laws and customs of merchants". It has been argued that this formula, as applied by this particular judge, ensured the application of Roman Law in the Admiralty Courts.[4] It so happened, and this is one of those historical oddities, that at this particular time the Court of Judicature had not been formally reconstituted after the overthrow of the rebellion, so Dr St John was able to assume the office of *defacto* judge for all civil and criminal matters in addition to his Admiralty jurisdiction. Naturally enough, his concept of justice was not bound either by the common law on the one hand or by the company's laws on the other.

This particular period came to an end in 1687 when Dr St John was recalled to England. At this point in the history of the British administration in Bombay there appears to have been a three-cornered struggle. First, the administrators in Bombay wished to have recourse to English law, both common law and statute. Second, the company officers in London wished to rule by direct order through letters.[5] Third, there was Dr St John who, before his recall, wished to extend the civil law (or Roman law) so that all suits would be administered according with its provisions.

The administration of justice in Bombay was interrupted once again in 1689 by an invasion by the Moghul navy. The court was not reconstituted until 1718 when, by proclamation, the Governor and Council of Bombay empowered the justices to "hold pleas, hear and determine all causes, suits, actions and trespasses as well Civil as Criminal whatsoever, in this Island of

---

[4] See J.D.M.Derrett, "Justice, Equity and Good Conscience", in J.N.D.Anderson (ed), *Changing Law in Developing Countries*, (London, 1963) p.130.

[5] One particular letter from the London office talks about the laws of England being a "heap of nonsense".

Bombay . . . according to Law, Equity and Good Conscience". In addition, the judges were required to pay due regard to caste customs, "the principles of common right, the orders of the Right Honourable Company, the policy and known and established law of the Realm of Great Britain, provided the same be conformable to the Instructions given to the court".

One provision of the 1718 proclamation resulted in requiring the Court of Judicature to be the Court of Appeal from the caste courts. It will be recalled that thirty years or so before this date the caste courts had been directly recognised. If this provision had not been introduced at this time, the development of Indian law, both the reception of English law as such and the development of what can be called Anglo-Mohammedan law and Anglo-Hindu law, would have been very different.

This proclamation of 1718 was the beginning of the involvement of the colonial court structure in the administration of local justice. Other colonial powers have followed significantly different models, and delegated the administration of all personal law matters to the courts of the indigenous communities.[6] But in 1718, the British had not made the complete commitment which was to develop later. Indeed, both the proclamation itself and the early reported cases prove that the British settlers in this period were fully prepared to allow the indigenous inhabitants to settle disputes, up to a point, according to their own laws. The Muslim courts at this period were better organised than the Hindu courts but, none the less, Hindu caste courts did exist, and were recognised by the British.

In 1726, the authority of the Court of Judicature was changed by a Charter establishing a Mayor's Court in Bombay, deriving authority from the King. At the same date, Mayor's courts were constituted in the two other important settlements, in Madras and in Calcutta. In passing, it should be mentioned that the British had derived authority in Calcutta from the acquisition of three villages in 1694 by which they became landowners with jurisdictional responsibility, and in Madras, Indian rulers in 1639 had allowed the company's courts to exercise jurisdiction by grants of sufferance. In effect, the 1726 charters ended the threefold struggle of the 1685-7 period by laying down the authoritative introduction of English law for the first time. The courts were authorised to "try, hear and determine all civil suits, actions and pleas between party and party" and to give "judgment and sentence according to justice and right". It has been pointed out by Professor Derrett from London University, amongst others, that the Charter and the Letters Patent of 1726 expressly

---

[6] See generally M.B.Hooker *Legal Pluralism* (Oxford, 1975).

avoided the phrase "justice, equity and good conscience", or "equity and good conscience", with its Roman law/civil law flavour from the days of Dr St John, and substituted the term "justice and right". Thus, historically, the term "justice and right" is different in scope from "justice, equity and good conscience", but from the legal point of view the two phrases do not differ in their meaning.

The introduction of English law into the three Presidency towns raised the question of jurisdiction over the indigenous population. On the whole, the company had encouraged the application by caste courts of the relevant indigenous laws. For instance, in reply to a petition of the castes of Madras, the company laid down the following principles:

> We say in the next place that such differences that happen between the Natives, in which the King's subjects are not involved, they may and should be decided among themselves, according to their own Customs, or by Justices or Referees to be appointed by themselves or otherwise as they think fit; but if they request and choose them to be decided by English laws, those and those only must be pursued, and pursued too according to the directions in the Charter and this likewise must be the case when differences happen between Natives and subjects of England, where either party is obstinate and determined to go to Law.

This reply foreshadowed the 1753 Charter for the three Mayor's courts, which expressly excepted from the jurisdiction all suits and actions between natives which were "to be determined among themselves unless both parties submitted them to the determination of the Mayor's courts". There is no doubt that the Mayor's courts continued to be extremely popular amongst the Indian population, and, although recognised by the law, the caste courts were resorted to infrequently.

This reluctance on the part of the Indian population to use the caste courts was acknowledged twenty years later when civil courts were established by the company in the newly acquired Mofussil, the area beyond the three Presidency towns. In 1765, the Company had obtained the Diwani of Bengal, Bihar and Orissa, and in 1772, the Governor, Warren Hastings, determined to carry out the decision of the Company to "stand forth as Dewan". In pursuance of this policy, he established civil courts to govern both Europeans and Indians. By the 27th Article of the Regulation II of 1772 Hindus and Muslims were to be governed by their own laws (but not administered in their own courts) in disputes relating to inheritance, marriage and caste and other religious usages and institutions. In 1781, the word "succession" was added to the list of subjects within the control of the indigenous laws. Another interesting development at this time was that Hindu and Muslim experts (Pandits and

Maulvis) were empowered to instruct the courts as to the nature of the Hindu or Muslim law, whenever a matter of Hindu or Muslim law came to be decided upon.

Regulation II placed the Hindus and Muslims on an equal footing. This must be seen as an enlightened decision, bearing in mind the nature of the Diwani grant which had been given to the Company and the strict Moghul interpretation of that grant. The Pandits and the Maulvis were bound by the "laws of the Shastras" in the former case and "the laws of the Koran" in the latter case. In 1793 this Regulation was replaced by Section 15 of Regulation IV to read "Hindu laws" and "Mohammedan laws".

In 1781, Regulations were enacted providing procedural instructions for the judges of the Mofussil courts. It is interesting to note that these instructions use the formula "justice, equity and good conscience" after an interval of nearly a hundred years. Section 60 of the 1781 Regulation lays down "that in all cases, within the jurisdiction of the Mofussil Dewannee Adaulut, for which no specific directions are hereby given, the respective judges thereof do act according to 'Justice, Equity and Good Conscience'".

There was also in this period an interesting development in the Presidency towns. In 1773 in Calcutta, the Mayor's court was replaced by a Supreme Court. It is not necessary to describe in detail the conflicts which existed at this time between the Supreme Court on the one hand and the Governor and Council in Calcutta on the other hand, and it will suffice for present purposes to state that the dispute arose out of the assumption by the Supreme Court of jurisdiction over the indigenous population. The judges of the Supreme Court, whenever they were confronted with a dispute involving Indians, probably applied Hindu or Muslim laws rather than English law. The Act which created the Supreme Court did not regulate either the extent of the jurisdiction or the applicable laws to be applied. In 1781, this particularly unfortunate state of affairs was resolved, when the Supreme Court was granted jurisdiction over all Indian inhabitants of Calcutta. By Section 17 of this Act, however:

> inheritance and succession to land, rent and goods and all matters of contract and dealing between party and party were to be determined in the case of the Mohammedans and Hindus by their respective laws.

The striking point to make about the Act of 1781 dealing with the Presidency towns is that the "reservation" section, that is the section which deals with the laws regulating Hindus and Muslims, differs from the "reservation" section of the Regulations enacted both in 1772 and in 1781 for the Mofussil courts. The actual position between the Presidency towns and Mofussil, however, was not too different, despite the apparent divergence between the Act and the Regulations.

The Indian Subcontinent

It should be added also that whereas in the Mofussil the judge applied in the case of a conflict between a Hindu and a Muslim the principles of "justice, equity and good conscience", the Calcutta Act of 1781 introduced in the case of conflict between Muslim law and Hindu law the concept of the application of "the laws and usages of the defendant".

In 1801 a Supreme Court was established in Madras, and in Bombay a Supreme Court was established in 1823. Then, in 1853, the Company's courts were abolished, and the Crown assumed direct responsibility. As a result, there was a fusion between the Mofussil and the Presidency jurisdictions. By 1853, the position had been reached where the jurisdiction of the British courts extended to Hindus and Muslims, with the important proviso that these people were governed by their own laws in disputes falling roughly into the categories of family law and caste usage.

So far we have only considered the personal laws of Hindus and Muslims. There were, of course, as there still are, many other personal systems of law being applied in India. The Charter Act in 1833, which provided for a Law Commission to consider the enactment of law which would be common to all the peoples of India, maintained the prevalent attitude of the time by directing the Commissioners to pay due regard to the "rights, feelings and peculiar usages of the people of India". The first Law Commission is remembered largely because of a report it brought out in 1840, known as the Lex Loci Report which, together with the subsequent Draft Act of 1841, proposed the extension of English substantive law (excluding procedural laws, the law of tort and the criminal law) to all non-Muslims and non-Hindus living in the Mofussil. The Law Commission hoped to reduce the confusion and chaos which existed at that time in the Mofussil whereby numerous personal laws governed non-Hindus and non-Muslims. The Draft Act, however, did not suggest the introduction of a uniform law for all situations. Nothing in the Act was to apply to Hindus or to Muslims; non-Christians were to retain their law of marriage, divorce and adoption; the immemorial customs of the people subject to the uniform law were to be safeguarded; and English law was to be applicable only to the extent that it conformed to the "situation" of the people.

The Draft Act received far from unanimous approval, and, in the result, the only provision which was introduced into law was the regulation abolishing the application of any personal law which demanded the loss of inheritance rights on conversion to another religion. This provision was introduced in 1850 by the Caste Disabilities Removal Act.

The second Law Commission extended the policy by recommending that a body of substantive civil law should be enacted for India which would be no less applicable to the transactions of the Hindus and the Muslims than to the rest of the Indian population. It goes further than the first recommendations, but the Commission was prepared to accept that certain unspecified exceptions should be made to the uniform law concept.

The dawn of the codification era commenced with the Code of Civil Procedure (1859), followed by the Limitation Act (1859), the Indian Penal Code (1860) and the Code of Criminal Procedure (1861). The report on the Law of Succession in 1863 by the third Law Commission was enacted into law by the Indian Succession Act of 1865 which excluded Hindus, Muslims and Buddhists. In 1872, the Evidence Act and the Contract Act were passed. The work of the fourth, and final, Law Commission resulted in the enactment, in particular, of the Negotiable Instruments Act of 1881 and the Transfer of Property Act of 1882. The Transfer of Property Act contained a special provision in Section 2 that nothing in the Act relating to transfer of property should be deemed to effect any rule of Hindu, Muslim or Buddhist law. The same respect for personal laws was expressed in the Trust Act of 1882, Section 1. Indeed, the British believed at this time that the personal laws were so interconnected with religious feelings that any attempt at large-scale reform, or any attempt to codify the personal laws, would necessarily involve injury to religious susceptibilities, and for this reason reform was invoked only after considerable pressure from the communities themselves. For example, in 1856 the Hindu Widow's Remarriage Act, designed to make legally possible the remarriage of Hindu widows, was enacted. This cautious approach was followed, in particular, in the case of Muslim law. It has been commented that of the few acts dealing with Muslim law enacted by the British, a number of them restored traditional Muslim law. For example, we can note the Wakf Act of 1913, as perhaps the best example of this trend, and which will be commented upon in detail later.[7] It should be mentioned in addition that the orthodox Muslim community was responsible, in part, for the enactment of the Shariat Act (1937) which destroyed the application of a considerable section of customary law. The only major reform of the Muslim personal law in the British period occurred in 1939 with the enactment of the Dissolution of Muslim Marriages Act.

The uniform law approach of the nineteenth century succeeded in codifying, in particular, the Criminal Law, the Law of Contract and the Law of Evidence. The Law Commissioners maintained intact, however, the principle that the Muslims and the Hindus were to be governed by their own personal laws in the area of the law which falls broadly within the 1772/1781

---

[7] This Act overruled the Privy Council decision of *Abul Fata Mahomed Ishak v. Russomoy Dhur Chowdhry* 1894/5, 22 LR IA 76.

Regulations. The Government of India Act (1915) accepted this necessary exclusion from the uniform law concept.

2.1.1 *The Formulas*

It is necessary to consider in more detail the question of "justice, equity and good conscience" and "justice and right". Examples have been cited of the use of the formulas; in 1668, the judges of the Court of Judicature at Bombay were directed to administer justice to all persons "according to the principles of common right"; the Mayor's court charter for Madras in 1687 enacted that "all causes, whatsoever, civil and criminal, between party and party, whoever they shall be, shall be adjudged according to equity and good conscience"; the Proclamation of the Governor and Council of Bombay reconstituting the Bombay Act was in similar terms. Again, in 1726 the charter establishing the Mayor's courts in Bombay, Madras and Calcutta enacted that judgment was to be given according to "justice and right", and this formula was repeated in 1753. Moving into the nineteenth century the Supreme Court in Madras was invested with jurisdiction to give judgment according to "justice and right". The concept appears also in the Mofussil: in the regulations of 1781; in the Bengal Civil Courts Act of 1871; and in the Bengal, Agra and Assam Civil Courts Act (1887). Thus the formula appears constantly in the Regulations, Acts and Charters of India from the seventeenth century to the nineteenth century.

In 1886 the Privy Council held that the formulas, "justice, equity and good conscience" or "justice and right" implied the application of English law if found applicable to Indian society and circumstances.[8] In every situation where, by Regulation or by the Act, the court had to apply this particular formula, if a rule of English law was relevant to Indian society, or to Indian circumstances, then English law was applied. In this manner substantive rules of English law found their way into the body of Indian law indirectly through the principles of "justice, equity and good conscience" and "justice and right".

How did the judges deal with matters in accordance with "justice, equity and good conscience" when the situation was completely unknown to English experience? One line of decisions deals with the effect of a religious conversion by one of the parties to a marriage. By Sunni Islamic law as applied in India, a Muslim male has capacity to marry either a Muslim girl or a Jewish or Christian girl. Jews and Christians (Kitabiyya) are deemed to possess revealed scriptures. A Muslim male, however, cannot marry a

---

[8] *Waghela Rajsanji v. Sheikh Masludin* 1886/7 14 LR IA 89.

polytheist, and a Muslim girl can marry no one other than a Muslim male. Thus, the conversion to Islam of a man married either to a Jewish or to a Christian girl will not affect the validity of an existing union.[9] In contrast to this position, the conversion to Islam of a man married to a polytheistic girl or the conversion to Islam of a girl married to a non-Muslim (regardless of his faith), will bring into play the Islamic law rule which demands either the conversion to Islam of the non-Muslim or the termination of the union.

Two decisions of some consequence which deal with this question are *Robaba Khanum v. Khodadad Boman Irani* [1948][10] and *Rakeya Bibi v. Anil Kumar Mukherji* [1948].[11] In the first case, the parties were Parsees who had married in Iran in 1927. Subsequently they settled permanently in Bombay, and, in 1944, the wife converted to Islam and requested that her husband should adopt her new faith. The husband refused the wife's request. She therefore instituted proceedings in the High Court for divorce, or, in the alternative, for a declaration that her marriage was at an end. The wife argued that by the classical Islamic law as applied in India, a marriage celebrated in non-Muslim form between non-Muslims is brought to an end usually three months after the wife's conversion to Islam, without any intervention from the court.[12] The wife argued that this legal result applied to her situation. She submitted that after her conversion she became a Muslim governed by Muslim personal law. The judge, Mr Justice Blagden, rejected the plea. He said:

> The Law of India is not Mohammedan Law any more than it is Hindu Law or Christian Ecclesiastical Law, but the Mohammedan Law is by virtue of the general law of India the personal law of the minority of Indians, regulating their relations with one another. It differs in degree, but not in kind from (say) the bye-laws of the Willingdon Club.

He went on to say: "It is true that a convert is generally subject to the personal law appropriate to his new religion as against that appropriate to his old one. But why should this apply to the wife or the husband of the

---

[9] However, see the case of *Viswalingham v. Viswalingham* [1979] 1 F.L.R.15 where the Court of Appeal in England considered a different view of this area of the law in the context of the Shafi'i law as applied in Malaysia.

[10] 1948 ILR Bom 223.

[11] 1948 ILR 2 Cal 119.

[12] If the conversion takes place in Dar al-Islam (where Islamic law is the law of the land), and if the husband is resident there as well, then by classical law the Muslim judge offers the Islamic faith to the non-Muslim partner. If the faith is refused three times, the judge has the authority (indeed the duty) to separate the parties.

convert?" Having held Muslim law to be inapplicable to the case, he went on to decide the case according to "justice, equity and good conscience". According to this criterion, the wife's contention, he said, "was so monstrous an absurdity that it carried its own refutation with it". The wife appealed and, on appeal, Mr Justice Blagden's decision was upheld. The Appeal Court found that the Muslim personal law was inapplicable and thus decided the case in accordance with "justice and right".

It is not in accordance with justice and right that on the conversion of one of the parties to the marriage to Islam, it should be held that the marriage stands dissolved.

A similar result was reached in *Rakeya Bibi v. Anil Kumar Mukherji*.[13] The parties, both of them originally professing the Hindu faith, married each other in 1944 in accordance with Hindu rites. The marriage was never consummated and in 1945 the wife embraced Islam. She offered Islam to her husband who refused the invitation. She then petitioned the court for a declaration that her marriage be dissolved. Mr Justice Ormond submitted the case to a Special Bench. The Bench examined the relevant rule of Muslim law relied upon by the plaintiff, but rejected her plea. Mr Justice Chakravartti, on giving the decision of the Special Bench, said:

If one of the parties to a marriage brings about a conflict of personal law by forsaking their common religion and adopting another, can the new personal law of the converted spouse prevail over the old personal law retained by the unconverted partner, under which the marriage was celebrated?

He answered his question by deciding that the personal law of the converted spouse did not govern the case. The plaintiff was unable to prove to the satisfaction of the Bench that there was any law in force in India which brought the rule of Muslim law into prominence as the law governing the dissolution of the marriage. It was not "just nor right" to apply the rule of Muslim law to the case. The Bench decided, therefore, that the extrajudicial Muslim law could not govern the dispute. It could be argued that the formula "justice, equity and good conscience" was used in this case in a negative sense; the refusal to recognise an alleged accomplished act.

Further examples can be given of the use of the formulas "justice, equity and good conscience" or "justice and right" as used in this context. In *Sayeda Khatoon v. M. Obadiah* [1944][14] both parties were members of the Jewish

---

[13] 1948 ILR 2 Cal 119.
[14] 1944/45 49 Cal WN 745.

community domiciled in India. They married in Calcutta in 1943 according to Jewish rites. In December 1943, the husband deserted the wife, and in 1945 the wife embraced Islam. She petitioned the court for an order that her marriage be declared at an end by reason of the conversion. Mr Justice Lodge said, however: "Why should Islamic Law be preferred to the Jewish Law in a matrimonial dispute between a Mohammedan and a Jew, particularly when the relationship was created under the Jewish Law?" He decided, first, that Muslim law should not govern the dispute, and second, that by the principle of "justice and right" the marriage still subsisted.

There is a Pakistani case of some interest, namely *Farooq Leivers v. Adelaide Bridget Mary* [1958].[15] This case must be read in the light of *Jatoi v. Jatoi* [1967][16] which is discussed in detail in chapter 10. In *Jatoi v. Jatoi* the husband was a Muslim at all times. He contracted a civil ceremony with a Christian wife in England. The divorce by talaq was recognised by the Pakistan Supreme Court. *Farooq Leivers v. Adelaide Bridget Mary* was referred to in the judgment of the majority but the case was not expressly overruled. The husband and the wife in the earlier case were Christians married according to Christian rites. The husband converted to Islam, asked his wife to embrace the Muslim faith and, on her refusal, he purported to divorce her by "talaq". The husband sought a declaration that he was no longer married to his former wife. Changez J. thought that there was no reason why Muslim law should govern the dissolution of the marriage. He fell back on the Punjab Laws Act 1872 Section 5 and Section 6, holding that "it would be against the dictate of justice, equity and good conscience to grant a decree to the plaintiff in terms of the relief sought for". Once again, in effect, the formula is being employed by the court in order to determine the legal system governing the question before it.

There are a few isolated cases where the courts in this situation have applied the Muslim law as the governing law. The most important case, so far as India is concerned, is *Ayesha Bibi v. Subodh Chandra Chakrabarty* [1945].[17] This case was a decision of Mr Justice Ormond in the Calcutta High Court. The husband and wife in this case both came from

---

[15] 1958 PLD (WP) Lah 431.

[16] 1967 PLD SC 580.

[17] 1945 ILR 2 Cal 405. See also the two unreported cases; *Ayesha Bibi v. Bireshwar Ghosh Mazumdar* (noted briefly in 1929 33 Cal WN 179) and *Chelimutnessa v. Surrendra* [1924]. These cases are referred to by K.K.Basu in "Hindu-Muslim Marriages", *Indian Law Review* 2 (1948/9) p.249. See also the older case of *Budansa Rowther v. Fatma Bi* 1914 26 Madras LJ 260.

backgrounds referred to in the judgment as "respectable" Brahmin families. They were married according to Hindu rites in 1941. They then went to live in the wife's parents' house and the husband became (as the judgment puts it) "a domesticated son-in-law". Nevertheless, the husband mistreated his wife. In 1943, perhaps in desperation, the wife converted to Islam and invited her husband to accept her new faith. On his refusal, she petitioned for a declaration that the marriage had been dissolved. Mr Justice Ormond granted her the declaration. Clause 19 of the 1865 Letters Patent establishing the High Court directed him to give judgment according to "justice and right". The Government of India Act of 1915 directed him that in certain matters he must decide according to the laws of the defendant, but he held that the Government of India Act did not apply to the case before him because it did not cover suits relating to marriage; thus the case must be governed according to "justice and right". In his view it was "just and right" to apply the Muslim law, primarily because, in his opinion, under the Hindu law the wife-apostate would be reduced to the position of an untouchable menial servant. It was "just and right" therefore to separate the parties. No rights of the husband would be transgressed and the husband would be liberated from an intolerable position.

One can draw the conclusion from these cases that when the courts apply "justice, equity and good conscience", or "justice and right" in a situation which is peculiar to Indian circumstances, the judges apply the formula along lines which they, as English or English-trained judges, consider to be just. In this way, English law is introduced on what can be termed a "third level". The "first level" is obviously codification of English rules; the "second level" is by "justice and right" or "justice, equity and good conscience" when English law acts as the "reservoir law" in a case which is similar to an English situation. The third, and perhaps most interesting level, occurs in situations very different from English type circumstances.

2.2 Muslim Law and Customary Law

As early as 1847, customary practice was recognised as being relevant in situations where the courts were directed to apply the personal law of the parties as a governing law.[18] The leading case is the decision involving Khoja and Memons decided in Bombay in 1847.[19] The Khoja community is referred to in the judgment as "a small caste in Western India who appear to have

---

[18] See generally, C.Rankin, "Custom in the Muslim Personal Law of India", Transactions of the Grotius Society (1939) vol. 25 p.89.

[19] 1847 Perry's Oriental Cases 110.

originally come from Sind or Kutch (the western seaboard), [now in Pakistan], and who, by their own traditions, which are probably correct, were converted from Hinduism about four hundred years ago". The plaintiff in the action, the daughter of the intestate, claimed a share in the inheritance of the father on the grounds that Muslim law governed the dispute and that under Muslim law she was entitled, as a daughter, to a share in the inheritance. The defendants countered the claim of the plaintiff on the grounds that although the Khojas are a Muslim community, and that normally Muslim law would govern them, nonetheless there are Khoja customs whereby females are not entitled to any share of the father's property on his death.

The Chief Justice, Sir Erskine Perry, considered, in the first instance, the enforceability of the customary rule in principle. He concluded that if a custom had been proved to exist "from the time whereof the memory of man runneth not to the contrary", if it is not injurious to the public interest, and if it does not conflict with any express law of the ruling power, such a custom was entitled to receive the sanction of a court regardless of the general Muslim law to the contrary. The Charter of the Bombay Court lays down that "in the case of Mohammedans, or Gentoos (Hindus), their inheritance and succession shall be determined in the case of the Mohammedans by the laws and usages of the Mohammedans". The Chief Justice thought it clear that this particular clause did not mean the adoption of the Qur'anic law without regard to the usages of the Muslims in India, whether they be Shi'i, Sunni or sectarian. In this sense, the Chief Justice restricted the application of the personal law otherwise applicable:

> I am clearly, therefore, of opinion that the effect of the clause in the Charter is not to adopt the text of the Koran as law, any further than it has been adopted in the laws and usages of the Mohammedans who came under our sway, and if any class of Mohammedans, Mohammedan dissenters, as they may be called, are found to be in possession of any usage which is otherwise valid as a legal custom, and which does not conflict with any express law of the English Government, they are just as much entitled to the protection of this clause as the most orthodox Sunni who can come before the Court.

The petition of the daughter failed and, as the price of an unsuccessful experiment, her claim was dismissed with costs.[20]

In the Punjab, custom is given statutory recognition by the Punjab Laws Act (1872) Section 5, which states:

---

[20] In matters other than succession it is important to point out that the Khoja community is governed by the personal law of the Shi'i Isma'ili school.

> In questions regarding . . . [a list of matters pertaining to family law] the rule of decision shall be (a) any custom applicable to the parties concerned, which is not contrary to justice, equity and good conscience, and has not been by this or any other enactment altered or abolished, and has not been declared to be void by any competent authority, (b) the Mohammedan Law, in cases where the parties are Mohammedans . . . except insofar as such law has been altered or abolished by legislative enactment; or is opposed to the provisions of this Act or has been modified by any such custom as is above referred to.

There is no doubt that in the Punjab as in Bombay provable custom takes precedence over Muslim law when the court has to determine the issue before it in accordance with the personal law.

Custom was allowed to derogate from the Muslim personal law in other areas of British India beside Bombay and the Punjab. In Madras, for example, the Civil Courts Act (1873) contained a provision in Section 16 similar to the Punjab Laws Act. The problem whether custom or the personal law is applied as the governing law has been particularly relevant with respect to the small Mappilla Muslim community from Malabar. The leading case concerning this group is the decision of Tyabji J in *Kunhambi v. Kalanthar* decided by the Madras court in 1915.[21] The question before the court was whether the Mappilla community was governed by its normal personal law, the Muslim law, or by a particular variation of Hindu law with respect to the dispute in issue. Tyabji J argued that the question was primarily one of fact: "whether the particular parties have adopted the one system of law or the other and whether they have been governing their conduct in accordance with the one system or the other." If a custom is proved then there is no doubt that the Muslim personal law is not applicable.

In contrast to the position in Madras, in Bombay and in the Punjab, custom was not granted statutory recognition in other areas of British India. This was particularly the case in Bengal, in the United Provinces and in Assam. The Allahabad High Court at first read the lack of a statutory mention of custom in the Civil Courts Acts of these areas to imply that no customary deviation should be permitted from the purity of the personal laws. These early cases were overruled in 1913 in *Muhammad Ismail v. Lala Sheo-mukh Rai*.[22] From this case, the position is that custom does not have any less effect upon the Muslim law in Bengal and Assam than in other areas where it is expressly

---

[21] 1915 ILR 38 Mad 1052.
[22] 1913 15 Bom LR 76. This is a Privy Council decision.

mentioned as the primary rule of decision.

It has already been seen that there was a desire by the religious Muslim community to reduce the role of custom. As a direct result of appeals by the Muslim community, the Shariat Act of 1937 was enacted in order to reduce the instances where custom was the rule of decision. The text of the Act lays down that in a number of specified areas of law regarding intestate succession and the law of marriage and divorce, the rule of decision in cases where the parties are Muslims shall be the Muslim personal law (Shariat) save for questions relating to agricultural land. If a person satisfies the prescribed authority that he is a Muslim, he can declare, in addition, that the personal law by which he wishes to be governed is Muslim law in relation also to testate succession and adoption.[23]

The Act has been extended to all parts of independent India, except for Jammu and Kashmir. According to an Act of 1977, however, the courts in Jammu and Kashmir apply Muslim law in all cases specified under the terms of that Act, subject to any contrary legislation or custom.[24] The Act has been adopted by the acceding states to independent India, such as Rajasthan.

In Pakistan it was adopted, although it is now substantially amended, and the amendments now apply to all areas of Pakistan. So as far as Bangladesh is concerned, the governing statute is the 1937 Shariat Act.

It will be apparent that even after the passing of the Shariat Act, custom is still the determining law in many cases. In particular, as legislation relating to agriculture was not within the competence of the central legislature, agricultural land was excluded from the purport of the Act. In so far as custom governs the law of testamentary succession, the individual has the right to opt for Muslim law, but if the option is not taken testamentary succession is governed by the customary law.

There have been one or two amendments in India to the Shariat Act. In Madras, in 1949, Section 2 of the 1949 Act reworded the parent Act so as to include within the scope of the personal law all waqfs and agricultural land. In these circumstances, the position in Madras is that the rule of decision in all questions relating to intestate succession and the other specified matters, including waqfs, where the parties to the dispute are Muslims is the "Muslim Personal Law". Similar extensions have been introduced, in the case of of

---

[23] Adoption is not recognised as carrying any legal consequences in Islamic law.

[24] Sri Pratap Jammu and Kashmir Laws Consolidation Act (1977). I am grateful to Professor Tahir Mahmood of New Delhi for directing my attention to this Act which I overlooked in the first edition of this book.

agricultural land only, in Kerela.[25] Further details on this and other local Acts are outside the scope of this book and readers are referred to Professor Tahir Mahmood's book entitled *The Muslim Law of India*.[26]

Turning to Pakistan, Muslim law has been introduced to a much greater extent by the West Punjab Muslim Personal Law (Shariat) Application Act 1948 and the Punjab Muslim Personal Law (Shariat) Application (Amendment) Act 1951.[27] Section 2 of the 1948 Act stated that in all questions regarding succession, including agricultural land, the decision in cases where the parties are Muslims shall be the Muslim personal law. Complications were experienced in applying the 1948 Act, in particular in ascertaining the meaning of the word "succession". Did it include both intestate and testate succession, or was it restricted to intestate succession as in the parent Act ? This problem was overcome in 1951 by Section 2 of the Shariat Act of that year which stated that notwithstanding any rule of customary usage, in all questions regarding succession, whether testate or intestate, the rule of decision shall be the Muslim personal law, in cases where the parties are Muslims.

If all the events in dispute occur after 1951, in so far as Pakistan is concerned, there is no major problem of classification. The Pakistan legislature has extended the original 1937 Act to a point where a choice between the personal law as laid down by the Act and the customary law is no longer necessary. The amendments to the Shariat Act in Pakistan, more than any other reform, illustrate the attempts by the legislature to reduce the role played by custom and to introduce the Shari'a law as the rule of decision in a large area of personal law governing Muslims.

2.3 Muslim Law and the General Law

Another issue of considerable importance relating to classification difficulties is the relationship between the personal law on the one hand and the general law of the land on the other hand. An example of the problem facing the court arises in respect to the laws of evidence.

Section 112 of the Evidence Act (1882) relating to presumptions of legitimacy provides an example of this conflict. Does the court classify the dispute as one which falls under the substantive law to be governed by the

---

[25] Kerela Act XLII of 1963.

[26] 2nd. ed. (Allahabad, 1982).

[27] These and other Acts were repealed and consolidated by the West Pakistan Muslim Personal Law (Shariat) Application Act (1962), as amended by the Muslim Personal Law (Shariat) Application Act 1983.

The Indian Subcontinent

personal law, or as one which falls under the law of evidence to be governed by the Indian Evidence Act?[28]

Section 112 of the Indian Evidence Act introduced into this area of law the English law rule, namely:

> The fact that any person born during the continuance of a valid marriage between his mother and any man, or within 280 days after its dissolution, the mother remaining unmarried, shall be conclusive proof that he is the legitimate son of that man, unless it can be shown that the parties to the marriage had no access to each other at any time when he would have been begotten.

It is the general opinion in India that Section 112 abolished the Hanafi law relating to the presumption of legitimacy.[29] In the Hanafi law, a man is presumed to be the father of a child who is born to his wife not less than six months from the date of the marriage (unless he disclaims the child) and within two years after the dissolution of the marriage, either by death of the man, or by divorce. If a child is born within the period of six months from the date of the marriage, according to Hanafi law, that child is illegitimate (unless he claims it to be legitimate.) The Hanafi law is classified as evidential and thus has now been superceded by the Indian Evidence Act.

This view, however, has not been accepted in Pakistan. In the case of *Abdul Ghani v. Taleh Bibi* [1962][30] the question before the court was whether the claimant was the legitimate child of Allah Bakhsh. If she were, then she would be entitled to inherit. On the other hand, if she were illegitimate, she would have had no claim to the inheritance. The claimant in this case was born to her mother within the first six months of her mother's marriage to Allah Bakhsh. The trial judge at first instance found that as the claimant was born during the marriage between her mother and the husband Allah Bakhsh, in accordance with the provisions of Section 112 of the Evidence Act, she was presumed to be the legitimate daughter of Allah Bakhsh.

The other heirs appealed on the ground that the trial judge was wrong in law to apply Section 112. The Appellate Court held, first, that the rule of Muslim law in question was a rule of substantive law. Having held that the Muslim law was a rule of substantive law, the court applied the substantive rule of the personal law. It will be recalled that, according to Muslim law, if a

---

[28] The details of Pakistan law in this area of the law of evidence are discussed later in chapter 6.

[29] See *Sibt Muhammad v. Muhammad Hameed* 1926 ILR 48 All 625; *[Mst.] Rahim Bibi v. Chiragh Din* 1930 A.I.R. Lah 97.

[30] 1962 PLD (WP) Lah 531.

child is born within the first six months of the date of the marriage of its mother, the child is an illegitimate child (unless the man claims it to be legitimate.) The important date is the date of conception and not the date of birth. Thus the Appellate Court held that the claimant was not the legitimate daughter of Allah Bakhsh because she was born within the first six months of the marriage. Consequently she was not entitled to the property in dispute. The interest of this Pakistan case lies in the way in which the court classified the Muslim rule relating to the legitimacy as a rule of substantive law.[31] If the facts of the case were to occur before an Indian court, the Indian court no doubt would apply the Indian Evidence Act, on the basis that the rule of Muslim law is a rule of evidence and thus has been superseded by the codified Indian Evidence Act.

Another section of the Evidence Act has created a similar conflict and is illustrated by an early decision from Allahabad in 1885; *Mazhar Ali v. Budh Singh*.[32] Sections 107 and 108 of the Evidence Act deal with the burden of proving the death of a person known to have been alive. According to Muslim law a missing person is to be regarded as alive till the lapse of ninety years from the date of his birth.

The Indian Evidence Act introduces an English law concept of proof. If it is shown that the man was alive within thirty years of the date of the presentation of the case, then the burden of proving he is dead is on the person who affirms it. If it is proved that he has not been heard of in the last seven years, by those who would naturally have heard of him if he had been alive, then the burden of proving that he is alive is shifted to the person who affirms that he is alive.

The dispute in *Mazhar Ali v. Budh Singh* resolved itself into whether to apply the rule of Muslim law (in accordance with Section 24 of the Civil Courts Act) or the rule of evidence as contained in Section 108 of the Evidence Act. After an exhaustive analysis of the Muslim law sources, Mr Justice Mahmood concluded that the Muslim rule in question fell within the topic of evidence. Although before the enactment of the Evidence Act there might have been some justification for applying the Muslim law to Muslim cases, there was no doubt in the judge's mind that he was bound by Section 108 of the Evidence Act. If he had concluded otherwise to the effect that the Muslim rule was a rule of substance, then he undoubtedly would have applied

---

[31] The case was discussed and expressly approved by the Pakistan Supreme Court in *Hamida Begum v. Murad Begum.* 1975 PLD SC 624.

[32] 1885 ILR 7 All 297.

the Muslim law as directed by Section 24 of the Civil Courts Act.[33]

It remains to be seen how this case would be dealt with if it ever came up before a Pakistan judge. One has a feeling that the decision probably would go the other way.

Since 1962, institutions have existed in the Pakistan constitutions for attempts to be made to bring all existing laws into conformity with the injunctions of Islam as laid down in the Holy Qur'an and Sunna. As early as 1966, the Interest Act of 1839 and the Negotiable Instruments Act of 1881 were being criticised by these constitutional bodies as being contrary to the principles of Islamic law. Major changes have been introduced since 1977 to the received laws. Details of some of these changes will be considered at a later stage in the book, but it is opportune to comment at this point that the Islamicisation of the laws in Pakistan, on one level at any rate, is an attempt to fuse into *one* what can be termed the "Muslim law" with the "general law". In such an attempt to unify the legal system, it is perhaps only natural in the present stage in the development of the State of Pakistan that the "Muslim law" would come out the victor.

---

[33] See chapter 7 for a discussion of the Dissolution of Muslim Marriages Act (1939). By section 2(1) of that Act, a woman married under Muslim law can obtain a decree for the dissolution of her marriage if the whereabouts of her husband have not been known for a period of four years. This section of course is confined to divorce petitions brought by the wife, and to that extent it has a limited effect on the traditional law, although it does change the Hanafi law in that respect.

3. Marriage: Form and Capacity

3.1 The Nikah

This chapter describes the legal framework of the marriage contract in Muslim law. We concentrate on the formal requirements in the first instance, and then go on to consider the prohibitory rules which prevent certain relationships from being given the imprint of a valid and lawful union. The marriage ceremony is often referred to as the nikah. It is to a consideration of this ceremony that we first turn.

3.1.1 Formal Requirements

The nikah is effected quite simply by an offer (ijab) and an acceptance (qabul), before Muslim witnesses (either 2 male or 1 male and 2 female). The first speech, from whichever side it emanates, is the offer, and the second speech constitutes the acceptance. The declarations, which must be made conceptually "at the same meeting" are pronounced by the parties themselves, or by an attorney (vakil) acting on their behalf, or by their guardians when they lack the capacity to contract themselves in marriage. We consider this question later in the chapter. However, this simple form of marriage is almost always accompanied by religious ceremonials. A description of the usual marriage ceremony in Northern Pakistan appears in the case of *Ghulam Kubra v. Mohammad Shafi*.[1] It is customary for a relation of the bride to be sent to the bride accompanied by two witnesses. The relation asks the bride within the hearing of the witnesses whether she authorises him to agree to the marriage offered by the prospective husband. When the bride signifies her consent, the relation and the two witnesses go to the prospective husband, who is in another house, another part of the building, or in the mosque. The Muslim religious leader (the Mullah) asks the prospective husband whether he is offering to marry the bride. After an affirmative reply, the Mullah will then ask the relation if he is the agent of the bride and to communicate to him the views of the bride. As soon as both the prospective husband and the relation have replied in the affirmative, the marriage is complete. Normally, certain scriptures are then read before the conclusion of the ceremony although this is

---

[1] 1940 AIR Pesh 2.

not essential.[2]

The traditional concept of marriage and the informality of the ceremonies does not take account of the need in a complex and highly mobile society to have definitive proof of the existence of marriages. Registration is therefore of paramount importance. Attempts to introduce registration, however, have met opposition. The present position in most Muslim countries is that facilities exist for registration of marriages, non-compliance with which involves criminal sanctions. However, a marriage which is not registered can be often proved by the production of other evidence.[3] Registration of the marriage, of course, will always be the best evidence, and in the absence of registration, it will be extremely difficult to prove a valid marriage. Another device which has been employed, and which will be the subject of later comment, has been to remove the ability of the court to adjudicate over matrimonial disputes, inheritance problems and the like, in cases where the marriage has not been registered.

3.1.2 Capacity

We turn now to consider the questions relating to the capacity of persons to contract a marriage valid by Islamic law. By Hanafi law, a person can contract a marriage as soon as he or she has attained the age of puberty. The presumption is that puberty is reached at 15 years, but evidence can certainly be produced to the effect that it is reached at an age earlier than this. Minimum periods would appear to be 12 in the case of males and 9 in the case of females.[4] If an under-age boy or girl contracts himself or herself in marriage without the consent of the guardian then, so long as he or she has attained "discretion" (intellectual maturity) at the time of the marriage, the union can be validated by acts of ratification after the minor has attained

---

[2] See *Shahzada Begum v. Sh. Abdul Hamid.* 1950 PLD Lah 504. Rashida Patel in her book *Women and Law in Pakistan* (1979) recalls that in Pakistan the families resort to what she describes as "wild spending and feasting and singing, dancing and music." In contrast, given the nature of the marriage as a civil contract it is possible for the contract to be concluded entirely by proxy, for instance over the telephone. A number of English cases on immigration law have expressly recognised this form of marriage. See *Nasreen Akhtar v. Secretary of State for the Home Department* (1981) No. 2166. (unreported).

[3] For Pakistan cases, see *Nasim Akhtar v. The State* 1968 PLD Lah 841; *Habib v. The State* 1980 PLD Lah 791; *Abdulla v. R.Khatoon* 1967 PLD Dacca 47; and *Sher Afzal v. Shamin Firdaus* 1980 PLD SC 228. Registration was introduced by the Muslim Family Laws Ordinance 1961 s.5.

[4] For cases in Pakistan; see *Bakshi v. Bashir Ahmed* 1970 PLD Lah 386, and *Sughran Mai v. The State* 1980 PLD Lah 386.

Marriage: Form and Capacity

sexual maturity. In Hanafi law, of course, the marriage guardian can actually contract in marriage his under-age ward.

There has been legislation in the Indian subcontinent since 1929 designed to restrain the solemnisation of child marriages. Such marriages were perceived as socially undesirable, and legislation was enacted to prevent the solemnisation of such unions in all the communities in India. Thus criminal penalties were introduced. Initially, a "child" was defined as a male under 18, and a female under 14. The criminal sanction which is now imposed is that if a male above 18 in Pakistan or 21 in India contracts a "child marriage" he shall be punishable with imprisonment or with a fine or both. In addition, whoever performs, conducts or directs any "child marriage" shall be punishable with imprisonment and/or a fine, unless he proves that he had reason to believe that the marriage was not a "child marriage".[5] The girl who contracts a "child marriage" is not liable to any punishment under the Act. Most importantly, the definition of a "child marriage" for the purposes of this Act has been raised to under 16 for a girl and under 18 for a boy in Pakistan and Bangladesh,[6] and under 18 for a girl and under 21 for a boy in India.[7] It is important to emphasise that a marriage solemnised in contravention of the relevant Act is nevertheless valid.

In contrast to the Hanafi law, in both Shafiʻi and Maliki law, an adult virgin has no capacity to contract herself in marriage. She needs the consent of her guardian, and indeed it is possible for a guardian to contract into marriage his daughter who has reached puberty without any necessity of obtaining prior consent. The girl only becomes capable of contracting herself in marriage when she ceases to be a virgin by reason of a consummated marriage or an

---

[5] Child Marriage Restraint Act 1929 as amended in Pakistan by Muslim Family Laws Ordinance ss. 12(2)(3).
[6] Muslim Family Laws Ordinance (1961) s.12(1).
[7] Child Marriage Restraint (Amendment) Act 1978.

illicit sexual relationship.[8]

Although Hanafi law does permit a guardian the right to contract his minor ward in marriage, the child on attaining puberty has a right himself or herself, under certain conditions, to avoid the union by exercising an option (Khiyar al-bulugh). In classical Hanafi law this option exists only in cases where the child is married by a guardian *other than* the father or grandfather.[9] The option is lost by the affirmative act of consummation of the marriage, at least if consummation has taken place without duress and after the acquisition of puberty. This principle was applied in the Bombay case of *Abdul Rahimin v. Aminabai*.[10]

In India, Pakistan and Bangladesh the doctrine of the Khiyar has been affirmed in its classical mould, and, at the same time, there is an additional right available only to the girl to avoid the marriage within the terms laid down by Section 2(vii) of the Dissolution of Muslim Marriages Act (1939). Section 2(vii) states that a woman married under Muslim law shall be entitled to obtain a decree for the dissolution of her marriage on the ground that she, having been given in marriage by her father or other guardian before she attained the age of 15 years, repudiates the marriage before attaining the age of 18 years. In Pakistan the age of 15 has been increased by the Muslim Family Laws Ordinance (1961) to 16.[11] Again the option is not lost when consummation occurs without her consent.[12]

---

[8] See for the Shafi'i law, the decision of the Singapore Appeal Board in *Syed Abdullah Shatiri v. Sharifa Salman* (1959) MLJ 137. A different view of the Shafi'i law appears to have been taken by the High Court of Kerela in the case of *Kammu v. Ethiyumma* 1967 Kerela Law Times 913, and again in the case of *K.Abubukkur v. V.Marakkar* 1970 AIR Ker 277. In the latter case, the Judge said as follows: "Marriage among Muslims being a contract and the contracting parties being the husband and the wife the consent contemplated in the Shafei sect is that of the wife and not of the father or grandfather or any other person who acts as the wali at the time of the marriage. The person who acts as the wali only communicates the consent of the wife to the Kazi who conducts the marriage and the husband."

[9] The option exists, however, when fraud or negligence can be proved by the father or grandfather. For an interesting case from Pakistan see *Noor Muhammad v. The State* 1976 PLD Lah 516. See also *Muhammad Sharif v. Khuda Bakhsh* 1936 AIR Lah 683.

[10] 1935 ILR 59 Bom 426.

[11] Section 13(b).

[12] *Behram Khan v. Akhtar Begum* 1952 PLD Lah 548; *Muhammad Bibi v. Raja* 1962 PLD Azad Jammu and Kashmir 7.

Marriage: Form and Capacity

In addition to the ground now available under the Dissolution of Muslim Marriages Act, the classical law would still appear to be applicable. If a girl given in marriage by a guardian *other than* her father or grandfather attains puberty before 15 (or 16 in Pakistan) she has a right of repudiation at that point. The classical law and the statutory law exist side by side.[13]

One problem brought about by the 1939 Act is whether the option operates by itself to bring the marriage to an end, or whether it is mandatory to obtain a decree from the court. A reading of the Act would make it appear that the latter position prevails; however, there is now a line of Pakistani authority which decides that a court decree is not necessary. In *Muni v. Habib Khan*[14] the judge said:

> Repudiation of marriage by the exercise of [the] option of puberty puts an end to the marriage without the aid of any court, and when the matter comes to court, the court does not dissolve the marriage by its own act but recognizes the termination of the marriage.

A similar point was made in *Noor Muhammad v. The State*.[15]

In this case, the husband brought a private complaint under the Pakistan Penal Code alleging that Noor Muhammad, the father, had committed a criminal breach of trust under Section 406 of the Pakistan Penal Code by arranging a second and bigamous marriage between the wife and another man. The husband alleged that he had married the girl, Amiran, in 1958 and that there had been an agreement that they would commence living together in 1974. Ten days before the girl was due to move to the husband's house, Noor Muhammad told the "husband" that he was giving the girl in marriage to Bashir Ahmad, a marriage which was duly performed. The court decided that there was no bigamy, thus no criminal breach of trust; the girl had exercised her option of puberty. "The mere fact of her entering into a subsequent marriage on attaining puberty amounts to repudiation of her earlier marriage." There is no need to communicate the decision to exercise the option to a court, and any court decree is only confirming an established fact.

The exercise of the option of puberty is the only situation in Hanafi law where a marriage can be avoided unilaterally and extra-judicially at the option of one of the parties. A marriage made by way of jest, or under duress, or without any intent to contract a marriage is, in Hanafi law, nevertheless

---

[13] *Daulan v. Dosa* 1956 PLD (WP) Lah 712.
[14] 1956 PLD (WP) Lah 403.
[15] 1976 PLD Lah 516.

lawful.[16]

The other Sunni schools recognise the right of khiyar in the area of jest and duress. The person who was induced into performing the marriage, for instance through tahdid (threat), can in effect rescind the contract by the exercise of the khiyar.

3.2 Classification

We now turn to a classification of the kinds of marriage found in Sunni law. Most modern jurists in India and Pakistan adopt a threefold classification between sahih (the valid union), batil (the void union) and a middle classification, namely fasid (the irregular union). This type of classification is not necessarily acceptable to non-Hanafi Muslims and even some Hanafi jurists, not least the two disciples (Abu Yusuf and Shaybani), were not prepared to adopt such a rigid demarcation. Nevertheless, the classification technique has gained acceptance. At the very least, it does provide a framework within which one can discuss the effects of irregularities in the forms of the marriage or the capacity of the parties to contract a marriage.

The sahih marriage is a valid and fully effective union. It has a total effect in law in that sexual intercourse is lawful. In addition, the wife is entitled both to a dower and to be maintained by the husband. The husband acquires certain specific rights relating to the organisational aspects of the relationship based primarily upon his patriarchal power to control the activities of his wife (although she still has notional rights with respect both to ownership and control over her own property).

At the other end of the spectrum is the batil or void marriage which does not create any rights or obligations between the parties other than that there is no zina (illicit sexual relations) if the parties were unaware that the marriage was void (shubha). If there is consummation in a batil marriage, it could be argued that there should be a right of dower (similar to a consummated fasid marriage). However this is a doubtful proposition. The factor which makes the union batil is that there is a permanent irregularity preventing the relationship from being regularised.

A fasid marriage, like a batil marriage, is also no marriage at all. There is a clear irregularity in a fasid relationship although, in contrast to the batil

---

[16] There is one Pakistan case which suggests that when a woman above the age of puberty has not consented to the marriage, then there is no valid subsisting marriage for the simple reason that there has been no effective acceptance. *Sughran Mai v. The State* 1980 PLD Lah 386.

Marriage: Form and Capacity

relationship, the irregularity in this situation is of a temporary nature; thus if the parties were to separate and the temporary bar removed there would be no reason why the marriage between the parties should not be reconstituted as a sahih union. If the fasid marriage is consummated, certain legal effects arise, primarily that children of the union are legitimate (nasab), a dower is due to the wife, and on separation (which must occur) the wife is obliged to observe an 'idda period from the date of separation.[17] The amount the wife receives by way of dower is the customary (proper) dower or the specified sum whichever is the less.[18] The parties are not liable to any penalties for committing zina. The fasid marriage, however, is not capable of ratification by simple approbation. There must be a separation. The distinction between batil and fasid was well described in 1950 by Professor Anderson who, in commenting upon Abu Hanifa's view, stated:

> In Batil, the contract was vitiated in essence and there was no legal effect; in Fasid, the contract was good in itself and would have been valid in different circumstances, but was illegal in this particular instance by reason of some divine prohibition.[19]

A fasid marriage therefore is good in itself, but the particular circumstances render it irregular; thus it is the responsibility of the parties, or in the absence of any move by the parties themselves, the responsibility of the qadi, to separate the couple.

The two disciples, as the Shi'i schools and the other Sunni schools, recognise no real distinction between batil and fasid unions. Rather they recognise the doctrine of "semblance" (shubha) of the marriage. In a case where the husband and the wife acted in good faith and were ignorant of the irregularity, or at least of its effect in law, the concept of shubha removes the possibility of a charge of zina, and it establishes both the right to a dower and the duty of an 'idda period imposed after the separation.

Although the distinction between batil and fasid marriages is a blurred one, and has been rejected even by some in the Hanafi school, it is generally recognised in India as the basis of jurisprudential discussion; thus it is adopted in these pages. We turn now to consider the particular defective unions which are the subject of this discussion.

---

[17] This doctrine is discussed later in this chapter.
[18] Hedeya vol I book II ch.III.
[19] 1949/50 13 Bulletin of S.O.A.S. p 357.

3.3 Batil Marriages

3.3.1 Blood Relatives (Nasab)

The first heading of batil marriages relates to the prohibitions which stem from consanguinity. In outline, the rules prohibit a man from marrying his own ascendants or his own descendants; or his father's or mother's descendants (that is his sister and her descendants). A complete list of the prohibitory degrees is as follows. There is a permanent impediment between a man and:

```
(i) his mother and all female ascendants;
(ii) his daughter and all female descendants;
(iii) his sister, whether germane, consanguine, or
uterine;
(iv) his paternal aunt and the paternal aunt of any
ascendant;
(v) his maternal aunt and any maternal aunt of any
ascendant;
(vi) his brother's daughter (of whatever degree of
descent);
(vii) his sister's daughter (of whatever degree of
descent).
```

The only immediate relatives with whom the man is free to marry are his mother's brother's/sister's daughter and his father's brother's/ sister's daughter; i.e. his cousin. Such marriages, of course, are of frequent occurrence on the Indian subcontinent.

3.3.2 Relationship by Affinity (Musahara)

Relationships by affinity are, in certain circumstances, likewise prohibited. A man is prohibited from marrying, first, any ascendant or descendant of his wife and second, any former wife of any ascendant or descendant. The only exception which is permitted in Hanafi law is that a man, if he so desires, can marry a descendant of his wife by another marriage so long as he had not consummated that marriage with her.[20] If the first marriage is itself fasid or batil, then there is no prohibition on marrying a descendant of that woman from the first batil or fasid marriage *unless* the union had been consummated. If this has in fact occurred, then the prohibition is operative.

---

[20] Hedaya. vol I book II ch.1.

Marriage: Form and Capacity

3.3.3 Relationship by Fosterage (Rada'a)

Historically, a third prohibition arises in a situation where there is a relationship of what is called "fosterage". This prohibition, introduced by jurists, stemmed from the not uncommon situation of the woman providing breast milk not only for her own child but for someone else's child as well. The two children are prohibited from intermarrying, as are the male child with the foster mother. The link arising out of the mother's milk is given a force similar to the blood tie. In Hanafi law, at least, even one drop of milk will create the bar. The Hedaya lays down the prohibition in the following way:

> It is not lawful for a man to marry his foster-mother, or his foster-sister, the Almighty having commanded, saying, "Marry not your mothers who have suckled you, or your sisters by fosterage", and the Prophet has also declared, "Everything is prohibited by reason of fosterage which is so by reason of kindred."[21]

3.3.4 Illicit Sexual Impropriety

The next prohibition to be considered arises out of an act of impropriety between a man and a woman. Although the man, at least in the Sunni schools, can marry the girl in question, the improper association is seen by the Hanafi and the Hanbali jurists in particular as an association which creates a permanent bar to a marriage between the man and those relatives of the girl with whom he is prohibited by the bar on affinity (musahara). The man can however marry the girl's sister; for there is no such bar in that situation based on musahara.[22]

Moreover, the impropriety is caused not only when there is actual proof of sexual intercourse. It arises also when there is privacy (khalwat) between the man and the girl. The Hanafi and the Hanbali jurists, therefore, treat the sexual act, or an actual period of privacy, as equivalent to a nikah to create a musahara impediment.

This view of illicit sexual contact being equated to a nikah is rejected by the Shafi'i and the Maliki jurists. The Shi'i jurists accept the Hanafi view with regard to actual illicit intercourse; but, if there is privacy only, the Shi'i jurists do not have any consensus view, some favouring the Hanafi viewpoint and others favouring the Maliki law.

---

[21] Hedaya vol I Book II ch.1.

[22] For a Pakistan case on this area of the law see *Mst. Sakina v. The State* 1981 PLD FSC 320.

Marriage: Form and Capacity

3.3.5 Remarriage to a Triply Divorced Wife

We shall consider later, in the chapter on divorce, the various forms of repudiation, known as the talaq. It can happen, indeed the most frequent repudiation is in this very form, that a man repudiates his wife for a third time. If this occurs, the man cannot constantly keep his wife "as if she were hanging in the air". There has to be some finality to the question. Thus any marriage between the couple *inter se* (after a triple talaq) is void unless and until, first, the woman has observed her 'idda (or waiting period);[23] secondly, that there has been a supervening marriage between the woman and another man; and thirdly, that this supervening marriage has itself been consummated and effectively terminated. The Hedaya goes into great detail on the possibility of an intervening marriage with a person who marries her solely to free her from the impediment of a remarriage with her former husband. In particular, attention is given to a marriage with a boy below the age of puberty. In these cases, the intervening marriage is valid and a second marriage with the first husband (after a valid dissolution of the intervening marriage) is sahih; *but* it is necessary for penetration actually to take place.[24]

There is some dispute as to whether a remarriage between the man and his first wife without the intervening union is batil or fasid. One opinion is based on the point that as the impediment is actually temporary – the marriage would be correct so long as the procedures with regard to the intervening marriage are gone through – the remarriage after a triple talaq and without any intervening marriage should be fasid rather than batil. Indian case law, however, treats such marriages as batil.[25]

3.3.6 Polyandry

Although polygamy within certain limits is permissible, polyandry (the woman taking a second husband whilst still married to her first husband) is reprehensible and such a second union is batil.[26]

3.3.7 Differences of Religion

In Hanafi law, a man may marry a Muslim woman or a Kitabiyya (a woman of the book). A Muslim female can marry no one other than a Muslim

---

[23] See later.
[24] vol I book IV ch. 11.
[25] See the Indian case of *Rashid Ahmad v. Anisa Khatun* 1931 59 LR IA 21.
[26] See *In the Matter of Ram Kumari* 1891 ILR 18 Cal 264; *Budansa Rowther v. Fatma Bi* 1914 26 Mad LJ 260.

male. Most Shi'i sects, traditionally, do not permit any flexibility. The status of Kitabiyya is granted to Jewish and Christian girls, and also to Magians (or Zoroastrians).[27] The important question is whether a marriage solemnised between a Muslim husband and a non-Kitabiyya or between a Muslim girl and a non-Muslim is batil or fasid. In Qur'an, Sura II, verse 221, it is said: "Do not marry unbelieving women until they believe". This is generally taken to show that a union of the type referred to is a batil union. The Indian jurist, Ameer Ali, did not accept this viewpoint. He suggested that these marriages should be considered fasid. He placed the emphasis on the temporary nature of the irregularity.[28]

An interesting if slightly puzzling case in this area is the Privy Council decision of *Abdool Razack v. Aga Mahomed Jaffer Bindaneem*.[29] The case concerned the inheritance claim brought by a Muslim (Abdool Razack) to the property of his uncle. On the death of the uncle, no immediate Muslim heirs could be discovered. Abdool Razack was the son of a relationship between the half-brother of the deceased and a Burmese Buddhist (Mah Thai). The case is somewhat coloured by the peculiar circumstances in which it was brought before the court. When the uncle died, certain Calcutta gentlemen "discovered" Abdool Razack – who was living rough in the jungle – and adopted his claim as a speculative enterprise. The success of the action, of course, depended on whether there had been a valid marriage between the half-brother and the Burmese lady (Mah Thai). Out of this curious case, two principles appear to be established. First, a marriage between a Muslim male and a polytheistic female is batil. Thus the classical view of the Qur'anic texts is accepted, and the views of Ameer Ali, the nineteenth-century Indian jurist, rejected. Second, the issue of such a batil relationship is illegitimate – and, as such, no such child is capable of being acknowledged as a legitimate child.

Unfortunately, both these principles were really *obiter* in the particular case for, on the facts, the court decided that the half-brother and Mah Thai had simply cohabited and had not married. It could be argued, therefore, that it is

---

[27] Although see *Viswalingham v. Viswalingham* [1979] 1 F.L.R. 15, where the English Court of Appeal decided that the unilateral termination of a marriage, under the law of Malaysia, by the husband's change of religion from Hindu to Muslim did not constitute a divorce within the meaning of the English legislation. In the context of this case, the court heard evidence of a restrictive approach taken by Shafi'i law to the definition of a Kitabiyya.

[28] Many modern Pakistan writers adopt a similar viewpoint. See for instance A.A.Qadri *Muslim Personal Law* (Lahore, 1969); Shaukat Mahmood *Principles and Digest of Muslim Law* (rewritten Lahore, 1967).

[29] 1893/4 21 LR IA 56.

still an open question whether by Muslim law as applied in India and Pakistan the marriage of a Muslim man to a Hindu or Buddhist girl or maybe even of a Muslim girl to a non-Muslim is a fasid rather than a batil union.

The point is, perhaps, academic in India – for the Special Marriage Act 1954 as amended in 1976 permits a marriage to be solemnised under its provisions between any two persons regardless of religious affiliation so long as it is a monogamous marriage and so long as both parties have capacity in fact to enter into a monogamous relationship. The position in Pakistan and Bangladesh, however, is very different. If a Muslim wishes to marry a Hindu girl, for instance, in either of the countries, the couple can do one of three things – all possibly unattractive. First, the girl can adopt Islam; secondly, the couple can marry in a secular form outside the country;[30] thirdly, the couple can take advantage of the provisions of the Special Marriage Act (1872) still in force both in Pakistan and in Bangladesh. The 1872 Act, however, is very limited in its scope. It is available, first, for persons both of whom profess one or other of the Hindu, Buddhist, Sikh or Jaina religions. Second, it provides a form of marriage for persons neither of whom professes the Christian, Jewish, Parsi, Muslim, Sikh, Buddhist or Jaina religions. In effect, therefore, two people, (unless they are both members of the Hindu or associated faiths) who wish to marry under the Act, are forced to renounce their religion. It is a matter of controversy whether such a renunciation, made solely for the purposes of enabling a solemnisation of an inter-community marriage, is valid. Indian cases decided before partition suggest that it is not necessary to enquire into the *bona fides* of a renunciation; the test therefore is purely subjective. For example, in the case of *Mohan v. Mohan*[31] it was decided that whether the parties to a marriage solemnised under the terms of the 1872 Act were or were not at heart adherents to a particular faith was irrelevant for the purpose of the Act and the only relevant criterion was the declaration made at the time of the celebration of the marriage. The Dacca bench of the old Pakistan High Court was not as tolerant and the authority which would presumably prevail today both in Bangladesh and Pakistan is the case of *Muhammad Mustafizur Rahman Khan v. Rina Khan.*[32] In this case, both parties at the time of the marriage which was celebrated under the 1872 Act, declared that they did not belong to a specified religion. Subsequently, however, they denied having renounced respectively the Muslim and the Christian religions. It was held, therefore, that

---

[30] It is necessary to state that capacity of the parties to marry outside the country in this way has not yet been tested in the Pakistan or Bangladesh courts.
[31] 1943 AIR Sind 311.
[32] 1967 PLD Dacca 652.

the marriage which was purported to have been solemnised under the 1872 Act was null and void.

3.4 Fasid Marriages

3.4.1 Marriage Without Witnesses

It will be recalled that one of the few formalities which has to be observed is that witnesses, 2 male or 1 male and 2 female, must be present at the moment the marital tie is created. Thus the absence of witnesses invalidates the union. The witnesses must be adult, sane and Muslim. A man and a woman who contract a marriage without witnesses are under a duty, as in all fasid marriages, to separate. The bar, however, is not permanent — and the matter can be resolved by the husband and wife contracting a fresh marriage in the presence of the appropriate witnesses.

There are many cases where the formalities of marriage are beyond positive proof. Quite a few of these cases have come for determination before the British courts and tribunals. They have also been considered by Pakistan courts. All the decisions tend to lean in favour of a valid sahih marriage. Thus in one case, the court said:

> There is ample evidence to show that both Mst. Qadul and Haji Qadir Bakhsh had for years lived as husband and wife in the eyes of the public and nobody seems to have raised his little finger on the nature of their relationship which by no means appears promiscuous.[33]

Islamic law permits the proof of marriage on the basis of a prolonged and continuous cohabitation by the parties. There must be evidence that the man acknowledged the woman as being his lawful wife, and equally acknowledged any children by the relationship as being his legitimate children. The presumption does not arise in a case where no lawful marriage could have been solemnised in any event.

3.4.2 The 'Idda

The second situation we discuss of a fasid relationship arises when a man marries a woman who is in her 'idda period. We have mentioned this doctrine on two occasions so far in this chapter. 'Idda must be observed by the woman after her divorce from the former marriage or on the death of the first husband. The 'idda provides a period of time for the parties to "ascertain the state of the womb" at the moment of divorce or death. This is important in

---

[33] *Mst Qadul v. Allah Bachaya* 1973 PLD BJ 48.

order to establish parentage and thus to protect the rights both of the first as well as of a potential second husband. In addition, the 'idda period enables the wife to observe mourning in the case of her husband's death. If the wife indeed be pregnant, it is seen to be correct for tenderness to be shown to the foetus. During the 'idda period the wife cannot remarry. If she does so, the marriage is fasid, there must be a separation, and the parties must contract a fresh ceremony of marriage. The need to observe an 'idda period is linked closely with the Islamic notion of consummation, and it is interesting to note that no 'idda period is required when a marriage, dissolved by a talaq, has not been consummated. However, as we have seen, Islamic law does not demand definitive evidence of the sexual act. If it is shown that the husband and the wife were together in a room on their own, and that the circumstances of their meeting were such that there was no possible impediment to the performance of the sexual act, then this situation (khalwat) (often referred to as "undue familiarity", "privacy" or "valid retirement") is, at least for certain purposes including the matter at present under discussion, deemed to have the same consequences as consummation. If the marriage has not been "consummated" in the extended sense as explained above, no 'idda period is necessary on divorce; thus the wife on divorce can immediately remarry. Otherwise, she has to observe an 'idda period of three menstrual cycles (or 3 months in the case of a woman who does not menstruate or whose menstruations are irregular) before she can remarry. Furthermore, the prohibition extends to cases of separation from a fasid union itself. If the woman is pregnant at the time of repudiation (or death of husband) the 'idda period is prolonged until the delivery. And if the husband dies, an 'idda period of death (4 months and 10 days) has to be observed in any event regardless of whether the marriage has or has not been consummated. Thus any marriage solemnised by a man with a woman who is observing an 'idda period is fasid.

3.4.3 Polygamy

The third prohibition which results in a fasid marriage arises when a man, whilst already married to his maximum of four wives, marries a fifth wife. This fifth contract of marriage is fasid. This topic is discussed in Chapter 5.

3.4.4 Unlawful Conjunction (Jam')

This prohibition is simply stated. A man may not validly contract in marriage his existing wife's sister or any woman so related to his wife that if one of them were male they could not lawfully marry. The source for this rule is Sura IV, verse 23 in the Qur'an. "And two sisters in wedlock at one and the same time, except for what is past; for Allah is oft-forgiving." This verse includes the prohibition based on consanguinity, and some interpret the verse collectively as creating permanent prohibitions based on nasab (consanguinity) and sabab (other cause – namely affinity and conjunction). Such indeed was the view of early Indian decisions such as *Aizunnissa Khatoon v. Karimunnissa Khatoon*[34] Logically, the prohibition of "unlawful conjunction" should be characterised as a temporary prohibition. On the separation of the parties to the second union and a subsequent divorce from the first wife, there would be no reason why the man should not remarry his second partner. This indeed is the more appropriate solution in modern jurisprudence; and has been accepted by Indian cases.[35]

3.4.5 Kafa'a (Equality)

The doctrine of kafa'a is different from the other fasid situations so far discussed. The inequality of the parties provides the guardian in certain circumstances with the right to exercise the khiyar (option) to set the marriage aside. Thus, kafa'a is closely analogous to the khiyar al-bulugh (the option of puberty). Nonetheless, the effect of the successful exercise of the khiyar and its application by the court produces a separation of the parties. Thus kafa'a is best discussed today within the context of fasid marriages.

The principle of kafa'a was peculiar to the ancient school of law of Kufa, where, because of the freedom of an adult girl to contract herself in marriage, it was seen to be necessary to protect the interests of the wali (the guardian). After Shafi'i's thesis had been accepted by the scholars, the principle of kafa'a found its way into Maliki law, although in a rather restricted sense. In Maliki law, as we know, the wife requires the consent of her guardian. Thus, there was no real danger that the girl would be influenced to marry a man not her equal, unless there was fraud. Thus, fraud came to be regarded as essential in Maliki law on an application by the wali for a separation of the parties based upon inequality. This is not the case, of course, in Hanafi law.

Six matters, all to some extent interrelated, would appear to provide grounds in Hanafi law for inequality. These are: family, Islamic adherence, occupation, freedom, character and financial resources. As to family and freedom, these are of no real significance today. Slavery is of course abolished and the view that only a man of the tribe of Qur'aysh (Mohammed's tribe) is suitable for a woman of that tribe cannot really be extended to a system which, in theory, although not in practice, is caste-free. As to Islamic

---

[34] 1895 ILR 23 Cal 130.

[35] See for instance *Tajbi v. Mowla Khan* 1917 ILR Bom 485.

adherence, a Muslim husband whose father is a non-Muslim would seem not to be kafa'a with a woman whose parents were both Muslim. This form of kafa'a must be of only limited application today. Certainly it is not observed in countries such as Egypt.[36] With regard to the other three factors, namely occupation, character and financial resources, certain guidelines were developed by the jurists. First, the husband should have the probability of matching the financial means of the wife's father. Second, the husband should have a similar occupation as the wife's father, and third, if the wife's father is pious, the husband must not be irreligious. A misalliance is not of itself fasid, and acquiescence by the guardian will enable the marriage to continue. Only the guardian can apply for separation, although in at least one Pakistan case the court appear to have given the wife *locus standi* to apply on her own behalf for separation based on kafa'a. The application was unsuccessful.[37]

The courts of India and Pakistan have a wide discretion, and they will only terminate the marriage when it would be inequitable to permit continuation having regard to the interests both of the two parties and their respective families.

3.4.6 Conclusion

It is as well to complete the description of batil and fasid unions by returning to the question of shubha (semblance) which was mentioned briefly earlier in this chapter. It has already been said that although a systematic distinction between batil and fasid appears from some of the texts, none the less this distinction is blurred at the edges. Other jurists state that neither an irregular nor a void marriage has *any* validity whatever in law unless it is consummated. If the union is consummated in a situation where the parties were acting in good faith, then any children of such a union is legitimate and there is no zina. The "wife" is entitled to the appropriate dower and the 'idda period has to be observed by her on the separation.

What has been discussed so far is often classified by jurists under five different conditions (shurut). These conditions are:

(a) shurut al-in'iqad

---

[36] M.K.Khadduri and H.Liebesny (eds.) *Law in the Middle East* (Washington, 1955), Chapter VI by Abu Zahra.
[37] *Shazada Begum v. Sh.Abdul Hamid* 1950 PLD Lah 504. In *Sughran Mai v. The State* 1980 PLD Lah 386 at p.397 the Judge said kafa'a might provide a ground for annulment for the wife herself "if she was misrepresented by the husband regarding any element of his social status".

Marriage: Form and Capacity

(b) shurut al-sihha
(c) shurut al-madaidh
(d) shurut al-luzum
(e) shurut al-sijill

The first shurut, the in'iqad, deals with the necessity to comply with the formal conditions – namely the offer and acceptance must be pronounced at the same meeting, and must issue from persons competent to make the contract. In contrast the second shurut, the sihha, deals with the conditions which decide whether the contract, valid as to form, actually creates a marriage valid as to essence. For instance, are the parties outside the prohibited degree of relationship? Third, the shurut al-madaidh, which deals with the matter of effectiveness, relates primarily to questions of capacity of slaves and, as such, is no longer of significance. Fourth, the al-luzum concerns itself with the question whether the contract is binding – for example, the option of puberty and the ability of the husband to consummate the marriage.[38] The fifth shurut – the al-sijill – refers to the modern innovation of registration. Here, a new category has been created – the illegal marriage – whereby criminal penalties and sanctions are imposed in the absence of registration; although the marriage may well be valid, if it can be proved by other means.[39]

Having considered the questions relating to form and capacity and itemised circumstances when a defective marriage is contracted, we must now turn our attention to the legal effects which arise on the solemnisation of a valid marriage.

---

[38] See later in the chapter on divorce.
[39] See *Nasim Akhtar v. The State* 1968 PLD Lah 841.

4. Marriage: Legal Effects

A sahih marriage is a contract. It is also a status and carries with it a number of rights, duties and responsibilities. Many of these fall into the domain of the religious and the spiritual. However, strictly legal consequences play a significant part in the description of the totality of a marriage in Islamic law. A leading Pakistan writer and judge puts it this way:

> The rights arising out of an Islamic marriage contract are not the gifts of any legislative body of a country; they emanate from the proposal and acceptance of the parties made at marriage time. The rights and obligations arising thus are a cohesive whole based on the biddings of God and traditions of the Prophet. Hence Muslim jurists regard Nikah to be both temporal and religious at the same time.[1]

It is nonetheless true that the Islamic marriage complies with a patriarchal pattern firmly based on its historical and geographical roots. Although the status of marriage should be seen as a composite unit, for discussion purposes it is possible to separate a number of specific issues. Five matters require some discussion.

```
(1) sexual intercourse and the procreation of children;
(2) the husband's control over his wife;
(3) the dower;
(4) the entitlement of the wife to maintenance;
(5) the question of ownership of property.
```

4.1 Sexual Relations

The Qur'an contains many verses outlawing the sexual connection between a man and woman outside a valid (sahih) or a fasid union. Typical of such verses are Sura XVII, verse 32:

```
Nor come nigh to adultery:
For it is a shameful (deed)
And an evil, opening the road
(To other evils)
```

and Sura XXIV, verses 2-3:

---

[1] Tanzil-ur-Rahman *A Code of Muslim Personal Law* vol. I p. 18. (Karachi, 1978).

Marriage: Legal Effects

```
The woman and the man
Guilty of adultery or fornication
Flog each of them with a hundred stripes.
```

Sexual intimacy is only permitted, therefore, in the context of the marital union. Outside this union, sexual connection is referred to as zina, and endangers the perpetrators to the hudud (compulsory) punishment. We shall have occasion to discuss this aspect later.

4.2 The Right of Control and Guidance

A wife who leaves the husband's home without permission or legal reason is seen by Islamic law to be a rebellious wife (nashiza). The power of the husband, however, certainly does not extend to refusing the wife the right to visit her parents or other close relatives. Equally, unreasonable requests by the husband that the wife should accompany him on long journeys can be refused by the wife. The corresponding duty of the husband, of course, is to provide a dower (mahr) and maintenance for his wife. The Muslim law sees the system of rights and duties within the marriage as a carefully balanced appraisal of the needs of both men and women. One Pakistani decision, *Sahi Bi v. Khalid Hussain*,[2] serves by way of example to illustrate this balance. The Supreme Court of Pakistan considered a case which one suspects occurs all too frequently. Irshid Begum was married to Khalid. They lived together for a month after their marriage. It was then suggested by the wife's mother that the husband was cruel to her daughter, and she therefore left the marital home and returned, indeed "took refuge", in the maternal home. It is alleged that some time later, the girl was forcibly removed by the husband and his family. The mother brought an application under the Pakistan Penal Code s. 491. In effect, this criminal action complained that the husband was not allowing the girl to move freely, that she was confined within the four walls of the house, that she was maltreated, and indeed that she was tortured. The court took the view that a wife cannot be forced to live with her husband against her wishes. The Judge said:

> [A]ccording to Mohammadan Law, if there is disagreement between the husband and the wife, the wife is entitled to live separately from her husband.

However, notwithstanding this statement of general principle, the Judge went on to state that it was open to the husband to file a suit for restitution of

---

[2] 1973 S.C.M.R. vol. 6 p. 577.

conjugal rights. In that context, unless the wife is able to show that the husband has treated her with cruelty, a decree will be ordered. Although the decree can not be enforced, and to that extent the remedy may not be viewed as effective, refusal by the wife in these circumstances to return to the husband releases him from any obligation to provide maintenance. In addition, any property owned by the wife can be attached. Thus it is clear that the general principle is that a wife is bound to reside with her husband unless there is a valid reason for her refusal to do so.[3]

4.3 The Dower (Mahr)

4.3.1 Definitions

The dower (mahr) is paid by the husband to his wife. It needs to be emphasised at the outset that the mahr is not a *consideration* for the contracting of the marriage. The dower must be clearly seen as the *effect* of the contract of marriage rather than the price paid by the husband for acquiring the various rights which accrue to him on marriage. Mahr is often discussed also in terms of a sum paid to the wife as a mark of respect to her. If, therefore, no mahr is agreed by the parties, the contract of marriage is neither fasid nor batil. It is still a sahih marriage, and what is referred to by the expression "proper dower" created by operation of law will become payable. The concept of the "proper dower" is discussed later. Thus early Indian cases must be read with caution. For instance, Lord Parker described a dower in the following way in *Hamira Bibi v. Zubaida Bibi*.[4]

> Dower is an essential incident under the Musulman law to the status of marriage; to such an extent this is so that when it is unspecified at the time the marriage is contracted, the law declares that it must be adjudged on definite principles. Regarded as a consideration for the marriage. . . .

Mahmood J's dictum in *Abdool Kadir v. Salima* [1886][5] is similarly misleading. He said:

> Dower, under the Muhammadan Law, is a sum of money or other property promised by the husband to be paid or delivered to the wife in consideration of the marriage, and even where no dower is expressly

---

[3] Another case of interest which discusses this area of law is *Mohd. Zaman v. Irshid Begum*. 1967 PLD Lah 1104.
[4] 1915/16 43 LR IA 294.
[5] 1886 ILR 8 All 149.

fixed or mentioned at the marriage ceremony, the law confers the right of dower upon the wife.[6]

A more accurate description which expresses clearly the basis of the dower in Islamic law is the definition adopted by Abu Zahra writing in Chapter VI of the book *Law in the Middle East*.[7] Abu Zahra says:

> The Mahr is a due which the husband must pay to the wife in accordance with the marriage contract, but it is not a condition which affects the validity of the contract nor is it an essential requisite. Therefore, if the Mahr is not mentioned in the contract, the contract is still valid.

In a case in Karachi in 1980, *Siddiqui v. Family Judge Court III Karachi*[8] the Judge defined the dower as:

> a right which comes into existence with the marriage contract itself except that in case the dower is deferred its enforcement is held in abeyance till a certain event, i.e., dissolution of marriage by death or divorce occurs.

Another Pakistan judge, from Peshawer, has referred to the mahr as "a mark of respect" to the wife.[9]

Having underlined the point that the obligation to pay a mahr is an *effect* of the marriage, rather than an *incident* to it, we must now turn our attention to the question of classification. The mahr is usually classified either as a specified or as an unspecified ("proper") mahr. The specified mahr is itself subclassified into prompt and deferred.

4.3.2 Specified Mahr

The early Hanafi and Maliki jurists developed a minimum limit to the specified dower, by the use of analogy with the minimum value of stolen goods which rendered a thief liable to one of the hudud penalties; namely amputation of the hand. The sum was 10 dihrams in Hanafi law and 3 dihrams

---

[6] See Winn J in the English case of *Shahnaz v. Rizwan* 1965 1 QB 390: "What is being sought to be enforced here is a contract entered into in contemplation of, by reason of, and – as has been said in at least one decided case, though some doubt it to be very accurate – in consideration of a marriage..."

[7] M.K.Khadduri and H.Liebesny (eds.), *Law in the Middle East* (Washington, 1955).

[8] 1980 PLD Karachi 477.

[9] *Zarin Qaisha v. Arbub Wali Mohd* 1976 PLD Pesh 128.

in Maliki law.[10] The use of analogy raises the suspicion that the dower is a consideration for the marriage; rather it should be seen, however, as we have already stated, as an effect of the creation of the relationship. No maximum limits were laid down by the early jurists. In South Asia, as in some Middle East countries, the recent trend has been for very large mahr sums to be announced. There are probably three reasons for this trend. First, the fathers of brides will often demand high mahr sums for status purposes. Second, in many cases the bridegrooms themselves encourage the insertion of large mahr sums in the nikahnama (marriage contract) for their own aggrandisement. Finally, and obviously a more valid reason, a large dower sum can be viewed as an insurance against the possibility of an unjustified divorce by the husband or his early death.

If the dower is *intended* to be paid, then the dower is enforceable against the husband. Indeed, it is only in Oudh (Uttar Pradesh), under the Oudh Laws Act (1876) section 5 and in both Jammu Kashmir and Azad Kashmir (Pakistan) under the Muslim Dower Act (1920) that a dower is enforceable only if it is a reasonable figure in the circumstances of the particular parties. It is not necessary to do more than comment that the system imposes substantial financial strains on young men who often find that it is simply impossible for them to raise the money required, and who in consequence delay their marriage for considerable periods of time.

Another unfortunate result of the lack of a maximum sum of dower is that publicly acclaimed mahr, in many cases, is never intended to be paid, for there is a private agreement for a lesser sum agreed between the parties. In any dispute over the payment of dower, there is ample scope for the husband to allege such an agreement. If the court believes him, it is the private agreement (the as-sum'at) which will be enforced.

A comment on the institution of as-sum'at was made by the Pakistan Marriage Commission in its report in 1955. The Commission stated:

> The result [of the as-sum'at] is that even in cases where a larger amount of Mahr has been genuinely fixed, a defence is taken, if litigation ensues, that the Mahr was not meant to be paid, and that the intention of the parties was that it should never be claimed. This necessitates the framing of a number of unnecessary issues by the court, and the civil suit relating to dower lasts sometimes for ten years.

The Commission believed that the possibility for husbands to argue that the agreement in the nikahnama was really a sham had created a social evil. It

---

[10] In *Asma Bibi v. Abdul Samad Khan* 1910 ILR 32 All 167, ten dihrams is treated as equivalent to three or four Rupees.

Marriage: Legal Effects

recommended that the law should require the husband to pay the fixed mahr no matter how high it was set in the document. This view was criticised, and it never became law. The principle was discussed more recently by Daud Khan J in the Peshawar case, *Nasir Ahmad Khan v. Asmat Jehan Begum*:[11]

> Broadly speaking, this principle recognized that when a real dower has been fixed between the parties privately and in some cases publicly the second dower is fixed in inflated amount just for the enhancement of the prestige of the family of the bridegroom, and for its glorification, but in such a case the intention was never to enforce the dower announced in public and the real intention was to enforce the dower agreed upon privately between the parties. It is abundantly clear that the principle of as-sum'at recognizes the fixation of two agreements with respect to the dower – one agreement is in private for a real amount and the other agreement for the inflated amount is in public for the glorification of the bridegroom and his family, and if this is proved then the real dower which has been fixed in private should alone be allowed.

Thus, the presence of the dower must be seen in the context of the absence of alimony after divorce, and within the background that although the dower can be either prompt or deferred, the greater part of it is usually deferred. It is important to distinguish the dower (mahr) from "dowry and bridal gifts". The latter are sums of money and presents given either by the bride's family (jehaz or dowry) or by the groom's family (bridal gifts). In Pakistan, under the Dowry and Bridal Gifts (Restriction) Act 1976 s.5, all such property vests absolutely in the bride. Furthermore, section 3 places a restriction on the amounts that can be given as dowry presents and bridal gifts, and there has to be a display of these articles. Criminal penalties are laid down for breach of the Act. The dower (mahr) is expressly excluded from the operation of this Act.[12]

4.3.3 The Prompt and the Deferred Specified Dower

The prompt dower is payable immediately after the marriage; so long as the wife demands it. More commonly some of the dower, if not the entire amount, will be deferred; payable on the dissolution of the marriage by divorce or death, or on the happening of a specified event. Many marriage contracts, of course, do not specify whether the dower is to be prompt or

---

[11] 1967 PLD Pesh 328.
[12] For a discussion see R.Patel *Women and Law in Pakistan* at pp. 24 ff.

deferred. In these circumstances, the presumption, in the absence of any usage of the particular community, is that the dower is prompt. This is certainly the position in Pakistan, for Section 10 of the 1961 Muslim Family Laws Ordinance 1961 lays down that when no details of the mode for payment of dower are specified, the entire amount of dower shall be presumed to be payable on demand.

4.3.4 The Unspecified Dower

As we have had occasion to state already, if no mahr sum is specified in the marriage contract, the husband is not thereby released from his liability to pay a dower. Even a statement that no dower shall be paid does not change the position. In these circumstances, what is known as the "proper dower" (the mahr al-mithl) becomes due. The mahr al-mithl is worked out on the basis of the mahr paid to women of a similar social status to the wife. Particularly relevant will be the mahr paid to other female members of the wife's family; for instance, sisters, paternal aunts and female cousins.

One must distinguish the pre-nuptial agreement releasing the husband from his obligation to provide the wife with a dower – which is a void contract in Muslim law – from the remission of the dower which can be made after the marriage by the wife. She can enter into an agreement remitting the obligation to pay the dower either in whole or in part. Such a remission in this context is equivalent to a gift. She is the owner of the dower, and she can do with it what she likes.

All gifts of course are subject to the general rules relating to ikrah (threats). If coercion is proved, the remission will be involuntary, and the remission will be set aside by the court.[13]

4.3.5 Reduction of Dower

If the husband divorces his wife before the marriage has been consummated the dower which he owes to the wife is reduced by one-half, even in the case of a prompt dower.[14] If the wife, having received the prompt dower, remits the dower after the marriage, and then prior to consummation of the marriage the husband divorces his wife, it would seem that she is entitled

---

[13] See *Shah Bano v. Iftikhar Muhammad Khan* 1956 PLD (WP) Karachi 363. In this case the wife remitted the dower so as to prevent the husband from taking a lover. It was held by the court that in the circumstances of the case the remission or waiver was void and it was therefore of no effect.

[14] *Tajbi v. Nattar* AIR 1940 Madras 888. In this case the court applied the provision stated in the Hedaya vol.I Book II chapter 3 at p. 124.

to one-half of the dower. In contrast if the wife, having never received the dower, remits the sum after the marriage, and then the marriage is dissolved by the husband prior to consummation, the dower debt is completely absolved. If the dower is a "proper dower", the wife will be entitled to a present (mut'a). If the wife divorces the husband before consummation, which although rare will be possible in certain cases, the dower will be cancelled. In the event of the husband's death, in Hanafi and Hanbali law the wife will nonetheless be entitled to the dower payment (or in appropriate cases the "proper dower") notwithstanding the fact that the marriage may not have been consummated. There are particular rules which apply to the fasid marriage. If the fasid marriage is consummated, the husband is under an obligation to pay a dower, although the obligation is restricted to the payment of either the specified dower or the proper dower whichever is the lesser sum. This rule would enable a husband to pay a more realistic amount in these admittedly few cases. It needs to be added, also, that for the purposes of payment of the dower, the wife does not need to prove actual consumption. Valid retirement (khalwat) will suffice.

4.3.6 Enforcement of Dower
For an excellent discussion of this highly complex topic see an article by Dr. D. Hinchcliffe entitled "The widow's dower-debt" written in 1973.[15]

4.3.6.1 The Deferred Dower
An unpaid dower represents an unsecured debt. On the death of the widow, either her own heirs or her legal representatives are entitled to sue for the debt.[16] A widow also has a right to retain possession of the deceased husband's property until the dower debt is paid to her. This right, which must be distinguished from the right to the dower itself, was discussed in the leading case of *Maina Bibi v. Chaudhri Vakil Ahmad.*[17] A Muslim husband, Muin-ud-Din, died in 1870 survived by a widow, Maina Bibi. The widow remained in possession of certain immovable property. In 1902, the other heirs sued the widow, claiming immediate possession of their share of the estate. The widow defended the application on two grounds. First, she said that the property had been gifted to her. Second, and in the alternative, she argued that she was entitled to remain in possession of the property until the dower had been paid.

---

[15] (1973) vol. IV, Islam and the Modern Age, p.1.
[16] See *Janudul Haque v. Zubair Haider.* AIR 1981 Patna 345.
[17] 1924/5 52 LR IA 145.

The judge made a decree for possession on condition that the heirs paid to the widow Rs25387/- within six months. The decree provided that in default of payment the suit should be dismissed. The heirs did not pay the money and the widow remained in possession.

In 1907, well before the case had been finally decided, the widow, Maini Bibi, executed gifts of the property in favour of a third party. She gave possession of the property to this third party. In 1915, the heirs filed a further suit against the widow and the alienees. The Judicial Committee of the Privy Council, before which the case eventually arrived, advised that although the widow had a right to remain in possession of her former husband's property until the dower debt had been paid, she had no *absolute right* in the property.[18] Thus the alienation in this case is treated as *ultra vires*. Further, the failure of the heirs to comply with the original order did not "convert her into the absolute owner of the immovable property of her deceased husband".

Although a widow's right is a personal right, and she is not able to convey a good title to third parties, the right is heritable and a wife's heirs can themselves remain in possession.[19] The right to remain in possession is of course conditional on being in possession of property at the moment of the husband's death. In all other respects, the widow is in the same situation as other creditors of the estate. Indeed, if there are any profits arising from the property in her possession, she has to account the profits to the other heirs.[20]

---

[18] The Judicial Committee followed the decision of Sir Montagu Smith in *Bachun v. Hamid Husain* (1871) 14 Moo I.A.377. The Judge in that case defined the right to retain possession in the following manner: "It is not necessary to say whether this right of the widow in possession is a lien in the strict sense of the term...whatever the right may be called, it appears to be founded on the power of the widow as creditor for her dower to hold the property of her husband of which she has lawfully, and without force or fraud, obtained the possession until her debt is satisfied, with the liability to account to those entitled to the property subject to the claim for the profits received." See also *Zobair Ahmad v. Jainandam Prasad Singh* 1960 AIR Patna 147.

[19] *Kapore Chand v. Kidar Nissa Begum.* AIR 1953 SC 413. There is a Mysore case which has held that the right to retain possession was not only heritable but also transferable, provided it was done by a deed of conveyance, and the transferee is put in possession. *Hussain v. Rahim Khan* 1954 AIR Mysore 24.

[20] A useful article on this area of the law is Nisar Ahmad Ganai, "Heritability of the Widow's Right of Retention under Muhammadan Law", (1979) vol. III Cochin University Law Review p.493. See also the case of *Syed Yusuf Akbar Hussaini v. Syed Mirturza Akbar Hussaini* (1983) 1 An.W.R. 273.

4.3.6.2 *The Prompt Dower*

Problems arise also in relation to the payment of the prompt dower, not least when wives refuse to have sexual relations until the prompt dower has been paid. The matter usually will be aired by the court on the basis of a suit initiated by the husband for a decree for restitution of conjugal rights. The defence raised by the wife will invariably be that she has denied sexual intercourse to the husband because the dower has not been paid.

Such a defence will be accepted by the court in cases where the marriage has not been consummated. The wife in these circumstances will not be forced to live with her husband until such time as the prompt dower has been paid. Thus refusal to have sexual intercourse under these circumstances does not constitute disobedience (nashuz), and the husband remains under a duty to continue to provide his wife with maintenance.

Difficulties arise, however, in cases where the marriage has actually been consummated and, subsequent to the consummation, the wife refuses any further sexual contact until the prompt dower is paid. Abu Hanifa argued that the wife can always refuse consortium until such time as the dower is paid. The two disciples, Abu Yusuf and Shaybani, as so often, disagree with the view of their teacher and give priority to the actual consummation of the union. The wife's right to demand the payment of the prompt dower by refusing consortium comes to an end as soon as the marriage has been consummated. The right "to refuse consortium", therefore, is in the view of the two disciples a very limited right indeed.

The problem was discussed in India in *Anis Begum v. Muhammad Istafa Wali Khan*. The case followed the normal pattern of a petition by the husband for restitution of conjugal rights, defended by the wife on two grounds, namely, first, that the husband had been guilty of cruelty and second, that the husband had not paid the prompt dower to the wife. On appeal Sulaiman J adopted the views of the Disciples and, to that extent, dismissed the wife's appeal. Sulaiman J said:[21]

> To allow to the wife the right of refusing to live with her husband, even after consummation, so long as any part of the prompt dower remains unpaid would, in many cases, where the husband and wife quarrel, amount to an absolute option to the wife to refuse to live with her husband and yet demand a maintenance allowance. This would dislocate domestic life.

---

[21] 1933 ILR 55 All 743 at pp.752, 753.

Marriage: Legal Effects

A petition for a decree for restitution of conjugal rights is similar to an application for specific performance. Sulaiman J, therefore, was able to exercise his discretionary powers when granting the remedy and he attached a condition that the decree be granted subject to the condition that the prompt dower be paid.

The same question was argued before the court in *Rahim Jan v. Muhammad*.[22] In this case the wife petitioned for divorce on the ground that the husband had failed to maintain her without reasonable cause for two years.[23] The husband defended the petition arguing that the wife had not given him "the benefit of her conjugal society"; thus he was under no obligation to maintain her. In reply, the wife said that the prompt dower had not been paid to her. The court had to decide whether, in Hanafi law, the wife is entitled, even after consummation, to refuse to live with her husband when the prompt dower has not been paid to her. The court dissented from *Anis Begum v. Muhammad* and adopted the view of Abu Hanifa.[24] The court said:

> I do not find any principle of justice or reason by which the right of the wife to refuse the performance of marital obligations on account of non-payment of prompt dower may come to an end by her once surrendering herself. I would hold that even after consummation the wife retains the right to refuse the performance of marital obligations till the prompt dower is paid.[25]

Pakistan and Bangladesh are almost certain to follow the *Rahim Jan* case; but in India, it seems that *Anis Begum* is the better authority.

4.4 Maintenance (Nafaqa)

The Qur'an, Sura IV v. 34 states:

---

[22] 1955 PLD Lah 122.

[23] This ground is available to the wife under the provisions of the Dissolution of Muslim Marriages Act (1939) Section 2. See later.

[24] Kaikus J stated that in his opinion when there was a difference in approach between Abu Hanifa and the two disciples, regard should be taken of the authority and reasons in support of each view. The approach which had the stronger support should then be followed.

[25] See also to the same effect, the following two cases. *Nur-ud-Din Ahmad v. Masuda Khanam* 1957 PLD Dacca 242, and *Muhammadi v. Jamil-ud-din*. 1960 PLD (WP)Karachi 663.

Marriage: Legal Effects

```
Men are the protectors
And maintainers of women
Because God has given
The one more (strength)
Than the other, and because
They support them
From their means.
```

This verse is the basis of the law in this area. A wife is entitled to maintenance (food, clothing and lodging) during the subsistence of a valid (sahih) marriage and during the period of 'idda. As we shall see, there is considerable controversy as to whether the obligation extends beyond the 'idda period. But there is no dispute that the husband remains under the duty to support his wife during the period of 'idda following a revocable pronouncement of talaq by him. So far as the irrevocable talaq is concerned, there is a difference of opinion between Hanafi law and Maliki law on the point. In Hanafi law, a woman divorced by her husband in a form which is held to be irrevocable, is entitled to full maintenance during the 'idda period for as long as she does not leave the home. In contrast to this view, the Maliki law states that such a person is entitled to full maintenance only when she is actually pregnant. Maintenance is extended in such circumstances, that is to pregnant women, even when they leave the former matrimonial home. According to the Maliki view, a non-pregnant woman is only entitled to *lodging* during the 'idda following a pronouncement of an irrevocable divorce.

In the case of a co-wife, she must have a separate apartment from the other wife. We discuss questions relating to co-wives in the next chapter.

One of the problems regarding nafaqa concerns the standard of maintenance which is required. All schools agree that if both the husband and wife come from wealthy backgrounds, then the level of maintenance should be in accordance with their standard of living. Likewise, if both are from poor backgrounds, the level of maintenance will reflect this position. If, however, one party is from a poor background and the other one from a wealthy background, the schools have arrived at slightly differing interpretations of the level of the appropriate maintenance. The Maliki and Hanbali schools adopt the view that the average and medium level should be maintained in all cases. The Hanafi school adopts the same position when the husband is wealthy and the wife poor. When the wife is wealthy and the husband poor, however, the Hanafi school believes that it is unreal to look to an average position. This school adopts the view that the husband's condition alone should be the guiding factor.

Marriage: Legal Effects

As we have seen, a wife loses her right to maintenance if she is "disobedient" (nashiza).[26] This certainly occurs when she *leaves the home* without the husband's consent or without a "lawful excuse". The non-Hanafi schools are of the opinion that even if she stays at home she will not be entitled to maintenance if she refuses sexual intercourse.

Past maintenance is not easy to claim in classical Hanafi law. In this school past maintenance only becomes a true debt if the court has authorised the wife to borrow money on the strength of the debt.[27] The Shafi'i, Hanbali, Maliki and Shi'i schools are more flexible in this area, and arrears are seen as being a debt on the husband which can be claimed however much time has elapsed. Pakistan cases appear to have adopted the flexible attitude of the non-Hanafi schools. For instance, in *Rashid Ahmad Khan v. Nasim Ara*,[28] it was decided that maintenance which is awarded to the wife after the reconciliation and arbitral procedures implicit in Section 9(3) of the Muslim Family Laws Ordinance (1961) can include payment for past maintenance as well as future obligations.[29]

Section 488 of the 1898 Code of Criminal Procedure enables the wife to apply for maintenance if she can prove that her husband, having sufficient means, neglects or refuses to maintain his wife. In Pakistan, the Family Court now has exclusive jurisdiction to entertain, hear or adjudicate upon matters relating to maintenance.[30] In *Hajiran Bibi v. Abdul Khaliq*[31] it was held that this court could award past maintenance. Although this case produced a result contrary to the generally held view of the law under section 488, its effect is certainly welcome. It provides consistency between the arbitral procedures under the Muslim Family Laws Act (1961) and the judicial proceedings in the Family Court.

---

[26] For a discussion of "nashiza" see *Ahmad Ali v. Sabha Khatun Bibi* 1952 PLD Dacca 385.

[27] See *Abdool Futteh v. Zabunnessa* 1881 ILR 6 Cal 631.

[28] 1968 PLD Lah 93.

[29] Section 9 of the Muslim Family Laws Ordinance (1961) states that where a husband fails to maintain his wife adequately, then the wife may apply to the Chairman (of a local Union Council) who shall constitute an arbitration council to determine the matter.

[30] See *Adnan Afzal v. Sher Afzal* 1969 PLD S.C. 187. West Pakistan Family Courts Act 1964 ss 5, 20.

[31] 1981 PLD Lahore 761.

Marriage: Legal Effects

4.4.1 Maintenance after Divorce

We turn now to discuss a question which has caused considerable difficulty in India in particular and which indeed has been the cause of a remarkable series of protests against the Government culminating in the Indian Government in 1986 steering through a Bill which completely undermines the judgment of a special 5 bench Supreme Court ruling.

Section 488 of the Code of Criminal Procedure was amended in India by Section 125 of the Code of Criminal Procedure (1973) which enables maintenance to be awarded to a woman who has been divorced from her husband until her remarriage. As we have seen, however, in classical law, maintenance to a divorced wife ceases after the 'idda period. An additional provision, Section 127(3)(b), was inserted into the Code as a result of political pressure. This section states:

> Where any order has been made under s. 125 in favour of a woman who has been divorced by, or has obtained a divorce from her husband, the Magistrate shall, if he is satisfied that
>
> (b) the woman has been divorced by her husband and that she has received, whether before or after the date of the said order, the whole of the sum which, under any customary or personal law applicable to the parties, was payable on such divorce, cancel such order.

The meaning of Section 127(3)(b) was the subject of much litigation. In Bombay, it was originally held that the payment of the dower on the divorce will satisfy Section 127(3)(b), and that therefore the magistrate would have no jurisdiction to make an order under Section 125.[32] However it was held in Kerela that the dower payment is outside the purview of Section 127(3)(b). In *Muhammed v. Sunabii*,[33] the Judge said that:

> Mahar is an amount payable by the husband to the wife either prompt or deferred. Payment of Mahar will not effect a discharge of a claim for maintenance, because the claim for Mahar is a valuable right available to the wife and this claim is a charge over the properties of the husband.

Three Supreme Court cases resolved the debate in favour of the Kerela

---

[32] *Ruckhsana Parvin v. Sheikh Mohamed Hussein* (1976) 79 Bom LR 123. See generally the article by Professor Derrett in (1977) 80 Bom LR 4.

[33] 1976 KLT 711. See also the case of *Kunhi Moyin v. Pathumma* 1976 KLT 87. A further case of interest is *Madapathi v. Susheda* 1978 Andh LT 7, where it was held that a woman whose marriage is void *ipso jure* has no right to seek maintenance under section 125.

decisions, namely *Bai Tahera v. Ali Husain*,[34] *Fuzlunbi v. K.Khader Vali*,[35] and finally, *Mohd Ahmed Khan v. Shah Bano Begum*.[36] Krishna Iyer J, giving judgment of the court in *Fuzlunbi*, where the husband had paid his wife R500/- by way of a dower, said:

> No one in his senses can contend that the Mahar of R500/- will yield income sufficient to maintain a woman even if she were to live on city pavements! What is the intendment of s.127(3)(b)? What is the scheme of relief for driftwood and destitute wives and divorcees discarded by heartless husbands?[37]

He answered his question, as he had done in *Bai Tahera*, by stating categorically that the payment of illusory amounts by way of customary or personal law requirements would be considered in the reduction of maintenance awarded, but that it could not "annihilate" the rate unless it was a reasonable substitute.

Another case in the Supreme Court in India, *Zohara Khatoon v. Mhd. Ibrahim*[38] permits a wife who has obtained a divorce under the Dissolution of Muslim Marriages Act (1939) to obtain maintenance under Section 125. The court in this case refer to s.127(3)(c) which states that where a woman obtains a divorce from her husband, the amount of maintenance cannot be cancelled until she voluntarily relinquishes or surrenders her rights. Unfortunately, various *obiter* remarks in this judgment appeared to contradict the views of Krishna Iyer J in the earlier cases. There was therefore still some doubt as to the exact extent of s.127(3)(b). As Dr.Tahir Mahmood stated in his contribution to the 1980 Annual Survey of Indian Law about the *Fuzlunbi* decision:[39]

> Whilst some Indian and foreign scholars have strongly supported it, an overwhelming section of the Muslim community have viewed the case with greater anxiety shown earlier for the parent ruling (*Bai Tahera*).

It was hoped that this chapter of uncertainty would be brought to an end by the Supreme Court decision, *Shah Bano's case* [1985] about which some comment is required. Mohd Ahmed Khan, an advocate by profession, was

---

[34] AIR 1979 SC 362.
[35] AIR 1980 SC 1730.
[36] AIR 1985 SC 945.
[37] See also *Thilothama v. Kunjappan* 1983 KLT 90 to the same effect.
[38] AIR 1981 SC 1243.
[39] at p. 72.

Marriage: Legal Effects

married to the respondent, Shah Bano, in 1932. Three sons and two daughters were born to the marriage, which was never a happy one. In 1975, the husband drove the wife out of the house. She filed a petition for maintenance against the respondent in April 1978 under the provisions of the Code of Criminal Procedure. Then, on November 6 1978, the appellant divorced the respondent by irrevocable talaq. Thus the man's defence to the respondent's claim for maintenance was that she had ceased to be his wife, that he had paid her Rs3000/- by way of mahr, and that he was now under no further obligations in the matter. The High Court of Madhya Pradesh awarded the ex-wife maintenance at the rate of Rs179.20 per month. The husband appealed. A two-bench Supreme Court were of the view that *Bai Tahira* and *Fuzlunbi* were incorrectly decided. Thus they referred the matter to a Bench of five justices, headed by the Chief Justice, Chandrachud C.J. This Court dismissed the appeal, and confirmed the decision of the High Court. The Chief Justice stated that s.125 overrides the personal law if there is any conflict between the two. He referred specifically to the proviso to s.125(3) of the Code. The proviso says that if the husband offers to maintain his wife on condition that she should live with him, and she refuses to live with him, then the magistrate may consider any grounds for refusal. He may make an order of maintenance notwithstanding the offer of the husband, if he is satisfied that there is a just ground for passing such an order. The Explanation expressly states that "if a husband has contracted marriage with another woman ... it shall be considered to be just ground for his wife's refusal to live with him." Chandrachud C.J. expressly refers to this provision and states that this shows:

> unmistakably that section 125 overrides the personal law, if there is any conflict between the two.

But Chandrachud C.J. goes on to argue that there is in fact no such conflict in any event. He says that the Muslim personal law, in his opinion, does not countenance cases where the wife is unable to maintain herself after a divorce. He goes on:

> Since the Muslim Personal Law, which limits the husband's liability to provide for the maintenance of the divorced wife to the period of 'idda, does not contemplate or countenance the situation envisaged by section 125, it would be wrong to hold that the Muslim husband, according to his personal law, is not under an obligation to provide maintenance, beyond the period of 'idda, to his divorced wife who is unable to maintain herself...The true position is that, if the divorced wife is able to maintain herself, the husband's liability to provide maintenance for her ceases with the expiration of the period of 'idda. If she is unable to maintain herself, she is entitled to take recourse to

section 125 of the Code.

Thus there is no conflict between the provisions of the Code and Muslim personal law. There is of course little justification for describing the Muslim law obligation in this way. It is an unorthodox approach, and the Qur'anic authorities cited by the Judge are given by him a novel interpretation.

The contrary argument does less than justice to the teaching of the Quran.

The Chief Justice is able to disregard s.127(3)(b) on the simple ground that even if there is a deferred mahr payable on divorce, this cannot justify the conclusion that it is payable "on divorce." He considers the two propositions that mahr is consideration for the marriage or a mark of respect for the wife. As to the first proposition: "No amount which is payable in consideration of the marriage can possibly be described as an amount payable in consideration of divorce." As to the second proposition: "[H]e may settle a sum as a mark of respect for her. But he does not divorce her as a mark of respect. Therefore, a sum payable to the wife out of respect cannot be a sum payable 'on divorce.' "

In one respect, Chandrachud C.J. goes further than the court in *Bai Tahera*. In that case, mahr was seen as being within the cognizance of s.127(3)(b) as it was a customary discharge; it was not sufficient to discharge the obligation however if the amount was illusory. Chandrachud C.J. states that mahr does not fall within the meaning of the provision at all.

This decision produced concern amongst sections of the Muslim community in India. Fundamentalists urged amendment in two directions. First, it is suggested that in a situation where a Muslim divorced woman has no blood relatives who would normally support her, the magistrate should ask a Waqf Board to make a monthly allowance for her maintenance. Second, Waqf Boards should be authorised to raise money for this purpose from waqfs in the state.[40] The problem here of course is that the Waqf Board is unable to help a woman who has a living relative, but one perhaps who simply does not wish to maintain his divorced kinswoman. The Muslim community in India is divided on the issue, but political considerations clearly contributed to the passing of an Act in May 1986 which in effect prohibits a Muslim woman from going to court to seek a maintenance payment from the man who divorces her.[41] Whether this Act is struck down as being unconstitutional remains to be seen. There is perhaps an attempt to protect the Act from allegations of unconstitutionality by Section 5 which enables the husband and

---

[40] For the law on waqfs see later.
[41] Muslim Women (Protection of Rights on Divorce) Act 1986.

Marriage: Legal Effects

the wife (or ex-wife as she would be) to opt jointly to be governed by sections 125-128 of the 1974 Code of Criminal Procedure. Section 4 enables a Muslim divorcee who is unable to obtain her ex-husband's consent to an election under Section 4, to apply for an order for maintenance from relatives of hers as would be entitled to inherit her property. If she has children alive, who are able to pay, then an application must be made to these relatives. In the absence of children of sufficient means, an application is made to the parents. If there are no available relatives, then application is made to the State Waqf Board.

4.5 Property

The fifth of the legal effects of marriage relates to ownership of property. The wife is entitled to full ownership of property. There is no concept either of a doctrine of unity between husband and wife as known in common law, or the concept of community in matrimonial property. The Qur'an Sura VI states:
  To men Is allotted what they earn, And to women what they earn.

Such sentiments of course fully support a patriarchal and dependent structure for the simple reason that women have few opportunities to obtain financial rewards other than through inheritance, and even here the entitlement is often much smaller than the male members of the inner family circle. By custom, the management of her property will often fall into the hands of the husband, or the wife will readily give up her rights to own property in return for other privileges, for example the right to visit relatives. This is common in Bangladesh in particular. Mutual rights of inheritance accrue on the solemnisation of a valid sahih marriage. Competence to inherit generally is dealt with in Chapter 8.

4.6 Shi'i Law

By way of a postscript to this chapter, it would be useful to discuss in brief some of the peculiar incidents of the Shi'i law in this area of domestic relations law.

There are three basic differences in Shi'i law compared with the mainstream of the Sunni law. First, no witnesses are required to create a formal marriage in Shi'i law. Second, and perhaps more important, the Shi'i jurists recognise only the sahih and the batil marriage. There is no concept of fasid. Third, there is a peculiar doctrine recognised only by the Shi'i, namely

Marriage: Legal Effects

the mut'a marriage.[42] This form of marriage is contracted for a period of time which comes to an end at the expiry of the time limit. The Sunnis see it as equivalent to legalised prostitution. Indeed the Sunnis point to the remarkable characteristic of the mut'a that the husband can make a gift of the term left (hiba-i-muddat).

The husband certainly in this institution pays a sum of money as consideration for entering into the union.[43]

There is in fact a narrow line between the mut'a marriage and the sahih marriage. If the ijra is specified, but no time is mentioned, the marriage may operate as a permanent sahih marriage.

In pre-Islamic customary law, the mut'a was certainly commonplace and it is probable that Mohammed tolerated the system.[44]

'Umar suppressed the practice; indeed it is thought by some that it is for this reason if for no other that mut'a is held to be lawful by the Shi'i Ithna 'Ashari branch. Today mut'a hardly exists, except perhaps in the conservative towns of southern Iraq.

Like a sahih marriage, a mut'a marriage is contracted by ijab al qabul (an offer and an acceptance). In Shi'i law, as we have already stated, no witnesses are necessary. This is indeed especially convenient in the mut'a ceremony. The rules relating to capacity, especially with regard to non-Muslims, are similar to sahih marriages. The restriction on four wives, however, does not apply in the mut'a marriage; thus men are permitted to contract any number of mut'a marriages at one time.

The children of a mut'a marriage are legitimate. The wife, however, is not entitled to inherit property on the man's death or to receive maintenance – other than, of course, the remuneration (ijra).

---

[42] See N.J.Coulson, *A History of Islamic Law* (Edinburgh, 1964) pp.110, 111; A.A.A.Fyzee, *Outlines of Muhammadan Law* (4th ed. Oxford, 1974), pp.117-121; J.Schacht, *An Introduction to Islamic Law* (Oxford, 1964), pp.266, 267.

[43] This reward, known as the ijra, is clearly different from the institution of the mahr in a sahih marriage.

[44] Qur'an Sura IV, verse 24.

5. Polygamy

Before the advent of Islam, unlimited polygamy was a general practice in the Arabian tribes. Mohammed restricted the right of polygamy to four concurrent wives. It has been said of Mohammed that:

> [he] was not an impractical visionary who simply made high-sounding moral pronouncements. It was a central function of the Prophet and his mission, after having made these moral pronouncements, to be effective in society and to move it in a certain direction. In other words, the Prophet was the seer-cum-reformer. But at any given time a reformer, however zealous, cannot change society beyond a certain point.[1]

The Qur'anic text relating to this subject is Sura IV, verse 3:

> If ye fear that ye shall not
> Be able to deal justly
> With the orphans,
> Marry women of your choice,
> Two, or three, or four;
> But if ye fear that ye shall not
> Be able to deal justly (with them),
> Then only one, or (a captive)
> That your right hands possess.
> That will be more suitable,
> To prevent you
> From doing injustice.

All schools are agreed that a Muslim man does not require permission to enable him to contract a second or subsequent marriage up to a maximum of four. The requirement in Sura IV, verse 3, (to treat the two or more wives equally) is construed, again by all schools, as a requirement to be decided upon by the husband himself. It is his responsibility and he has no need to submit himself to examination by any person or institution in advance of the final decision to contract a second or subsequent marriage.[2] Again, the moral injunction – for such it is – to treat four wives equally relates to nafaqa (support and maintenance) and not to equal affection; for the Qur'an itself

---

[1] Fazlur Rahman in E.D.Smith (ed.), *South Asian Politics and Religion* (Princeton, 1966) p.418.

[2] See generally D.Hinchcliffe, "Polygamy in Traditional and Contemporary Islamic Law", (1970) Islam and the Modern Age p. 28.

Polygamy

admits this is an impossible task. The rights of several wives to equal and impartial treatment arise after the marriage. The husband is obliged to provide all wives with nafaqa on exactly the same basis. He must also provide them with separate living quarters. It is important to stress here, however, that the undoubted rights of the wives in no way whatsoever limit the capacity in law of men to enter into polygamous marriages.

There are essentially two factors which make the issue of polygamy so contentious. First, it is the view of many women's groups, for instance in Pakistan and in Egypt that the existence in law of the right to take a second wife severely hinders the progress towards the emancipation of Muslim women. Second, and as a contrary factor, the orthodox and more conservative sections of the community have been challenged into issuing a continuous stream of apologetics and polemics directed against the antagonism of some Western Orientalists. The controversy is all the more unfortunate bearing in mind the fact that polygamy is decreasing in all Muslim countries. Indeed, it may well be argued that the introduction of external checks on the system of polygamy in many Muslim countries has simply regulated a trend towards monogamy already apparent, as Western concepts of monogamy and of romantic love spread across the Muslim world. It is also true that restrictions on polygamy which are not accompanied by similar restrictions on the power of a husband to divorce his wife unilaterally can actually work to the disadvantage of women. Is it better to be a discarded and divorced elderly woman, or a respected first wife in a polygamous household? However, those who would wish to reject legislative amendments to the law of polygamy are today in a minority; indeed only Egypt and Muslim India, together with the more observant Saudi Arabia and North Yemen, stand outside the move towards restrictions. The Egyptian reforms in 1979 in the area of polygamy were very limited indeed, restricted simply to notification being required to the Registrar of Marriages of the intention to contract a second marriage. Evidence of capacity to support the two wives must be provided as well, and the Registrar is responsible for notifying both the first wife and the second wife of each other's existence. He cannot prevent the second marriage, although the first wife has a ground for divorce.

Only in the cases of Turkey, Israel and Tunisia has the capacity to contract a second polygamous marriage been completely abolished. Restrictions there are; and the following extracts from legislation will illustrate the differing ways the problem has been tackled.

Polygamy

Jordanian Law of Family Rights 1951 (amended 1976)
(now called the *Jordanian Law of Personal Status.*)

21. If a stipulation is made in the marriage contract for the benefit of either party, it must be complied with, *eg* a stipulation that the wife should have the power to divorce herself in specified circumstances or should live in a specified place or that the husband should not have a co-wife. But such a stipulation can be enforced only if it is incorporated in the registered marriage-deed and also in the certificate by the *Qadi*. Violation of such a stipulation shall give to the wife a right to seek dissolution of marriage.

The Iranian Family Protection Act 1967
(This Act, consolidated into the *Family Protection Act 1975*, has now been repealed.)

14. If a husband wishes to marry another woman, he must seek permission of the Court to do so. The Court shall give such permission after it satisfies itself, through all necessary measures including examination of the existing wife, regarding the financial capability of the husband and his capacity to do justice.

If a person, without obtaining the Court's permission, contracts a second marriage, he shall be punishable with the penalty laid down in article 5 of the Marriage Law of 1310-1316 (1931-37).

Iraqi Law of Personal Status 1959

(4) Marriage with more than one wife is not permissible except with the permission of the *Qadi* and the granting of such permission shall depend on the following conditions:

(a) the husband's financial position should be sound enough to have more than one wife, and

(b) any lawful interest *(maslihat al mashru'a)* should be involved.

(5) Where injustice between the wives is feared, plurality is not permissible, and determination of this fact is left to the *Qadi*.

(6) All those who enter into a contract of marriage with more than one woman in contravention of clauses (4) and (5) shall be liable to imprisonment for a period not exceeding one year, or to fine not exceeding hundred dinars, or to both.

Moroccan Code of Personal Status 1958
Impediments to Marriage

30.(1) If any injustice between the wives is feared, plurality of wives is not permitted.

(2) Where a husband contracts a second marriage, and the wife had not stipulated against such an act in the marriage contract, the

Qadi may consider whether the second marriage has caused any injury to the first wife; marriage with a second wife shall not be contracted unless she is informed that the husband is already married to another woman.

31. A wife may stipulate in the marriage contract that her husband shall not marry a second woman along with her, and if the husband violates such a stipulation she will have a right to seek dissolution of her marriage.

Tunisian Code of Personal Status 1956

18. Plurality of wives is prohibited. Any person who, being already married and before the marriage is lawfully dissolved, marries again, shall be liable to imprisonment for one year or for a fine of 240, 000 francs, or to both, even if the second marriage is in violation of any requirements of this law.

Syrian Law of Personal Status 1953

17. The *Qadi* can refuse to a married man permission to marry another woman if it is proved that he is not capable to maintain two wives.

Readers are referred also to Article 13 of the Somali Family Law (1975) and the interesting reforms in Indonesia of the same year.[3] Under the Indonesian legislation, a man may receive permission from a court to contract a second marriage if, and only, if;

(i) his wife cannot carry out her conjugal duties, or
(ii) his wife becomes crippled or terminally ill, or
(iii) his wife cannot give him children, and
(a) his present wife or wives give him permission,
(b) his ability to support all his wives and children is certain,
and (c) his ability to be fair to all his wives and children is certain.

The Somali law[4] requires prior permission of the court before a second and polygamous marriage can be contracted. Such permission can be contracted on the grounds of (i) medically certified sterility of the wife, (ii) her contagious or chronic ailment which is incurable, (iii) her imprisonment for over two years, and (iv) desertion by the first wife for more than a year. The court can, in addition to these specific grounds, grant permission on the ground of "social

---

[3] For a discussion of the Indonesian law see the article by J.S.Katz and R.S.Katz "The New Indonesian Marriage Law: A Mirror of Indonesia's Political, Cultural and Legal Systems." (1975) vol. 23 A.J.C.L.p.653.

[4] see T.Mahmood "The Somali Experiment with Family Law Reform", (1982) vol. II Islamic and Comparative Law Quarterly p. 251.

Polygamy

necessity".

The Jordanian Law of Family Rights (1951 now 1976) is an illustration of limited reform. The Jordanians adopt the prevalent Hanbali doctrine that a stipulation in the marriage contract restricting the husband to one wife is valid and if the husband violates the stipulation the wife has a right to seek a judicial dissolution. Article 31 of the Moroccan Code (1958) introduces a similar procedure to that of the Jordanian reform. The Moroccan Code states that if there is no stipulation and a second marriage takes place the Qadi may consider whether the second marriage has caused any injury to the first wife. Iran, Iraq and Syria – in differing forms – have accepted the need for an external check on the right of the husband to marry a second time. In all cases a marriage is not permitted without the express approval of the court or the Qadi. Furthermore, approval will be refused in cases where the court is not satisfied that the husband is capable of maintaining a second wife. In Iraq, the husband also has to satisfy the court that there is a "lawful benefit." Similar requirements exist in Algeria by virtue of the Family Code (1984). A man who wishes to take a second wife must establish a clear and genuine need. The court will grant him such permission if it is satisfied of such need, and further if there is evidence that the man is able and willing to treat the wives and the children with equality. The first wife may obtain a divorce on the sole ground of the husband's second marriage.[5] Only time will tell how detailed an examination is made by the court. Certainly, it is the probable position that in Iraq at least a proper investigation will rarely be carried out, since the first wife is seldom called upon to give evidence and the testimony of the husband usually goes unchallenged. In Iraq, as in the law which once existed in Iran, the husband has to satisfy the court as to his capacity to "do justice between the two wives". In all cases, however, it would appear that a marriage without permission or possibly in direct contravention of a refusal to sanction a second marriage will nonetheless be valid.

The position is similar in Pakistan and Bangladesh to that in other countries except that there the permission granting authority is an administrative body which, under the Muslim Family Laws Ordinance (1961), is provided with certain judicial functions. In a pilot study of Quetta (Baluchistan), a town of 100,000, it was found that in the period 1966-8, 32 applications for permission to contract polygamous marriages were forwarded to the Union Committees – the administrative bodies. Of these 32

---

[5] For information on Algeria, see T.Mahmood's essay on "The Islamic World" in (1983/4) Annual Survey on Family Law p. 81 (International Society on Family Law).

applications, permission to take a second wife was granted to all but one case.[6] The Union Committee is responsible for setting up an Arbitration Council, made up of a representative of the existing wife, a representative of the husband, and the Chairman of the Union Committee. If the Arbitration Council is satisfied that the proposed marriage is "necessary and just" it may grant permission to contract the second union. Rule 14 of the Rules states that in making a judgment on what is "just and necessary" and without prejudice to its general powers, the Arbitration Council should have regard to the following circumstances: sterility, physical infirmity, physical unfitness for the conjugal relationship, wilful avoidance of a decree for restitution of conjugal rights, and insanity on the part of the existing wife. If a second marriage is solemnised without the approval of the arbitration council, the man is subject to the possibility of criminal proceedings being instituted against him, but the second marriage is clearly valid. The second marriage, however, *cannot* be registered; and the absence of registration would make it extremely difficult to prove the existence of a valid marriage. The original Rules state that the complaint has to be brought by the Union Committee.[7] In *Fauzia Hussain v. Khadim Hussain*,[8] the husband married his wife in Birmingham, England in a civil ceremony. Both parties were dual nationals of Pakistan and the United Kingdom. The husband married a second wife in Pakistan without the permission of his first wife or of the Arbitration Council. The High Court rejected the argument of the husband that no complaint could be brought against him for the reason that the first marriage had been contracted in the UK:

> Such marriage conforms to requirements of Muslim marriage and would be recognized as a valid marriage under Muslim law.[9]

Mst. Fauzia Hussain was an aggrieved party and she could therefore file a complaint directly in a court of competent jurisdiction.

---

[6] D.Pearl, (1971) vol. 13 JILI p. 561 at p. 564.

[7] As the Union Committees were abolished for a time in 1972, it was decided in one case that no organisation had *locus standi*. See *Fateh Muhammad v. Chairman, Union Committee, Ward 14/15*. 1975 PLD Lah 951. This position was amended at least in the Punjab, and now the court can take cognizance of an offence on a complaint brought by the aggrieved party. West Pakistan Rules under the Muslim Family Laws Ordinance 1961 reproduced in 1977 PLD (Provincial Statutes; Punjab) p. 30.

[8] 1985 PLD Lahore 166.

[9] at pp. 172/173 per Muhammad Munir Khan J.

Polygamy

There has been no direct legislative reform of Muslim personal law in India on the subject of polygamy. Although it is certainly the case that many in the middle-class Muslim community in the large urban areas have married (or registered their existing unions) under the procedure laid down under the Special Marriages Act 1954 (amended in 1976) and therefore invoked a monogamous regime on the union, the majority of Muslims still solemnise their marriages in the classical religious form. Thus the only real protection at the time of the marriage is a stipulation in the contract that the husband shall not take a second wife – which is enforceable in that the wife should be entitled to claim a dissolution under the 1939 legislation (Dissolution of Muslim Marriages Act) if the husband does indeed marry a second time in contravention of the stipulation. Moreover, the decision in *Itwari v. Asghari*[10] suggests that a second marriage in a case where there has not been a stipulation may constitute cruelty by the husband against the first wife entitling the wife to obtain a divorce under the Act.[11] In addition s.125 (3) of the Code of Criminal Procedure states that it is a just ground for refusing to live with your husband when he has contracted a marriage with another woman.

It would be appropriate in this context to consider the question of the enforcement of conditions within the marriage contract. In the classical Hanafi law, very few stipulations are recognised as valid if they interfere with the rights and duties of the parties to the marriage. Three conditions in particular would be deemed contrary to these rights and duties:

(1) any stipulation of a time limit,

(2) any stipulation of the right of the husband to take an additional wife or wives up to the maximum of four,

(3) the restriction on the right of the husband to exercise a talaq.

Hanbali law, in contrast, lays stress on the injunctions for Muslims to abide by their stipulations. It is, therefore, one of the ironies of recent Muslim legal history that the rigid and somewhat doctrinaire attitude of Hanbali scholars has been utilised in Hanafi countries to reform the Hanafi law and give greater

---

[10] 1960 AIR Allahabad 684.

[11] Not surprisingly, this view has not been accepted in Pakistan. *Resham Bibi v. Muhammed Shafi* 1967 PLD AJK 32. In *Muhammad Khan v. Zarina Begum* PLD 1975 AJK 27, a first wife obtained a divorce under the principle of the case of *Khurshid Bibi* (see later). There are important restrictions in this area of the law, and the judgment did not consider whether the taking of a second wife amounted to cruelty against the first wife.

rights to women. Hanbali law was adopted in the Ottoman Empire (1917) when, in the Law of Family Rights of that year, stipulations inserted in the marriage contract against a second marriage were declared valid and enforceable. Similarly, the 1951 (1976) Jordanian Law of Family Rights states, very widely indeed, that "any stipulation of benefit to one of the parties" is valid.

The overall position in most Hanafi countries therefore is that if the husband breaks one of the conditions, and the usual one relates to polygamy, the wife will herself be released from her obligations and will be able to claim a dissolution of the marriage.

In the Indian subcontinent, the same result has been obtained by the application of principles of public policy laid down by Section 23 of the Contract Act 1872. Contracts are enforced unless contrary to public policy.

The difference between the Middle East and the subcontinent illustrates clearly a difference in approach apparent in the dynamic development of the law. The Middle Eastern countries rely upon reforming legislation, often hidden behind the concept that it is really codification aad restatement; the subcontinent adheres to the English common law tradition of judicial developments within the context of a loose enabling statute.

6. Parent and Child

In this chapter we turn our attention to the issues relating to the parent-child relationship, and, in particular, we consider the questions of legitimacy, custody and guardianship. It is important to mention at the outset that the problems arising out of the legal relationship of parent and child in Muslim law are subsidiary by and large to the major issue of inheritance; indeed the law relating to parental rights over children and the legitimacy of children becomes a feature of litigation in many situations because of the overwhelming importance of inheritance.

6.1 Legitimacy

The illegitimate child has no right to inherit property through his father, and, in the classical law, the mother of the illegitimate child may well find herself subject to the draconian punishment imposed on those found guilty of illicit sexual relations (zina). Thus, the status of legitimacy in Islamic law has very important consequences for the child and his parents.

Legitimacy is established either by the birth of a child in a marriage which is sahih or fasid (but not in a batil marriage) or alternatively, through the application of the doctrine of acknowledgement.

6.1.1 Legitimacy by Birth (al-Walad l'il Firash)

Perhaps in order to avoid the consequences of being stigmatised as illegitimate, all the Sunni schools recognise gestation periods well beyond the medically proved maximum. Thus Hanafi law concedes that there can be a gestation period up to two years between the conception of the child and its birth. Hanbali, Shafi'i and the consensus of the Maliki extend this period to four years, and there is a divergent opinion in Maliki law that would even extend the period to five years.

There is also a minimum period of gestation, which in this case is accepted by all the schools, that a child will be illegitimate if he is born *less than* six months from the date of the marriage. If the child is born after six months from the marriage, the legitimacy of the child cannot be rebutted either by proof that there was no physical access between the parties or indeed even by proof that the marriage had never been consummated.

There is only one method available to a husband to challenge the legitimacy of a child and disown his own paternity; namely the doctrine of the li'an. The husband swears four oaths that the child is not his child. He then invokes the curse of Allah if he has sworn falsely. After the oath-taking by the husband, the wife can confess to the adultery or deny her guilt by herself swearing four oaths as to her innocence and calling upon herself the curse of Allah if she is guilty. The procedure amounts to a permanent divorce. In Egypt, in 1929, this procedure was placed on one side and modern notions of the proof of non-access were introduced in its place. Thus, the child will be illegitimate if it can be established that the union had never been consummated or that there was no access for more than one year from the last act of intercourse.[1]

The position on the Indian subcontinent is slightly confusing, and the case law is a little inconclusive. The questions raised have already been referred to in Chapter 2. The Indian Evidence Act (1872), Section 112, states:

> the fact that any person born during the continuance of a valid marriage between his mother and any man, or within two hundred and eighty days after its dissolution, the mother remaining unmarried, shall be conclusive proof that he is the legitimate son of that man, unless it can be shown that the parties to the marriage had no access to each other at any time when he would have been begotten.

It is the general opinion that Section 112 has abolished the Hanafi law relating to the presumption of legitimacy. As we have already seen, in the Hanafi law, a man is presumed to be the father of a child who is born to his wife not less than six months from the date of the marriage and within two years after the dissolution of the marriage, either by the death of the man or by divorce. The opinion that the old law has been replaced rests on the view that the Hanafi law in this area is an aspect of the law of evidence, and therefore it has been superseded by the Evidence Act.[2]

---

[1] Law no.25. (1929) Article 15 states: No disputed claim of paternity shall be heard regarding the child of a divorced or widowed woman who gave birth to him more than a year after her divorce or widowhood. Article 17 states: No claim of maintenance shall be heard in respect of an 'idda period in excess of one year from the date of divorce. (Nor shall any disputed claim of inheritance on the grounds of marriage be heard regarding a divorced woman whose husband died more than a year after the date of the divorce).

[2] See the following old Indian cases: *Muhammad Allahdad Khan v. Muhammad Ismail Khan* 1888 ILR 10 All 289 (where the question whether section 112 supercedes the rules of Muslim law was left open); *Sibt Muhammad v. Muhammad Hameed* 1926 ILR 48 All 625; *Ismail Ahmed Peebadi v. Momin Bibi* AIR 1941 PC 11; *Mst. Rahim Bibi v. Chiragh Din* AIR 1930 Lah 97; *Ghulam Mohy-ud-Din Khan v. Khizar Hussain* 1929 ILR 10 Lah 470. In the last four cases, it was held that s.112 supercedes the Muslim law.

Parent and Child

There is a further difficulty in Pakistan in relation to the Shariat Act 1951. Section 2 of that Act states that "legitimacy or bastardy" is henceforth to be governed by Muslim law. Notwithstanding the provision in the Act, the general academic view at least was that the Muslim law had not been reactivated by this provision for the simple reason that the Muslim law in this area is classified as evidential rather than substantive. However this view has not been accepted by the Lahore High Court in *Abdul Ghani v. Taleh Bibi*.[3] The following table is reproduced from the judgment.

Table 1

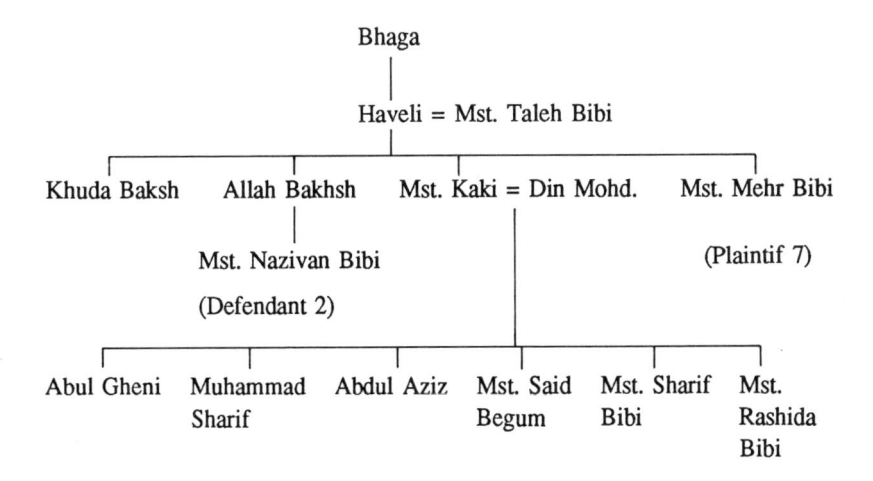

```
                        Bhaga
                          |
                Haveli = Mst. Taleh Bibi
                          |
  ┌─────────────┬─────────────┬──────────────────┬──────────────┐
Khuda Baksh   Allah Bakhsh   Mst. Kaki = Din Mohd.         Mst. Mehr Bibi
                   |                                         (Plaintif 7)
             Mst. Nazivan Bibi
              (Defendant 2)
  ┌───────────┬──────────────┬─────────────┬──────────────┬──────────┐
Abul Gheni  Muhammad      Abdul Aziz    Mst. Said    Mst. Sharif   Mst.
            Sharif                      Begum        Bibi          Rashida
                                                                   Bibi
```

(Plaintiffs Nos. 1 to 6)

Mst. Taleh Bibi was the first defendant and Mst. Naziran Bibi was the second defendant in an action brought by Mst. Mehr Bibi and Abdul Ghani and the other 5 children of Mst. Kaki and Din Mohammed. The facts of the case were as follows. The land in dispute was owned by Allah Bakhsh who died in 1936 leaving his mother, Mst. Taleh Bibi, and a daughter, Mst. Naziran Bibi (who at that time was four years old) as his surviving heirs. The entire property was mutated into the name of the daughter as requested by

---

[3] 1962 PLD (WP) Lah 531. See before chapter 2.

Taleh Bibi, although Taleh Bibi continued to manage the land on behalf of her granddaughter. Some time afterwards, Taleh Bibi gave the land on lease to Din Mohammad (Taleh Bibi's son-in-law), the father of the first six plaintiffs. In 1953, the plaintiffs filed a suit to seek a declaration that they were the owners of the land in dispute. They alleged that Taleh Bibi was solely entitled to the land on the death of Allah Bakhsh, and that she had relinquished her right in their favour. They alleged further that Mst. Naziran Bibi was disentitled to a share in the property because she was born within six months of the date of marriage of her mother, Aishan Bibi, with Allah Bakhsh, and so therefore, according to Muslim law, she was not the legitimate daughter of Allah Bakhsh. The suit was contested by Mst. Naziran Bibi, who claimed, *inter alia*, that she was the legitimate daughter of Allah Bakhsh and she was therefore entitled to the land in dispute.

The trial judge found that Naziran Bibi was born within six months of the marriage of her mother, Aishan Bibi, with Allah Bakhsh, but that in accordance with the provisions of section 112 of the Evidence Act, she was presumed to be the legitimate daughter of Allah Bakhsh. The plaintiffs appealed on the ground that the trial judge was wrong in law to apply section 112 of the Evidence Act.

The complex argument accepted by the Appellate Court in this case is as follows. First the rule of Muslim law in question is a rule of substantive law. In Muslim law:

> if a child is born six months after the marriage of its parents, or within two years of the dissolution of the marriage, by death or divorce, it is considered to be the legitimate child of its father, unlike the rule of evidence in s.112 of the Evidence Act, under which only a presumption of legitimacy can be raised under certain circumstances.[4]

The court went further and advanced the view that the decisions to the contrary in *Sibt Muhammad v. Muhammad Hameed*[5] and other cases which state that the Muslim law is a rule of evidence, have been materially altered by the repeal of section 2(1) of the 1872 Act by section 2 of the Repealing Act 1938. The argument which found favour with, for instance, Kayani J, in *Ghulam Bhik v. Hussain Begum*[6] (namely, that the continued demise of the Muslim law is ensured by the General Clauses Act 1936 notwithstanding the repeal of section 2 of the 1872 Act by the Repealing Act 1938) was not

---

[4] at p. 541 (Masud Ahmed J.).
[5] 1926 ILR 48 All 625.
[6] 1957 PLD (WP) Lah 998. This case does not appear to have been cited before the court in *Abdul Ghani*.

accepted by the court. In the opinion of the court in *Abdul Ghani v. Taleh Bibi*, the rules of Muslim law are not part of a Central Act or Regulation and for this reason the repeal of Section 2 of the Evidence Act is not saved by the General Clauses Act.[7]

Thus, even if Muslim law is a rule of evidence as opposed to substantive law, the Muslim law is reactivated by the repeal of s.2 of the 1872 Act. The major thrust of the *Abdul Ghani* litigation however is to define the rules of Muslim law as substantive rules. Having held that the rule of Muslim law regarding legitimacy is a rule of substantive law which, even if it had been affected by the Evidence Act, had been revived by the repeal in 1938 of Section 2 of the Evidence Act, it was open for the court to apply Muslim law. The court held, therefore, that Naziran Bibi could not be the legitimate daughter of Allah Bakhsh because she was born within six months of the marriage of her mother Aishan Bibi with Allah Bakhsh. She was not entitled, therefore, to the property in dispute, although at the end of the day the court concluded that because she had been in possession of the land for more than 12 years, she had become owner of the property in dispute by reason of adverse possession. The interest of the case lies in the way in which the court classified the Muslim rule relating to legitimacy as a rule of substantive law.

Another case which can be cited although its reasoning is somewhat different is the Supreme Court decision *Hamida Begum v. Murad Begum*.[8] The reasoning of the court in this case was as follows. The shortest period of gestation is six months. If therefore a child is born within six lunar months of the marriage then no affiliation is permitted unless the husband acknowledges the child to be his issue. Thus the case suggests that it is the right of the husband to legitimate a child born within the first six months of the marriage. The case really adopts the principle that the "child follows the bed". It was common ground that Hamida Begum was born during the subsistence of the marriage between her mother and Mehar Din. Thus the court decided that the

---

[7] General Clauses (Amendment) Act 1936 s.6A reads: where any Central Act or Regulation made after the commencement of this Act repeals any enactment by which the text of any Central Act or Regulation was amended by the express omission, insertion or substitution of any matter, then, unless a different intention appears, the repeal shall not affect the continuance of any such amendment made by the enactment so repealed and in operation at the time of such repeal. The section in issue before the court in this case was s.2 of the Indian Evidence Act (1872) which stated as follows: The following laws shall be repealed – (1) All rules of evidence not contained in any Statute, Act or Regulation in force in any part of British India.

[8] 1975 PLD SC 624.

plaintiff would be presumed to be a legitimate child; unless it was proved that there was no valid marriage between her mother and Mehar Din, or that she was born within six months of that marriage *and* she was not acknowledged as a legitimate child by Mehar Din. This judgment adopts a different approach to *Abdul Ghani's* case. It also appears to differ from the traditional Indian cases on acknowledgement; to which we now turn.

6.1.2 Acknowledgement (Iqrar)

The doctrine of acknowledgement can be used to establish legitimacy only when real paternity is possible. Thus the acknowledged child must be at least 12 years 6 months younger than the acknowledgor. This represents the minimum period of gestation added to the minimum period of puberty.

A father can acknowledge paternity if the following three conditions are met:

(1) the child is of unknown paternity;

(2) there is no definite proof that the child is the offspring of zina; and

(3) there can be no rebuttal of the presumption of paternity of another by the acknowledgement.

These principles are clearly rules of substance. In the Indian and Pakistani context, therefore, the rules have not in any way been affected by the Indian Evidence Act. The leading case is *Muhammad Allahdad Khan v. Muhammad Ismail Khan.*[9] The parties in this case were Sunni Muslims. Muhammad Allahdad Khan and his alienee Musammat Hakim-un-Nissa brought a suit against Muhammad Ismail Khan, his three sisters, and others, for a declaration of right to and possession of two shares in villages left by one Ghulam Ghaus Khan, who was the father of Muhammad Ismail Khan and his three sisters. Muhammad Allahdad Khan asserted that he was the eldest son of Ghulam Ghaus Khan; thus he was entitled to shares in the estate in accordance with the Islamic laws of inheritance. In reply, Ismail Khan and the three sisters contended that Allahadad Khan was no more than a step-son of Ghulam Ghaus. According to Muhammad Allahdad Khan, even if he failed to prove that he was the full son of Ghulam Ghaus, he argued that nonetheless Ghulam Ghaus had *acknowledged* him as his child, which gave him the status of a legitimate child. The latter argument found favour with the judge, Mahmood J. A child born of zina (illicit sexual relations) can never be legitimated, and is

---

[9]   1888 ILR 10 All 289.

barred from inheriting from the father. Illegitimacy, in those circumstances, is a proved and established fact, and no amount of acknowledgement of the child can change the situation. Mahmood J expressed the rule in the following manner:

> The doctrine [of acknowledgement] applies only to cases of uncertainty as to legitimacy, and in such cases acknowledgement has its effect, but that effect always proceeds upon the assumption of a lawful union between the parents of an acknowledged child.

On the basis of the facts in *Muhammad Allahdad Khan's* case, Mahmood J was able to hold that the case presented all the conditions to which the law of acknowledgement is most appropriately applicable; thus Allahdad Khan could inherit together with the brother and the three sisters.

Another interesting case is *Habibur Rahman Chowdhury v. Altaf Ali Chowdhury*.[10] In this case the plaintiff submitted before the court that he was the son of one Nawab Sobhan of Bagba by the second wife, a Mozelle Cohen. He said that his mother was a Jewess who had converted to Islam. The respondent, the Nawab's grandson, denied the claim of Habibur to any share in the Nawab's estate. The respondent argued that Habibur was the illegitimate son of the Nawab and Mozelle Cohen. There were therefore three interlinked questions. First, did Mozelle Cohen marry the Nawab? Second, if so, was Habibur the legitimate son of the Nawab and Mozelle?, and third, was there an acknowledgement? The Judicial Committee of the Privy Council discussed the plaintiff's contentions. The court advised that there was no proof whatsoever of a marriage between Mozelle and the Nawab. Thus, Habibur was illegitimate and no amount of acknowledgement could make him legitimate.

6.1.3 Adoption

It will be recalled that Sura XXXIII, verse 37 abolished the pre-Islamic custom of adoption whereby an adopted child could be assimilated in a legal sense into another family. It can be suggested that the acknowledgement of paternity of a person of unknown origin amounts, in a way, to a form of adoption.[11] Moreover, there are some Muslim scholars who argue that Sura XXXIII, verse 37 does not prohibit adoption, but merely classifies it into the category of acts known as mubah – the acts towards which religion is indifferent. Such arguments have not found favour with the legislators in the

---

[10] 1920/21 48 LR IA 114. See also the case of *Sadik Hussein v. Hashim Ali Khan* 1915/16 43 LR IA 212.

[11] See for example the argument by J.Schacht *An Introduction to Islamic Law* (Oxford, 1964 reprinted Oxford, 1982) p. 166.

Muslim countries, and, by and large, there is no law of adoption in the Muslim world. Certainly, statements by the Pakistan Ministry of Foreign Affairs to the effect "that adoption is not known under Muslim Law" have been accepted by immigration tribunals in England to deny entry to young persons who are alleged to have been adopted under Pakistan law by their sponsors settled in UK.[12] The law of adoption was discussed in the Pakistan Supreme Court in *Sher Afzal v. Shamin Firdaus*[13] where, in the context of a dispute relating to the validity of a marriage and the legitimacy of the offspring, the Supreme Court stated:

> it is well known, that there is no institution of adoption in Islamic law.[14]

Adoption has been introduced however into Somalia by the Family Law (1975) Article 110. Adoption is restricted to cases where the parents are unknown. Adoption is also now part of Tunisian law as a result of reforms in 1958. It is undoubtedly the case that reformers in many Muslim countries feel that a legal transfer of responsibility for children in certain cases through a process of adoption serves an essential social function for destitute children and often also for childless couples. *Defacto* arrangements exist as a result of custom across the Muslim world, and legislative changes in this area can be expected in the future.

6.2 Custody (Hadana)

In all schools of Islam, the mother of a child has the responsibility for care and control of the child for the first few years of the child's life. The father, who has rights over the child as the wali, retains the overall rights and indeed powers of guardianship. If the mother dies, the responsibility falls on other female relatives.[15] There are certain situations in a Muslim state were the qadi may well consider it necessary to remove the child from the care of the mother. In particular the carer must be sane, trustworthy and of good morals.

---

[12] See the Immigration Appeal Tribunal cases of *Rafiq v. Secretary of State for the Home Department* [1972] Immigration Appeal Reports p. 167; *Malik v. Secretary of State for the Home Department* [1972] Immigration Appeal Reports p. 37; *Tohur Ali v. Entry Clearance Officer, Dacca* [1985] Immigration Appeal Reports p. 33.

[13] 1980 PLD SC 228.

[14] p. 266.

[15] In the Shi'i law of the Ithna 'Ashari school, in the absence of the mother, priority in custody is given to the father, and failing him, to the paternal grandfather.

Parent and Child

On the Indian subcontinent, Section 17 of the Guardians and Wards Act 1890 sets out the procedure for applications for removal of custodians and carers. It states, *inter alia*, that the court "shall be guided by what, consistently with the law to which the minor is subject, appears in the circumstances to be for the welfare of the minor". A distinction must be drawn between the provisions of s.17 and of s.7 of the Act. Under s.7, an application is made to the court for the appointment of a guardian. Under that provision, in order to decide whether a guardian should be appointed or not, all that the court has to take account of is the welfare of the minor. The personal law of the parties does not appear to be relevant to the guidelines. In s. 17 cases, where an adult is being removed, the personal law is clearly of considerable importance. The distinction between the two provisions is apparent from a consideration of the case of *Rashida Begum v. Shahab Din*.[16]

In Pakistan, the courts have developed the presumption that the minor's welfare lies in granting custody in accordance with the personal laws of the minor. Mahmud J said in *Atia Waris v. Sultan Ahmad Khan*:

> In considering the welfare the Court must presume initially that the minor's welfare lies in giving custody according to the dictates of the rules of personal law, but if circumstances clearly point that his or her welfare dominantly lies elsewhere or that it would be against his or her interest, the Court must act according to the demand of the welfare of the minor, keeping in mind any positive prohibitions of the personal law.[17]

In the *Atia Waris* case, custody was given to the paternal grandparents in order to ensure that the minor child was brought up as a Muslim, despite the positive rule of Muslim law which states that if the mother is found unsuitable to have the custody of her female child, the right of custody devolves on the maternal grandmother.

Sometimes it is difficult to decide which law is indeed the personal law. A preliminary question, therefore, is raised. An example of this problem is contained in *Mrs Moselle Gubbay v. Kwaja Ahmad Said*.[18] Two children were born to Moselle and her husband Ahmad when they lived together in Calcutta. It appears that the parties contracted a Muslim marriage in Calcutta in 1943 at a time when both parties were Muslim, although Moselle's parents were both Jewish. In 1954, the marriage was terminated as a result of a petition brought

---

[16] 1960 2 PLD Lah 1142.
[17] 1959 PLD (WP) Lah 205 at p. 214.
[18] 1957 PLD (WP) Karachi 50.

by Moselle presumably under the provisions of the Dissolution of Muslim Marriages Act 1939. Custody of the children was given to the petitioner. The husband, however, kidnapped the children and took them to Karachi in Pakistan. Contempt proceedings were drawn up in the Calcutta High Court against Ahmad and he was sentenced *in absentia* and committed to prison. Moselle then travelled to Pakistan, instituted a criminal prosecution under Section 368 of the Pakistan Penal Code, and, in addition, filed a petition for a writ of *habeas corpus* praying that the two children be brought before the court and dealt with according to law. Although the petition was not filed under the Guardian and Wards Act, the principles applied by the court relate to the jurisdiction under the Guardian and Wards Act, for in the result the court held that it was "improper to give the custody of the two Muslim children to a Jewess mother who is an Indian national and is residing in India".[19] The preliminary problem was not raised by the court. In Jewish law, children are presumed to follow the religion of the mother. In Muslim law, the children are presumed to follow the religion of the father.[20] In Pakistan, the personal law governing the father is certainly applied on grounds of public policy, but there is no reason why in India, where the mother was both domiciled and a national, the law of the father should be preferred to the law of the mother.

Another Pakistan case, *Grace Abdul Haqani v. Abdul Hadi Haqani*[21] illustrates the problem of the selection of the personal law of the child for the purposes of the Guardians and Wards Act. Abdul Hadi Haqani, the father, had married Grace Rodrigues, a Muslim convert, according to Muslim rites. Notwithstanding her conversion to Islam, however, the mother continued to attend church. In 1955, a female child was born to the couple. Soon afterwards, the father was court-martialled for an offence under the Official Secrets Act. He was convicted and sentenced to three years' rigorous imprisonment. Before the conviction, the parents signed a joint statement whereby they gave an undertaking that they would provide a Catholic education for their child. After the undertaking was signed, the child was baptised. Whilst the husband was in prison, Grace Rodrigues commenced an affair with another man, and she left the matrimonial home to live with this man. As soon as Haqani was released from prison, he filed an application,

---

[19] 1957 PLD (WP) Karachi 50 at p. 52.
[20] *Atia Waris v. Sultan Ahmad Khan* 1959 PLD (WP) Lah 205 at p. 215. "Under the law, the minor must be presumed to have the father's religion and corresponding civil and social status."
[21] 1961 PLD (WP) Karachi 296.

with his mother as co-petitioner, under the terms of the Guardians and Wards Act, for custody of the child.

The first question was to ascertain the personal law of the child. Mr Justice Faruqui held that despite the baptism the child was a Muslim governed by the Muslim law. "The minor was born a Muslim and the fact of her baptisement [sic], particularly in the circumstances in which it took place, does not change her religion unless after coming of age she chooses to do so."[22]

In the result, the judge held that it was in the interests of the welfare of the child and consistent with her personal law, to be brought up as a Muslim. Custody was given, therefore, jointly to the father and the paternal grandmother. If the personal law of the child had been applied exclusively, the mother would have had custody until the child attained puberty. If she were unsuitable, the right of custody would have devolved on the maternal grandmother.

Substantive Muslim law, as applied on the subcontinent, lays down that apostasy from Islam is a sufficient ground for taking custody of infant children away from the mother, or the custody away from the father. The Caste Disabilities Removal Act (1850)[23] however, established the statutory choice of law rule which ensures that apostasy itself is not a sufficient reason for denying the rights of the mother or of the father.[24] The cases of *Atia Waris v. Sultan Ahmad Khan*, *Mrs Moselle Gubbay v. Kwaja Ahmad Said* and *Grace Abdul Hadi Haqani v. Abdul Hadi Haqani*, however, illustrate that in Pakistan the principle of the Caste Disabilities Removal Act is subsidiary to the overriding rule of "the general welfare of the child".

The classical law based upon hadith is that the right to custody will be lost when the mother or other custodian marries a man who is not related to the child within the prohibited degrees. This rule was followed in Pakistan in

---

[22] 1961 PLD (WP) Karachi 296 at p.300. See also the case of *Emperor v. Maha Ram* 1918 ILR 40 All 393.

[23] This Act was passed to extend the principle of section 9 of Regulation VII (1832) of the Bengal Code throughout the territories subject to the government of the East India Company. The 1832 Act refers to "Property". In contrast, the 1850 Act refers to "Right or Property." See later for amendments to the 1850 Act in Pakistan.

[24] *Muchoo v. Arzoon* 1866 5 WR 235; *In Re Muhammad Alam Md Ibrahim* AIR 1939 Sind 311. But see *In the matter of Mahin Bibi* 1874 13 Bengal Law Reports 160, where the father's consent as guardian to his daughter's marriage was considered. It was held in this last mentioned case that because the father had renounced Islam and re-embraced his former faith (Judaism), consent by him to the marriage of his minor daughter was not necessary.

Muhammad Bashir v. Ghulam Fatima,[25] even though the judge said that "welfare of the minor remains the dominant consideration and the rules only try to give effect to what is (the) minor's welfare from the Muslim point of view". The judge in that case did say however that the father must deposit Rs 10,000/- in the name of the minor, and allow all reasonable facilities to the mother for seeing the child. He concluded by saying that if the husband did not abide by the conditions or acted in any way to the detriment of the child, then it would be open to the mother to reapply to the court. The judge certainly envisaged cases when the classical law would be departed from.

The rationale for the departure from the traditional law is contained in another Pakistan case from Lahore, *Fahmida Begum v. Habib Ahmad*.[26] The judge in that case summarised the conclusion of a Full Bench in the earlier decision of *Zohra Begum v. Latif Ahmad Manawwar*.[27]

> It is permissible for Courts of law to differ from the rules of custody as stated in the text-books of Muslim law since there was no Quranic or Traditional Text on the point, and courts which have taken the place of Qazis can, therefore, come to their own conclusions by process of Ijtihad. . . . Therefore it would be permissible to depart from the rules stated therein if on the facts of a given case, its application is against the welfare of the minor.

An example of a case where the rule was departed from is that of *Amar Ilahi v. Rashida Akhtar*.[28] In this case, it appears that the husband, in order to avoid his liability to maintain his minor daughter, and also to avoid paying his dower debt to his wife, gave up all claim to the custody of his daughter when she was very young and took no further interest in her until the time came to arrange for her marriage to someone of his choice. The court rejected the application made by the husband under the Guardians and Wards Act for an order that the child be returned into his custody. The remarriage of the mother in this case did not prohibit the mother from being appointed both as her carer and as her guardian.

In Hanafi law the mother retains the right of custody until age seven for boys and nine for girls. In India and Pakistan, this limit for girls appears to have been extended to the onset of puberty – which may well be later than nine. The father who retains rights as guardian (or wali) of the child will then

---

[25] 1953 PLD Lah 73.
[26] 1968 PLD Lah 1112.
[27] 1965 PLD (WP) Lah 695.
[28] 1955 PLD Lah 413.

assume custodial powers. The ages in Maliki law when mothers lose the right of care and control are puberty for boys and marriage for girls; in Hanbali law it is seven years for both boys and girls; and in Ithna 'Ashari law it is only two years for boys and seven years for girls. The Shafi'i law lays down no fixed limits. In Shafi'i law, on the attainment of discretion, the child is given the opportunity to decide which parent to live with.

These rules, of course, are unimportant in an undivided family where the husband and wife live together. In a divided family however, problems will be bound to occur. The Shafi'i rule, with the inbuilt flexibility, has been adopted in recent years in Muslim countries. For instance, in Egypt (1929) the law states that the "Qadi may give permission for women's rights to the custody of a boy to be extended from the age 7 up to 9 and of a girl from the age of 9 up to 11, if it appears that their welfare so requires". Sudan extended this departure from Hanafi law (in 1932) to enable the mother to keep custody up to puberty for boys, or marriage for girls. Syria (1953) states that "if a wife deserts her husband, and her children are more than 5 years old, the Qadi may place them with whichever of the spouses he sees fit, provided he has regard to the welfare of the children". Similar provisions have been enacted in Tunisia (1957) and Iraq (1961). Classical law rules on the whole have not been followed in the case law of Pakistan.[29] Finally, readers are referred to Articles 62 ff of the Somali Family Law (1975) which illustrates the flexible Shafi'i approach in statutory form.

6.3 Guardianship

Although the mother is the custodian of young children, the right of guardianship remains with the father. There are two types of guardianship; guardianship over property and guardianship over the person.

6.3.1 Property

The leading case is *Imambandi v. Mutsaddi*.[30] A Muslim by the name of Ismail Ali Khan died in March 1906 leaving three widows and numerous children.

---

[29] See for instance the cases of *Zohra Begum v. Latif Ahmad Manawwar* 1965 PLD (WP) Lah 695, *Niaz Bibi v. Fazal Ilahi* 1953 PLD Lah 442 (where the classical law was applied), *Harbai v. Usman* 1963 PLD Kar 868, *Tahera Begum v. Saleem Ahmad* 1970 PLD Kar 619.

[30] 1917/18 45 LR IA 73. See also the case of *Sulaiman v. Iqbal* 1981 PLD AJK 33, where the court decided that the mother was not the guardian in law of the ward's property and therefore had no right to transfer the property to a third party. No good title could be passed in these circumstances.

The third wife had two children from Ismail Ali Khan. In June 1906 this wife conveyed to purchasers the property which not only she, but also the children, had inherited. The purchaser then applied for mutation (substitution) of the names in the local land register. The first two wives and the children of the first two wives successfully opposed this mutation. It was held by the Privy Council that the mother had no power to alienate the property for she was not the legal guardian. She was really no more than the *defacto* guardian, and she had acted as a fuduli or meddler.

After the father's death, guardianship falls on the following persons in the following order; the father's executor, the paternal grandfather and the paternal grandfather's executor.

The guardian stands in a fiduciary relationship to his ward. Only in the most exceptional circumstances, when it is in the interests of the child, will the court allow a guardian to buy or sell a ward's property.[31]

6.3.2 Guardianship of Person (Jabr)

The major point of note in this connection, of course, is rights of the marriage guardian (the wilayat al-ijbar). The guardian has the power to contract his minor ward in marriage without her consent, although as we have seen, in Hanafi law this right ends as soon as the minor attains puberty. If the father is dead, the right of guardianship of the person shifts to the grandfather, and in his absence to the brother.

Guardianship (jabr) includes the duty to maintain the ward. This duty, however, is not an absolute one. A good description of the way in which maintenance can be restricted is contained in the Lahore case *Ghulam Fatima v. Sheikh Muhammad Bashir*.[32] The judge said in this case:

> a father's liability to maintain his children extends only to such of them as are really in need of maintenance. It follows that a child who is being already voluntarily maintained by another and therefore does not stand in need of his food, clothing or lodging cannot require his father to pay maintenance.

Similarly, if a person maintains the child of another voluntarily, he is not entitled to reclaim the maintenance from the father.

---

[31] *Rahimuddin v. Abdul Malik Bhuyia* 1968 PLD Dacca 801.
[32] 1958 PLD (WP) Lah 596.

Parent and Child

It needs to be said also that the obligations to maintain one's parents are enforceable in Islamic law if the son is comparatively in easy circumstances and the parents are indigent. The same is true also of the obligation to maintain an unmarried sister.

7. Dissolution of Marriage

Two general observations need to be made at the outset with regard to the Islamic law of divorce in general and the Hanafi law of divorce in particular. First, divorce at the instance of the husband is relatively simple. Second, and in contrast, divorce at the instigation of the woman is particularly difficult. Both these points will become apparent in the course of this chapter.

7.1 The Rights of the Husband (the Talaq)

7.1.1 The various forms of talaq

Before entering into a general discussion it may be useful to summarise at the outset the most important aspects of the institution of the talaq. In its essence, the talaq is a repudiation or a cutting off of the marital tie. It is a power which is available exclusively to the husband, although it is possible for the husband to delegate the power to pronounce the talaq to some other person. No consent is required by the wife; and the pronouncement or declaration of talaq is extra-judicial, in no way subject to any external check. In classical Hanafi law, a talaq can be pronounced in one of a number of forms. The more meritorious forms (the talaq as-sunna) offer the opportunity of revocation (rajih). In contrast, the least meritorious forms (the bid'a forms) are irrevocable from the moment of pronouncement. The bid'a talaq can be instituted either as a triple pronouncement or as a single talaq but accompanied by some expression of finality. In Hanafi law the bid'a talaq can be either pronounced orally or it can be reduced into writing.

7.1.1.1 Talaq as-sunna (ahsan form).

This form is the most approved method of repudiation. When the wife's cycle falls into what is known as the "tuhr period", that is when she is free from her menstrual flow, the husband pronounces a talaq. He must then refrain from sexual intercourse during the 'idda period of three menstrual cycles (or, if she be beyond the age for menstruation, or if she has not menstruated, or if her periods are irregular, then three lunar months). At the end of this 'idda period, the marriage is terminated; the dissolution arising directly from the unilateral talaq pronounced three months earlier. This form of repudiation provides an opportunity for revocation, as the husband can take back his wife during the period of this 'idda. The ahsan formula is categorised therefore as rajih

Dissolution of Marriage

(revocable). Revocation can be implied by conduct, and naturally a resumption of intercourse clearly constitutes sufficient evidence of an intention to revoke.

The ahsan talaq is often referred to also as a sughra method (the little method). Only one pronouncement has taken place; thus the man has the capacity to remarry his wife by contracting another marriage with her after the expiry of the 'idda period.

7.1.1.2 Talaq as-sunna (hasan).
The hasan form of talaq, like the ahsan, is an approved method of repudiation. However, this form is not considered as acceptable as the ahsan form. The procedure is as follows. The husband repudiates his wife 3 times; the first talaq takes place during a tuhr period and he pronounces 2 subsequent talaqs during the following two tuhr periods. As soon as the husband pronounces the third talaq, the talaq becomes irrevocable. The talaq is rajih (revocable) up until the third pronouncement. In the hasan form, the marriage does not come to an end until the pronouncement of the third talaq. The wife has to observe an 'idda period after the third pronouncement; but at this time the husband cannot revoke the decision to divorce the wife. Furthermore, if he wishes to remarry her, he can only do so if she goes through a ceremony of marriage with another man which is consummated and is itself validly dissolved. (For this reason this form of talaq is referred to as a kubra or big talaq.)

7.1.1.3 Talaq al-bid'a.
The talaq al-bid'a, although disapproved by classical jurisprudence, has the advantage, for the husband at least, of simplicity and finality. The most common method of talaq al-bid'a is for the triple pronouncement of talaq hasan to be brought together into a single sitting. Such a divorce creates an irrevocable termination of the status of marriage. As the divorce pronouncement has been effected three times, it is not possible for the parties to remarry each other unless, and until, the wife has gone through another marriage which has itself been consummated and dissolved. A talaq al-bid'a is effected also when a husband repudiates his wife during her menstrual flow, or also when he accompanies a single talaq with some expression of finality. An example of this last type of talaq is graphically illustrated where the husband says: "I divorce you like the point of a needle or of a mountain."[1] Finally, if

---

[1] See Tyabji, "Muslim Law" (Bombay, 1968) p. 168. Such a pronouncement creates an irrevocable talaq according to the opinion of both Abu Hanifa and Abu Yusuf. If the word "magnitude" is *not* mentioned, the pronouncement is only revocable according to Abu Yusuf.

the marriage has not been consummated, a single talaq without any additional words will constitute a completed and immediate divorce.

7.1.2 Effect of Talaq

An important point to bear in mind is the exact moment in time when the divorce takes effect, for this moment differs depending on the form of talaq which is under discussion. In the ahsan form, the talaq is effective at the expiry of the 'idda period. In the hasan form, it is effective on the third pronouncement. And, of course, in the bid'a form, the talaq is effective at once. As soon as the divorce is irrevocable, the marital relationship must cease. Indeed, any intercourse at this stage will be viewed as zina. The revocable divorce, of course, is subject to the 'idda period. One important effect which arises as a result is that if either party dies during this period of 'idda, the rights of inheritance are preserved. Inheritance rights *inter se* do not exist after the pronouncement of talaq al-bid'a, even if one of the parties dies during the 'idda period following the bid'a divorce. The 'idda period both of the talaq al-bid'a and of the third pronouncement of the talaq as-sunna (hasan) enables the wife to obtain maintenance from her former husband, and she of course has no capacity to contract herself to another man in marriage during this period.

7.1.3 Formalities

There are no real formalities required in the classical Sunni law laying down the manner in which the repudiation is pronounced. There is no requirement that there be witnesses, and the wife need not be present. The talaq can be either oral or it can be reduced into writing. Any words can be used. In one old Indian case the husband said to his wife, "Thou art my cousin, and daughter of my uncle, if thou goest."[2] Evidence was presented to the court and accepted by it that what was meant by this statement was that if or when the wife left the house, she would be no other relation to him than a cousin (which she was) for she would no longer be his wife. In this case, therefore, effect was given to the intention of the husband to pronounce a talaq al-bid'a.

Examples of talaq pronouncements can be obtained from the English decisions on the subject. In *Mahbub v. Mahbub* the husband wrote to his wife in these terms: "I divorce you with immediate effect. I repeat you are hereby

---

[2] *Hamid Ali v. Imtiazan* 1872 ILR 2 All 71.

divorced. You are hereby divorced."[3] In the important case of *Qureshi v. Qureshi*, the following statement was made by the husband to his wife:
> This is to inform you that as irreconcilable differences have arisen between you and myself I have formed an irrevocable intention to divorce you and I am divorcing you under Pakistan law. I divorce you. I divorce you. I divorce you.[4]

A slightly different form of words was used by the husband in the leading case of *Quazi v Quazi* which eventually reached the House of Lords. The husband pronounced the talaq in this way:
> I do hereby on my free will give and pronounce irrevocable TALAQ, TALAQ, TALAQ, 3 times to my wife...[5]

The leading case on the Indian subcontinent is *Ahmed Kasim Molla v. Khatun Bibi*.[6] This decision reiterates the Hanafi law that, no matter how disapproving Islam is of a man who divorces his wife without cause, nonetheless a Muslim may repudiate his wife "at his mere whim and caprice".[7] Such a repudiation is good in law, although it is bad in theology.[8]

The husband in *Ahmed Kasim's* case sent the talaq document by registered post to his wife. The letter came back to the husband endorsed by the postal authorities with the word "refused". There was no evidence that the wife had actually received notification of the talaq by this letter. Notwithstanding the absence of communication of the talaq, Costello J decided that the talaq was effective:
> a talaq is valid, where it is made by a written instrument, notwithstanding that it is not brought to the knowledge of the wife; and the only question which can arise is with regard to the wife's maintenance during such period as may elapse until the fact of the execution of the talaknama actually comes to the knowledge of the wife.[9]

---

[3] 1964 108 Sol.Jo 337.
[4] 1972 Fam 173.
[5] The House of Lords judgment is at 1980 AC 744 [HL].
[6] 1932 ILR 59 Cal 833.
[7] at p. 840.
[8] See the judgment of Batchelor J in *Sarabai v. Rabiabai* 1906 ILR 30 Bom 537.
[9] See 1932 ILR 59 Cal 833 at pp. 846-847. However, there are a number of Indian cases which adopt a different point of view. Thus in *Abdul Khader v. Azeeza Bee* 1944 A.I.R. Mad 227 it was held that a talaq pronounced in the absence of the wife would be effective only when it became known to the wife.

Indeed, as we have already stated, witnesses are not strictly essential, even though clearly it may well be impossible to prove a talaq in the absence of witnesses to the pronouncement.

Professor Tahir Mahmood in his book *Muslim Law in India* makes the important point that the talaq as-sunna (ahsan), the talaq as-sunna (hasan), and the talaq al-bid'a are not "modes" or "forms" of talaq in the true sense. He states the position as he sees it as follows:

> The law of Islam simply prescribes a procedure for pronouncing talaq, keeping all chances of reconciliation and reconsideration open.

He particularly states that the talaq as-sunna (hasan) need not be given in three consecutive tuhr periods, but that the requirement of the "next tuhr" for the second and the third talaqs, "prescribes the minimum limitation, *not* the maximum limitation". His comments clarify this area of the law and it may well be true that the procedures have been misunderstood both by text book writers in India and elsewhere as well as by the courts. It is nonetheless the case that the Indian courts, as Tahir Mahmood himself admits, base their judgments on this "misunderstanding" of the "modes" of talaq.

7.1.4 Shi'i Law

There are a number of important differences between the Sunni law and Shi'i law, but the most significant of these is the legal disability which accompanies a bid'a divorce in Shi'i law. In Sunni law, the difference between the approved divorce (the as-sunna) and the disapproved (the al-bid'a) is simply based on the spurious morality of divorcing one's wife by talaq al-bid'a. The Shi'i law, however, does not recognise the talaq al-bid'a. Only the talaq as-sunna divorces are recognised in Shi'i law.[10] Moreover, the pronouncement of talaq in Shi'i law must be declared orally in the presence of two witnesses with the exact term "talaq" being used. In Shi'i law, there has to be a definite intention to repudiate. In contrast with this position, in the Hanafi law a divorce pronounced by way of jest is valid. Indeed, in this law even a divorce pronounced when drunk, or by mistake, or under duress is valid. The justification for this rule in Hanafi law is that this law looks to the *act* rather than the *intent*. This emphasises the sanctity of the marriage tie.

7.1.4.1 Other forms of repudiation

There are two other forms of repudiation, the Ila' and the zihar. Neither are of importance today, and it will suffice if a short comment is made on

---

[10] See the Pakistan case *Syed Ali Nawaz Gardezi v. Lt.Col. Muhammad Yusuf* 1963 PLD SC 51.

Dissolution of Marriage

both. Ila' is really a variant form of repudiation. The husband swears on oath to abstain from marital relations for four months. If the husband keeps his oath it is equivalent to one irrevocable pronouncement of divorce. However, it can be withdrawn against the performance of a self-imposed penalty. The zihar is an impious declaration. An example which is often cited is the phrase; "You are for me as the back of my mother." Zihar requires a particularly heavy expiation. Zihar, however, by itself is not a divorce.

It is also necessary to mention that the challenge to the legitimacy of a child by a husband (li'an), which has been described briefly in the last chapter, amounts to a permanent divorce. The procedure has been introduced into Pakistan law by the Pakistan Ordinance (1979) referred to as the Offence of Qazf Ordinance. Section 14 reads as follows:

(1) When a husband accuses before a Court his wife who is muhsan within the meaning of section 5, of zina and the wife does not accept the accusation as true, the following procedure of lian shall apply namely:-

    (i) the husband shall say upon oath before the Court: "I swear by Allah the Almighty and say I am surely truthful in my accusation of zina against my wife (name of wife)" and, after he has said so four times, he shall say: "Allah's curse be upon me if I am a liar in my accusation of zina against my wife (name of wife)"; and

    (ii) the wife shall, in reply to the husband's statement made in accordance with clause (a) say upon oath before the Court: "I swear by Allah the Almighty that my husband is surely a liar in his accusation of zina against me"; and, after she has said so four times, she shall say: "Allah's wrath be upon me if he is truthful in his accusation of zina against me."

(2) When the procedure specified in subsection (1) has been completed, the Court shall pass an order dissolving the marriage between the husband and wife, which shall operate as a decree for dissolution of marriage and no appeal shall lie against it.

(3) Where the husband or the wife refuses to go through the procedure specified in subsection (1), he or, as the case may be, she shall be imprisoned until –

    (i) in the case of the husband, he has agreed to go through the aforesaid procedure; or

(ii) in the case of the wife, she has either agreed to go through the aforesaid procedure or accepted the husband's accusation as true.

A wife who has accepted the husband's accusation as true shall be awarded the punishment for the offence of zina liable to hadd under the Imposition of Hudood for the Offence of Zina Ordinance, 1979.[11]

7.1.5 Reform in the Muslim World

As can be imagined, the institution of talaq has been subjected to severe criticism. One Western observer has commented: "Without doubt it is the institution of talaq which stands out in the whole range of the family law as occasioning the gravest prejudice to the status of Muslim women."[12] The reservations made by Islam both in the Qur'an and in the Hadith on the unilateral right of the husband, in particular the disapproval of the bid'a forms of divorce, and the introduction of the dower and the 'idda period, provide only limited checks on the husband's powers. In all Muslim countries there has been pressure to introduce reforms which will safeguard the wife's rights, and enable a proper opportunity to attempt a reconciliation.

The first major reforms were in Egypt in the 1920s. Article 1 of Law No. 25 (1929) repealed the Hanafi doctrine which had looked to the act of the talaq and ignored the intent of the talaq. Article 1 states: "Any divorce uttered in intoxication or under compulsion is henceforth invalid." The dominant Hanbali view was therefore adopted. Article 4 has a similar emphasis: "Ambiguous expressions which might or might not imply divorce shall only have the effect which the speaker actually intended."

Article 5 of the 1929 law is of considerable importance, for this article restates the circumstances where a talaq al-bid'a will be acceptable; "every repudiation is revocable except a repudiation pronounced for the third time, a repudiation pronounced before consummation of the marriage, a repudiation in exchange for compensation, and repudiations considered irrevocable by the 1929 law and the 1920 law." Moreover, by Article 3: "A repudiation coupled with words or gestures indicating a number is equivalent to a single repudiation." Thus the Egyptian reformers adopt the hasan and ahsan methods

---

[11] A muhsan in this context is a woman who has consummated a marriage. The punishment laid down in the Ordinance is stoning to death in a public place. A similar procedure to that in Pakistan has been introduced into Libyan law by Law number 52 (1973), Article VIII. See A.Mayer "Libyan Sex Laws" (1980) 28 AJCL 287 at p.311.

[12] Professor N.J.Coulson, *A History of Islamic Law*. Edinburgh University Press (1964), reprinted 1978, at p. 209.

Dissolution of Marriage

and effectively abolish the triple talaq al-bid'a. The Egyptian reforms were themselves subjected to further changes in that country in 1979, but the general scheme of the law as laid down in 1920/29 remained unchanged. All that was effectively added in 1979 in this area is the requirement to register the talaq, and the requirement on the husband to give notice of the talaq to the wife. Divorce does not take effect if the notice does not reach her. The current position of the 1979 reforms is a little unclear for in April 1985, the Supreme Court in Egypt held the 1979 reforms to be unconstitutional.[13]

The 1920/1929 reforms in Egypt were influential in other Islamic countries and formed the basis for change elsewhere, especially in countries which are predominantly Hanafi. Thus Article 92 of the Syrian Law of Personal Status states: "If a divorce is coupled with a number, expressly or impliedly, not more than one divorce shall take place." Other reforms in the Syrian law follow the Egyptian pattern. Article 117 of the Syrian law, however, introduces a novel and highly significant concept into the Hanafi world. This article states that where the Qadi considers that a husband has repudiated his wife without reasonable cause, and the wife has suffered material damage, the Qadi may ask the husband to pay the wife compensation, limited to one year's maintenance and support. Professor Coulson has said of this provision:

> [it] represents the first real attempt, in thirteen centuries of legal tradition, to control the husband's power of repudiation. For the first time, his motive in exercising his power was subject to scrutiny and the wife's position is protected to some extent in the event of its abuse.[14]

The reform, of course, does not attempt to subject the man to any external control of his right to repudiate his wife. Notwithstanding its limited nature, however, it does serve as a valuable expedient in discouraging men from unilaterally and unjustly divorcing their wives. The justification for the provision can be found in the Qur'an in Sura II, verse 241: "for divorced women, maintenance on a reasonable scale"; although the ijma' is that this verse is abrogated by later revelations. In effect the Syrian reformers have exercised ijtihad to reinterpret the Qur'anic provision. Section 18 of the 1979 Reforms in Egypt extended the principle just a little further by stating that where the wife is divorced by the husband without any fault on her part, she shall be entitled to compensation (muta'ah) which should be an amount not less than two years' maintenance. It can be paid by instalments. Again, this provision is now subject to the ruling of the Supreme Court on its

---

[13] For the reforms introduced by Law no 44 in 1979 see Abdullah Abu Bakar (1980) 7 J Malaysian C.L. p.65.

[14] Professor N.J.Coulson *A History of Islamic Law*, pp. 209, 210.

constitutionality.

A more dramatic reform was the Tunisian Law of Personal Status, 1956. This provision will be considered in more detail later in the chapter. Article 30, however, states categorically that extrajudicial divorces are no longer to be effective: "Any divorce outside a court of law is without legal effect." It is important to make clear that the Tunisian legislation does not completely remove the right of the individual to obtain a divorce on his own volition, for the court *must* issue a divorce if the husband (or indeed the wife) remains obdurate. In these circumstances, the court can order the husband to pay compensation to the wife, no limit being laid down in the law. The transference to judicial decrees is justified by the Qur'anic verse Sura IV, verse 37: "where discord arises between spouses then appoint arbitrators". The verse, however, has been reinterpreted by the Tunisians, for the consensus has been that the verse relates to an "optional obligation" prior to a consensual divorce.

No other Arab Muslim country except South Yemen in 1974 has gone quite as far as the Tunisians. In Africa, however, the Somali legislation (1975) requires the man to obtain the permission of the court to divorce his wife by talaq. This permission will be granted only after the failure of a conciliation body to reconcile the parties. In the case of failure in the attempted reconciliation, the committee shall transmit its findings to the court within 60 days of its appointment. The Somali law by article 36(4) expressly states that the court shall not authorise more than one talaq at a time. Moreover, by Article 44, the court is empowered to award maintenance from a husband to a former wife, in all cases where the talaq results through the fault of the husband, for a period not less than three months and not more than one year. Turning to Iraq, the law was changed in that country in 1959. The reforms of that country adopt a slightly different approach. They require the husband who seeks a divorce from his wife to obtain a judgment in the court. However, if the domestic dispute is not brought before the court, the repudiation must be registered during the wife's 'idda period. If this is done, the talaq is valid and effective. This is true also of Algeria by the reforms in that country in 1959 (now 1984). In Algeria, the court has the duty of attempting to arrange a reconciliation.

One Muslim country which took a position similar to the Tunisian law was Iran where, in 1967, they, like the Tunisians, abolished the right of the husband to repudiate his wife without any judicial intervention. In Iran, by Article 11 of the Act, the party to a dispute must apply to the court for arbitrators to be appointed on one or more of a number of grounds based primarily on the culpability of the other party. The arbitrators attempt reconciliation and, in the event of failure, submit a report to the court. The court issues what is referred to as a "certificate of impossibility of reconciliation". The certificate remains valid for a three-month period, and during this time it can be produced before a notary who is responsible for registering the certificate and effecting the divorce. The usual procedure is for the man to pronounce a talaq in the notary's office.

An interesting aspect of the Iranian legislation was Article 17 which stated that the provisions of Article 11 were inserted by mandatory provision into all marriage documents drawn up in Iran. This factor enabled the Iranians to say that a divorce is still the right of the husband who, in his marriage contract, has delegated his right, first to the court, and second to the wife in the event she can prove one of the grounds of culpability. The law has been repealed by the current regime in Iran.

It is with this background of reform in mind that we must turn our attention now to changes which have occurred on the Indian subcontinent.

7.1.5.1 Reform in South Asia

In Pakistan, a Marriage Commission report had recommended as early as 1955 that the triple formula of the talaq al-bid'a should be made equivalent in law to one single pronouncement, and that the talaq as-sunna should become obligatory. The opponents of the report's recommendation, like the proponents, accepted that the Prophet regarded the talaq as-sunna as the favoured method of divorce. They believed, however, that legislation was not the correct approach. In effect, these fundamentalists deny legislative authority to humanity on this earth. Education against the talaq al-bid'a was permissible, indeed to be encouraged. However, legislation against the system was reprehensible.

President Ayub Khan proved sufficiently strong to discount the orthodox protagonists and changes were introduced in 1961 by an Ordinance of that year. Section 7 states:

> Any man who wishes to divorce his wife must immediately after the pronouncement of talaq in any form whatsoever give the Chairman of the Union Council notice in writing of the talaq.

The effect of the notice is to "freeze" the talaq for 90 days, during which time the chairman of the council plus representatives both of the wife and the husband constitute an arbitration council for the purposes of bringing about a reconciliation. After the expiry of 90 days, the talaq takes effect *unless* a reconciliation has been successful. No further procedure is required, and no

Dissolution of Marriage

court or arbitration council order is necessary. Section 7, therefore, has converted the talaq al-bid'a into a revocable divorce.

Pakistan courts have considered the implication of the Ordinance on a number of occasions. In 1963, the Supreme Court considered the operation of the Ordinance in the leading case of *Syed Ali Nawaz Gardezi v. Lt.Col. Muhammad Yusuf*.[15] The case is important for a number of reasons. It considers the interesting issues relating to the internal conflict of laws which are discussed in chapter 10. The facts are worthy of note at this stage. Syed Ali Nawaz Gardezi was a Shi'i Muslim domiciled in Pakistan. In July 1951 he married a German girl, Christa Renate Sonntag. The marriage was solemnised at a register office in Kingston-upon-Hull, England. The couple came to Pakistan for the first time in 1953, where the husband took up employment as manager of the Pakistan office of a German engineering company. The couple travelled abroad on frequent occasions and, in August 1961, they returned to Pakistan from one of their visits abroad, and broke their journey at Quetta, Baluchistan. On this visit, the couple met Lt.Col. Muhammad Yusuf, and they all became friends. The wife and the lieutenant-colonel grew fond of each other, and a relationship developed. Letters passed to and fro. One such letter was intercepted, and was produced in evidence in the subsequent litigation. It illustrates the relationship.

Commissioners House, Quetta. 9 November.

My Dearest Love, Your letters of Tuesday morning and night delighted me. But the deliberations of this afternoon and tonight, I find, almost exhausting. I am ready for you as soon as you are. My own love, my desire for you knows no bounds. I love you more and more every moment I breathe, and I am finding the suspense too much to endure. Au revoir my own darling. I love you and need you most desperately.

Your Yusuf.

In November 1961 the husband again went on tour, and on his return to the matrimonial home in Lahore, he found that Renate had disappeared to Quetta. However, on this first occasion she did return to Lahore. She left Lahore for good at the end of 1961, and the husband brought proceedings against the lieutenant-colonel under the Pakistan Penal Code (Sections 497, 478) for enticement. The lieutenant-colonel defended the action, *inter alia*, on the ground that Renate had been divorced by her husband on 29 December 1961. He said in evidence that Renate had produced a draft document of

---

[15] 1963 PLD SC 51.

Dissolution of Marriage

divorce for her husband to sign on 29 December 1961. The document read:

> While in full possession of my senses and having considered the matter objectively, I ...son of...hereby divorce my wife...daughter of...of my own free will and set her at liberty to marry whomsoever she likes. I shall have no case for any complaint or litigation against her or the person whoever she may marry.

The lieutenant-colonel said that the husband freely signed the document which, in effect, was a talaq pronouncement. The husband denied having ever signed the divorce deed. On 2 January 1962, the lieutenant-colonel and Renate were married at Quetta according to Muslim law; Renate declared that she had become a Muslim and that she was now called Ruquiyya.

One of the issues in this case centred around the validity and effectiveness of the divorce document. The trial judge held that it was a fabricated document. The Appellate Bench, in contrast, disagreed. The Supreme Court, on an examination of the contemporary evidence, held that the evidence was indeed inconclusive and that the court was thus unable to arrive at a positive finding about the genuineness or otherwise of the divorce document.

The court examined the legal implications of the talaq document, as well as the effect of the 1961 Ordinance. First and foremost, the talaq purported to be in the form of a talaq al-bid'a which, of course, for a Shi'i (as the husband was) was not recognised as valid. In Shi'i law, as we have had occasion already to consider, the talaq has to be pronounced orally in the presence of two witnesses in a set form of Arabic words; a written talaq is not recognised.

The Supreme Court also discussed the basic reasons for the enactment of the Ordinance. S. A. Rahman J said:

> The object of s.7 is to prevent hasty dissolution of marriages by talaq, pronounced by the husband unilaterally, without an attempt being made to prevent disruption of the matrimonial status. If the husband himself thinks better of the pronouncement of talaq and abstains from giving a notice to the chairman, he should perhaps, be deemed, in view of section 7, to have revoked the pronouncement and that would be to the advantage of the wife.

The notice to the chairman, therefore, is of mandatory form. Thus if the husband abstains from giving notice to the chairman, the Supreme Court takes the view, in the light of section 7, that the husband has necessarily revoked the pronouncement of the talaq. One aspect of this case will be discussed in Chapter 10, for the decision which led to a pronouncement of guilty provides the most interesting discussion on internal conflict of law in Pakistan. The statement about the mandatory nature of the notice to the chairman, however, has been followed in a number of Pakistan cases, notably *The State v. Tauqir*

Dissolution of Marriage

Fatima,[16] *Fahmida Bibi v. Mukhtar Ahmad*,[17] and *Abdul Mannan v. Safuran Nessa*.[18] This line of authority has been confirmed by decisions both in the Supreme Court and in the Lahore High Court in the early 1980s. Particularly important is the Supreme Court case of *Ghulam Fatima v. Abdul Quyyum*[19] There are authorities however which adopt a different view.[20] Thus, in *Chuhar v. Ghulam Fatima*[21] in the context of a case involving the legitimacy of a child, the court decided that "as the main object of s.7...is to prevent hasty dissolution of marriage by talaq" in this particular case this object would not be defeated by the "non giving" of the notice. The case is clearly understandable on its facts, for the talaq was pronounced some 15 to 18 years before. Nonetheless, the case runs counter to previous authority. One must assume that the case will be distinguished by future cases on the grounds that the point in issue primarily related to legitimacy of a child rather than to the the validity of a divorce. The law leans in favour of legitimacy, and over reliance on the technicality of section 7 would have an adverse effect.

A similar consideration forms the basis of another case which is of interest in this context, *Noor Khan v. Haq Nawaz*.[22] This was a case which eventually went to the Federal Shariat Court under the Offence of Zina Ordinance 1979. The facts are worthy of report. On 18 November 1979, Noor Khan filed a report in a police station alleging that some ten years before the wife of his uncle Fatah Khan had gone on to her fields to cut grass when a certain Haq Nawaz forcibly took her away. It was stated that the woman in question, Naziran Bibi, had given birth to three children and that Haq Nawaz was the

---

[16] 1964 PLD (WP) Karachi 306: "As no such notice had been given [to the chairman] the talaq could not have become effective."

[17] 1972 PLD Lah 694: "A divorce thus does not become effective unless the notice is served on the Chairman of the Union Committee or Council and ninety days expire from the date of the receipt of the notice by him."

[18] 1970 SCMR 845: "The learned counsel for the petitioner concedes that no notice of the alleged divorce was given to the chairman as required by section 7(1) of the Muslim Family Laws Ordinance. That being so the alleged divorce, in view of the express provision of subsection (3) of section 7 of the said Ordinance, is yet to become effective."

[19] 1981 PLD SC 460.

[20] See *Amanullah Khan v. Eidat Shah* 1981 [NLR] 164; *Muhammad Latif v. Hanifan Bibi* 1980 P.Cr.J 123 (Lahore); *Muhammad Rafique v. Ahmad Yar* 1982 PLD Lah 825; *Chuhar v. Ghulam Fatima* 1984 PLD Lah 235; *Noor Khan v. Haq Nawaz* 1982 PLD FSC 265.

[21] 1984 PLD Lah 235.

[22] 1982 PLD FSC 265. See also *Amanullah Khan v. Eidat Shah* 1981 [NLR] 164.

father. It was further stated that Haq Nawaz had not returned her to Fatah Khan and that he had committed zina with her. Noor Khan's uncle told the police that he had married Naziran Bibi some thirty years before and that she had borne him children, five of whom were still alive. He asserted that he had not divorced Naziran Bibi.

The Additional Sessions Judge acquitted the accused. He formed the view that Fatah Khan had indeed divorced Naziran Bibi. Notification of the talaq to the chairman had clearly *not* taken place, yet the judge held that the provisions of s.7 of the Ordinance were against the injunctions of Islam "to the extent of giving notice of talaq to the chairman by the husband and in respect of the notice becoming effective within ninety days". The Judge had relied on the provision of Article 227 of the Constitution. This provision will be discussed in chapter 11, but it obliges the Pakistan law maker to bring all laws into conformity with Islam as laid down by the Qur'an and the Sunna. The Federal Shariat Court had no hesitation in repelling that proposition of law.

> Article 227 of the Constitution is controlled by Article 230 and unless Parliament enacts laws in accordance with the recommendations of the Islamic Council the provisions of Article 227 do not have the effect of rendering existing laws unislamic automatically...this view that s 7 of the Muslim Family Laws Ordinance is against Muslim personal law or against the Constitution is evidently unjustified.

However, this aspect of the decision of the court is *obiter* for the court decided that none of the parties was conscious of the requirements of notice under section 7 and therefore it was not really material for the purposes of a criminal case. The Federal Shariat Court went on to say:

> it would be making a technicality of the provisions of notice under section 7 of the Muslim Family Laws Ordinance too cumbersome on the parties who have been living together as husband and wife without any challenge for 10/12 years.

It would thus appear that for the purposes of legitimacy and the criminal prosecution of zina, emphasis on the mandatory obligation to inform the chairman might produce a harsh result. In those circumstances, the courts appear willing to waive the consequences on the status of any subsequent children from another relationship or the commision of zina by the wife.

However, attempts to attack the validity of section 7 on the grounds that it

Dissolution of Marriage

is contrary to the Qur'an and the Sunna have failed.[23] And in disputes between the parties *inter se*, the requirement to inform the chairman has on many occasions been held to be mandatory. A recent statement is the Supreme Court case, *Muhammad Salah-ud-Din Khan v. Muhammad Nazir Siddiqui*[24] In this case, the court said:

> Where the husband does not give a notice of Talaq to the Chairman, it can be deemed that he has revoked the Talaq.

There is however a difficult problem surrounding the appropriate Chairman. The West Pakistan rules, amended in 1965, are complex. In essence, notice should be given to the chairman of the district where the wife was residing at the time of the pronouncement of the talaq (rule 3). If the wife has left Pakistan, notice is to be given to the chairman of the council where the wife last resided with the man in any part of Pakistan (rule 3bi), or where the person pronouncing the talaq permanently resides (rule 3bii). There are a number of problems relating to the interpretation of these rules. For instance, what are the meanings of the words "residence" and "permanent residence"? In addition, it is not entirely clear from a reading of the rules whether a man can serve notice on a chairman in a place where he and his wife resided together in Pakistan, if in fact their last place of residence is in another country. When both husband and wife reside out of Pakistan, there are enormous difficulties. The Ordinance is extraterritorial in scope, and is applicable to all Pakistan nationals wherever they may be living. Pakistan missions abroad have been given authority to act as chairmen of union councils, but their exact constitutional status is far from clear.[25]

The rules were considered by the Lahore court in *Masood Khan v.*

---

[23] See for instance *Aziz Khan v. Muhammad Zarif* 1982 PLD FSC 156. In this case Aftab Hussain J said "... [it] is not within our jurisdiction to declare s.7 of the Muslim Family Laws Ordinance as repugnant to the Holy Qur'an in view of the embargo placed on our jurisdiction in this respect by article 203(B) of the Constitution".

[24] 1984 SCMR 583. disapproving *Muhammad Rafiq v. Ahmad Yar* 1982 PLD Lah 825. and reversing *Muhammad Nasir Siddique v. Muhammad Salahuddin Khan* 1984 CLC 879 [Lahore].

[25] S.R.O.1086(K) 61 dated 8 November 1961 states:
"In exercise of the powers conferred by clause (b) of section 2 of the Muslim Family Laws Ordinance, 1961 (VIII of 1961), the Central Government is pleased to authorise the Director General (Administration), Ministry of External Affairs to appoint officers of Pakistan missions abroad to discharge the functions of Chairman under the aforesaid Ordinance."

Dissolution of Marriage

Chairman, Arbitration Council, Wah.[26] The facts of this case were as follows. The husband and the wife married at Wah, District Campbellpur (now called Attock) in 1975. The husband at the time was employed in the United States and soon after the marriage he returned to his job there. The wife stayed with the husband in the matrimonial home in the United States from August 1975 until sometime in 1977 when she returned to Pakistan. According to the evidence submitted by the husband, he visited his wife in Pakistan, and indeed resided with his wife in the house of his in-laws until March 1978 when he returned once again to his post in the United States. On 4 November 1978, the husband pronounced a talaq in the United States. He sent a notice of this talaq to the Chairman, Arbitration Council, Wah and he posted a copy of this notice to his wife at her address in Wah as well as to her address in the United States where she had by then moved. The notice was returned to the husband by the secretary of the Union Council, Wah with the following endorsement: "that in pursuance of rule 3(b) of the rules framed under the Muslim Family Laws Ordinance, the notice of talaq could not be registered in that Union Council as [the wife] did not reside within its territorial limits". The husband appears to have sent off two further notices which met with the same fate as the first notice. Having failed to invoke the jurisdiction of the particular Chairman, the husband then sought a directive from the High Court under the provisions of Article 199 of the Constitution for an order directing the Chairman to constitute an arbitration council and to declare the talaq as pronounced by him to be valid and in accordance with the law.

In the argument before the court, the parties both conceded that rule 3(b) did not apply as the wife was residing in the United States at the time of the pronouncement of the talaq. Thus the court concerned itself with whether either rule 3(b)(i) or rule 3(b)(ii) were applicable. It adopted a very liberal interpretation of the words "last resided".

> It is but natural to presume, that after her marriage, the third respondent [the wife] must have lived together with the petitioner presumably in his house, for some time, maybe for a couple of days only, before he left for the USA. In our view, where a person has a permanent or quasi-permanent abode, howsoever short his stay therein may be, that would constitute residence for the purposes of subclause (i) of rule 3, but where a person is obliged to leave his place of residence and goes to some other place on an occasional visit, the place of such visit cannot be considered as his residence.

---

[26] 1982 PLD Lah 532.

Dissolution of Marriage

Thus it does not matter that the parties had last resided together outside Pakistan. As to the other rule, 3(b)(ii), the court decided that even if the petitioner had established himself in the United States, and at present was permanently residing there, he still had a strong attachment to his birth place, and he had not abandoned his home in District Attock. The court accepted that it was possible for a man to have two permanent residences at the same time.

The question of jurisdiction was remitted to the administrative processes as constituted under the Ordinance to determine whether there was jurisdiction in the light of the observations made by the court. It will be apparent that the approach taken by the court in this case makes it almost certain that a chairman will have jurisdiction even though the parties have left the country a considerable time before. If the marriage were solemnised in Pakistan, it is likely that the parties stayed together in Pakistan prior to both of them or one of them leaving for abroad; and even if the marriage were solemnised abroad, the husband is likely to have retained an "attachment" to his ancestral home, and, according to the judgment, he may well have two permanent residences.

The issues which arise in the interpretation of the rules have been considered from time to time by English courts. The leading case is the House of Lords judgment in *Quazi v. Quazi*.[27] We shall comment on the English cases in chapter 10, but suffice it to say at this stage that the *Masood Khan* case would now be applied by the English courts as representing Pakistan law. Thus it would be difficult to challenge the validity of a talaq on the sole ground that the husband had not complied with the Pakistan rules.

The Ordinance states that the husband *shall serve* on the wife a copy of the notice of talaq which he serves on the chairman. This provision has caused considerable difficulty also. Is the notice to the wife mandatory or permissive? In the Lahore decision, *Inamal Islam v. Hussain Bano*,[28] the court gave mandatory force to the need to inform the wife: "The supply of a copy of notice to the wife is a necessary part of the requirement of service of notice on the Chairman." Unfortunately, the Karachi bench in an *obiter* remark in *Parveen Chaudhry v. VIth Senior Civil Judge, Karachi*[29] appears to have taken the opposite view.

> The only impediment to immediate effectiveness of the divorce is information to the Chairman and the forming of the Arbitration Council. To such extent it is very clear to us that the mere fact of

---

[27] 1980 AC 744.
[28] 1976 PLD Lah 1466.
[29] 1976 PLD Karachi 416.

Dissolution of Marriage

absence of communication of the divorce before moving the Chairman under subsection (i) of section 7 of the Ordinance does not invalidate the divorce.

Did the Judge mean by this that it was not mandatory to inform the wife of the divorce (which is indeed the position in the classical law) or also that it was not mandatory to inform the wife of the notice to the chairman telling *the chairman* that a divorce had been pronounced? In any event the comment was *obiter* for the court found as a fact that a copy of the divorce (and presumably of the notice also) was sent to the wife.[30]

Another recent case is *M. Zikria Khan v. Aftab Ali Khan*.[31] Zikria Khan married his wife in 1972. Their relationship deteriorated, the husband pronounced a talaq, and he despatched notice of the talaq to an administrator of a union committee in Lahore. The administrator transmitted the notice to the Chairman of Union Committee Ward 5 where it was received on 13 April 1983. The Chairman initiated the procedure under s. 7 and asked the parties to nominate representatives. On receipt of the notice, the wife appeared and contested the validity of the proceedings on the ground that the notice of the talaq had not been given to her by the husband, and that in the absence of such notice the proceedings were in effect a nullity. The matter eventually reached the Lahore High Court by way of a writ petition. The court decided that the argument of the wife was without foundation:

> The effect of non-supply of copy of divorce notice to the wife *qua* the period when the divorce would become effective is not traceable from the provisions of the Ordinance or the Rules framed thereunder. The whole emphasis is on the date of the receipt of the notice by the Chairman of the Union Committee/Council. *Terminus a qua* is date of receipt of notice by the Chairman.

However, on the facts of this case there was evidence that the husband had sent a copy of the notice to the wife who had refused to receive it, and in any

---

[30] This case involved a talaq pronounced by the husband in New Jersey, the United States. The talaq was attested by a notary public in New Jersey. The document was then forwarded to the Consulate General of the Pakistan mission in New York. The Consulate General forwarded the papers to the Deputy Commissioner in Karachi who in turn sent them to the District Judge in Karachi who at the time had jurisdiction as a chairman of a union council under the Muslim Family Laws Ordinance 1961. The dispute was subject to judicial proceedings both in Pakistan and in New Jersey. The New Jersey court recognised the talaq as effectively terminating the marriage. *Parveen Choudry v. M. Hanif Choudry* 159 N.J.Super. 566.

[31] 1985 PLD Lah 319.

event she was informed of the pronouncement when she was summoned to send a representative to the proceedings initiated by the Chairman of the Union Council.

It could be argued that the correct position is a middle one where the husband has to show that the wife had notice of the talaq through the chairman (or in some other way). The Pakistan court in those circumstances would be likely to uphold the talaq notwithstanding that she had not actually been supplied direct with a copy of the notice to the chairman.

What is entirely clear, however, is that the provisions of the Ordinance relating to the formation of the arbitration council and the functions of the chairman of the arbitration council are directory only. Thus, if the chairman does not summon the council, or if the parties fail to turn up, the talaq is none the less valid 90 days after notice has been received. This fact has been accepted on numerous occasions in Pakistan. A few examples will suffice.

In *Sobhan v. Ghani*[32] Sayam J said:

> Nothing has been said in section 7 or anywhere else in the Act providing as to what will happen if upon receipt of such written notice of the talaq, the Chairman does not constitute an Arbitration Council or if the Arbitration Council does not take any steps to bring about a reconciliation. Failure of the Chairman to constitute an Arbitration Council or that of a duly constituted Arbitration Council to take necessary steps to bring about a reconciliation is thus inconsequential.

The same view was expressed in *Fahmida Bibi v. Mukhtar Ahmad*

> If reconciliation does not succeed or the husband does not revoke the talaq before the expiry of ninety days, it becomes *automatically* operative and effective. If the Chairman issued the certificate, it was not under any provision of law and had no legal effect.[33]

A similar view was highlighted in *Maqbool Jan v. Arshad Hassan*[34] In that case, Muhammad Afzal Zullah J said:

> [I]f the talaq is otherwise valid [i.e. if under the personal law of the parties the talaq is valid] it would become effective under that law; but the only clog thereon is that the effectiveness would be postponed for

---

[32] 1973 Dacca LR 227. This case is fully known as *(Abdus) Sobhan Sarkar v. Md. Abdul Ghani*.

[33] 1972 PLD Lah 694.

[34] 1975 PLD Lah 147. See also *Akhtar Hussain v. Collector Lahore* 1977 PLD Lah 1173; *M. Zikria Khan v. Aftab Ali Khan* 1985 PLD Lah 319. This view has been accepted on numerous occasions in English courts, in particular in *Quazi v. Quazi* 1980 AC 744.

ninety days under sub section (3) of section 7 of the Ordinance. Similarly ... there is no provision either in the Ordinance or the Rules requiring the chairman or the Arbitration Council to give decision on the question of validity or otherwise of the talaq under the relevant law applicable to the parties or even to issue a certificate to make the divorce effective.

The Pakistan law, therefore, is limited in its effect. Arbitration is not compulsory; thus the system appears no more than equivalent to a form of registration. It does not prevent a man from divorcing his wife, and it does not introduce universal judicial divorce. Neither is there anything in the Ordinance which changes the classical law as respects a talaq being pronounced under compulsion or by way of a jest.[35] The husband can revoke the talaq either by words or by deeds within the ninety day period notwithstanding either that the talaq was in the bid'a form or that he had informed the chairman of the union council. Although such a power will on occasion work to the benefit of the wife, it is not hard to think of circumstances where the husband will use this power of revocation, or at least the threat of the exercise by him of a revocation, to obtain an unacceptable concession from his wife, such as a waiver of a dower right and so on.

However unsatisfactory the law is in Pakistan and Bangladesh, there is at least an opportunity that the hasty repudiation will be thought over, and the marriage will not be dissolved. No such reform has taken place in India, and all legislative attempts to reform this area of Muslim law, as indeed other areas as well, have been met by allegations of interference in the political and religious rights of the Muslim minority community. However, there have been a number of judicial attempts in India to restrict the unfettered rights of the husband. Most important of these is the case from Gauhati, *Jiauddin Ahmed v. Anwara Begum* [1978] where the judge stated that it was his view that

> talaq must be for a reasonable cause and be preceded by attempts at reconciliation between husband and wife by two arbiters... if the attempts fail, talaq may be effected.

A few words need to be said about the position in Azad, Jammu and Kashmir. Although Pakistan case law is respected in this territory, the correct position would appear to be that the Ordinance does not apply; for it has not yet been extended to this region. The traditional law of talaq is therefore still

---

[35] See for example a case decided before the enactment of the Ordinance, *Muhammad Azam Khan v. Akhtar-un-Nisa Begum* 1957 PLD (WP) Lah 195. In this case Changez J said that the rule "emphasized the sanctity of the marriage tie amongst Muslims."

in force.[36]

7.2 The Rights of the Wife

We are here still concerned with the extrajudicial form of divorce. The husband's right of talaq can be either suspended (ta'liq at-talaq) or delegated. In the suspended or conditional talaq, the repudiation occurs automatically after a particular event. The most common example of this form of delegated talaq occurs when the husband contracts a marriage with a second wife. It is fairly common to see a marriage document stating that a second marriage will activate a ta'liq at-talaq. If such a condition is agreed upon, then to that extent the wife will have some protection. The right of talaq in this situation, is of course still very much the right of the husband.

The delegated talaq (the talaq-i-tafwid) is also recognised by the schools of law. In this form of divorce, the husband has delegated to the wife the power to pronounce a talaq. The grant of the power to pronounce a talaq can be made either at the time of the marriage (and be inserted in the marriage contract) or after the marriage. A leading case on talaq-i-tafwid is *Buffatan v. Sh. Abdul Salim*.[37] In this case the husband sought a decree for restitution of conjugal rights. The wife contested the suit on the grounds that under the terms of the marriage contract which was executed by the husband before the marriage, she had validly divorced herself from her husband and thus she was no longer the wife of the petitioner. The court accepted that as a precondition to the effectiveness of a talaq-i-tafwid the wife must clearly establish that the condition entitling her to exercise the power had been fulfilled. The case was remitted to a lower court for a reconsideration of the evidence. But in the course of the judgment, the court made clear its opinion that an antenuptual agreement where the wife is given power to exercise the talaq in the event of failure to pay maintenance for a certain period is not against public policy and is clearly enforceable.[38]

---

[36] See the English case, *Chaudhary v. Chaudhary* (CA) [1985] 2 W.L.R.350. In *R. v. Immigration Appeal Tribunal ex parte Secretary of State for the Home Department* [1984] 2 W.L.R. 36, the case was decided on the footing that the Ordinance applied in Kashmir because the point was conceded by counsel for the Secretary of State in the pleadings.

[37] 1950 AIR Cal 304.

[38] See also *Sufuddin v. Sureka* 1955 AIR Assam 153.

Dissolution of Marriage

7.3 Divorce by Consent of Both Parties

A marriage in the classical Hanafi law is a contract which can be terminated by the agreement of both parties. A divorce which is effected by a mutual agreement where the aversion is on the side of the wife is known as a khul'. Usually the wife will offer to pay a certain sum (normally the amount of the dower either given to her or promised to her) in return for the agreement of the husband to release her from the marriage tie. It is possible for the husband to initiate the procedure, although in most instances the wife will be the one who is desirous of a khul'. Financial compensation provided by the wife releases her from her marital tie. The jurists differ on the interpretation of the Qur'anic verse "if you fear that they would be unable to keep the limits ordained by Allah; there is no blame on either of them if she gives something for her release". Some suggest that a husband can demand a sum larger than the mahr given by him to his wife. Other jurists forbid the taking by the husband of more than the mahr. All the debts, however, which exist between the parties are cancelled by the khul'.

If the husband is the one who makes the initial offer of khul', his offer may not be retracted before the wife has given an answer. This is the case primarily because the offer by the husband is deemed equivalent to an oath of repudiation. This oath becomes effective immediately the wife signifies her consent and acceptance of the offer. Contrariwise, if the wife initiates the matter, she may retract that offer at any time before the acceptance by the husband. Thus in the classical Hanafi law the khul' is equivalent to one irrevocable pronouncement of talaq and it is necessary for the parties to contract a fresh marriage if they wish to resume a marital relationship.

An essential prerequisite of the khul' is that it is a consensual divorce; thus it could be argued that the khul' is voidable if it can be illustrated that either of the parties lacked necessary consent or was induced into accepting the khul' by fraud or duress of sufficient gravity. Duress (ikrah) in Muslim law envisages a threat (tahdid). This threat is recognised only if one party is in a position to carry out the threat and the other party fears that it might actually happen. A threat based on death, physical injury or deprivation of liberty makes the khul' voidable, at the option (khiyar) of the person subjected to the threat. Old Indian decisions suggest that the khul' obtained by duress results in a valid divorce, but that the compensation payable by the wife cannot be enforced by the husband. Perhaps a more appropriate way to look at this matter would be to say that in such circumstances, unless there is clear evidence of a repudiation by the husband so as to constitute a talaq, the decision whether to acquiesce in a divorce should be that of the party

Dissolution of Marriage

subjected to the fraud or duress.

As the khul' may be the only effective method in the classical Hanafi law for a wife to obtain a divorce, the law of khul' has been often abused by husbands who demand very large sums in return for consenting to the khul'.

7.3.1 South Asia

The leading case on the subject from the subcontinent is the Privy Council decision *Moonshee Buzul-ul Raheem v. Luteefut-oon-Nissa*.[39] The facts of this case were as follows. In 1842, the husband married the respondent. A dower was fixed at R10,000/- and 1,000 gold pieces. In 1847, the husband married a second wife, a lady referred to in the judgment as a "rich widow". The judgment continues the story in these terms:

> From that time, the appellant did everything he could to get rid of the respondent; treating her with great harshness, refusing to permit her to see her mother, denying her food and clothing adequate to her station, in the hope of inducing her to ask for a divorce, to which she would forfeit her right in respect of her dower, and to force her to return the marriage settlement, which was at this time deposited with her mother for safe custody.

There was a dispute on the facts as to what happened next. The wife claimed that the husband divorced her by talaq, and that she was therefore entitled to the dower which she had not received. The husband claimed that he did not divorce her by talaq but that, on her initiative, there had been a khul' agreement amounting to a consensual divorce. Furthermore, declared the husband, as consideration for this khul' agreement, the payment of dower was waived. The Privy Council, where the dispute was eventually to reach, advised that the decision of the court below should not be disturbed. The lower court had decided that no divorce other than a khul' had been proved by the evidence, but that the plea of the appellant admitted that there had been a divorce by khul'. The lower court held further that the documents put in evidence by the husband purporting to show that the wife had released him from the duty to pay a dower were fraudulent and therefore of no effect. As the marriage was admittedly dissolved, the wife was entitled to recovery of the unpaid portions of the dower.

In the Privy Council, Lord Kingdown, supporting the lower court decision, said:

> A divorce by khoola is a divorce with the consent, and at the instance

---

[39] 1859/61 8 LR IA 379.

Dissolution of Marriage

of the wife, in which she gives or agrees to give a consideration to her husband for her release from the marriage tie. In such a case the terms of the bargain are a matter of arrangement between the husband and wife, and the wife may, as the consideration, release her [mehr]...or make any other agreement for the benefit of the husband.

7.3.2 Pakistan Developments

Judicial and legislative developments in Pakistan have produced important developments in the law of khul'. First, after some hesitation, the Supreme Court in *Khurshid Bibi v. Muhammad Amin* has decided that khul' can be effected without the consent of the husband, in that the wife can demand from the court *as of right* a termination by khul' provided that she can show that married life has, in effect, irretrievably broken down.[40] Secondly, Section 8 of the Muslim Family Laws Ordinance (1961) has introduced the arbitral provisions of Section 7 of the Ordinance into the khul' procedure.

The court is involved in Pakistan primarily because Section 2(ix) of the Dissolution of Muslim Marriages Act (1939) enables a Muslim wife to seek a judicial divorce "on any other ground which is recognised as valid for the dissolution of marriages under Muslim law". The Pakistan court decisions will now be considered. In *Sayeeda Khanam v. Muhammad Sami*[41] the court was concerned with the question whether a wife could be granted a divorce, notwithstanding the absence of the spousal approval, on the sole basis of incompatibility of temperament. The court in this case refused to acknowledge such a petition, and upheld the traditional Hanafi law: "a divorce by khul' is effected with the consent of the parties and at the instance of the wife in which she gives or agrees to give consideration to the husband for her release". Thus incompatibility of temperament, dislike, or even hatred on the part of the wife for the husband was held not to be a valid ground for divorce unless the husband consented to the divorce. The question was raised again for consideration in *Balqis Fatima v. Najm-ul-Ikram Qureshi*, where the court came to the opposite conclusion.[42] It was held in this case that the wife may demand a khul' as of right, provided the court is satisfied that the marriage has broken down and provided she is willing to return the benefits she has received from the marriage. Although the wife may demand a divorce as of right, Kaikus J does not equate the khul' with talaq, but rather he classifies

---

[40] 1967 PLD SC 97.
[41] 1952 PLD Lah 113.
[42] 1959 PLD Lah 566.

the khul' as a faskh (a judicial divorce).

The conflict between these two cases was resolved in favour of the latter case when the Supreme Court examined the whole issue in the leading case, *Khurshid Bibi v. Muhammad Amin*.[43]

Khurshid Bibi was contracted in marriage to Muhammad Amin, whilst at the same time her brother was contracted in marriage with Muhammad Amin's sister. No children were born to Khurshid Bibi, and, as a result, Muhammad Amin took a second wife. After this second and polygamous marriage, the relationship between Muhammad and his first wife became very strained. Khurshid Bibi demanded a separate house which her husband promised to provide. He did not actually take positive steps to implement this promise. After complaining of ill-treatment by her husband and, indeed, after her brother took out a warrant for his arrest under Section 100 of the Pakistan Criminal Procedure Code, the wife left the matrimonial home. The wife petitioned for divorce under the Dissolution of Muslim Marriages Act on grounds alleging cruelty of treatment. The husband, at the same time, instituted a successful suit for restitution of conjugal rights. The wife then brought an action for a khul' divorce "on consideration of giving up her dower, since it was impossible for the spouses to live together". Her appeal to the Supreme Court was successful. In an exhaustive judgment, the Supreme Court examined the relevant Qur'anic verses and Hadith literature. The verse of prime importance is Sura II, verse 229:

> If ye do indeed fear that they would be unable to keep the limits ordained by Allah, there is no blame on either of them if she give something for her freedom. These are the limits ordained by Allah; so do not transgress them. If any do transgress the limits ordained by Allah, such persons wrong themselves as well as others.

The Supreme Court interpreted "if ye do indeed fear" as a reference to the judges. They could find nothing in the verse which indicated that the consent of the husband is necessary. They go on to say, in support of the decision in *Balqis Fatima's* case, that the divorce should be granted by way of judicial dissolution (faskh) rather than a talaq (repudiation). It has been argued, notably

---

[43] 1967 PLD SC 97.

Dissolution of Marriage

by Dr Doreen Hinchcliffe,[44] that the Supreme Court interpreted Sura II, verse 229 in a fashion which has no authority for it in any school. In Maliki law, the court can order a khul' on certain occasions, but the Maliki jurisprudence is firmly based on the "judicial talaq", whereby if the husband is to blame, the court exercises the talaq on behalf of the husband, and the wife keeps her dower. If the wife is to blame, the court (in its discretion) exercises the talaq conditional on the wife giving up her rights to the dower.

The question of culpability under Pakistan law is clearly a vexed problem. In *Siddiq v. Sharfan*, in a case where the wife was wholly to blame for the break-up of the marriage, the court refused the wife a khul' divorce, for to do otherwise would be contrary to the policy of Islam.[45] Yet in *Hakim Zadi v. Nawaz Ali*[46] where admittedly the wife was *not* at fault, it was held that it was not necessary to prove that each and every allegation was true, but only to show that her marriage had broken down and that there was no hope of reconciliation. One of the more interesting recent cases is *Rashidan Bibi v. Bashir Ahmad*.[47] This case arose out of a writ petition filed by the wife. She had instituted an unsuccessful suit for dissolution of marriage based on khul'. The Judge of the Family Court formed the view that:

> she had not proved that there was hatred between the parties to such an extent that they cannot live within the limits prescribed by God.

In the writ petition the wife stated that "she would not live with her husband even if she was shot with a bullet". The Lahore High Court decided that there was certainly sufficient material to satisfy the conscience of the Court that the parties could not live together. The Judge stated the legal position as he saw it in the following way:

> The principle of khul' is based on the fact that if a woman has decided not to live with her husband for any reason and this decision is firm, then the Court, after satisfying its conscience that not to dissolve the marriage would mean forcing the woman to a hateful union with the man, it is not necessary on the part of the woman to produce evidence of facts and circumstances to show the extent of hatred to satisfy the conscience of the Judge, Family Court or the Appellate Court.

---

[44] "Divorce in Pakistan: Judicial reform." 1968 vol. 2 Journal of Islamic and Comparative Law vol. 2 p. 13.
[45] 1968 PLD Lah 411.
[46] 1972 PLD Karachi 540.
[47] 1983 PLD Lah 549. See also *Bilquis Fatima v. Noor Muhammad* 1978 PLD Lah 1109, and *Akhlaq Ahmad v. Kishwar Sultana* 1983 PLD SC 169.

Dissolution of Marriage

This is clear authority that the rather restrictive approach taken in *Siddiq v. Sharfan* is not likely to be followed in Pakistan today. In *Rashidan Bibi*, the case was remitted to the district judge to consider the facts anew in the light of observations made by the Appellate Court.

Other decisions on khul' deal with the question of compensation.[48] *Shamshad Begum v. Abdul Haque*[49] states the position that the payment of compensation is not a prerequisite to the validity of the khul', and the court can grant a khul' divorce under the *Khurshid Bibi* line of authority notwithstanding that the husband and the wife agree privately that she will not repay the full dower back to the husband. In *Parveen Begum v. Muhammad Ali*,[50] The Lahore High Court supported the view that it is not appropriate for the husband to demand more than he has given his wife by way of dower. In this case, it was held that khul' should have been allowed in consideration of the wife giving up her right to recover dower money remaining unpaid.

The other issue which must be discussed is the relationship between the khul' divorce granted by the court under the *Khurshid Bibi* case, and Section 8 of the Ordinance. Section 8 of the Ordinance lays down

> where the right to divorce has been duly delegated to the wife and she wishes to exercise that right, or where any of the parties to a marriage wishes to dissolve the marriage otherwise than by talaq, the provisions of section 7 shall, *mutatis mutandis,* and so far as applicable apply.

The mandatory requirement of Section 7 is, as we have already seen, for notice of the talaq to be given to the appropriate Chairman. The *Khurshid Bibi* type of khul' requires a court decree. One case, *Muhammad Ishaque v. Ahsan Ahmad*,[51] decided that after the decree for dissolution has been made by the Family Court, that court must send a copy of the decree to the chairman, but that at the same time it is necessary also for the wife, in whose favour the decree is passed, to inform independently the Chairman about the decree, as also to send a notice thereof to the husband. Thus Section 8 applies to the

---

[48] See *Muhammad Khan v. Zarina Begum* 1975 PLD AJK 27; *Shamshad Begum v. Abdul Haque* 1977 PLD Karachi 855; *Parveen Begum v. Muhammad Ali* 1981 PLD Lah 116.
[49] 1977 PLD Karachi 855.
[50] 1981 PLD Lah 116.
[51] 1975 PLD Lah 1118.

Dissolution of Marriage

Khurshid Bibi khul'.[52]

There is a view that the truly consensual divorce, which today should be called in Pakistan *mubara'a* rather than khul', does not require judicial investigation under Section 2(ix).[53] The khul' and the mubara'a can be distinguished, primarily on the basis that in the former case the aversion is on the side of the wife and she desires a separation, whereas in the latter case the aversion is mutual and both sides desire a separation.

Thus there is an additional problem. Assuming that the truly consensual divorce does not require judicial investigation under Section 2(ix), is the wife or the husband required to give notice to the chairman of the union council under Sections 7 and 8 of the Ordinance? In *Muhammad Nawaz v. Mst. Faiz Eliahi*,[54] Muhammad Afzal Zullah J, stated that the consensual khul' did not fall within the requirement to inform the chairman, and that Section 8 was not applicable. He arrived at this decision because of the irrevocable nature of the khul'. He said:

> Islamic law does not permit revocation of dissolution of marriage through khula' or mubara'at. Subsection (3) of section 7 has not changed the Islamic law. The expression 'unless revoked earlier' used therein carries the implication that the revocation should be lawful . . . In this case it is not denied that under Islamic law, revocation is not permissible.

This is not a convincing argument, indeed the whole purpose of Sections 7 and 8 is to provide an opportunity for revocation in a situation where, under classical law (as in the triple form of talaq) the divorce is irrevocable.

---

[52] There is one rogue decision. In *Muhammad Amin v. Surraya Begum* 1970 PLD Lah 475, the court in a rather confused judgment appear to have held that it was not necessary to inform the chairman of a union council after it had granted a decree under s.2(vii) on the basis of the "option of puberty". This view is perhaps justifiable, because in the context of an "option of puberty" application, the court is really granting a declaration that the marriage has been terminated; and in those circumstances it may be felt that a reference to an arbitral body empowered to attempt reconciliation is a pointless exercise. The judgment in this 1970 case is contradictory in parts, and actually in the *Muhammad Ishaque* case in 1975, the earlier 1970 decision is cited, perhaps surprisingly, as an authority for the proposition that a declaratory suit filed on the basis of the exercise of option of puberty is essentially a suit for a petition for a dissolution of marriage as envisaged by Section 8 of the Muslim Family Laws Ordinance 1961, and therefore the arbitral provisions applied.

[53] See *Ghulam Sakina v. Umar Bakhsh* 1964 PLD SC 456.

[54] 1978 PLD Lah 38. See also *Mumtaz Mai v. Ghulam Nabi* 1969 PLD Baghdad-ul Jadid 5.

Dissolution of Marriage

A second argument in favour of the inapplicability of Section 8 would be as follows: that further reconciliation attempts available under the arbitration procedures are irrelevant in a case where both parties freely agree to dissolve the union. This argument, however, is similarly unconvincing, not the least reason being because in the case of judicial proceedings under the Dissolution of Muslim Marriages Act 1939 the Family Courts are obliged to attempt reconciliation on two occasions during the proceedings. Yet such attempts do not prevent the superimposing of the Section 7 and Section 8 provisions on to the judicial application for a divorce. Likewise surely in the case of the traditional consensual khul', the opportunity for reconciliation, which has already been available, should not prevent the further mandatory communication to the chairman of the union council.

The practice in Pakistan is for notice of the consensual khul' to be given to the chairman, and this indeed was done in the *Muhammad Nawaz v. Mst Faiz Eliahi* litigation.[55] The whole question was discussed in *Princess Aiysha Yasmien Abbasi v. Maqbool Hussain Qureshi*.[56] The judgment in *Muhammad Nawaz* was distinguished on the basis that the chairman in that former case had conducted proceedings on a notice by the husband of a revocation of the procedure leading toward the divorce, and the chairman had given a certificate of cancellation of the notice. According to Islamic law, the husband has no authority to revoke a khul' unilaterally, and therefore any "decision" of the chairman was necessarily without authority. The Judge in *Princess Yasmien Abbasi* went on to state:

> The spirit of the law would be satisfied if a notice of dissolution of marriage in the form of Khula/Mubara'at is sent to the Chairman by virtue of the provisions contained in section 8 read with section 7 of the Ordinance.

The Judge accepted that the form of the notice might be different from the notice in relation to a talaq. In the case before him, the parties had agreed mutually to dissolve their marriage, and the communication to the chairman was sent by them both. The notice read:

> We, the undersigned...have mutually decided and agreed to dissolve the marriage under the Muhammadan law and within the purview of the Muslim Family Laws Ordinance of 1961.

Then there was set out the agreement concerning the dower, and the document concluded:

---

[55] 1978 PLD Lah 38.
[56] 1979 PLD Lah 241.

Dissolution of Marriage

we...have also decided and agreed not to have any resort to any Reconciliation Council for purpose of bringing about reconciliation or settlement of any dispute, and this decision of both parties is final and conclusive.

The Judge decided that this notice was in accordance with the provisions of Section 8 of the Ordinance.[57]

Assuming that Section 8 does apply to the consensual khul', the next question which arises is to consider who is responsible for informing the chairman of the council. If the husband made the initial offer, notice must be given by the husband, although if he does not do so, one may assume that the wife may give notice. In any event, notice must be given, and, if no notice is given, the analogy with cases decided under Section 7 would make the khul' (or mubara'a) ineffective.

No time limits are laid down by the Pakistan law about when notice is to be given. Section 7 states "as soon as may be after the pronouncement . . ." The question is raised, therefore, as to how long the parties can wait before the lack of registration will be considered to be a revocation of the khul'. There is no easy answer to this question. The case law, unfortunately gives no clues. In *Inamal Islam v. Hussain Bano* (a case on talaq)[58] the husband told the court that he had notified the chairman of the pronouncement of talaq on 10 September 1971. The wife denied that this had been done, but admitted that she was divorced by talaq on 12 May 1972, and that there may well have been notification on that date. There is no suggestion in that case of any other notice after 12 May 1972, and the court treated the marriage as terminated three lunar months (the 'idda period) after that date. The case is very unsatisfactory, but it is certainly no authority for the proposition that a talaq or khul' can be "reactivated" years later simply by giving notice. It is possible that the Pakistan court would consider the resumption of cohabitation together with the passing of the 'idda period (or three lunar months) as sufficient evidence that the divorce, either by talaq or by consensual khul' (on the assumption that judicial cognisance under Section 2(ix) of the 1939 Act is not strictly necessary) had been revoked. If contrary to this view, the

---

[57] In *Quazi v. Quazi* 1980 AC 744 at 772, at first instance in the English High Court, the Judge took the view that ss 7 and 8 were not relevant to the traditional khul'. He said: "It seems clear to me therefore that the mischief aimed at by sections 7 and 8 of the Muslim Family Laws Ordinance 1961 does not exist in the case of a khula which is extra-judicial and where every opportunity of reconciliation has occurred."

[58] 1976 PLD Lah 1466.

Dissolution of Marriage

consensual khul' (now called mubara'a) is indeed subject, on a correct construction of the Pakistan law, to Section 2(ix), then the rule in *Muhammad Ishaque v. Ahsan Ahmad* would of course apply and a copy of the decree would be sent to the chairman, and subsequent reconciliation attempts would be carried out by him at that stage.

It may be useful to summarise the position of Pakistan law at the present time. We have to await judicial comment before we can accurately state whether the consensual divorce is, or is not, subject to the provisions of Section 2(ix). It is submitted, however, that the consensual divorce operates *outside* the framework of Section 2(ix), but that, in contrast, it operates *within* the framework of Sections 7 and 8 of the 1961 Ordinance. The *Khurshid Bibi* case has not changed this position. A *Khurshid Bibi* divorce operates of course *within* the framework of both the Dissolution of Muslim Marriages Act 1939 Section 2(ix) and Sections 7 and 8 of the Muslim Family Laws Ordinance 1961.

7.4 Divorce by Judicial Authority (Faskh)

In Hanafi law, the only ground on which a woman may obtain a judicial termination of her marital status occurs when she can prove to the court that her husband is incapable of consummating the marriage. The other classical schools, besides acknowledging this ground, provide additional bases. Thus the Ithna 'Ashari school enables the qadi to grant a judicial decree in cases where the husband is suffering from insanity, leprosy or venereal disease. The Shafi'i school in addition to these grounds, considers wilful refusal to maintain to be a sufficient reason for a judicial divorce. The Hanbali school recognises the various physical and mental defects, and recognises also the following: failure to maintain, desertion for more than six months without just cause, and the failure to comply with a condition in the marriage contract. Even more liberal than the Hanbali school is the Maliki school. Physical and mental defects, failure to maintain, desertion, absence for more than one year for *whatever reason,* and ill-treatment (darar) are all acknowledged as grounds for dissolution in this school. Maliki law, therefore, is the only classical school which permits a divorce on the basis of cruelty or ill-treatment by the husband. The important point to make, however, is that when the Maliki qadi grants the wife a decree he does so by way of exercising the right of talaq on behalf of the husband; thereby continuing the legal fiction of the exclusive right of the husband to repudiate his wife. The other schools recognise the doctrine of the faskh. The reason for the difference in approach is the emphasis placed by the Maliki school on Sura IV, verse 35. This verse reads as follows:

Dissolution of Marriage

```
If ye fear a breach between them twain,
Appoint two arbitrators,
One from his family
And the other from hers . . .
```

In Shafi'i, Hanbali and Hanafi law, the arbitrator's role is no more than conciliatory and, if possible, reconciliatory. In Maliki law, however, the arbitrators are representatives of the court. Thus, according to Maliki law, if the arbitrators fail to reconcile the parties, they can decide that the marriage should be terminated; which they can do by way of ordering the husband to divorce his wife by talaq.

7.4.1 Modern Reforms

Given the limited facilities available to women in Hanafi law, it is not surprising that most of the legislation which has taken place in the Muslim world in this area in the last sixty years or so has been in Hanafi countries. It was the 1917 Ottoman Law of Family Rights which really opened the floodgates of legal reform. This law was enacted in the aftermath of the First World War, in particular in order to alleviate the difficulties created by foreign husbands marrying Turkish girls, and then deserting them. In Hanafi law, of course, girls in this position had no chance of remarriage. The 1917 law provides for judicial dissolution in cases where the husband is suffering from serious disease and in cases where the husband has failed to provide maintenance and has deserted the wife.[59]

The early Egyptian reforms of 1920 (Law no. 25) and 1929 (Law no. 25) introduce Maliki law in place of the predominant Hanafi doctrine. Article 4 of the 1920 Act states:

> Where a wife demands dissolution of the marriage with the husband who fails to support her and who has no known property from which a maintenance order could be executed, her demand shall be granted forthwith unless the husband proves by evidence that he is destitute, in which case he may be given a respite not exceeding one month.

Articles 12 and 13 of the 1929 law enable the wife to obtain a divorce in the case of desertion by her husband for a continuous period of one year. Affliction of a serious disease "making the continuance of marriage injurious to the wife" (1929 Act, Article 9) constitutes grounds for a "single irrevocable

---

[59] The law is applicable today amongst the Muslim communities both in Israel and in the Lebanon. [Articles 119, 121, 126 of the 1917 law].

divorce" granted by the court. Failure to maintain and desertion, in contrast, constitutes ground for a revocable divorce in that the situation can be saved by the husband who proves during the 'idda that he is now able and willing to maintain his wife.

The most important reform of the Egyptian legislation, however, is contained in Article 6 of the 1929 law which introduces the Maliki law of darar (harm) in relation to cases where the wife can obtain a divorce on the grounds of the husband's impeachability. The Maliki law of khul' which enables the wife to obtain a judicial divorce even in cases where she herself is at fault is not, however, introduced. The explanatory memorandum accompanying the law states:

> It was, therefore, considered in the interest of general welfare to adopt the doctrine of Imam Ibn Malik concerning disagreement between spouses except in the case where the arbitrator finds that the fault was exclusively with the wife.

The procedure under the 1929 law is as follows. The wife alleges that her husband is guilty of cruelty in a way "which makes the continuance of the marital relationship impossible for people of their class". If the allegation is proved the qadi grants a dissolution by way of an irrevocable divorce. If she is unable to provide proof of the allegation, an arbitration procedure is established to attempt a reconciliation. The arbitrators are able to make recommendations involving a dissolution of the marriage, although such a recommendation can be made only if they find that the fault for the discord lies with the husband.

Similar provisions to the earlier Egyptian reform have been introduced both in Jordan (1951) and in Syria (1953). The Jordanians, however, have gone further than the 1929 Egyptian law by enabling a termination to be decreed in the event of an allegation of ill-treatment even if the fault for the breakdown is determined to be that of the wife. The Jordanian law was consolidated in 1976 by the Law of Personal Status (no. 61) of that year. The Syrian law does not adopt this solution, and in contrast to the Jordanian law, stays closely to the Egyptian reforms. Further reforms were introduced in Egypt in 1979 by Law no. 44 of that year. Article 10 of the 1929 Law is amended to state that if the arbitrators determine that the fault is that of the wife, then the court can dissolve the marriage on payment of compensation by the wife. Thus the Egyptian law is brought into line with the Jordanian law and moves closer to the Maliki law in this regard. As we have already had occasion to remark, at the time of writing, the status of the 1979 reforms is in jeopardy as a result of a judicial determination in 1985.

Dissolution of Marriage

One of the more comprehensive codes is the Somali Family Law no. 23 (1975). This code is similar to the family law legislation in South Yemen (1974) and Algeria (1984). The Somali Code deserves citation in full:

Article 42.
Dissolution (faskh)

(1) Dissolution (faskh) means the rescission of the marriage contract brought about by the court.
(2) Dissolution has the same legal effects as revocable divorce.
(3) A suit for dissolution of the marriage shall deprive the husband of his right of divorce.

Article 43.
Cases for Dissolution

(1) Both the husband and wife are entitled to file a petition in any of the following cases for dissolution of the marriage:
   (a) If one of the spouses is suffering from an incurable disease which does not allow cohabitation or even if possible, it causes harm, on condition that the fact is proved by a medical practitioner.
   (b) If the whereabouts of one of the spouses are not known for more than four consecutive years; but if the missing person reappears before the dissolution judgment is delivered, the dissolution petition shall be rejected.
   (c) If one of the spouses, though able to provide maintenance, habitually fails to provide maintenance where the petitioner is actually in need of such maintenance.
   (d) If both husband and wife do not own anything and therefore none of them is able to meet the maintenance obligations, the Court shall decide the case only after six months from the date the dissolution was filed.
   (e) If disagreement between the spouses has become so serious as to make conjugal life impossible. In this instance the court shall follow the procedure laid down in Article 36.

Dissolution of Marriage

(f) Perpetual impotency or sterility of one of the spouses.

(g) If one of the spouses is sentenced to imprisonment for a period exceeding four years, provided the petition of dissolution is submitted after the imprisoned spouse has completed his sentence.

(2) The wife is entitled to apply for dissolution of her marriage if her husband has been authorised, according to Article 13, to contract another marriage and on condition that no children were born.

Article 44
Maintenance Where Divorce (talaq) or dissolution (faskh) results through the fault of the husband, the Court shall order him to maintain the former wife for a period not less than three months and not more than one year. If the divorce or dissolution results through a fault on the part of the wife the Court shall order her to pay to the husband a sum not less than her dower.

7.4.1.1 Reforms in South Asia
Reforms on the Indian subcontinent have been nowhere near as comprehensive. Reforms came in 1939 by the Dissolution of Muslim Marriages Act of that year, which is still in force in all three countries on the subcontinent. Although the Act introduces concepts similar to Maliki law, the Maliki interpretation of Sura IV, verse 35 is not incorporated into the law. Section 2 of the Act enables a woman married under Muslim law to obtain a decree for the dissolution of her marriage on any one or more of a number of grounds.

(i) The whereabouts of the husband have not been known for a period of 4 years. A divorce passed on such a ground shall not take effect for a period of six months from the date of the decree. If he or his agent appears within the six months, and satisfies the court that he is prepared to perform his conjugal duties, the decree is set aside.

(ii) The husband has neglected or has failed to provide for her maintenance for a period of two years.

One problem of this provision is that it does not deal with the difficulty of a situation where the husband alleges that the wife is disobedient and that, therefore, he is released from his duty in Islamic law to maintain his wife. The consensus view is that such a husband is entitled to refrain from maintaining his recalcitrant wife without laying himself open to divorce proceedings. In two cases, however, Krishna Iyer J decided that a divorce may be granted on this ground even where the husband is under no legal duty to support his wife.[60]

>   (iii) The husband has been sentenced for a period of seven years or upwards. No decree shall be passed on this ground until the sentence has become final.
>
>   (iv) The husband has failed to perform, without reasonable cause, his marital obligations for a period of 3 years.
>
>   (v) The husband was impotent at the time of the marriage and continues to be so. Before passing a decree on this ground, the court shall, on application by the husband, make an order requiring the husband to satisfy the court within a period of one year from the date of such order that he has ceased to be impotent. If the husband satisfies the court within the one-year period, no decree shall be passed. The wife does not need to show that she was ignorant of the husband's impotence at the time of the marriage.
>
>   (vi) The husband has been insane for a period of two years or is suffering from leprosy or a virulent venereal disease.
>
>   (vii) The husband treats her with cruelty.

Six illustrations are given of cruelty, and it is incumbent on the wife-petitioner to bring her allegations under one of these headings. The most general heading is the first: "habitually assaults her and makes her life miserable by cruelty or bad conduct, even if such conduct does not amount to physical ill-treatment". The conduct has been defined as "conduct of the husband which would cause

---

[60] *Aboobacker Haji v. Mamu Koya* 1971 KLT 663 and *Yusuf Rowthan v. Surramma* 1970 KLT 477. In the latter case, Krishna Iyyer J states that it is his view that "where there has been actual failure to provide for the maintenance of the wife even if it be because the wife has improperly declined to live with the husband, section 2 clause (ii) is fulfilled." Professor Anderson states that such an approach appears to him to be an "wholly unjustifiable interpretation" of the Statute. See T.Mahmood (ed) *Muslim Personal Law in India.* (New Delhi, Indian Law Institute, 1972). A similar approach however has been taken recently in *Ittochalil Meethal Moosa v. Pachiparambath Meethal Fathima & Pathumma* 1983 KLJ 610.

such bodily or mental pain as to endanger the wife's safety or health".[61] The other examples of the "cruelty" ground are more precise, namely: association with women of ill repute; attempting to force the wife to lead an immoral life; disposal of the wife's property (or preventing her from exercising rights over it); obstructing her in the observance of her religious profession or practice; if, having more than one wife, he does not treat her equitably in accordance with the injunctions of the Qur'an. In Pakistan, a further "ground" has been added: taking an additional wife in contravention of the provisions of the 1961 Ordinance.

The other two subsections, dealing with the option of puberty and the general provision "on any other ground which is recognised as valid for the dissolution of marriages under Muslim law" have already been dealt with in the course of this chapter and earlier chapters.

The arbitration procedure, available in classical Maliki law, and introduced, for example, in Egypt, Jordan and Syria, is not mentioned in the 1939 Act. However, by Order XXXIIA (1976) the Code of Criminal Procedure has been amended so far as Pakistan is concerned to make it the responsibility of the Court where it is possible to do so consistent with the nature and circumstances of the case, to assist the parties in arriving at a settlement in respect of the subject-matter of the suit. The court has power to adjourn the proceedings for such period as it thinks fit to enable attempts to be made to effect such a settlement. We have already commented on the position in Pakistan that the effect of Section 8 of the Ordinance is to introduce the arbitral procedures of the Pakistan Code in all circumstances (except the exercise of the option of puberty, and possibly the consensual mubara'a).[62]

It is appropriate to conclude the discussion of judicial divorce in particular, as indeed the chapter on the law of divorce as a whole, by returning to the Tunisian law of 1956. Articles 25-33 state that a divorce can be obtained only by judicial means. The grounds are as wide as any other country in the world – on the demands of the husband or the wife on grounds specified in the code; when agreed upon by both spouses; when insisted upon by either spouse. In the last situation, the court shall determine the indemnity due to the wife as compensation for injuries suffered or the indemnity she shall pay to the husband. Article 32 introduces the arbitral process; thus it is laid down that "the court shall not grant a decree of divorce until it has exhausted all means

---

[61] *Itwari v. Asghari* 1960 AIR All 684, where the husband married a second wife without divorcing his first wife.

[62] *Muhammad Ishaque v. Ahsan Ahmad* 1975 PLD Lah 1118; *Muhammad Amin v. Surraya Begum* 1970 PLD Lah 475.

Dissolution of Marriage

of establishing the causes of conflict between the spouses and has failed to reconcile them". The Tunisian law is clearly an example of social engineering. It is justified by Tunisians themselves as being within the spirit of the Islamic jurisprudential process – how this is achieved will be the subject of the last chapter in this book. We must turn our attention at this stage, however, to the problems of inheritance.

8. The Laws of Inheritance

This chapter discusses the basic rules of Islamic succession law. Emphasis is given to the the Hanafi law of Sunni succession. The details of the law have been the subject of a major study by Professor Coulson, and it is therefore necessary only to provide a general review of the subject. Readers are referred to Professor Coulson's book for the detailed provisions.[1]

In Islamic law, succession is of two kinds, namely optional and compulsory. Optional succession (testamentary succession) is limited to one-third of the property owned by the propositus (the deceased). This principle is based firmly on Sunna. The remaining two-thirds of the property, together with any property which has not been bequeathed, is distributed according to a fixed and compulsory set of rules which represent the synthesis of the Qur'anic verses with the pre-Islamic customary law, and the interpretation of these verses as accepted by ijma' (consensus).

8.1 Administration of the Estate

Before the bequests can be paid to the beneficiaries the debts must be accounted for. The order of priority of debts, perhaps irrelevant in a fully solvent estate, takes on considerable importance in an insolvent estate. Most jurists will give priority to the burial expenses. After these expenses have been paid out from the estate, the next charges on the estate are the secured debts (such as a pledge which is secured to a part of the property), followed by the unsecured debts. It will be recalled that the widow's unpaid mahr ranks as an unsecured debt.

According to Hanafi law, the unsecured debts which are incurred during sound health prior to the deceased entering what is referred to as the "disease of death" take priority over debts where the only evidence for their existence is an admission by the deceased whilst suffering from the "disease of death". This concept is explained later. Dr. Tanzil-ur-Rahman in his book entitled *A Code of Muslim Personal Law*[2] gives a useful illustration of this principle

---

[1] N.J.Coulson, *Succession in the Muslim Family* (Cambridge, 1971). A major analysis of the Islamic law of inheritance, which includes a detailed commentary on certain aspects of Coulson's work appears in D.S.Powers, *Studies in Qur'an and Hadith: The formation of the Islamic Law of Inheritance*, (California, 1986).

[2] (Karachi, 1978) at p. 430.

which explains the operation of the rule.

> A person dies and there is a residue of R2000/- of his estate after the expenses of his funeral rites and ceremonies. There is a debt due .... of the same amount incurred during his sound health. Besides, there is the admission of a debt of R1000/- during his death-illness (for which there is no proof except his own admission). According to Hanafis, the debt incurred during sound health shall, in the circumstances, be paid first. In that event no residue of the estate remains and the creditors whose debts were admitted by the deceased during the death-illness shall get nothing.

The other schools do not operate such a system of priority, and, in the example taken from Tanzil-ur-Rahman's book, all the creditors would receive some payment out of the estate in proportion to the amount of the respective debt. The only concession made by the Hanafi law to equality occurs when the debt which is incurred during the "disease of death" can be proved by evidence in addition to a mere admission; otherwise the debt incurred at this time is treated in the context of the law of wills, a topic to which we shall return.

In the classical system, responsibility for administering the estate lay with the government, with the qadi acting as the agent. There is no executor of the estate in the Islamic system. The classical doctrine is that the deceased fictitiously survives and remains the owner of the estate until all his obligations have been discharged; thus in an insolvent estate, the property does *not* pass to the heirs unless and until the debts have been paid.

On the Indian subcontinent, however, to adopt Professor Coulson's terminology, "the courts betrayed a total ignorance of the doctrine of the deceased's fictitious survival". Influenced by English concepts, the Indian courts held that the deceased's estate devolved at death on his heirs irrespective of whether the estate was solvent or insolvent. In India, therefore, in contrast to the Muslim world elsewhere, the heir's ownership is acquired immediately and is subject to a personal liability to pay the debts of the deceased in proportion to the respective shares in the estate.

The leading case on the subcontinent is *Jafri Begam v. Amir Muhammad Khan*.[3] The facts of this case were as follows. Ali Muhammad Khan left considerable wealth. He died in 1878 leaving behind him, as his heirs, his widow, two sons, three daughters, a brother, and his parents.

---

[3] 1885 ILR 7 All 822.

The Laws of Inheritance

Table 2

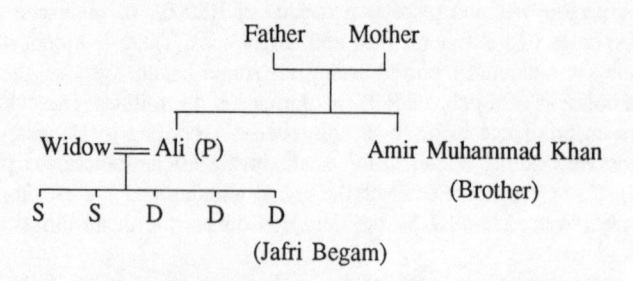

```
                    Father ── Mother
                          │
            ┌─────────────┴─────────────┐
  Widow ══ Ali (P)              Amir Muhammad Khan
     │                               (Brother)
  ┌──┬──┬──┬──┐
  S  S  D  D  D
     (Jafri Begam)
```

Abdul Rahman initiated proceedings and secured a court decree in his favour against the widow, two sons, and the three daughters for a debt which was due to him from the deceased. The decree was executed, and the village which originally belonged to the deceased was sold to Abdul Rahman. The brother (Amir Muhammad Khan) was not involved in this dispute, and, on becoming aware of the situation, brought an action to recover what he thought he was entitled to out of the estate. He submitted that he was entitled to a portion of the estate which he inherited on the death of his mother and his father; who of course were heirs of Ali Muhammad Khan. The defendants in the action were Ali Muhammad Khan's widow, the two sons, and the three daughters. The full Allahabad bench dealt with this case and, in giving judgment, Mahmood J enunciated the following three propositions:

(1) when a Muslim dies, leaving debts unpaid, his estate devolves immediately on his heirs, and such devolution is not suspended till or contingent upon the payment of debts;

(2) a decree for a debt passed against such of the heirs as are in possession of the estate does not bind the other heirs;

(3) if one of the heirs, who was out of possession, and who was not a party to the proceedings, brings a suit against the decree-holder for the recovery of his share of the estate, he must pay his proportionate share of the debt before recovering possession of his share of the inheritance.

It will be seen, of course, that rule (a) is directly opposed to the principle of Islamic law relating to the fictitious survival of the propositus. The essential difference between classical doctrine and the *Jafri Begam* rule is that under the *Jafri Begam* rule, an heir who alienates the property of which he has taken possession can pass a valid title, which would debar the claims of the

The Laws of Inheritance

creditor of the estate. Two cases, namely *Bazayet Hossein v. Dooli Chund*[4] and *Wahidunnisa v. Shubrattun*[5] illustrate very clearly this proposition. The facts in *Bazayet Hossein v. Dooli Chund* were as follows. A Muslim died leaving surviving him his widow and a son. The widow's dower had not been paid during the husband's lifetime. The son, in debt, mortgaged his share of the estate to M without paying the dower debt. Thus the widow applied for, and obtained, a decree against the son in possession for her dower debt. The estate was attached in execution of the decree. The mortgagor (M) then, in his turn, obtained a decree against the son on the basis of the mortgage in order to sell the son's property to recoup the mortgage amount. In execution of this decree, the property was sold to a third party (P). The question before the court, therefore, was who had the better right to the property; the purchaser (P), or the widow. It was held that the widow could not follow (trace) the property into the hands of the purchaser. The son had absolute capacity to dispose of his share of the inheritance; it was vested in him *immediately* on death, and there was no condition imposed that the debts must be paid prior to the property passing to the heirs.

The decision in *Wahidunnisa* is to the same effect.[6]

One of several heirs, though he may be in possession of the whole estate, has no power to alienate the share of co-heirs.[7] However, certain decrees of a court will nonetheless bind heirs not in possession. The Supreme Court of India considered this last issue in the case of *N.K.Mohammad Sulaiman v. N.C.Mohammad Ismail and others*.[8] The facts of this case were as follows. M, K, and L mortgaged certain property in 1933 in favour of NR to secure repayment of R20000/-. M died in 1937. In 1940, NR commenced proceedings for the enforcement of the mortgage against K, L, and the three widows and one daughter of M. A decree was obtained in 1941 and, in execution of this decree, the properties were sold at a court auction. The properties were purchased by NR with leave of the court. NR thereafter transferred the properties to P who in his turn alienated the properties to others. Subsequently, Muhammad Sulaiman (the plaintiff), claiming that he was the son of M, instituted a suit for a decree for partition of the mortgaged properties or, in the alternative, for a declaration that he was entitled to redeem the mortgage or

---

[4] 1877/78 5 L.R.IA 211.
[5] 1870/71 6 Bengal LR 54.
[6] 1870/71 6 Bengal LR 54.
[7] *Jan Mohammad v. Karam Chand.* AIR 1953 S.C. 2981.
[8] 1966 1 SCR 937.

portion thereof equal to his share in the mortgaged properties. The suit was resisted by NR and the alienees on two grounds. First, it was submitted that the plaintiff was not the son of M. Second, that NR had made a full enquiry and he was instructed that only the three widows and one daughter were the surviving members of the family of M.

Shah J, in the Supreme Court, set out what he referred to as the "well-settled principles" as follows:

> The estate of [a] Muslim dying intestate devolves under the Islamic law upon his heirs at the moment of his death i.e. the estate vests immediately in each heir in proportion to the shares ordained by the personal law and the interest of each heir is separate and distinct.

It follows from this statement, of course, that each heir is liable to satisfy the debts of the deceased only to the extent of the share of the debt proportionate to his share in the estate. So far as the creditor is concerned, he may sue all the heirs of the deceasd but he is certainly not *bound* to sue all the heirs. Where he sues all the heirs, he may execute a decree against the property as a whole without regard to the extent of the liability of the heirs. Where he sues only some of the heirs, liability for satisfaction of the decree may be enforced against individual heirs in the property held by them proportionate to their share in the estate.

The issue in this case is similar to the situation where a defendant dies during the pendency of the suit. In this context, the Judge said:

> if after bona fide enquiry, some but not all the heirs of a deceased defendant are brought on the record, the heirs so brought on the record represent the entire estate of the deceased and the decision of the court in the absence of fraud or collusion binds those who are not brought on the record.

Necessarily, therefore, the appeal by the son to the Supreme Court failed. The Supreme Court held that the son, on the assumption that he was a bona fide heir, was sufficiently represented in the 1940 suit and was bound by the decree of the court arising out of the suit. Bona fide enquiry had been made and, in any event, the defendant had no defence to put forward which had not been presented in 1940.

8.2 Testate Succession

Every adult Muslim with reasoning ability has capacity to make a will. A Hanafi, Hanbali or Shafi'i Muslim is adult for this purpose as soon as he has attained puberty; the presumption in Sunni law is 15 years at a maximum. The Shi'i law and the Maliki doctrine place the emphasis on the age of discernment; namely 10 years. The minimum age of capacity on the Indian subcontinent is established by the Indian Majority Act 1875 as 18.

If a will is procured, it will be void. Cases of procurement, such as undue influence, or even coercion, often occur in cases where heirs allege that the deceased was a woman who observed strict purdah (seclusion). In the Anglo-Mohammedan system, the rule in this situation is that the burden lies on the beneficiary of the estate to prove that the pardahnashin knew what she was doing. The burden is discharged if the beneficiary proves that the propositus acted after receiving independent advice.

8.2.1 Void and Ultra Vires Bequests

Certain bequests are void; other bequests are *ultra vires* in that they are subject to ratification. Void bequests are those that are opposed to Islam, such as a bequest to a gambling house or to a bar. Bequests which are outwardly unquestionable, but which have been made for an immoral purpose are not void in Hanafi law, where the emphasis is on the form; but are void in Hanbali law where, because of the strong moralism of that school, a bequest inspired by an improper motive is ineffective. An example of the Hanbali rule, which was adopted in Egypt in 1946, is a bequest by the testator to Mr X which, although not stated, is in gratitude for having kept him supplied with liquor, or a bequest to Miss Y, which is impliedly granted in recognition of her services as his mistress. Both bequests are void by Hanbali law.

The two rules dealing with *ultra vires* bequests in Sunni law are:

(1) no bequests can be made which involve disposition beyond one-third of the net estate.

(2) no bequest can be made in favour of an heir.

The second of these two rules is not applicable in Shi'i law. If the bequest, or if there is more than one bequest, the addition of all the bequests, exceeds one-third of the net estate, the rights of the compulsory heirs in the estate would be directly interfered with; thus the distribution of the estate to legatees beyond the one-third available for distribution by testamentary succession lies in the hands of the compulsory heirs. In Hanafi law, the consent of the heirs to such a distribution has to be obtained, if it can be, after the death of the propositus. In the Shi'i doctrine, however, where the legatee acquires a "contingent interest" as soon as the bequest is made, consent of the heirs can be obtained before the propositus dies. When some of the heirs grant their consent to such a distribution, but others do not, the bequests are payable beyond the one-third out of the shares of the consenting heirs alone.

The Laws of Inheritance

In cases where the legacies amount to more than one-third of the net estate, and when none of the surviving heirs consent, these legacies must be reduced. A testator can validly specify the order in which several bequests he has made are to be administered, and thus the bequests take effect in the order specified until the bequeathable one-third is exhausted. If no specification has been given by the testator, the abatement in Sunni law is proportionate; for as the will speaks from death, the rights of the legatees all mature at the same point in time. The only exception to this rule relates to an instance where two or more bequests have been made for a pious purpose. The abatement with respect to the pious purposes *themselves* is not proportionate; so-called "voluntary charities" abate before "recommended charities", which themselves take second place to "obligatory charities". In the Shi'i school, because of the emphasis given to the contingent rights of the legatees, the simple rule is "the first in time prevails". As between pious and secular bequests, normal rules of proportional abatement apply.

The restriction of the power to make bequests to one-third of the estate is seen, in the classical doctrine, as a fundamental rule deriving from the Hadith of the Prophet. Professor Schacht suggested[9] that the restriction is Umayyad in origin, connected as it is to a fiscal interest so important at that time. The rule, nonetheless, is of prime significance – and no Muslim country has restricted its scope.

In contrast, the second limiting factor; *no bequest in favour of an heir*, has been subject to important reform. The rule, in any event, is not followed in the Shi'i school which, because of the interpretation of Sura II verse 180 permits a testator, within one-third, to bequeath to whomsoever he desires.[10] The Sunnis believe that this verse has been abrogated by the verse which, as we shall see later in the chapter, details the specific fractions of the estate to particular relatives of the deceased.

In Sunni law, the bequest to an heir is *ultra vires*, and depends, as in the first limiting factor, on the agreement to the distribution by the heirs. The Shi'i law has been adopted in Egypt, Iraq and Sudan.

The leading case in India is the Privy Council decision *Ghulam Mohammad v. Ghulam Husain*.[11] A Hanafi Muslim made a will which included

---

[9] *Origins of Mohammedan Jurisprudence* op.cit. p. 201.

[10] Sura II verse 180:
It is prescribed, when death approaches any of you, if he leave any goods, that he make a bequest to parents and next of kin, according to reasonable usage this is due from the God-fearing.

[11] AIR 1932 PC 81.

the following term:

> I, Shaikh Khadim Husain, son of Munshi Aman Ullah, deceased..... I have two sons.......three daughters......and one wife. My elder son shall remain in proprietary possession [of certain property] acquired by my deceased father given to me under the will dated 1866.

Sir George Lowndes, in the Privy Council, said that it was not in dispute that under Hanafi law a will conferring beneficial interests to heirs is invalid unless consented to by other heirs after the testator's death. In a dispute between the two sons, the Privy Council formed the view that the younger son should be entitled to share equally with the elder son in the property mentioned.[12]

The legatee must be in existence at the time the bequest is made. This raises the particular problem of the child *en ventre sa mere*. Such a child has a legal existence and is entitled to take a bequest if born within the maximum period of gestation from the date of the bequest.

In Sunni law, the will must be accepted by the legatee after the legator's death: thus it is necessary for the legatee to survive the deceased. Acceptance may be either express or implied. If the legatee dies after the legator but before he has had the opportunity of accepting the will, the view of the Hanafi law is that the property devolves on the heirs of the legatee. Presumably, this situation is acceptable because the will is deemed to be completed on the death of the legator, and there can be no opportunity to repudiate the will. The other Sunni schools adopt a slightly different approach. They say that an option (khiyar) arises in this situation and the khiyar to accept or repudiate devolves on the heirs of the legatee. Thus if these heirs of the deceased legatee accept the legacy the legacy is valid; otherwise it is void (batil).

8.2.1.1 Sunni and Shi'i law

It may be convenient at this stage to summarise the major differences which have been noted so far between Sunni law and Shi'i law (of the Ithna 'Ashari school) on testamentary succession.

(1) *Capacity to make a will.*
    Hanafi law – puberty and sane.
    Shi'i law – 10 (age of discernment).

(2) *Consent of heirs to distribution of an otherwise ultra vires will.*
    Hanafi law – consent after the death of the testator.

---

[12] See also *Valanhiyal Kunhi Avulla v. Eengahil Peetikayil Kunhi Avulla* 1964 AIR Ker 201.

The Laws of Inheritance

Shi'i law – consent can be given either after the testator's death or during his lifetime.

(3) *Abatement.*
Hanafi law – proportionate reduction.
Shi'i law – first in time prevails.

(4) *Bequests to an heir.*
Hanafi law – bequests to an heir are *ultra vires*.
Shi'i law – a bequest can be made in favour of an heir within one-third of the distribution.

(5) *Legatee predeceases testator.*
Hanafi law – legacy lapses.
Shi'i law – the heirs of the legatee have the option of accepting or rejecting the legacy.

(6) *Homicide.*
Hanafi law – if the legatee caused the death of the legator in a direct manner, whether intentional or otherwise, the bequest is *ultra vires*.
Shi'i law – only intentional homicide will deprive the legatee of the bequest, although in this case the bequest is batil, and the legatee is absolutely barred.

For the views of the other Sunni schools, readers are referred to Coulson.[13]

8.3 Death Sickness

We have mentioned already the importance of the doctrine of marad al-mawt in relation to the administration of the estate. At the point in time when the propositus enters his "death sickness" the personal debts and the claims of the compulsory heirs attach to the property. The propositus, therefore, cannot defeat the expectancies of the claimants by donating, or selling below value, parts of the estate which amount to more than one-third of the net estate. Such a donation, like the bequests, is *ultra vires* and depends for its efficacy on the consent of the heirs. The limitations imposed upon bequests are thus extended to cover gifts made by dying persons. There would appear to be four major criteria to decide when, in Coulson's phrase, "the process of dying has irrevocably begun".[14] These criteria are as follows: the mental element, the

---

[13] op.cit. pp. 229 ff.
[14] Coulson. op.cit. at p. 227.

physical element, the causal factor, and finally the actual death. The mental element, which combines both a subjective and an objective test, causes the most problems. A few examples will suffice for present purposes. Thus, in one Indian case[15] a man was attacked by paralysis of the lower limbs and became a helpless invalid. He was a very old man and, as a result of his illness, he could no longer leave his bed either to say his prayers or to perform "the ordinary offices of nature". He executed a waqf[16] in March. He was bedridden for nine months, and he died in November. It was held by the court that he executed the waqf during his death sickness; thus the waqf was valid only to the extent of one-third of the estate. A contrasting case is *Muhammad Gulshere Khan v. Mariam Begam*.[17] In this case a donor suffered an attack of boils and carbuncles. At the time of the donation, it had lasted for over a year, and there was no evidence to suggest that he apprehended death. It was held that the gift was *not* made during death sickness. It is interesting to note that in Shi'i law, an illness which has lasted for over a year can never constitute death sickness.

In Pakistan, the emphasis has been placed firmly on the subjective element of the law. Indeed, in one case, *Shamshad Ali Shah v. Syed Hassan Shah*[18] Kaikus J observed *obiter* that the rules must apply so long as the donor believes he was dying even if, in fact, he does not in the event actually die.

This is perhaps an extreme view, although the proof of the subjective apprehension of death in the mind of the donor is clearly the crucial test in India as well as Pakistan. Thus in *Abdul Hafiz Beg v. Sahebbi*[19] when referring to previous cases, Masod Kar J said:

> [I]t may be taken as settled that the crucial test of marz-ul-maut is the proof of the subjective apprehension of death in the mind of the donor, that is to say, the apprehension derived from his own consciousness as distinguished from the apprehension caused in the minds of others, and the other symptoms like physical incapacities are only the indicia, but not infallible signs or a sine qua non of marz-ul-maut.

In this case, one Abdul Kadar, a man of 80 was taken seriously ill and he never recovered from this illness. Apparently, according to the judgment:

---

[15] *Karimanissa v. Hamedulla* 1925/26 30 Cal WN 129.

[16] A charitable endowment. Waqf is discussed in Chapter 9.

[17] 1881 ILR 3 All 731.

[18] 1964 PLD SC 143. See also *Jahan Khan v. Feroze* 1951 PLD Lah 433; *Asmat Begum v. Hussain Jan* 1956 PLD (WP) Pesh 5; *Safia Begum v. Abdul Rajack.* AIR 1945 Bom 438.

[19] AIR 1975 Bom 165.

[H]e had reached the mental low of such kind as he was asking for his near and dear ones to be by his side and when his daughters came near him he was even unable to express himself... All this raises the clear possibility that while he was making the gift which is about 24 hours before death, he was seized during or gripped by the subjective and imminent apprehension of his death.

In the Judge's own romantic language:

The bed on which he rested proved to be the death-bed and at the mellowed age of 80 this leaf fell from the tree of life.

8.4 Compulsory Succession

In pre-Islamic Arabia, the rules of succession were connected directly with the system of tribal warfare; that is the participation in combat of the man, and the non-participation in combat of the woman. Thus those who inherited the estate in the pre-Islamic system were able to trace their relationship with the propositus by male links exclusively. These relatives (the 'asaba) provided the cohesive unit of the Arabian tribe. In a competition between two male agnatic relatives, the simple rule was that the "nearest" to the propositus inherited to the exclusion of those more remote.

Table 3

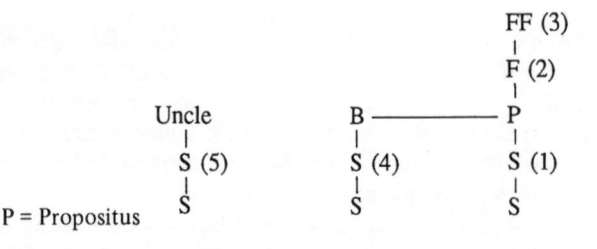

```
                                    FF (3)
                                      |
                                     F (2)
                                      |
        Uncle           B ─────────── P
          |             |             |
         S (5)         S (4)         S (1)
          |             |             |
P = Propositus S        S             S
```

(These rules will be discussed in a little more detail later.) One of Mohammed's major political objectives was to substitute the tribal unit by a family structure. The first Qur'anic provision, in time in this area is Sura II verse 180. This verse introduces the moral obligation that Muslims must make satisfactory provision for parents and next of kin. The revelation is general in scope and it is filled in by later verses in Sura IV which are revealed during the time of the early desperate battles with the unbelievers. Sura IV provides specific fractions of the estate, for the first time, to the widows and orphans

The Laws of Inheritance

and other relatives who were not entitled through the agnatic tie. The old agnatic system is not excluded by Sura IV. Indeed Sura IV verse 11 itself recognises that sons still inherit under the new system. Thus:

```
Allah thus directs you
as regards your children's
inheritance: to the male
a portion equal to that
of two females.
```

The Qur'anic system of inheritance, therefore, complements the old agnatic system. The synthesis of the two systems as worked out initially by the Sunna of Mohammed represents the Sunni law of inheritance; first, the Qur'anic heirs are given their share, and then the residue is distributed to the nearest agnate. Emphasis is here given to the Hanafi law. The Shi'i law will be considered later.

8.4.1 The Qur'anic Heirs

There are twelve Qur'anic heirs in Sunni law.[20]

```
(1) Husband.    (H)
(2) Wife.       (W)
(3) Father.     (F)
(4) True grandfather. (FF)
```

A true grandfather is a male ancestor between whom and the propositus no female intervenes, that is, a paternal grandfather. It is possible although obviously fairly unusual for inheritance to be claimed by an ancestor three or even more generations removed from the propositus. A false grandfather is a male ancestor between whom and the propositus a female intervenes, e.g. a maternal grandfather.

---

[20] Qur'anic heirs are sometimes referred to as class 1 heirs. The agnates comprise class 2, and more distant kinsmen constitute class 3. Distant kinsman very rarely inherit, and the rules of distribution within this group are not discussed in this book. Reference can be made to Coulson op.cit. generally for the detailed provisions in this area.

```
(5) Mother.          (M)
(6) True grandmother.   (MM;FM)
```

A true grandmother is a female ancestor between whom and the propositus no false grandfather intervenes. Both the maternal and the paternal grandmother can inherit. A false grandmother is a mother's father's mother (MFM).

She is excluded from any entitlement to inherit in this category in any circumstances.

```
(7) Daughter. (D)
(8) Son's daughter (however low so ever).
    (SD; SSD; etc.)
(9) Full sister.
```

(Sometimes referred to as the Germane Sister).

```
(10) Consanguine sister.    (Cons Sis).
```

(children of the same father but different mothers).

```
(11) Uterine brother.  (Ut Br).
(12) Uterine sister.   (Ut Sis).
```

(children of the same mother but different fathers).

We shall introduce discussion of each of these relatives in turn, in order to build up a picture of the Hanafi succession rules. Readers are referred also to the simplified chart of Hanafi succession which is annexed at the end of the chapter.

8.4.1.1 The Husband.
His share is one-quarter of the net estate. When there are no children, or agnatic grandchildren, his share is increased to one-half of the estate. It is immaterial whether the child belongs to the spouse relict or is issue of another marriage of the deceased spouse.

8.4.1.2 The Wife.
Her share is one-eighth of the net estate. If there are two wives, they share the one-eighth between them. Where there are no children, or agnatic grandchildren, the wife or wives take one-quarter.

The Laws of Inheritance

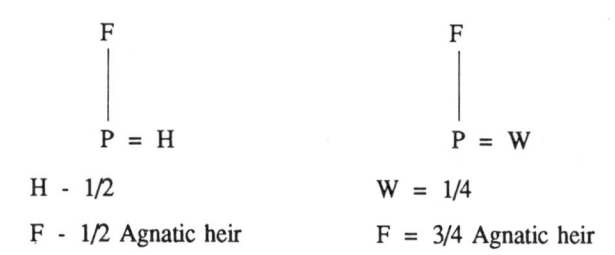

Table 4

```
        F                           F
        |                           |
        |                           |
       P = H                       P = W
  H - 1/2                     W = 1/4
  F - 1/2 Agnatic heir        F = 3/4 Agnatic heir
```

8.4.1.3 The Father.

The father can inherit in three possible categories. If the son is alive, the father's share is limited to one-sixth. If the daughter or son's daughter is alive (but not the son), he receives one-sixth plus any residue as the nearest agnate. If there is no son or daughter or son's daughter, he simply inherits as the nearest agnate.

Table 5

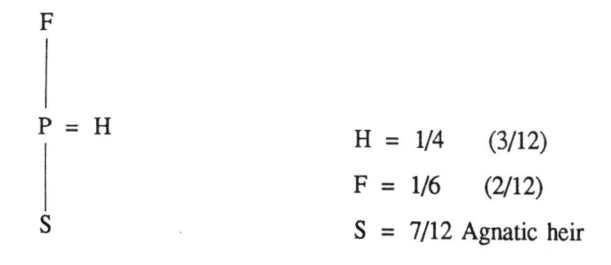

```
   F
   |
   |
  P = H               H = 1/4      (3/12)
   |                  F = 1/6      (2/12)
   |                  S = 7/12 Agnatic heir
   S
```

Table 6

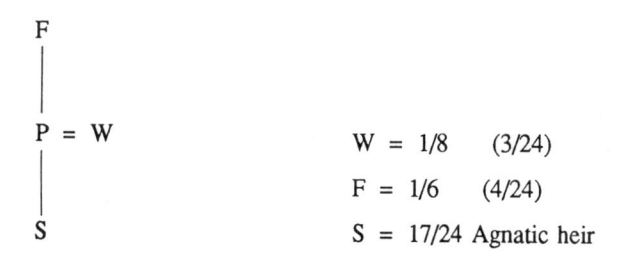

```
   F
   |
   |
  P = W               W = 1/8      (3/24)
   |                  F = 1/6      (4/24)
   |                  S = 17/24 Agnatic heir
   S
```

Table 7

```
F
|
|
P = W          W = 1/8    (3/24)
|              D = 1/2    (12/24)
|              F = 1/6 (Qur'anic heir)   +
D                  5/24 (Agnatic heir)
                 = 9/24
```

8.4.1.4 The True Grandfather.

As we have seen, this slightly archaic terminology refers to the single line of father's father, even though it is highly unlikely that an ancestor beyond the second generation from the propositus would ever inherit. The grandfather was added by Sunna, for he was not expressly mentioned in the Qur'an. His share is one-sixth. If, however, the father is alive, he is excluded. In the absence of the father, the son, daughter, or the child of the son, he will inherit as the nearest agnate. Like the father, the presence of the daughter or son's daughter and the grandfather enables the grandfather to inherit in both capacities.

Table 8

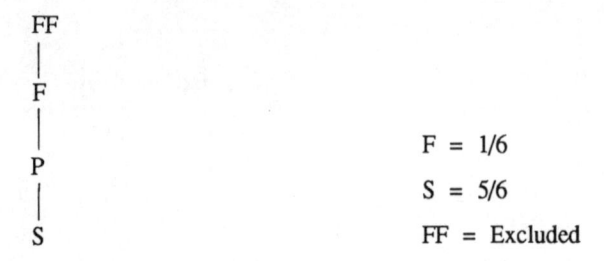

```
FF
|
F
|
P              F = 1/6
|              S = 5/6
S              FF = Excluded
```

8.4.1.5 The Mother.

The mother is given a "normal" share of one-sixth which she inherits when her child dies leaving surviving his or her own child or agnatic grandchild. The mother's share is capable of increase. In the event of no child or agnatic grandchild of the propositus being alive at the moment of the death of the propositus, then the share of the mother is increased to one-third of the estate.

The Laws of Inheritance

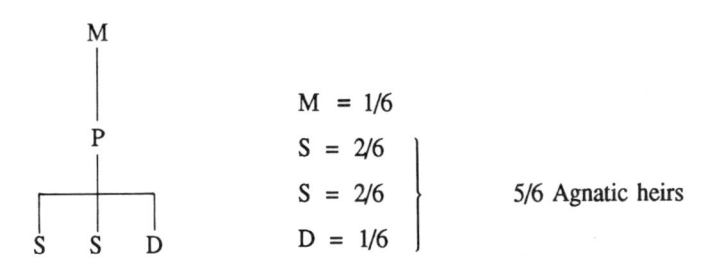

Table 9

```
       M
       |
       P
    ___|___
   |   |   |
   S   S   D
```

M = 1/6
S = 2/6 ⎫
S = 2/6 ⎬ 5/6 Agnatic heirs
D = 1/6 ⎭

The daughter, incidentally, inherits in this situation as the agnatic heir rather than the Qur'anic heir, for the presence of the son pulls her over to agnatic inheritance. She inherits in the proportion 1:2 with the son in accordance with the Qur'anic provision in Sura IV, verse 11. This concept, known as ta'sib, is an extremely important provision illustrating as it does the strength of the agnatic link. It will be the subject of comment later in this chapter.

Table 10

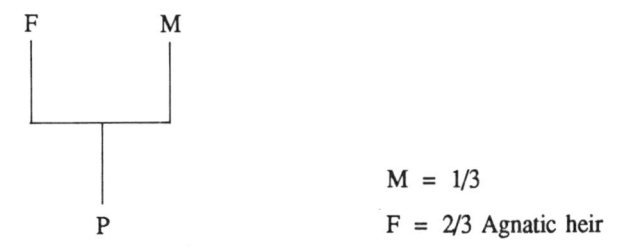

```
F       M
|_____|
    |
    P
```

M = 1/3
F = 2/3 Agnatic heir

Table 11

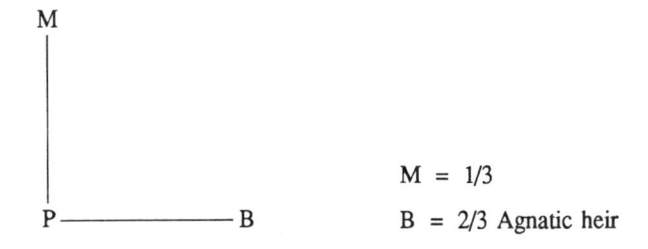

```
   M
   |
   P———————B
```

M = 1/3
B = 2/3 Agnatic heir

153

The Laws of Inheritance

Where the propositus dies survived by his mother and one brother or one sister, then the mother's share is one-third. If, however, there are two collaterals, be they brothers, sisters or a combination, the mother's share is reduced to the normal one-sixth.

Table 12

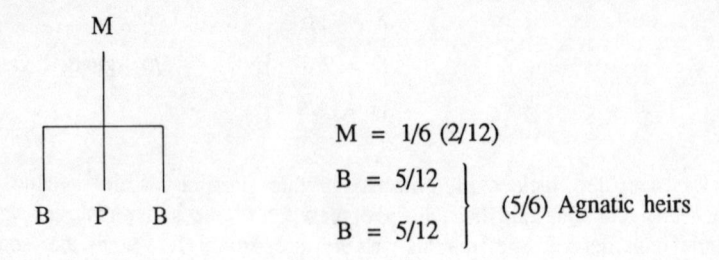

$M = 1/6\ (2/12)$

$\left. \begin{array}{l} B = 5/12 \\ B = 5/12 \end{array} \right\}$ (5/6) Agnatic heirs

A particular problem arises when the propositus is survived by the mother, the father, and the surviving spouse. If the *normal* rules are applied on the death of the wife, then the result of the distribution of the estate would be as shown in Table 13.

Table 13 (incorrect)

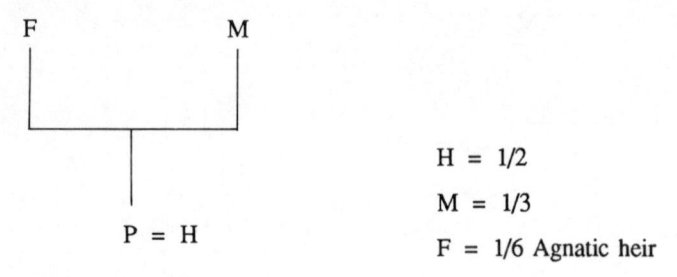

$H = 1/2$

$M = 1/3$

$F = 1/6$ Agnatic heir

This case was brought before Caliph 'Umar. Faced with the obvious illogicality in Islamic principle in this result, and bearing in mind the Qur'anic provision requiring a distribution of twice to the male of that to the female when they are of equal degree from the propositus, he solved the problem in the following manner. He first gave the spouse relict his share of the estate, and distributed to the mother one-third of the residue (i.e. 1/3 of 1/2 = 1/6). He then distributed the remainder of the estate (1/3) to the father as the aganatic heir. (Table 13 (correct)).

The Laws of Inheritance

Table 13 (correct)

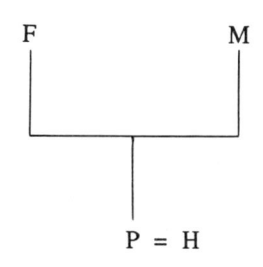

```
F           M
|           |
└─────┬─────┘
      |
    P = H
```

H = 1/2
M = 1/3 x 1/2 = 1/6
F = 1/3 Agnatic heir

The Qur'anic legislation, therefore, is subjected to a forced and restricted interpretation primarily to preserve the customary pre-eminence of the father as the agnatic heir.

The same approach is applied in the case of the death of the husband (Table 14).

Table 14

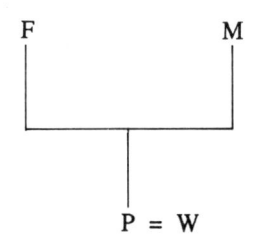

```
F           M
|           |
└─────┬─────┘
      |
    P = W
```

W = 1/4
M = 1/3 x 3/4 = 3/12 (1/4)
F = 1/2 Agnatic heir

It should be noted also that the paternal grandfather does not have the same capacity or authority to reduce the mother's share.

Table 15

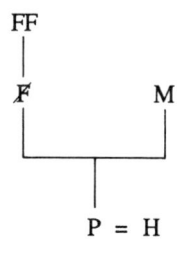

```
FF
|
F̶           M
|           |
└─────┬─────┘
      |
    P = H
```

H = 1/2
M = 1/3
FF = 1/6 Agnatic heir

Table 16

```
FF
│
F        M
│        │
└────┬───┘
     P = W
```

W = 1/4 (3/12)
M = 1/3 (4/12)
FF = 5/12 Agnatic heir

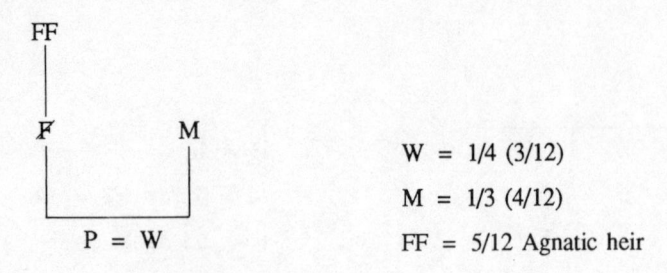

8.4.1.6 The True Grandmother.
The true grandmother is treated very much as a secondary heir. When the mother is alive, then the true grandmother is excluded entirely. The Hanafi school treats all true grandmothers as a group; when two are equally entitled they share the 1/6 share, although the basic principle is that the nearer in degree will exclude the more remote. Thus, the maternal true grandmother is excluded by the nearer maternal or paternal true grandmother. Also, at least in India, the paternal true grandmother is excluded by the father or the nearer true grandfather as well as the above mentioned relatives.

The true grandmother does not appear in the Qur'anic revelation and, like the grandfather, this category is added by the Sunna.

8.4.1.7 The Daughter.
The Qur'anic share for the daughter is one-half of the net estate. If two or more daughters survive the propositus, then that share is increased to a collective two-thirds. As we have seen already, however, the presence of the son agnatises the daughter, and she inherits with the son as an agnate, without regard to her Qur'anic status in the proportion two shares to the son and one share to the daughter.

The Laws of Inheritance

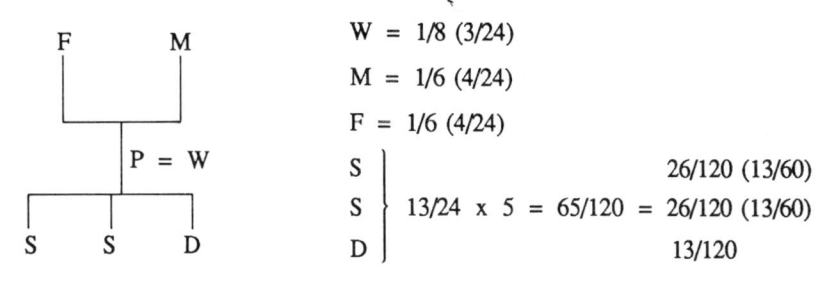

Table 17

```
F         M
└────┬────┘
     │
   P = W                W = 1/8  (3/24)
┌──┬─┴─┐                M = 1/6  (4/24)
S  S   D                F = 1/6  (4/24)
                        S ⎤                    26/120 (13/60)
                        S ⎬  13/24 x 5 = 65/120 = 26/120 (13/60)
                        D ⎦                    13/120
```

The daughter is described as the 'asaba bi ghayriha; the son as the 'asaba bi nafsihi. Two other examples will suffice to illustrate the principle (Tables 18 and 19).

Table 18

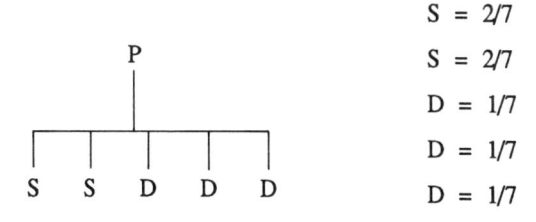

```
         P
    ┌──┬─┼─┬──┐          S = 2/7
    S  S  D D  D         S = 2/7
                         D = 1/7
                         D = 1/7
                         D = 1/7
```

Table 19

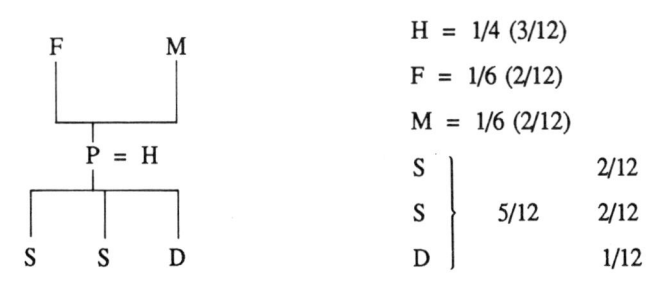

```
F          M
└────┬─────┘
     │
   P = H                 H = 1/4  (3/12)
┌──┬─┴─┐                 F = 1/6  (2/12)
S  S   D                 M = 1/6  (2/12)
                         S ⎤           2/12
                         S ⎬   5/12   2/12
                         D ⎦           1/12
```

8.4.1.8 *The Son's Daughter.*

The rules relating to the daughter are intertwined with the son's daughter (the son being deceased). The share of the son's daughter is one-half; if there are two or more it is two-thirds; but if there is a daughter and a son's daughter,

The Laws of Inheritance

the daughter and the son's daughter receive a collective portion of two-thirds in the proportion of one-half to the daughter as opposed to one-sixth to the son's daughter. If, however, there are more than two daughters, the collective portion of two-thirds is exhausted by the presence of the daughter, and nothing will remain for the agnatic granddaughter.

Table 20

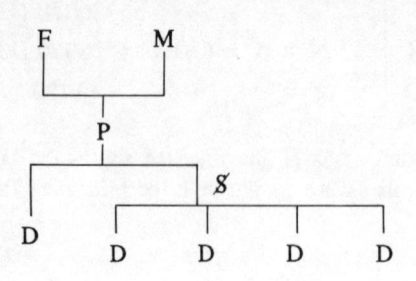

F = 1/6
M = 1/6
D = 1/2
SD 1/24
SD 1/24
SD 1/6 1/24
SD 1/24

Table 21

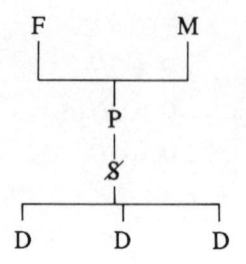

F = 1/6
M = 1/6

D   2/9
D   2/3 2/9
D   2/9

Table 22

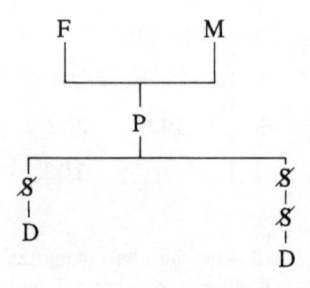

F = 1/6
M = 1/6
SD = 1/2
SSD = 1/6   } 2/3

The Laws of Inheritance

Table 23

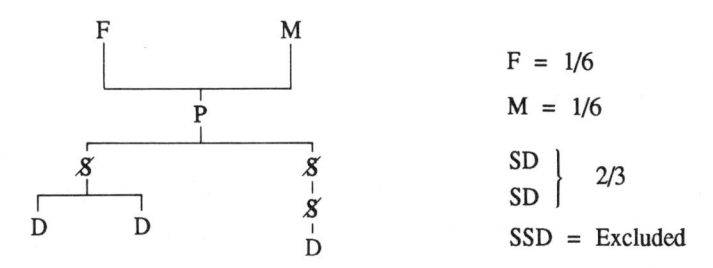

```
     F           M
     └─────┬─────┘
           P
     ┌─────┴─────┐
     S           S
   ┌─┴─┐         │
   D   D         S
                 │
                 D
```

F = 1/6
M = 1/6
SD ⎫
SD ⎬ 2/3
SSD = Excluded

An important point to make at this stage is that a son's daughter is agnatised by an equidistant son's son in exactly the same way as a daughter is agnatised by a son. This principle, that of ta'sib, may be to the advantage of the son's daughter, but on the other hand may in some instances operate to her disadvantage.

It would operate to her advantage in the case where, under the Qur'anic principles, the existence of two daughters exhausts the share of the Qur'anic estate available for distribution to the son's daughter. However, the existence also of the son's son 'reactivates' the son's daughter and she can thus participate in the distribution of the agnatic residue in the proportion of 1 share to the son's daughter to 2 shares to the son's son. This point is made clear in the second and correct version of Table 24.

Table 24(incorrect)

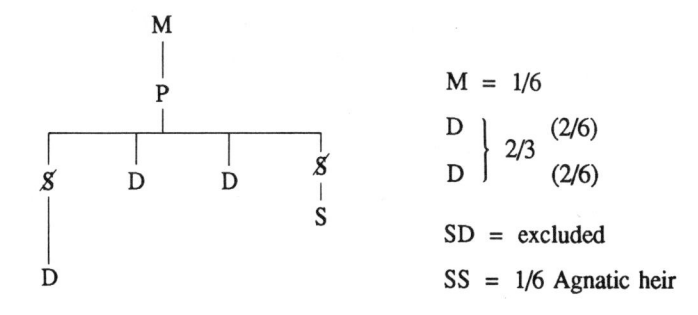

```
           M
           │
           P
     ┌───┬─┴─┬───┐
     S   D   D   S
     │           │
     D           S
```

M = 1/6
D ⎫   (2/6)
D ⎬ 2/3
        (2/6)
SD = excluded
SS = 1/6 Agnatic heir

The Laws of Inheritance

Table 24 (correct)

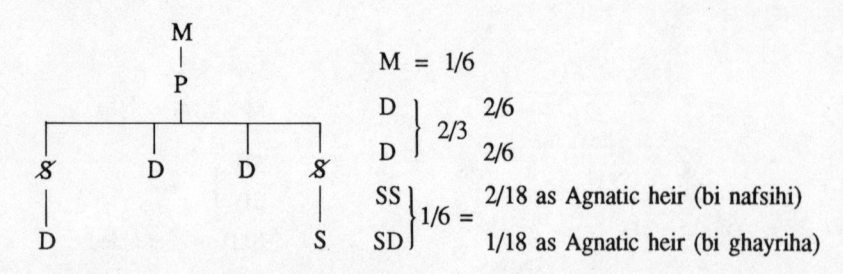

```
          M
          |
          P
  ┌───┬───┼───┐
  S̸  D   D   S̸
  |           |
  D           S
```

M = 1/6

D ⎱ 2/3   2/6
D ⎰   2/6

SS ⎱ 1/6 = 2/18 as Agnatic heir (bi nafsihi)
SD ⎰   1/18 as Agnatic heir (bi ghayriha)

If, in contrast, the son's daughter could inherit under the Qur'anic rules together with *one* daughter, the presence of the son's son nonetheless will pull her on to agnatic inheritance. In some instances the residue may in fact be very small; in other even more unfortunate circumstances, the residue available for agnatic inheritance may indeed be non-existent. If this is the case she is indeed an unlucky kinswoman (Table 25).

Table 25 (correct)

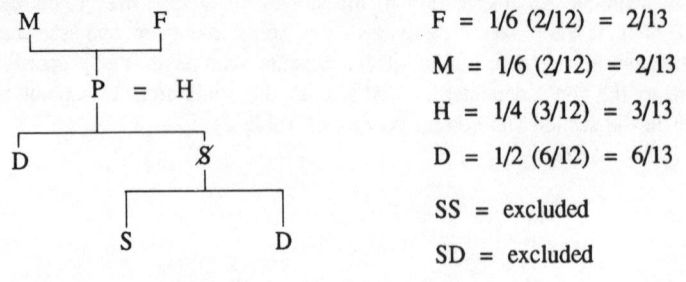

```
     M ─── F
        |
     P = H
      ┌──┴──┐
      D    S̸
         ┌──┴──┐
         S    D
```

F = 1/6 (2/12) = 2/13

M = 1/6 (2/12) = 2/13

H = 1/4 (3/12) = 3/13

D = 1/2 (6/12) = 6/13

SS = excluded

SD = excluded

It will be noticed that in this case there has to be a reduction according to rules which we shall consider briefly later in this chapter.

It must be mentioned, of course, that the presence of a son or indeed a higher son's son excludes the son's daughter completely.

Table 26

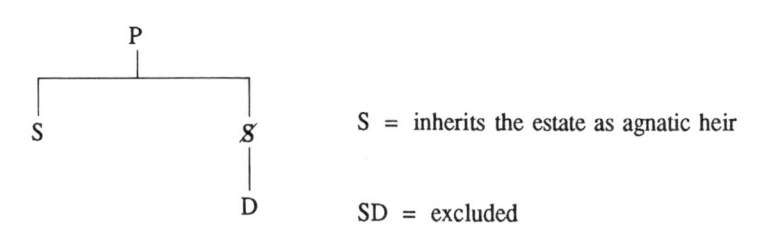

```
           P
    ┌──────┴──────┐
    S             S̸
                  │
                  D
```

S = inherits the estate as agnatic heir

SD = excluded

8.4.1.9 The Germane Sister; The Consanguine Sister

These two relatives can be considered together. The full (germane) sister's share is one-half of the estate, or, if there are two or more of them, two-thirds. Similarly, the consanguine sister's share is one-half (or if two or more of them, two-thirds). Like the grandfather, the grandmother and the son's daughter, the full and consanguine sisters are, at times, excluded entirely. The full sister and the consanguine sister are excluded by the son, the son's son however low in degree, the father, and (notwithstanding minority opinions) by the true grandfather. The view of Abu Bakr that in a competition between the grandfather and the full sister the grandfather excludes the full sister, is accepted by way of the consensus or ijma' in Hanafi law.[21] It needs to be emphasised that the full brother excludes the consanguine sister.

The presence of the brother, the daughter, or the son's daughter, together with the full sister, will affect the share of the sister; it does not, however, necessarily exclude her from the rights of inheritance. In each of these circumstances, the sister will be subject to agnatisation; although in different ways and for different reasons.

---

[21] For a detailed discussion of the minority opinions, and the juristic arguments which led the Hanafi jurists to accept Abu Bakr's solution to this problem, see Coulson op.cit. pp 78ff.

Table 27

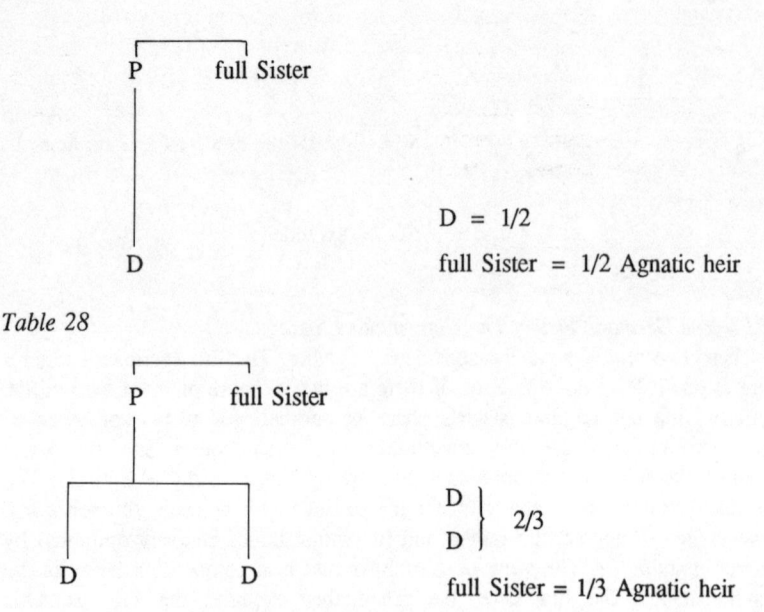

```
┌─────────┬──────────┐
P          full Sister
│
│                    D = 1/2
│                    full Sister = 1/2 Agnatic heir
D
```

Table 28

```
┌─────────┬──────────┐
P          full Sister
│
┌────┴────┐           D ┐
│         │           D ┘ 2/3
D         D
                      full Sister = 1/3 Agnatic heir
```

In these two illustrations, the daughter takes her primary share as a Qur'anic heir, forcing the sister on to agnatic inheritance. In the first illustration, of course, the sister is in no way disadvantaged. In the second illustration, however, the presence of two daughters will reduce the share of the sister to one-third of the estate as agnatic heir. The son's daughter has the same capacity to "push out" the collateral on to agnatic inheritance. The same rule applies also when the son's daughter or the daughter inherits with the consanguine sister.

When a full brother and a full sister coexist together, they take collectively as agnatic heirs, the brother taking the double share. Similarly, a consanguine sister coexisting with a consanguine brother take agnatically, the brother the double share of the sister. A full brother, as we have already stated, excludes the consanguine sister.

As in the case of the daughter and the son's daughter, the co-existence of the full sister and the consanguine sister enables the combined share of two-thirds to be distributed to these collaterals in the proportion of one-half to the full sister, to one-sixth to the consanguine sister. Where there are two full sisters, however, the consanguine sister is excluded; for the two-thirds of the estate available for distribution has been exhausted. The presence of a consanguine brother, however, affects the distribution for he has the capacity to agnatise the consanguine sister. There is, therefore, scope for distribution of the estate in such a way as would, in some cases, be to the advantage of the consanguine sister, and in other cases, to her disadvantage. There is a parallel here with the son's son co-existing with the son's daughter.

Thus we have the case of the lucky kinswoman (Table 29):

Table 29

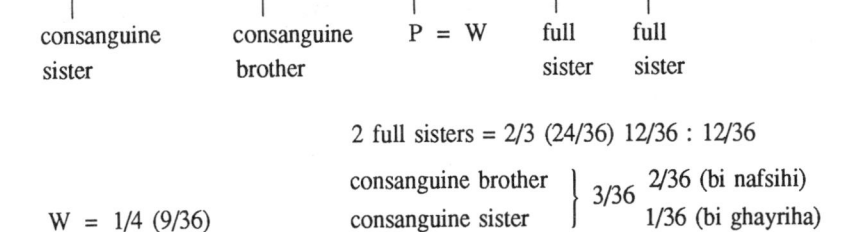

```
┌─────────────┬─────────────┬─────────┬─────────┬─────────┐
consanguine   consanguine   P = W    full      full
sister        brother                sister    sister
```

2 full sisters = 2/3 (24/36) 12/36 : 12/36

consanguine brother ⎫   2/36 (bi nafsihi)
                     ⎬ 3/36
W = 1/4 (9/36)   consanguine sister   ⎭   1/36 (bi ghayriha)

In contrast, there is the case of the unlucky kinswoman (Table 30):

Table 30

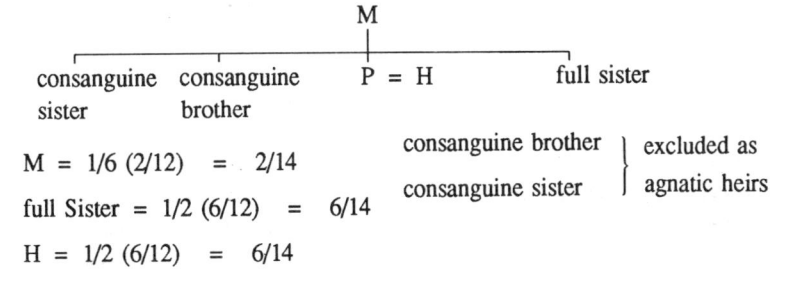

```
                        M
                        │
┌─────────────┬─────────────┬─────────┬─────────────────┐
consanguine   consanguine   P = H              full sister
sister        brother
```

consanguine brother ⎫ excluded as
M = 1/6 (2/12) = 2/14   ⎬
                          consanguine sister ⎭ agnatic heirs
full Sister = 1/2 (6/12) = 6/14

H = 1/2 (6/12) = 6/14

In this situation, the totality of the shares amounts to more than unity, there has to be reduction in the amounts received by the Qur'anic heirs, and the agnatic heirs (including the consanguine sister) are excluded from participating in the estate. A short description of how the reduction takes place is given later in this chapter.

8.4.1.10 Uterine Brothers; Uterine Sisters.

Our final Qur'anic heirs are the uterine collaterals. In a system of relatively easy divorce, uterine relationships are fairly common.

The Laws of Inheritance

As collaterals, the uterine collaterals are excluded by the superior heirs, namely son, daughter, son's daughter, father, true grandfather. If none of these people are present, the uterine collateral will take one-sixth; or if two or more survive, one-third. The uterines have equal shares in the estate. Thus the rule that a male participates in the estate to the extent of twice the amount of the female of equal degree from the propositus does not apply to the uterine relationships.

A particularly interesting problem occurs when the full brother co-exists with the uterine brother; for instance, when the propositus dies leaving surviving her a husband, the mother, and uterine and full brothers. One way to distribute the estate is to apply the normal principle of distribution; thus the Qur'anic heirs receive their fractions, and the residue if any is distributed to the 'asaba.

Table 31

```
                          M
                          |
      ┌───────────────────┼───────────────────┐
2 uterine brothers      P = H           2 full brothers
```

M = 1/6   2 full brothers = excluded as agnatic heirs

H = 1/2   nothing in the estate

2 uterine brothers = 1/3   remaining for distribution

With no superior heirs to exclude the uterine brothers, the full brothers are left without any portion of the estate, because there is nothing left in the estate for agnatic inheritance. The rights of the husband and of the mother are not in dispute, and thus the conflict is clearly between the uterine brothers and the full brothers. As Coulson observes, this conflict is, in effect, a head-on clash between the old tribal heirs (full brothers) and the new heirs introduced by the Qur'anic revelations (the uterine brothers).

The argument on behalf of the full brothers before 'Umar was to the effect that as the uterine brothers and themselves all had the same mother, they should be allowed to ignore their agnatic tie, and thus stand on a parity with the uterines. They put their argument in the following way:

> O commander of the faithful!
> Suppose our father were a donkey [a himar];
> Do we not have the same mother as the deceased?

We are told that 'Umar reversed his previous decision, and ordered that the one-third be distributed to all the brothers, both full and uterine.

The Laws of Inheritance

Table 32
The Himariyya Case

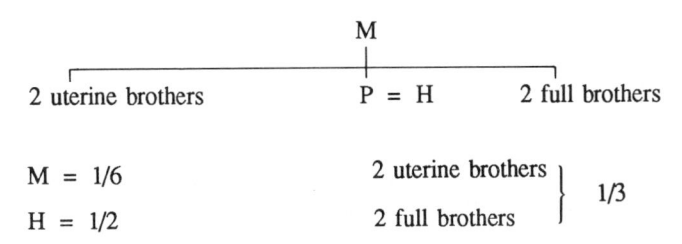

```
                        M
        ┌───────────────┼───────────────┐
  2 uterine brothers   P = H      2 full brothers


   M = 1/6                 2 uterine brothers ⎫
                                              ⎬ 1/3
   H = 1/2                 2 full brothers    ⎭
```

A further complication arises in the situation where the grandfather is alive together with the uterine and full brothers. Some opinion allows the grandfather to inherit collectively with the full brothers in agnatic inheritance. The grandfather, however, excludes the uterine brothers from inheritance, and therefore the full brothers attempt to move back to the agnatic link. Given the exclusionary powers of the grandfather, the full brothers are in a stronger position if they can be treated as agnates rather than as Qur'anic heirs. The rule which is known to us as Malik's rule prevents such a development. A brother, it is held, cannot be uterine for one purpose and germane for another; thus the grandfather takes the residue, and the full and the uterine brothers are excluded entirely.

Table 33
Malik's rule

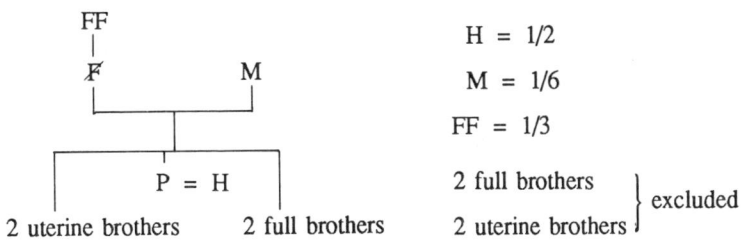

```
         FF
         │
         F̶              M              H  = 1/2
         └──────┬───────┘
                │                      M  = 1/6
                │
         ┌──────┴───────┐              FF = 1/3
         │              │
        P = H      2 full brothers     2 full brothers   ⎫
         │                                               ⎬ excluded
  2 uterine brothers                   2 uterine brothers⎭
```

These two rules, the Himariyya and Malik's rule, are applied in Maliki law, but they are not followed in the Hanafi law. The Hanafi jurists uphold the consistent view; once an 'asaba, always an 'asaba. Thus the full brother must remain as such, and in the situation illustrated by *Table 31* the full brothers are excluded.

The Laws of Inheritance

The Hanafis do not permit a full brother to inherit agnatically with the paternal grandfather. If the grandfather is alive at the opening of succession, together with uterine brothers and full brothers, then, in the Hanafi law, the uterine brothers are excluded by the superior heir, and the germane brothers are excluded because the Hanafi jurists acknowledge the pre-eminent agnatic claim of the paternal grandfather.

8.4.2 The Rules of Exclusion

Although the spouse relict is the primary Qur'anic heir in that he or she can never be excluded, the presence of the surviving spouse does not affect the rights of inheritance of any other heir. Some heirs, of course, do exclude others entirely, or at least have the capacity to push less fortunate relations onto agnatic inheritance. Sometimes the presence of relations reduces the share of others even though it does not benefit themselves. The best example of this is with the mother, father and two sisters. The two sisters reduce the share of the mother to one-sixth, even though they themselves do not benefit, for they are excluded by the father.

Table 34

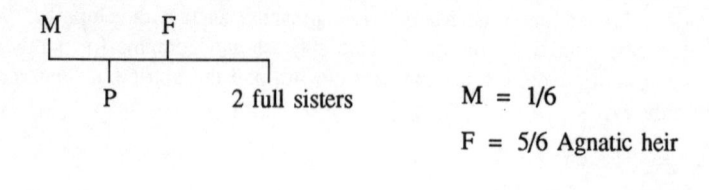

```
M         F
|_____|
    |
    |_____
    |                  |
    P            2 full sisters
```

M = 1/6

F = 5/6 Agnatic heir

2 full sisters = excluded

8.4.3 The Agnatic Link

The rules regulating agnatic inheritance have been considered at the beginning of the chapter. In summary form they are as follows:

(1) *Preference is given to the order:*
descendants, ascendants, collaterals.
(2) *Preference is then given to the degree:*
the nearer in degree excludes the more remote.
(3) *Preference is finally given to the blood tie:*
the full blood excludes the consanguine blood.

The Laws of Inheritance

8.4.3.1 The Order
The son of the deceased is a descendant, thus in a competition with the father, the son excludes the father. It is for this reason that the Qur'an lays down a specific fraction for the father when the propositus dies leaving both the son and the father. If the father co-exists with a collateral, the father excludes this collateral. In Hanafi law, notwithstanding variant opinions, the grandfather excludes the brother.

8.4.3.2 The Degree
The nearer in degree always excludes the more remote. Thus a son's son is excluded by a son.

Table 35

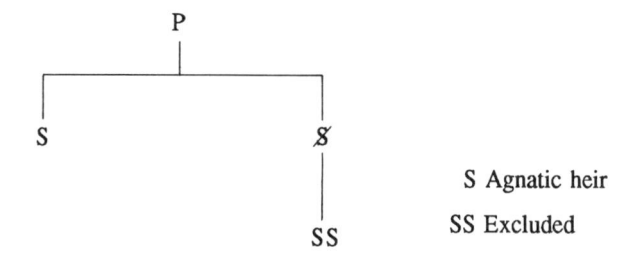

```
           P
      ┌────┴────┐
      S         S̸
                │
                SS
```

S Agnatic heir

SS Excluded

This problem has caused considerable difficulty, and indeed some hardship and suffering in the changed circumstances of today. The family is no longer the strongly cohesive unit that it was; and there is no guarantee that the nephews and nieces will be treated on an equality with sons and daughters. It is an area of succession law which has been the subject of reform; in Egypt, in Pakistan and elsewhere. We shall return to the problem, therefore, when the reforms in Islamic law are discussed later in the chapter.

8.4.4 Distant Kinsfolk and Associated Problems
When there is no Qur'anic heir other than possibly the spouse relict alive at the opening of the succession, and no agnates either, then the estate is distributed amongst any surviving distant kinsmen; that is those blood relations who are neither Qur'anic nor agnatic heirs. The most important distant kinsmen, of course, are female agnates, and male and female cognates. In Maliki law, the distant kinsmen are never admitted; and the problems of inheritance within the distant kinsmen category in Hanafi law can hardly be of common occurrence. Readers are referred to Coulson's treatise *Succession in the Muslim Family*, chapter 7, for the details of the distribution rules in this

The Laws of Inheritance

area.

When there are no members of the 'asaba or distant kinsmen alive at the moment of the death of the propositus in circumstances when the distribution to the Qur'anic heirs in their allotted fractions does not exhaust the estate, the problem arises as to what to do with the remainder? The simple answer, at least in the Hanafi law, is that the residue "returns" to the Qur'anic heirs in the proportion of their shares. This is known as radd. In the classical law, the husband or wife are not allowed to share in the return, unless there is no other heir alive at the opening of the succession, their share being expressly fixed in the Qur'anic revelations.[22] In the Maliki law, the doctrine of radd does not apply, not the least reason being because the propositus in Maliki law is never without an heir – the Treasury is seen as an heir in its own right, and will, therefore, inherit any residue.

When the fractions amount to more than unity, the estate is distributed by a system of proportionate reduction of the shares by a principle known as 'awl. So, for instance, in *Table 25*, the shares of the heirs add up to thirteen twelfths. (2/12 = mother;2/12 = father; 3/12 = husband; 6/12 = daughter). The denominator is adjusted to 13 and the mother's share is then 2/13, the father's share is 2/13, the husband receives 3/13, and the daughter receives 6/13. Similarly, in the situation reviewed in *Table 30*, the mother ultimately receives 2/14, the husband 6/14, and the sisters 6/14 collectively (1/7;3/7;3/7).

8.5 Competence to Inherit

We must now turn our attention to a number of problems relating to the competence of individual heirs to inherit the share allotted to them according to the rules of distribution which we have described. There willl be circumstances where an heir, otherwise qualified to inherit a share, will find himself or herself excluded from succession because of a particular rule of Islamic law.

---

[22] For a discussion of the position when the only heir alive at the time of the opening of the succession is the spouse relict, see the discussion by Tanzil-ur-Rehman J in *In Re Zainab* 1986 PLD Kar 269. He states the position as follows: "In case there is no [sharer by blood], asaba, or distant kindred, and that there is only a sole surviving Muslim widow, she is entitled to inherit one-fourth share in the estate of the deceased as heir/sharer and she takes the remainder, in case of the deceased and she being Shi'i if there is no Imam present or Bait-al-Maal in existence; and in case of her and the deceased being Sunnis there is no well-managed Bait-al-Maal." (A Bait-al-Maal is a chaitable house for the poor).

The Laws of Inheritance

8.5.1 Religious Differences

The first exclusion rule relates to religious differences. When a Muslim dies, all non-Muslim heirs are excluded from any entitlement to participate in the division of the estate. In contrast, it will be recalled that a bequest from the estate can be made to a non-Muslim.

On the Indian subcontinent, the law on intestate succession was changed with respect to apostate-heirs from Islam by the Caste Disabilities Removal Act 1850. An heir who leaves Islam will still be entitled to inherit on the death of a Muslim relation. The law, however, has not been altered with respect to a Muslim who subsequently dies. Thus if a person converts to Islam and then dies, his estate is distributed in accordance with Islamic law, and all the non-Muslim relations existing at the opening of succession are disbarred.[23]

In Pakistan, the effect of the Caste Disabilities Removal Act was altered by a 1963 amendment which states:

> nothing contained in this Act shall apply to the rights of inheritance to the property of a Muslim

The effect of the amendment is to restore the Muslim law; thereby excluding non-Muslim heirs, including those who were once Muslims and have apostacised, from any right to participate in the division of the estate. Finally, it is worth mentioning here that in India, if a Muslim marries under the provisions of the Special Marriage Act 1954 (as amended) the Islamic law of succession is thereby abandoned, and that law no longer applies to the distribution of either estate on their death.

8.5.2 Homicide

The detailed rules relating to homicide are discussed by Coulson.[24] It will suffice for our purposes to say that there is considerable difference of opinion amongst the Sunni schools. The Hanafi and Shafi'i doctrine excludes from inheritance not only the person who has deliberately killed the propositus, but also excludes the person who has killed the propositus by accident; so long as there is a causal connection. Thus, the Hanafi law concentrates on excluding the *direct* killer, emphasing the act rather than the animus. Thus, an heir who has murderous intent and leaves poison around is not excluded from inheriting from his victim. In contrast, if an heir shoots inadvertently, the killing is seen as direct, and the heir is not competent to inherit. In contrast, the Hanbali, Maliki, and Shi'i schools apply the rule that only the deliberate killer is barred

---

[23] See *Mitar Sen Singh v. Maqbul Hassan Khan* 1930 57 LR IA 313; *K.P.Chandrasekharappa v. Government of Mysore* 1955 AIR Mysore 26.

[24] op.cit. pp. 185 ff.

from rights of inheritance following the death of the propositus.[25]

8.5.3 Illegitimacy

The short point to make here is that the illegitimate child in Sunni law has no right of inheritance from his father. However, he can inherit from his mother.

8.5.4 A Child en Ventre sa Mere

A child *en ventre sa mere* has a right of inheritance even though he or she is not alive at the moment of death. Again, the detailed rules would not be an appropriate matter for discussion in a book of this kind and readers are referred to Coulson for the complexities of this subject, as also for the problems relating to illegitimacy.[26]

8.5.5 The Repudiated Wife

We return now to consider problems associated with the "disease of death", and in particular, the case of the unfortunate wife who is repudiated by talaq by her husband at a time when he is aware that his death is imminent. The presumption adopted by Hanafi law is that a repudiation pronounced during death sickness involves an improper motive; to interfere with the Islamic laws of succession. Thus, the wife's right of inheritance will not be extinguished. The presumption, however, is not absolute. In Hanafi law, it lasts only for the period of the 'idda. Thus a talaq in Hanafi law pronounced during the death sickness is treated as a revocable ahsan talaq regardless of the mode of the pronouncement. The other schools enable the wife's right of inheritance under these circumstances to last for one year.

There is an interesting Pakistan Supreme Court decision which discusses this particular issue, namely *Nazar Muhammad v. Shahzada Begum*.[27] The property the subject of the contentious litigation belonged originally to Ghulam Haider. He died on 10 November 1959, survived by his two widows, Shahzada and Musahiban. Musahiban had one son of whom Ghulam was the father (Nazar Mohammad), and Shahzada gave birth to a daughter (Khalida) shortly after Ghulam's death. Musahiban died prior to the action in the Pakistan courts. Shahzada Begum and her daughter Khalida claimed to be heirs of Ghulam. Nazar Mohammad denied their entitlement relying upon a document

---

[25] For an interesting case from Pakistan see *Beguman v. Saroo* 1964 PLD (WP) Lah 451.
[26] op.cit. pp 172-6, 204-210.
[27] 1974 PLD SC 22.

of divorce dated 6 November 1959, in which it was stated that eight or nine months before this date in November, the deceased had pronounced a talaq purporting to divorce Shahzada by whom he had no child and who did not carry a child at that time. In other words, it was claimed that Shahzada was not the widow of Ghulam in as much as the deceased had divorced her 9 months prior to his death. The deed executed in November was confirmation of the fact of divorce. Thus, as the daughter was born some two months after the man's death, she could not possibly be his daughter. In reply, Shahzada submitted that she had not been divorced. She submitted further, and in the alternative, that if indeed she had been divorced, then the relevant date was 6 November, when her husband was in his death sickness. As her daughter was born within 2 months of the death of the husband, the daughter was a legitimate child and therefore she was entitled to inherit.

On an examination of the evidence, the Supreme Court came to the conclusion that Shahzada Begum had been divorced on 6 November – but no earlier. It held also that the husband, suffering from severe paralysis, was in his death sickness. Shahzada, therefore, was entitled to inherit, as also was her daughter, the legitimate child of the deceased. The distribution of the estate was as shown in Table 36.

Table 36

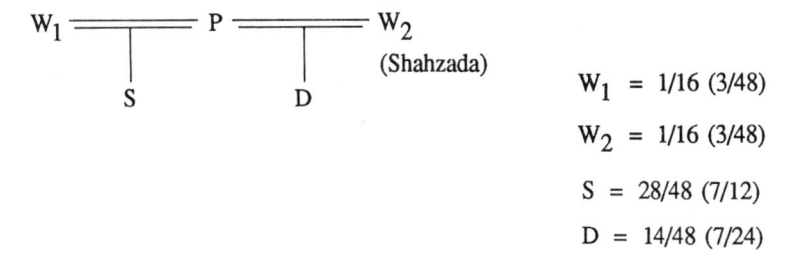

W_1 = 1/16 (3/48)

W_2 = 1/16 (3/48)

S = 28/48 (7/12)

D = 14/48 (7/24)

8.5.6 An Illustrative Case

Before we leave the discussion of the Sunni law of succession, it may be useful to discuss in some detail one particular case which will illustrate how the law works in practice. This is *Nur Ali v. Malka Sultana*.[28] The case concerned the entitlement to property which once was owned by a Hindu, one Sahib Ditta Mal, who had died in 1933. The precise family relationship between the Sahib and the disputants in the case is rather complicated, and a

---

[28] 1961 PLD (WP) Lah 431.

family tree should be of assistance (Table 37).
Table 37

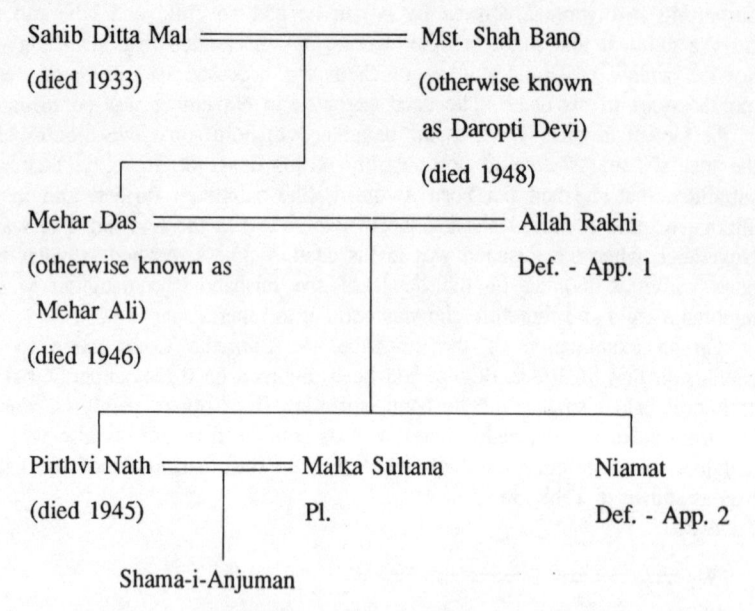

```
    Sahib Ditta Mal ═══════════╦══════════ Mst. Shah Bano
    (died 1933)                 ║           (otherwise known
                                ║           as Daropti Devi)
                                ║           (died 1948)
          ┌─────────────────────┘
    Mehar Das ═══════════════════════════ Allah Rakhi
    (otherwise known as                    Def. - App. 1
    Mehar Ali)
    (died 1946)
          │
    ┌─────┴─────────────────────┬──────────────────┐
    Pirthvi Nath ══════ Malka Sultana          Niamat
    (died 1945)         Pl.                    Def. - App. 2
           │
    Shama-i-Anjuman
```

It was common ground that Sahib Ditta Mal had been born a Hindu and had not embraced Islam during his lifetime. This was agreed notwithstanding Sahib Ditta Mal's allegiance to the Aga Khan. Apparently, the Aga Khan allowed "considerable liberty of religious profession to his followers". The parties were in agreement also that Sahib Ditta Mal's son (Mehar Das alias Mehar Ali) and his widow Shah Bano (alias Mst. Daropti Devi) had embraced Islam. Pirthvi Nath, the Sahib's grandson, had never embraced Islam but his death in 1945 during the lifetime of his father and his paternal grandmother enabled the court to overlook this particular complication. There was no doubt that all the parties to the present suit were Muslim.

The first issue, in point of time, arose out of a document executed by Sahib Ditta Mal in September 1933, some 10 weeks before his death, with which he purported to leave to his wife by will all the property the subject of the dispute. The dispute revolved around whether this document conferred an absolute title or only a limited life interest on the wife. The trial judge held that the document made the wife the full owner of the property. On appeal, the Lahore High Court came to the opposite conclusion after an examination of the terms of the document. The court held that the Sahib intended no more than to make his wife the manager of his property after his death. Having

The Laws of Inheritance

decided on this point, the court distributed the property to the various contestants using as the starting point, the personal law of Sahib Ditta Mal (Hindu law). The trial judge had distributed the estate using his starting point the personal law of Shah Bano (which at the time of her death was Muslim law).

The second issue involved the effect of the conversion to Islam by the widow and the son. Did their act of apostasy deprive them of their inheritance rights under Hindu law to the property of Sahib Ditta Mal? Any possible interpersonal conflict between substantive Hindu law and substantive Muslim law over this question was regulated by the Caste Disabilities Removal Act 1850. If in Hindu law Mehar Ali and Mst. Shah Bano could have inherited any property from Sahib Ditta Mal, they would not be deprived of these rights by reason of their change of religion. The estate is distributed in accordance with the personal law of the propositus, but no account is taken of any rule of the personal law which attempts to exclude from the succession an apostate from the religion.

According to the interpretation of the court of the Hindu law in force at that time (1933) in the then province of the Punjab, neither Shah Bano nor Malka Sultana, in any event, had any share in the property left by the Sahib. Mehar Das (Mehar Ali) was the only son and therefore, according to Hindu law, he became the owner of the whole of Sahib Ditta Mal's estate. Mehar, of course, had converted to Islam and for this reason, on his own death in 1946, the property devolved according to the rules of his personal law, Muslim law, thus excluding, as we have had occasion already to observe, non-Muslims who happened to be alive at the time.

The court had to take one more decision. It was contended that Mehar had been a Shi'i Muslim and that as a result Shi'i rules of inheritance should govern the distribution of the property on Mehar's death. In the result, the Lahore judge held that Mehar was a Sunni. The contesting heirs were those illustrated by *Table 38*.

Table 38

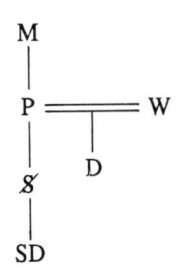

```
        M
        |
    P ===== W
    |    |
    S    D
    |
    SD
```

The Laws of Inheritance

The result of the application of the Sunni law was that Allah Rakhi (Mehar's widow) received one-eighth of the property, Mst. Niamat (Mehar's daughter) received one-half, and Mst. Shama-i-Anjuman (Mehar's granddaughter) received one-sixth. Strictly, the court should have considered the rights of the mother (Shah Bano) who was still alive in 1946 – the year of Mehar's death. The mother should have been entitled to her Qur'anic share of one-sixth which would have been distributed on her death in 1948 to the son's daughter (Niamat) and the son's son's daughter (Shama-i-Anjuman) in the proportion 1/2: 1/6. In fact, the position of the mother was ignored. The shares one-eighth, one-half and one-sixth add up to 19/24. The residue, 5/24, is distributed in proportion to the shares of Shama-i-Anjuman and Niamat. Allah Rakhi, as the wife, was held to be entitled only to a fixed Qur'anic portion of one-eighth which cannot be increased by any "return" of the residue. The final result is that Niamat receives 63/96 of the estate, Mst. Shama-i-Anjuman receives 21/96, and Ali Rakhi receives 12/96.

The trial judge, who had come to a different conclusion with regard to the document executed by the Sahib, came also to a different conclusion with respect to the school of Muslim law to be applied. He held that the parties had converted to Shi'i Islam. He applied the Shi'i law on the death of Shah Bano. According to the Shi'i law, the entire estate devolved on the nearest class I(ii) heir, the son's daughter, Niamat, who excluded all other competitors.

This remarkable difference in result between Sunni law and Shi'i law provides a useful point for us to transfer our attention to the Shi'i system of distribution.

8.6 Shi'i Law of Compulsory Succession

Whereas the Sunni law of entitlement rests on the sophisticated interaction of the Qur'anic and agnatic heirs, the Shi'i jurists recognise just one basis of entitlement, namely the Qur'anic rules.

In Shi'i law, the spouse always takes the Qur'anic share, but otherwise, all relatives fall into one of three classes, with sub-sections in each class (see Table 39). The agnate, therefore, has no distinctive place in the scheme of Shi'i inheritance, and indeed it is often said that the Shi'i treat the 'asaba with little sympathy: "dust into the jaws of the 'asaba". The son will always have the same entitlement in Shi'i law as in Sunni law, but other agnatic heirs are much less favourably placed in the Shi'i system.

The Laws of Inheritance

Table 39

> Class 1 a Parents
> Class 1 b Lineal descendants
> Class 2 a Grandparents
> Class 2 b Brothers, sisters and their issue
> Class 3 a Paternal uncles and aunts and those of parents and their descendants
> Class 3 b Maternal uncles and aunts and those of parents and their descendants

The general rules, subject to one exception, which we shall mention later, are as follows. In each section of class 1 and class 2, the nearest to the propositus absolutely excludes the more remote, and the nearest member of the two subsections inherit together regardless of their comparative degree removed from the deceased. The existence of an heir in class 1 will exclude any heir from class 2. Likewise, the existence of an heir in class 2 will exclude any heir in class 3. In class 3, the nearest in degree in either section excludes all other claimants. Unlike the Sunnis, the Shi'is include females and their descendants in all classes.

The best way to illustrate the operation of the Shi'i law, and to contrast it with the Sunni law, is to provide a number of examples.

Table 40

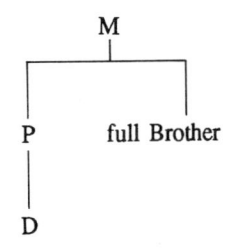

```
           M
           |
    ┌──────┴──────┐
    P         full Brother
    |
    D
```

In Hanafi law, the mother will receive one-sixth, the daughter will receive one-half, and the brother will receive one-third in his capacity as the nearest agnatic relative. In Shi'i law, mother and daughter are classes 1 (i) and 1 (ii) respectively. The brother (class 2 (ii)) is therefore excluded and the mother and daughter take their respective Qur'anic shares; 1/6 and 1/2 plus a return by radd. Thus the mother emerges with 2/12 + 1/12 and the daughter 6/12 + 3/12.

The Laws of Inheritance

Table 41

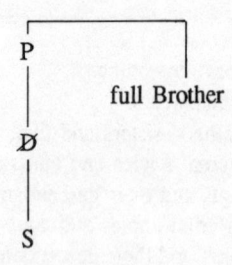

```
    ┌─────────┐
    P         │
    │     full Brother
    D̸
    │
    S
```

In Hanafi law, of course, the brother inherits the entire estate. The Shi'i school, however, reaches a result which is the exact opposite. The brother is a class 2 heir, whereas the daughter's son is a class 1 heir. The daughter's son, therefore, succeeds to the estate, a result which is unthinkable in this context in Sunni jurisprudence.

Table 42

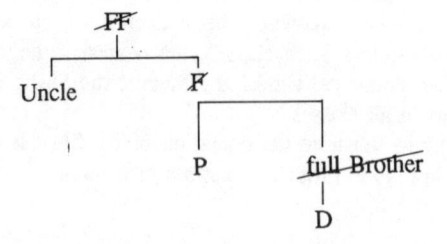

```
          F̸F̸
       ┌───┴───┐
     Uncle     F̸
              ┌─┴──────┐
              P    full Brother
              │
              D
```

The brother's daughter has no rights in Hanafi law, and the uncle, the nearest agnate, inherits the estate. In Shi'i law, however, the brother's daughter (as a class 2 heir) excludes the uncle (a class 3 heir).

These three examples illustrate that there are fundamental differences between Sunni and Shi'i law. Indeed, it is hard not to agree with Professor Coulson who asserts that the major reason for the difference is the rejection by the Shi'i jurists of the notion of the continuing validity of pre-Islamic practice. There are, of course, political reasons for the differences, not the least being to give priority to daughter's children. Perhaps the major reason for the disparity must be sought in the continuity of the tribal aristocracy of the Sunnis as compared with the limited family grouping of the Shi'i.[29] One important exception to the general Shi'i distribution, it must be conceded, is purely

---

[29] Professor Schacht in his writings tended to emphasise the political nature of the difference of approach. He minimised juristic divisions.

The Laws of Inheritance

political. This occurs when a man is survived by his consanguine uncle and his paternal full uncle's son. In this case, the paternal full uncle's son alone will inherit, notwithstanding that the consanguine uncle is nearer in degree to the deceased. When the Prophet died, the question arose whether 'Ali, the son of Abu Talib (a full paternal uncle of the Prophet), had priority over 'Abbas (a consanguine paternal uncle). The Shi'i, of course, accept the religious headship of the Imams descending from 'Ali and thus they make this exception to the general rule.

It would be useful to provide a number of other examples of the differences between the Sunni and Shi'i groups.[30]

Table 43

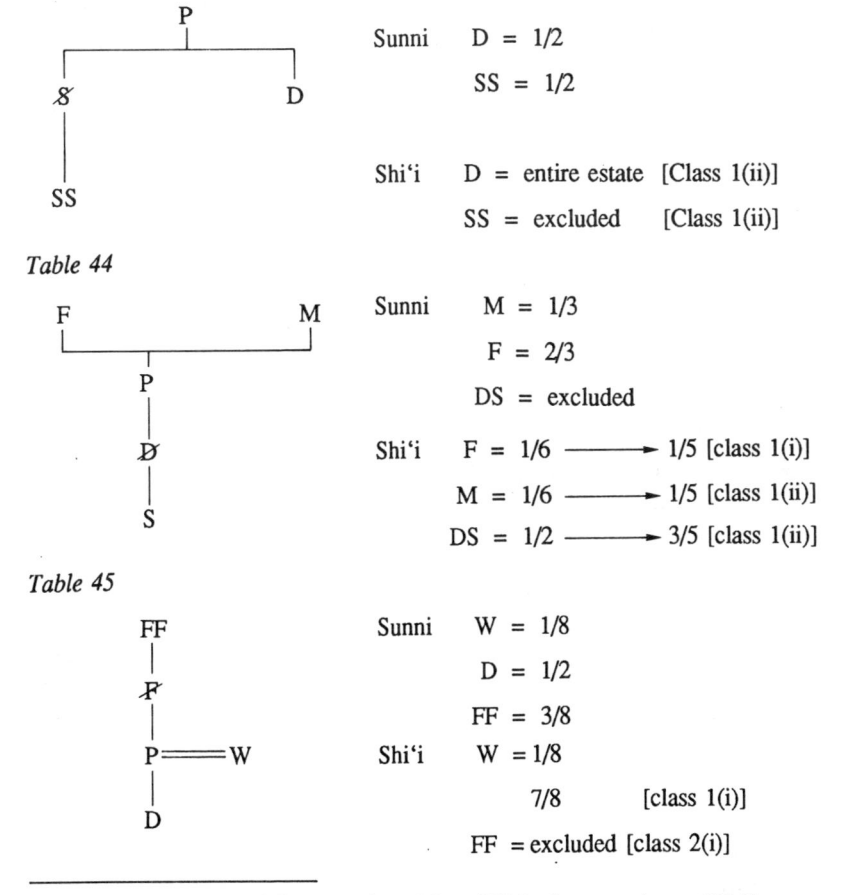

Sunni   D = 1/2
        SS = 1/2

Shi'i   D = entire estate   [Class 1(ii)]
        SS = excluded   [Class 1(ii)]

Table 44

Sunni   M = 1/3
        F = 2/3
        DS = excluded

Shi'i   F = 1/6 ⟶ 1/5 [class 1(i)]
        M = 1/6 ⟶ 1/5 [class 1(ii)]
        DS = 1/2 ⟶ 3/5 [class 1(ii)]

Table 45

Sunni   W = 1/8
        D = 1/2
        FF = 3/8

Shi'i   W = 1/8
            7/8   [class 1(i)]
        FF = excluded [class 2(i)]

---

[30] The examples that follow are adapted from N.J. Coulson op. cit. pp. 124 ff.

177

The Laws of Inheritance

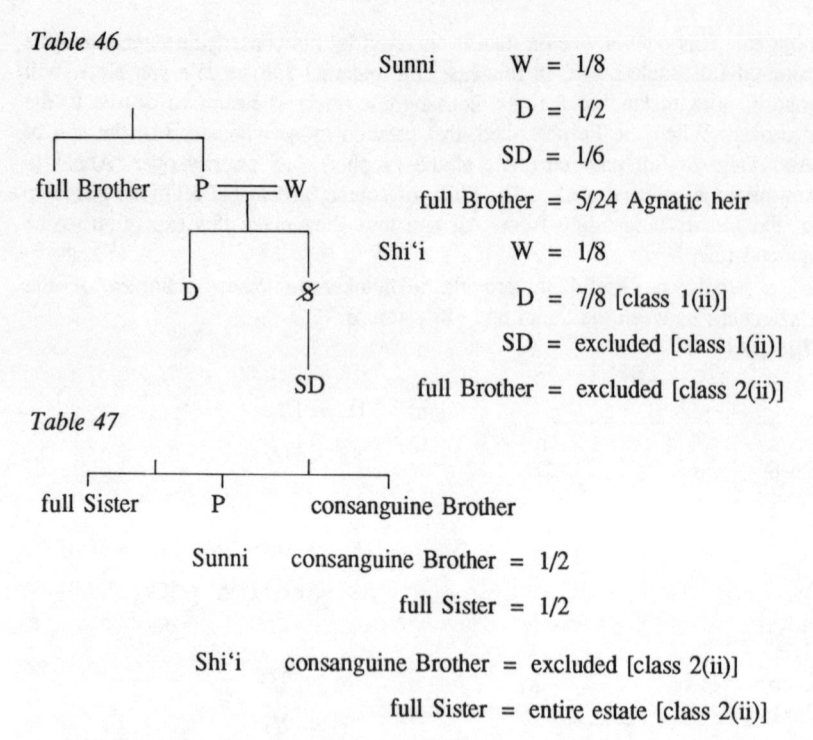

Table 46

```
                                Sunni     W  = 1/8
                                          D  = 1/2
                                          SD = 1/6
full Brother   P ══ W           full Brother = 5/24 Agnatic heir
                                Shi'i     W  = 1/8
          D         S           D  = 7/8 [class 1(ii)]
                                SD = excluded [class 1(ii)]
                    SD          full Brother = excluded [class 2(ii)]
```

Table 47

```
full Sister    P    consanguine Brother

         Sunni    consanguine Brother = 1/2
                  full Sister = 1/2

         Shi'i    consanguine Brother = excluded [class 2(ii)]
                  full Sister = entire estate [class 2(ii)]
```

The Shi'i permit a principle of representation, which is particularly relevant when the immediate children are dead leaving orphaned grandchildren. The grandchildren "step into the shoes" of their parents and receive the share their parents would have received if alive. The son's daughter is, therefore, not really an heir in her own right in Shi'i law, but will inherit the son's share if there is no surviving child of the propositus.

8.7 Reforms in the Islamic Law of Inheritance

It is no accident, of course, that the major reforms in the Islamic world in this area of law have taken place in the Sunni countries, for it is here that the extended distributory system with its emphasis on agnatic inheritance still continues to play an important role. Professor Sir Norman Anderson, writing in 1965, detected certain major criticisms of Sunni Islamic inheritance.[31]

---

[31] 1965 14 I.C.L.Q. 349.

The Laws of Inheritance

8.7.1 Rigidity

First, the system is far too rigid. It does not permit the prescribed shares to be augmented, even by will, however much the particular circumstances of the family may require such an augmentation. There have been changes, of course, notably in Sudan (1945), Egypt (1946) and Iraq (1959), permitting the testator complete freedom to make whatever legacies he likes within the bequeathable one-third.

8.7.2 The Wife's Share

Professor Anderson's second observation is that the wife has an inadequate share. An interesting attempt to improve this position occurred in Tunisia in 1959. The Tunisians, as Maliki, had no doctrine of radd (return). The Public Treasury in that system always *inherits* rather than acquires any residue by way of an administrative devise (escheat). In 1959, the Tunisians abandoned this rule, and adopted the principle of radd, but went beyond the Hanafi law by allowing the wife the right to participate in the return regardless of whether other heirs were alive at the opening of the succession. This extension of the radd doctrine applies also now in Sudan, Egypt and Syria.

A more radical reform has been introduced in Somalia, where males and females (including husbands and wives) are placed on a completely equal footing.

8.7.3 Daughter and Son's Daughter

A third criticism is that the daughter or son's daughter receives only one-half of the estate (or if two or more, two-thirds), and the residue will often vest in a distant agnate. This was felt to be wrong and unjust in modern conditions. Thus, in Iraq (1963) legislation was passed to enable female descendants of the deceased to exclude totally any collateral male agnate. This again is an adoption of Shi'i law and a rejection of Sunni doctrine; but, of course, in a country where there is an equal division anyway between Sunni and Shi'i adherents. The 1959 Tunisian legislation is not as wide as that of Iraq, although, by Tunisian law, a daughter or son's daughter now excludes a collateral male agnate.

8.7.4 Representation

The fourth major criticism relates to the lack of representation in Sunni law, and the very serious problem of the orphaned grandchild. We have already commented on this problem, and we must now return to discuss in detail some of the solutions which have been adopted. In Egypt, they adopted in 1946 a system generally referred to as "obligatory bequests". The Egyptian

The Laws of Inheritance

law provides that the propositus is obliged to make a bequest in favour of a grandchild by any son or daughter who has predeceased him (if they would not be entitled to any share on intestacy) provided that this bequest does not exceed the limit of one-third for legacies or the equivalent of the share of the predeceased son or daughter, whichever is less. The principle applies to all lineal descendants of the propositus on the male line, but in the case of predeceased daughters, only the immediate grandchildren can benefit. Should the grandfather fail to make a bequest, the court will act as if he had and such an implied or obligatory bequest will have priority over any voluntary bequests which the propositus may have actually provided for in his will.[32]

The justification for the Egyptian law is based on Sura II, verses 176-80, which, it will be recalled, enjoin Muslims to make bequests in favour of parents and close relatives. The consensus is that these verses have been abrogated by the later provisions in Sura IV. The Egyptians, however, exercise ijtihad and reinterpret the provisions in order to cope with the particular problem of the orphaned grandchild.

The "obligatory legatees" in the Egyptian system are never legal heirs in their own right, so the system appears to harmonise well with the general scheme of Sunni inheritance. Certainly, when legacies to the extent of one-third of the estate have been bequeathed the obligatory bequests can be extracted from the estate at the expense of the voluntary bequests, and the rights of the compulsory heirs are in no way affected. However, if bequests have not been made, the amount received by the heirs will be reduced; and the extraction of the obligatory bequest will change the quantified amounts, although not the fractions, received by the heirs.

There are a number of different ways to implement the scheme. By the "court method", so called because Egyptian courts initially adopted this method, the estate is distributed as if the deceased son or daughter were still alive, and that share, or one-third, whichever is less, is then allocated to the grandchildren. Under this method, as we shall later illustrate, the distribution produces an unfortunate distortion. Thus, a method suggested initially by the Egyptian jurist, Abu Zahra, is now applied by the Egyptian courts. In the Abu Zahra method, the distribution is as follows: rather like the classical 'Umariyyatan decision (spouse relict, mother and father), one ascertains the exact amount which the predeceased son or daughter would have received if

---

[32] See K.Faruki "Orphaned grandchildren in Islamic Succession Law." 1964 Islamic Studies, no. 4, p. 253; A.B.M.Sultanul Alam Chowdury "Problems of Representation in the Muslim Law of Inheritance." 1963 Islamic Studies, no. 3, p. 375.

The Laws of Inheritance

he or she had survived, and having subtracted this amount (or one-third) from the estate and allocated it to the grandchildren, the balance is divided up without regard to the predeceased son or daughter on the basis that he or she is in fact dead. Two examples can be given.[33]

Table 48

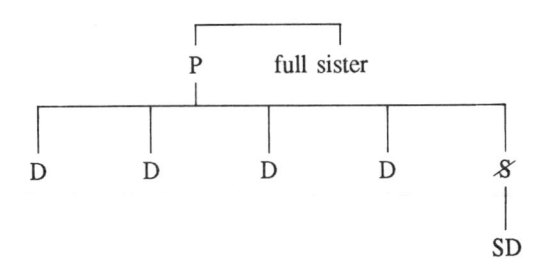

```
            ┌─────────┬─────────┐
            P         full sister
            │
    ┌───┬───┼───┬─────┐
    D   D   D   D    S̸
                      │
                     SD
```

By the "court method", the son is fictitiously reactivated in order to discover his interest. The son, if alive, would have excluded the sister and would have inherited agnatically with the daughters 2:1 (the son taking one-third and the daughters one-sixth each). The "court method" simply adopts a system of substitution. Abu Zahra's method, in contrast, gives the son's daughter one-third; and the residue two-thirds is distributed as if the son were not alive. The daughters, therefore, receive four-ninths between them (2/3 x 2/3) and the germane sister receives the residue two-ninths (1/3 x 2/3).

Table 49

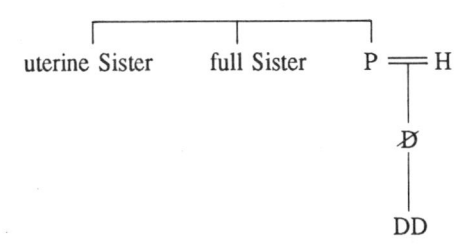

```
    ┌──────────────┬──────────────┐
    uterine Sister  full Sister    P ══ H
                                    │
                                    D̸
                                    │
                                    DD
```

In this example, the "court method" would produce the following fractions: H = 1/4; DD = 1/3 (the share of the D reduced down to 1/3); the uterine sister excluded by the reactivated D; and the surplus of five-twelfths given to the

---

[33] Adopted from N.J.Coulson op. cit. p. 147.

The Laws of Inheritance

germane sister as the residuary heir. The method proposed by Abu Zahra would provide a more equitable result, for there is no real justification for the uterine grandchild to exclude the uterine sister. Abu Zahra, therefore, would provide the one-third to the DD; 1/2 x 2/3 = 2/6 to the H; 1/6 x 2/3 = 2/18 to the uterine sister, and 1/2 x 2/3 = 2/6 to the germane sister. The shares would then have to be reduced by the principles of 'awl; but all surviving relatives would be entitled to part of the estate.

The system of obligatory bequests has been adopted in Syria, Morocco, Tunisia, and Kuwait; although in Syria and Morocco the reformers were a little more cautious for they confined the operation of the principle to children of the deceased's son. Children of the deceased's daughter do not benefit.

8.7.4.1 Pakistan

Pakistan tackled the problem a different way. Section 4 of the 1961 Ordinance states:

> In the event of the death of any son or daughter of the propositus before the opening of succession, the children of such son or daughter, if any, living at the time the succession opens, shall *per stirpes* receive a share equivalent to the share which such son or daughter, as the case may be, would have received if alive.

This provision has come in for considerable criticism. Coulson states: "The reform is obviously intended to operate within the framework of the traditional law, but its effect is so far reaching that one may perhaps be excused for wondering whether all its implications were fully appreciated." Sir Norman Anderson is equally critical: "Section 4 makes chaos of the Islamic system of inheritance." A simple illustration will perhaps make the point. The propositus is survived by a brother and a son's daughter.

Table 50

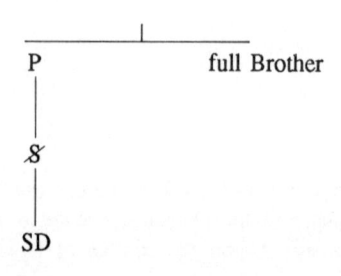

```
           |
   P              full Brother
   |
   S
   |
   SD
```

In the classical Hanafi law, the son's daughter will receive one-half of the estate and the brother receives the other half. The position, of course, is not altered in Egypt. In Pakistan, however, the son, if alive, would have excluded the brother; thus, the son's daughter takes the entire estate to the exclusion of the brother.

The 1961 Ordinance introduces also children of daughters as primary heirs. This dramatic change has certainly upset the religious elements in Pakistan society. Thus Chowdhury says

> The children of daughters are all distant kindred. The 1961 Ordinance, by invoking the principle of representation in the case of the daughter's children, aims at converting the distant kindred into sharers in contravention of the sacred law, causing innumerable anomalies by way of excluding many rightful claimants and including outsiders.[34]

Chowdhury has harsh words to say of the reform: 'If for the sake of finding a short-cut to these problems, we amend and abrogate the divine law for our convenience, then the sacrosanctity of and reverence for divine law will be gone for ever.'[35]

An attempt has been made in the Pakistan courts to attack the basis of section 4 of the Ordinance as being contrary to the principles of Islam as laid down in the Qur'an and Sunna.[36] However, all such attempts have failed, and the Supreme Court in *Federation of Pakistan v. Farishta*[37] held that the Ordinance was a special statutory provision intended to be applied only to Muslims in Pakistan and the court was thus without jurisdiction to review its constitutionality.

At this stage, more examples should be provided of the operation of the Egyptian and the Pakistan law.

---

[34] A.B.M.Sultanul Alam Chowdhury "Problems of Representation in the Muslim Law of Inheritance." 1964 Islamic Studies, vol. 3, p. 375.

[35] He is here speaking of the social problems experienced by the orphaned grandchild. See *Yusuf Abbas v. Ismat Mustafa* 1968 PLD Kar 480.

[36] Article 203D of the Constitution of Pakistan.

[37] 1981 PLD SC 120.

The Laws of Inheritance

Table 51

```
        P
       / \
      S   D
          |
          DD
```

Classical Law (Sunni)
　　Entire amount to S

Egypt
　　DD = 1/3
　　S = 2/3

Pakistan
　　DD = 1/3
　　S = 2/3

Table 52

```
        P
       / \
      D   S
          |
          SD
```

Classical Law (Sunni)
　　D = 1/2 + 1/4 (radd) = 3/4
　　SD = 1/6 + 1/12 (radd) = 1/4

Egypt　　Same as classical law

Pakistan
　　D = 1/3
　　SD = 2/3

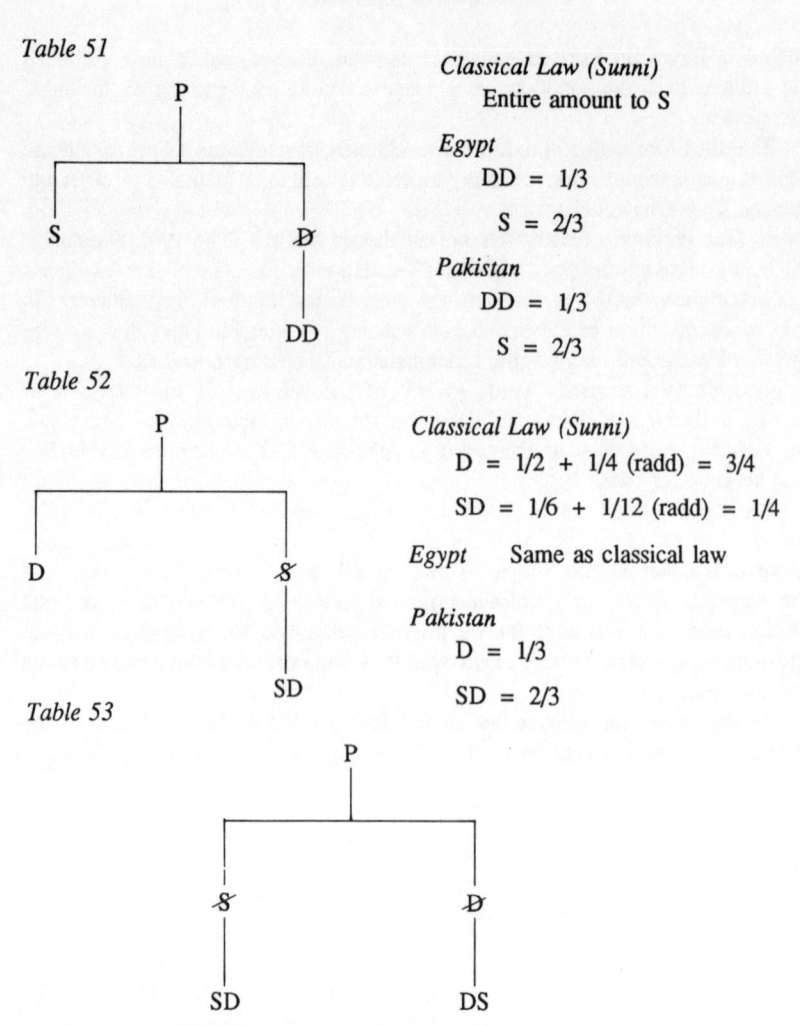

Table 53

```
            P
           / \
          S   D
          |   |
          SD  DS
```

Classical law. The SD excludes the DS.

Egypt. Under Abu Zahra's method, the D alone is reactivated. She would, of course, if alive have received 1/2 + 1/4 (radd) in the presence of the SD. This is well beyond the 1/3 available for distribution, thus the DS receives 1/3 only, and the SD receives 2/3.

Pakistan. The result is actually the same in Pakistan as in Egypt, although for very different reasons. Both the son and the daughter are reactivated, and their children receive the share their parents would have received if alive; thus the SD = 2/3 and the DS = 1/3.

Before we consider the next example, it will be useful to look at a recent Pakistan decision, *Kamal Khan v. Zainab*.[38] This case involved the distribution of the estate of one Sufaid Khan who died in 1972. In 1977, the entire estate was transferred to Zenib, the surviving granddaughter and the daughter of Rajoo, a predeceased son. An action was brought by the nephew, Kamal Khan, challenging this transfer.

Table 54

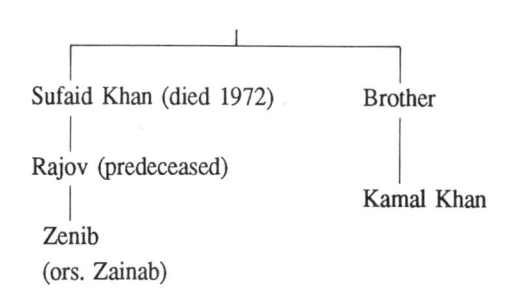

```
                    |
         ┌──────────┴──────────┐
  Sufaid Khan (died 1972)    Brother
         │                     │
  Rajov (predeceased)          │
         │                 Kamal Khan
       Zenib
    (ors. Zainab)
```

The Court held that Mst. Zenib, as a surviving grandchild, could not receive more than one half of the estate of her father, and the remaining half *must* revert to the collateral. The Judge said:

> The legislature never intended to give greater benefit to the grandchildren of a predeceased parent than would have been his due, if the parent was alive.

He then distributed the estate in the following manner:

> The starting point is that notionally the off-spring of the propositus is deemed to be alive for the purpose of succession at the time of the death of the propositus, and the succession of the grandchildren is to be calculated again notionally as if the parent of the grandchild died after the death of the original propositus.

Thus Zenib was entitled only to half the estate, and the rest of the estate (that is the other half) reverted to the nearest agnate, Kamal. Likewise in *Table 50*, the result would be that the classical law is applied notwithstanding section 4. The decision would appear to undermine the basis of section 4, and it remains to be seen whether it would be followed by other courts. In *Iqbal Mai v.*

---

[38] 1983 PLD Lah 546.

The Laws of Inheritance

Falak Sher,[39] the Supreme Court refused to consider the issue on the particular facts of that case. The question is raised in that case however as to whether it was the intention of the lawmaker to provide an opportunity of obtaining for the orphaned grandchild an Islamic law share, and not simply to provide a system of strict representation.

It is interesting to speculate on the result of a distribution of the estate in *Table 52* following the *Kamal Khan* system of distribution. The first distribution produces the following: D = 1/3; S = 2/3. The second distribution then produces the following: D = 3/4 x 2/3 = 1/2; SD = 1/4 x 2/3 = 1/6. It is then necessary to have a final distribution which produces the following result:

```
D = 1/3 + 6/12 = 5/6
SD = 1/6
```

It is seen that *Kamal Khan* actually leaves the son's daughter worse off than under the classical law.

Table 55

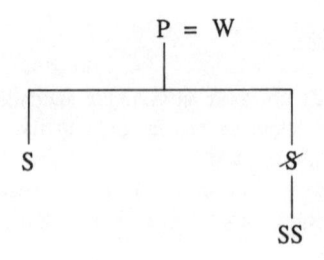

```
        P = W
        ┌───┴───┐
        S       S
                │
                SS
```

Classical law:

```
W = 1/8
S = 7/8
SS = X (excluded)
```

Egypt (court method):
```
W = 1/8 (3/24)
S = 13/24
SS = 1/3 (8/24)
```

---

[39] 1986 PLD SC 228.

```
Egypt (Abu Zahra):
W = 1/8 x 2/3 = 2/24
S = 14/24
SS = 1/3 (8/24)

Pakistan (usual method):
W = 1/8
S = 7/16
SS = 7/16

Pakistan (Kamal Khan distribution):
first distribution.
W = 1/8 (12/96)
S = 7/16 (42/96)
S = 7/16 (42/96)
second distribution.
(of 7/16)
W (M) 1/6 x 7/16 = 7/96
S (B) = X (excluded)
SS (S) = 5/6 x 7/16 = 35/96
final distribution.
W = 12/96 + 7/96 = 19/96
S = 42/96
SS = 35/96
```

8.7.5 Fragmentation

We must now return to the major criticisms levelled against the Sunni law, and consider a fifth matter, namely fragmentation. One often hears criticism that the Muslim law permits fragmentation below a viable economic unit. Certain countries have indeed tackled the problem within the framework of general land reform by laying down a minimum limit of land-holding. Below that limit, heirs must take as co-owners. Some apologists, of course, believe that fragmentation is a powerful check on capitalism and that it provides a sensible alternative to socialism on the one hand as well as capitalism on the other. A discussion of this topic is outside the scope of this book.

The Laws of Inheritance

Table 56

Heir	Share	Excluded by	Affected by	In Which Case	Notes
Husband	1/4	—	no child or child of son	1/2	
Wife	1/8	—	no child or child of son	1/4	
Father	1/6	—	no child or child of son	agnatised	Father is both an agnatic and a Qur'anic heir.
True grandfather	1/6	lower g/f or father	no child or child of son	agnatised	added by Sunna
Mother	1/6	—	1. no child or child of son 2. *one* brother or sister (and no child) 3. coexisting with father *and* spouse (and no child and not more than one collateral)	1/3 1/3 1/3 of residue	'Umariyyatam decision
True grandmother	1/6	*maternal true g/m*: mother, nearer maternal or paternal g/m *paternal true g/m*: these plus father, nearer true g/f.			added by Sunna (at least in India)
Daughter	1/2 (if 2 = 2/3)	—	son	agnatised	
Son's daughter however low ie SSD, SSSD	1/2 (if 2 = 2/3)	son, more than one daughter, more than one higher son's daughter	1. one daughter 2. one higher SD 3. equal son's son	1. 1/6 2. 1/6 3. agnatised	Reactivisation can operate lucky or unlucky kinsmen
Full sister	1/2 (if 2 = 2/3)	son, son's son, father, true g/f	full brother, daughter or son's, daughter	agnatised	in differing ways
Consanguine sister	1/2 (if 2 = 2/3)	son, son's son, father, true g/f, brother (full), more than one full sister	1. full sister 2. consanguine brother 3. daughter or son's daughter	1. 1/6 2. agnatised 3. agnatised	lucky and unlucky kinsmen cases,
Uterine brother Uterine sister	1/6 (if 2 = 1/3)	child, child of son, father, true g/f	—	—	See himmariyya decision and Malik's rule.

9. Gift and Waqf

9.1 Gift

Islamic law seeks to protect the lawful rights of heirs. Thus attempts to dispose of property *inter vivos* are accompanied by some strict legal requirements which must be satisfied in order to create an effective transfer of property. In this context, it is important to distinguish between a gift of the substance (hiba) and a gift of the usufruct or profits ('ariyya). Professor Fyzee defines a hiba as "the immediate and unqualified transfer of the corpus (the 'ayn) of the property without any return (iwad)". The basis of the doctrine of hiba is Sura II, verse 215 and hadith such as: "one who seeks to take back a gift is like a dog which takes back its vomit".

There are three important incidents to the law of hiba. There has to be ijab (declaration), qabul (acceptance) and qabda (delivery of possession). Until possession is taken by the donee, the property remains entirely at the disposal of the donor. If a donor makes a declaration of hiba which is accepted by the donee but without the delivery of possession, then, on the death of the donor, the property will descend to the donor's heirs. Hanafi law, however, permits constructive possession by the donee to be sufficient possession to fulfil the requirements of qabda. An illustrative case is *Zeenat Bi v. Zaman Mehdi*.[1] In this case, two successive husbands and a lover had attempted, in turn, to persuade Zeenat Bi to donate to them a gift of particularly valuable property. The judge in this case laid down the following principle:

> If the actual possession cannot be given by the donor to the donee, but the donor has done all that he could do to divest himself of the gifted property, the gift would be considered to be complete and effective according to law.

This is obviously a question of fact; and the judge held that the woman had intended to make a gift to her lover, Zaman Mehdi, who had taken constructive possession.

Another example is *Mohammad Abdul Ghani v. Fakhr Jahan Begam*.[2] The donor made a gift of the corpus of the property, but continued in physical possession enjoying the profits. The donee, however, paid all the government

---

[1] 1956 PLD (WP) Lah 760. See also *Eidun Nisa Begum v. Member, Board of Revenue* 1973 PLD Pesh 1.

[2] 1921/2 49 LR IA 195.

Gift and Waqf

taxes in respect of the land after the date of the gift. It was held that this factor amounted to constructive possession of the property, and thus there was indeed a valid gift. We can compare this case with *Ranee Khujooroonissa v. Mussumut Roushun Jehan*.[3] A father had attempted to defeat the operation of the law of succession by divesting himself before his death of some of his property to his son (there was no question of the father being in death sickness at the time). It was held that the intention of this deed was that the transfer of the corpus was only to operate after the death of the donor and, therefore, there was no actual nor constructive possession.

An interesting Supreme Court decision from India is *Maqbool Alam v. Khodaija*.[4] Shaik Ahmad Ali owned tenanted property in Dumraon. He died in 1910, leaving surviving him as his heirs the following: his mother, his second wife, three sons and two daughters from this wife, and two sons and four daughters from his first wife.

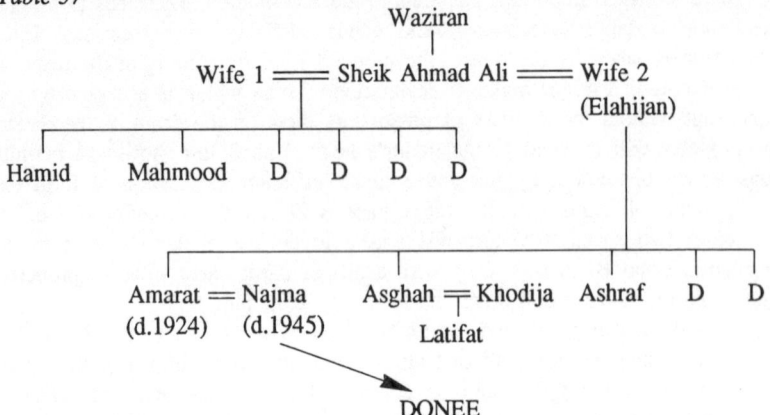

Table 57

```
                            Waziran
                               |
           Wife 1 ====== Sheik Ahmad Ali ====== Wife 2
                  |                             (Elahijan)
        ┌────┬────┬──┬──┬──┬──┐                    |
      Hamid Mahmood D  D  D  D                     |
                                      ┌──────┬──────┬──────┬──┬──┐
                                   Amarat=Najma  Asghah=Khodija Ashraf D D
                                   (d.1924)(d.1945)    |
                                                    Latifat
                                         ──────▶ DONEE
```

All the heirs were co-sharers of this property, but only the names of Hamid and Mahmud were recorded as tenure-holders in the "record of rights" published in 1911. In 1915, a decree for rent was obtained by the Maharaja of Dumraon against both Hamid and Mahmud. After considerable litigation connected with the rights and entitlements of the co-sharers in the tenure, Najma (the wife of Amanat) obtained by way of a compromise a share in the tenure.

Subsequently, the decree for rent was executed, and the son of Asghar (Latifat) purchased the tenure at the execution sale. Latifat, of course, was the

---

[3] 1875/76 3 LR IA 291.
[4] AIR 1966 SC 1194.

Gift and Waqf

Shaik's grandchild. The next stage of the litigation commenced in 1937 when Najma instituted proceedings against Latifat seeking a declaration that her share in the tenure was not affected by the sale. Subsequently, the Maharaja returned to the scene by seeking an order for rent against Latifat. The Maharaja was successful in this endeavour and obtained from the court a decree of execution. There was a further execution sale in 1940, on which occasion Khodaija, the second wife of Asghar, successfully purchased the tenure.

In February 1943, Najma died. After her death, a certain Maqbool Alam, the appellant in these present proceedings, filed a petition praying for the substitution of his interest in the property in place of Najma. on the ground that before her death Najma had made an oral gift of her share to him. Maqbool Alam was successful and thus, in June 1943, he obtained possession of the land dispossessing Khodaija in the process.

Further legal action continued during the 1940s resulting finally in a reversal of the substitution decision. This stimulated the appellant to bring the present suit. The appellant based his claim to title upon the alleged oral gift to him by Najma. In response, Khodaija disputed both the factum of and the validity of the gift. The appellant's evidence was that the gift was made on 10 February 1943, a fortnight before Najma's death, in the presence of witnesses. It was not shown, however, that he took possession of the properties; indeed this was not possible because at the time of the purported gift, Najma had already been dispossessed of the tenure.

In the context of these facts, Bachawat J, giving judgment for the Supreme Court, said:

> a gift of a property in the possession of a trespasser is not established by mere declaration of the donor and acceptance by the donee. To validate the gift, there must also be either delivery of possession or failing such delivery, some overt act by the donor to part with it within the power of the donee to obtain possession. If, apart from making a declaration, the donor does nothing else, the gift is invalid.

Najma had done nothing at all after the alleged declaration. She did not file any petition seeking a substitution of the appellant in her place in the context of the proceedings which were then before the courts. In these circumstances, the gift was invalid, and the appellant lost his case.

Two other important points need to be stressed. First, the property must be in existence at the point in time of the declaration of hiba. Secondly, the transfer must of necessity be an absolute one.

We turn now to consider the other institution with which hiba is often confused. Islamic law recognises a gratuitous transfer of the usufruct (manfa'a). This institution is known as 'ariyya. To make a person the owner of the substance of a thing without consideration is a hiba, while to make him the owner of the profits without consideration is an 'ariyya. The 'ariyya may be accompanied by conditions limiting the period of enjoyment of the property in the sense of creating a limited interest. Indian judges prior to 1948 ignored the distinction inherent in the Islamic law between hiba (the gift of the 'ayn) and 'ariyya (the gift of the manfa'a) and, when confronted with attempts by donors to make gifts for life, they declared such attempts as void because they saw such devices as imposing a void condition on the enjoyment of the 'ayn. The judges, therefore, struck out the limitation in the gift deeds, and allowed the donee to acquire an absolute interest. They were misled because of the English law concept of the "life estate" which is a transfer of ownership of the property for a limited period. Influenced by such English concepts, the Indian judges could not conceive that Islamic law permitted the transfer of the usus, and interpreted all the gifts as transfers of the corpus subject to a condition which was void for it was contrary to the Islamic law of hiba.[5]

The whole episode is now concluded by the Privy Council decision in *Sardar Nawazish Ali Khan's* case.[6] Sir John Beaumont stated the position as follows:

> Though the same terms may be used in English and Muslim law, to describe much the same things, the two systems are based on quite different conceptions of ownership. English law recognizes ownership of land limited in duration; Muslim law admits only of ownership unlimited in duration, but recognizes interests of limited duration on the use of property.

It is, therefore, a matter of construction whether the gift is intended as a transfer of the corpus or the usus. If it is the transfer of the usus only, any limitations imposed upon the duration of the donee's interest are valid and effective.

9.1.1 Revocation

Although revocation is frowned upon, it is possible to revoke a hiba in certain circumstances. It can never be revoked, at least in Hanafi law, however, if it is a gift to any of the donor's ascendants, descendants, brothers or sisters or their children, uncle or aunt, or spouse. Likewise, there can be no revocation if the donee has erected a building, or improved the property to such an extent that the increase cannot be separated from it. A gift to a charity (a sadakah) is also not capable of revocation. Finally, the death of either the donor or donee, the

---

[5] The early cases are complicated by the different views of the Shi'i as opposed to the Sunni law on the point.

[6] *Sardar Nawazish Ali Khan v. Sardar Ali Raza Khan.* 1948 75 LR IA 62.

sale or transfer of the property by the donee, if the property has perished, if there has been something given in exchange (iwad) – all these situations render the hiba incapable of revocation. In contrast to the hiba, an 'ariyya is revocable at any time by the donor.[7]

9.1.2 Musha'

When a hiba is of an "undivided part" (musha')[8] and the undivided part is in fact *divisible,* it is a fasid gift, rendered valid by subsequent separation and delivery. If the undivided part is indivisible, the gift is valid (sahih).[9]

There are three important exceptions, at least in India and Pakistan, to this general rule: first, a gift made by one co-heir to another; second, a gift to two or more persons; and third, a gift of freehold property in a town or shares in a land company. In all three cases, a gift of an undivided share capable of division is valid. In any event, the concept of musha' can be overcome by the use of hiyal (legal fiction). An undivided share capable of division is sold by A to B and immediately thereafter A absolves B of his debt.

Our discussion of hiba is concluded by the mention of two particular concepts: hiba bi'l-iwad and hiba bi-sharti'l-iwad.

9.1.3 Hiba bi'l-iwad

This is a transaction consisting of:

(a) a hiba
(b) an iwad (return)

As soon as the return gift is made, both gifts become irrevocable. In India, this type of transaction has evolved into a contract similar to sale. An example of hiba bi'l-iwad is the case of *Muhammad Faiz Ahmad Khan v. Ghulam Ahmad Khan.*[10] In this case, a widow surrendered her claims over her husband's estate in favour of her brother-in-law, but only after a transfer of other property was

---

[7] No revocation of hiba at all is permissible in Maliki law, and revocation is permitted in Shafi'i and Hanbali law only when the donee is a child of the donor.

[8] Every joint undivided property subject to the right of more than one individual is a musha'.

[9] See *Kasim Husain v. Sharif-un-Nissa* 1883 ILR 5 All 285. The gift in this case included the right to the use of a staircase used jointly by the donor and the owner of the adjoining house. As the musha' was *not* capable of division, the gift was valid.

[10] 1880/81 ILR 3 All 490.

made by the brother-in-law in her favour.[11] The Indian case law on this subject has been much criticised. In particular, Professor Tahir Mahmood lays down two propositions. He says in the first instance that where the transaction conforms to the Islamic form of hiba bi-l-iwad, then the courts should apply the Muslim personal law because of the overriding provision of the Shariat Act. Where however the transaction amounts neither to hiba nor to the Islamic concept of hiba bi'l-iwad, then the court should simply apply the Indian general legislation; namely, the Contract Act and the Transfer of Property Act 1882.

9.1.4 Hiba bi' sharti' l-iwad

This is a gift made with a stipulation (shart) for a return (iwad). The basic difference between this institution and hiba bi'l-iwad is that in hiba bi'l-iwad, a voluntary gift is followed by a voluntary return, whereas in the sharti'l-iwad, the gift itself is made with a stipulation. The donee is free to accept or to reject the stipulation. If he accepts the stipulation, then he is under a legal duty to complete the gift in favour of the donor. If the donee rejects the stipulated condition, the original gift is effective as a simple gratuitous transfer, and the stipulation simply does not take effect.

9.2 Waqf

9.2.1 Classical Law

Waqf is defined in the Encyclopedia of Islam as "A thing which while retaining its substance yields a usufruct and of which the owner has surrendered his power of disposal with the stipulation that the yield is used for permitted good purposes." In effect, the settlor withdraws from circulation the substance of the property ('ayn) and spends the proceeds (manfa'a) for a charitable purpose. If the income is devoted for charitable purposes from the beginning it is called a waqf khayri. If it is designed primarily for the benefit of the settlor's (waqif) descendants, with an ultimate benefit for a charitable purpose it is a family waqf (a waqf dhurri). The emphasis in these pages is placed on the second of these two institutions, referred to on the subcontinent as a waqf al-awlad.

Although there are Qur'anic verses recommending gifts of property to charity, the institution of waqf is not expressly mentioned in the Qur'an, and

---

[11] See also *Ashidbhai v. Abdullah* 1906 ILR 31 Bom 271.

Gift and Waqf

its development is really a product of the versatility of the jurists.[12] There are traces of non-Islamic influences in the law, and there may well be a direct link with the Byzantine system of Piae Causae.

There is an important hadith related by Bukhari to the following effect: 'Ibn Omar reported, Omar ibn-al Khattab got land in Khaybar, so he came to the Prophet...to consult him. He said "..I got land in Khaybar [more] than which I have never obtained more valuable property; what dost thou advise about it?" He said, "If thou likest, make the property itself to remain inalienable, and give [the profit] from it to charity."

The body of rules relating to waqf were built up around such hadith during the first two centuries of Islam on the basis of ijma'.

The essential requirements of waqf are as follows:

(1) The settlor (waqif) must have the full right of disposal of the property. He must have attained his majority and be of sound mind.

(2) The subject of the endowment must be of a permanent and tangible nature, and yield a usufruct. Moveables do not usually possess the quality of permanency, although it is possible that some moveables could yield a usufruct and thus fulfil at least part of this requirement.

It is accepted in Hanafi law that the following moveables can be the subject of a Waqf:-

```
(i) moveables permanently attached to immoveables,
(ii) animals such as horses and camels,
(iii) books and furniture,
(iv) at least in Pakistan; government securities,
shares in companies, debentures and stock.
```

(3) Overriding these considerations is the important point that the object of the waqf must be pleasing to Allah. This need only be achieved in the general sense. The charitable object need not be the immediate beneficiary. In the case of the waqf khayri the charitable object is the immediate beneficiary, but in the waqf dhurri the profits can be reserved first for the benefit of the settlor's children or indeed even for the benefit of strangers. A waqf dhurri devolves on the extinction of the beneficiaries to a charitable purpose. The examples of charitable purposes are very extensive, but will often include provision to benefit a mosque, a school, a hospital, or for the welfare generally of the poor.

---

[12] Sura II verse 215.

Gift and Waqf

(4) No particular form is required to create a waqf; indeed, there is no rule which states that the declaration of waqf has to be written. All that is necessary for the creation of a waqf is for the waqif to indicate his intention to make the property waqf property, and to specify the particular charitable purposes to which it is to be devoted. According to Abu Yusuf, the dedication of waqf is complete after the declaration. In his view, no delivery of possession to the guardian (the mutawali) is necessary. This is the general view of the Hanafi school, although there is a minority opinion of Imam Muhammad Shaybani to the effect that delivery of possession is necessary prior to the creation of the waqf. The Shi'i school demand a delivery.

(5) In Hanafi law, the waqf must be created in perpetuity. In the case of the waqf dhurri, the perpetuity principle is achieved by allocating the proceeds of the waqf to the poor after the death of the individuals who are to benefit from the waqf. If a waqf is created for a purpose which may fail, or indeed a purpose which is clearly limited in duration, the view accepted by the consensus in the Hanafi school is that the waqf is nonetheless valid. The perpetuity principle is not infringed, because there is an implied term in the waqf to benefit the poor in the event of the failure of prime purpose of the waqf. This view again constitutes the opinion of Abu Yusuf.

(6) Linked to the perpetuity principle is the other important factor namely, that the waqf, with a few exceptions, must be inalienable. The corpus of the property made the subject of the waqf cannot be sold, mortgaged, donated or alienated, even by inheritance, in any way. The only two exceptions are first, it can be exchanged or sold on the authority of the Qadi in order to purchase new property, and second, it can be leased, although usually for only a limited period of a year, or three years in the case of agricultural land. Long leases, akin to the disposition of ownership, could only rarely be authorised by the Qadi.

(7) One question, which disturbed the jurists, and which is indeed of troublesome complexity, relates to the question of the vesting of ownership of the waqf. The disciples of Abu Hanifa (Shaybani and Abu Yusuf) as well as Shafi'i propounded the theory that the waqif's right of ownership *ceased* on the dedication of the waqf. The Maliki school, however, as well as Abu Hanifa himself, considered that the founder and his heirs retained rights of ownership. The ijma' (consensus) of the Hanafi school, as so often, has been to adopt the view of Abu Yusuf and

Gift and Waqf

Shaybani.

But if the ownership of the waqif ceases, where is ownership vested? The two disciples answer that question simply by stating that ownership of the waqf, on dedication, vests in Allah. Others submit the view that the waqf is a juristic person in its own right. Still others, as in the case of particular jurists of the Shi'i school, vest ownership in the beneficiaries.

After dedication, the waqf, as we have seen, becomes inalienable and perpetual. It is for this reason that the waqf property is often referred to as the "dead hand".

(8) After dedication, the waqf comes into operation at once. There is one apparent exception to this rule. This exception relates to the waqf created by will. Such a waqf is subject to the law relating to testamentary succession (dedication beyond one-third is *ultra vires*). As the will speaks from death, the waqf only comes into operation on the death of the testator.

(9) The final matter which requires comment relates to the question of revocation. According to the views of the two disciples, the declaration of waqf by the waqif is irrevocable as soon as the dedication has been pronounced. A waqf cannot therefore be revoked after the declaration has been made; neither can the power to revoke be validly reserved. The view of Abu Hanifa, which represents a minority and divergent opinion within Hanafi law, is that waqf can be revoked up until the waqf is confirmed by a Qadi. The Maliki jurists also permit revocation.

It would be useful to conclude this discussion of the classical system of waqf by referring in brief to the powers and duties of the mutawali, the administrator of the waqf. The mutawali is the person who is appointed as manager of the trust property. No legal ownership vests in the mutawali, and it is this point which distinguishes the power of the mutawali from those of a trustee under an English trust. Essentially, the duty of the mutawali is to do everything necessary and proper for the protection of the waqf property and for the administration of the waqf. In particular, he is responsible for distributing the proceeds amongst the beneficiaries. Quite often, the founder himself will declare himself as the first mutawali. Indeed, if no mutawali is designated, according to Abu Yusuf at least, the waqif becomes the mutawali.[13]

---

[13] Abu Hanifa, again representing the minority opinion, states that failure to name the mutawali means that the waqf fails.

Gift and Waqf

With regard to succession to the position of mutawali, in the absence of any rules laid down in the waqfnama itself, the general rule is that during his own lifetime, the waqif possesses the power to designate a successor to the mutawali. Otherwise, the Qadi has responsibility to designate the mutawali. When the mutawali has been appointed, the settlor has no power to remove him, although in any particular case of unfitness, the general supervisory role of the Qadi would empower him to remove the mutawali.

9.2.2 India and Pakistan

The starting point to a discussion of the law of waqf on the Indian subcontinent is an examination of the leading case, *Abul Fata Mahomed Ishak v. Russomoy Dhur Chowdhry*.[14] The facts of this case are as follows. A waqfnama was purported to have been made in December 1868. The settlors were two brothers, Abdur Rahman and Abdool Kadir. The question before the court was simply this: was the settlement valid as a waqfnama? The settlement ran as follows:

> Committing ourselves to the mercy and kindness of the Great God, and relying upon the bounty of providence for the perpetuation of the names of our forefathers and for the preservation of our properties we have made this permanent Wakf according to Mohammedan law – for the benefit of our children, the children of our children and the members and relatives of our family and their descendants in male and female lines and in their absence, for the benefit of the poor and beggars and widows and orphans of Sylhet.

The two brothers took upon themselves the management and supervision of the waqf in the capacity of mutawali. '[We have] taken out the wakf properties from our ownership and enjoyment in a private capacity, and put them in our possession and under our control in our capacity as Mutawalis.'

Toward the end of the document, the general object of the waqf is stated:

> The object of this Waqf of properties is that the properties may be protected against all risks, the name and the prestige of the family maintained, and the profits of these properties appropriated towards the maintenance of the name and prestige of the family, the support of the persons for whose benefit the Waqf is made, and religious purposes, etc.

At first instance, the judge held the waqf valid, but on appeal the High Court reversed the decision, and the High Court's decision was upheld by the

---

[14] 1894/5 22 LR IA 76.

Gift and Waqf

Privy Council. Lord Hobhouse, in the Privy Council, was concerned by the illusory nature of the gift to the poor. Two passages are quoted here to provide the flavour of his speech:

> The motives stated are, regard to the family name, and preservation of the property in the family. Every specific trust is for some member of the family. The family is to be aggrandized by accumulations of surpluses, and apparently by absorption into the settlement of after acquired properties; and no person is to have any right of calling the managers to account.
>
> These possessions are to be secured for ever for the enjoyment of the family, so far as the settlors could accomplish such a result, by provisions that nobody's share shall be alienated, or be attached for his debts. There is no reference to religion unless it be the invocation of the deity to perpetuate the family name and to preserve their property, and the casual mention of unspecified, religious purposes etc. at the end. There is a gift to the poor and to widows and orphans, but they are to take nothing, not even surplus income, until the total extinction of the settlors' blood, whether lineal or collateral.

The other passage of Lord Hobhouse's speech deserving a full quotation is the following:

> Their Lordships asked during the argument how it comes about that by the general law of Islam, at least as known in India, simple gifts by a private person to remote unborn generations of descendants, successsions that is of inalienable life interests, are forbidden, and whether it is to be taken that the very same dispositions, which are illegal when made by ordinary words of gift, become legal if only the settlor says that they are made as a Wakf, in the name of God, or for the sake of the poor.
>
> To those questions, no answer was given or attempted, nor can their Lordships see any.

The Privy Council held the ultimate gift to the poor to be illusory. As we have seen, however, all schools are united in holding that the settlor's own family may be validly designated as beneficiaries (waqf dhurri) and that such a waqf *has* to be both perpetual and inalienable. No distinction is drawn between the waqf dhurri and the waqf khayri. Indeed, according to Abu Yusuf and accepted as Hanafi doctrine, the settlor can validly designate himself as the first beneficiary in that he can enjoy the income of the waqf property as life tenant. The Privy Council, however, places its own interpretation on the Sunna of the Prophet, rather than following by taqlid the authoritative interpretations of the Hanafi school. An important Hadith of the Prophet is the

following:
> A pious offering to one's family, to provide against their getting into want, is more pious than giving alms to beggars. The most excellent of Sadakah (gift) is that which man bestows upon his family.

The Privy Council placed its own interpretations on this hadith.
> These precepts may be excellent in their proper application. They may, for ought their Lordships know, have had their effect in moulding the law and practice of Wakf, as the learned Judge (Ameer Ali J) says they have. But it would be doing wrong to the great lawgiver to suppose that he is thereby commending gifts for which the donor exercises no self denial; in which he takes back with one hand what he appears to put away with the other.[15]

There was outrage in the Muslim community over this decision, and thus in 1913 the legislature enacted the Musalman Wakf Validating Act (1913) whose purpose was to restore the Hanafi law. Some Indian commentators have suggested that the major reason for the agitation was not to protect Muslim law as such, but rather to ensure the continuation of accummulation of capital, and to enable the Islamic rules of succession to be avoided by the language of the waqf. Thus Habibullah states:
> [is it not] a fact that the Act has been mainly used to deprive the daughter or some other legal heirs of a deceased Muslim, who were entitled to receive shares under Mohammedan law.[16]

Be that as it may, as we shall see, not all of the Hanafi law was restored by the Act. Section 3 of the Act states:
> It shall be lawful for any person professing the Musalman faith to create a Wakf which in all other respects is in accordance with the provisions of Musalman law, for the following among other purposes:-
> (a) for the maintenance and support, wholly or partially of his family children or descendants, and
> (b) where the person creating a Wakf is a Hanafi Musalman, also for his own maintenance and support during his life-time and for the payment of his debts out of the rents and profits of the property dedicated:
> Provided that the ultimate benefit is in such cases expressly or impliedly reserved for the poor or for any other purpose recognized by the Musalman law as a religious, pious or charitable purpose of a

---

[15] The reference in the speech to Ameer Ali J is to his judgment in *Bikani Mia v. Shuk Lal Poddar*. 1893 ILR 20 Cal 116.

[16] "The Law of Waqfs", Calcutta, 1976 at p. vii.

permanent character.

Three important points need to be made about this section.

(1) The ultimate benefit has to be reserved, either expressly or impliedly, for the poor or for any other purpose of a religious, pious or charitable nature. The view of Abu Yusuf is accepted, therefore, that the benefit can be impliedly reserved.

(2) The immediate purpose is for "maintenance and support". A reservation for members of the family *absolutely* is not valid as a waqf.[17] This restrictive interpretation of section 3 has not been followed in Allahabad on the basis that the *entire* income of the waqf property may be reserved for maintenance and support of the beneficiaries.[18]

(3) A line of Indian cases has considered the problem of the definition of "family". In *Ismail Haji Arat v. Umar Abdulla*,[19] it was held that a nephew who resided in the settlor's house could be considered to be within the term "family" so long as that person was dependent on the settlor. A "stranger", however, is not a member of the family within Section 3(a) of the Act. This restriction, of course, is contrary to the Hanafi law. In *Mohammad Afzal v. Din Mohammad*,[20] it was held that "kindred" also does not come within the definition of family. In contrast to this case, however, the Madras and Allahabad courts have taken a more liberal and generous interpretation.[21] The case law in India and Pakistan is confusing, and indeed it is difficult to lay down any guidelines with real certainty. In general, Madras and Allahabad have adopted a flexible approach; whereas other courts have been more restrictive.[22]

Under Section 3(b) a Hanafi is permitted to reserve the income of the property for his own maintenance and support. It must be remembered,

---

[17] *Abdul Karim Adenwalla v. Rahimabai* 1946 33 AIR Bom 342.

[18] *Mohammad Sabir v. Tahir Ali*, 1957 AIR All 94.

[19] 1942 ILR Bom 441.

[20] 1946 ILR 27 Lah 300.

[21] See for instance *Muhammad Azam Khan v. Hamid Shah*, 1946 ILR All 575, and *Asha Bibi v. Nabissa Sahib*, AIR 1957 Mad 583.

[22] See *Abdul Fazal v. S.Sayeeda Khatun*, 1963 PLD Dacca 343 where the expression "heir of the children" was used in a waqfnama. It was held that such an expression would include persons who are not members of the family, and thus the waqf was invalid.

however, that he is not permitted to reserve the property for himself absolutely. Under the Shi'i law, the waqif has no power to reserve the income for his own use, and Section 3(b) only applies to Hanafis.[23]

Section 4, in explaining Section 3, expressly repeals the *Abul Fata* decision. Section 4 states:

> No such Wakf shall be deemed to be invalid merely because the benefit reserved therein for the poor or other religious, pious or charitable purpose of a permanent nature is postponed until after the extinction of the family, children or descendants of the person creating the Wakf.

Section 5 of the Act deserves a mention. "Nothing in this Act shall affect any custom or usage whether local or prevalent among Musalmans of any particular class or sect." The application of section 5 is restricted by the Shariat Act (1937) section 2[24] to cases of waqfs to charities, charitable institutions, and charitable and religious endowments. Family waqfs are governed by Hanafi law as contained in the Wakf Act.

Finally, Section 2(i) defines waqf as "the permanent dedication by a person professing the Musalman faith of any property for any purpose recognised by the Musalman law as religious, pious or charitable". This definition, of course, throws us back on to the old texts for what is recognised as religious, pious or charitable – examples can be given such as money for Haj, money for the relief of poverty, for a school, for a mosque, for public purposes, etc.

9.2.2.1 An illustrative case

A Pakistan Supreme Court decision, *Ghulam Shabbir v. Mst. Nur Begum*[25] will serve to illustrate how the Act works in practice. The dispute in this case related to a house and three shops in Multan, Pakistan. On 10 May 1939, Haji Faiz Bakhsh executed a deed transferring a one-eighth share of the property in favour of Bakht Ilahi, wife of his son Hussain Bakhsh in lieu of a dower. On 30 November 1948, he registered a waqfnama with respect to the residue of the property, appointing himself as the mutawali and his brother-in-law (Abdul Ghafar) as his successor. He died in April 1949, leaving surviving him a son (Hussain), a widow (Hayat) and a daughter (Gulzar). After his death, Hussain started to "intermingle" with the property, and indeed he sold one-third of the property to a third party. The dispute in this case was between the third party and the mutawali as to the ownership of the property. Thus the court had to

---

[23] *Shahban Mohib v. Hemraj Raghavji,* 1942 AIR Sind 14.
[24] See above Chapter 2.
[25] 1977 PLD SC 75.

Gift and Waqf

determine whether there had been a valid waqf. It was held, first, that the waqf was not pronounced in death sickness. The Supreme Court then examined in detail the waqfnama. The waqif had declared that he had voluntarily decided to create the waqf. He had emphasised that henceforth he would have no right to sell the property and that he and his descendants would have only the right to the enjoyment of the income of the property and to reside therein. He stated that *he* would be the first mutawali and that he would feed himself and his family from its income. He stated also that his son (Hussain) would have no right to any of the money from the property except for 3 rupees a day as his wages.

The final paragraph of the waqfnama said:

> If, God forbid, his family became extinct then half of the income of the factory will be given to the orphanage and the other half to the school attached to the mosque.

It was obvious, of course, that the dominant, indeed the only, object with which the waqif executed the deed was to preserve and protect the property from the clutches of a son who, in his opinion, was reckless. The Supreme Court held that the waqf could not be struck down merely on the ground that it had as its object the exclusion of one who was profligate. There was one other difficulty preventing recognition for the waqf, namely that neither the orphanage nor the school attached to the mosque existed. Notwithstanding, the Supreme Court held that such a problem is overcome by applying a *cypres* rule.[26] The waqf, therefore, was valid, and as the son had no title in the property, the third party took no interest and lost his case.

So far as India is concerned, consideration needs to be given, in brief, to the taxation and land legislation which reduces significantly the importance of the Wakf Act. For instance, in *Ahmed G.H.Ariff v. Wealth Tax Commissioner*,[27] it was held that where a Hanafi creates a family waqf of properties, the right to receive the income of these properties is an asset within the meaning of section 2(c) of the Wealth Tax Act 1957, and is therefore subject to tax legislation. Likewise, the management of waqf property is controlled in India both by central and local legislation; namely the Waqf Act 1954 as amended by the Waqf (Amendment) Act 1984. This act is a central Act which applies across India except in Uttar Pradesh, Bihar, West Bengal, and Jammu and Kashmir where there is local legislation.

---

[26] The charitable basis of the waqf can be satisfied by ensuring that the ultimate benefit be for an object similar to the objects which had failed.

[27] AIR 1971 S.C. 1691.

Gift and Waqf

9.2.3 Waqf in East Africa

It is of considerable interest to discuss the development of waqf in East Africa, especially in Kenya. The British courts in the days before independence regarded themselves as bound by the case law of India prior to the Musalman Wakf Validating Act, thus following the discredited Privy Council decision of *Abul Fata*. The Privy Council itself followed its own previous decision in *Fatima binti Mohamed's* case.[28] Sir Norman Anderson describes this case as one of the "most regrettable judgements their Lordships have ever delivered". The criticism of the Privy Council decision was immediate, and an Ordinance was enacted which resulted in a statutory acceptance, with some improvements, of the legal position of India.

Section 4 of Wakf Commissioners Ordinance (1951) states that a waqf will be recognised if it is "for the maintenance and support, either wholly or partly, of any person *including* the family, children, descendants or kindred of the maker". The effect of Section 4, therefore, is to ensure that a waqf dhurri can be established in favour of a stranger – this, of course, returns to the classical position. The second improvement on the 1913 Act is contained in the proviso to Section 3 of the Ordinance. Section 3 lays down that the waqf dhurri will be valid provided that the ultimate benefit is reserved for a religious, pious or charitable purpose of a permanent nature. The proviso states:

> Provided that the absence of any reservation of the ultimate benefit in property the subject of a Wakf for a religious, pious or charitable purpose of a permanent character shall not invalidate the Wakf if the personal law of the maker of the Wakf does not require such a reservation.

The proviso was inserted in order to save the Shafi'i law on this point, for classical Shafi'i law provides that an express or even an implied reservation is not required. If the beneficiaries are exhausted, the proceeds of the waqf are to be diverted for the benefit of the poor generally, in the absence of any relatives of the waqif.

The East African courts, however, have ignored this proviso. In a Shafi'i case, the court held a settlement void because no reservation of the ultimate benefit for a religious, pious or charitable purpose of a charitable nature was made.[29]

The East African Ordinance, however, copied the 1913 Indian legislation in defining a waqf dhurri as one where the settlement is made for the

---

[28] *Fatima binti Mohamed v. Mohamed bin Salim*, 1952 AC 1.

[29] *Abdulla bin Said bin Hassan v. Halima binti Said bin Hassan*, 1957 EA LR 688.

"maintenance and support" of either the family or, if a Hanafi, himself. The Bombay court in *Abdul Karim Adenwalla v. Rahimabai*[30] had interpreted these words restrictively. Thus the waqif, if a Hanafi, cannot reserve for his absolute use during his lifetime the entire income of the waqf under Section 3(b). Notwithstanding that this case has not been universally followed in India,[31] *Abdul Karim* was applied in the East African context in *Sheika v. Halima*.[32] The terms of the settlement were construed in this case as being equivalent to an attempt to create an absolute gift, and not restricted to maintenance and support. It was not a waqf, thus it could be only valid, if at all, as a gift. It infringed, however, the law of perpetuities, and therefore the whole settlement was void. The case was heavily attacked, and in 1964 an amendment was introduced which had the effect of overruling *Sheika v. Halima* and adopting the principle in *Mohd Sabir v. Tahir Ali*.

A new section 4 is enacted. It is a valid waqf if it is:

(a) for the benefit, either wholly or partly of the family, children, descendants or kindred of the maker or of any other persons;

(b) if the maker of the wakf is an Ibadi or Hanafi Mohammedan for his own benefit during his lifetime.

Thus, the restrictions imposed initially by the 1913 Indian Act, and still apparent in the Indian subcontinent, that the waqf dhurri has to be confined to the "maintenance and support" of the beneficiaries have been abolished in Kenya by virtue of the 1964 Amendment.

9.2.4 Modern Reforms

It is perhaps ironic that whilst Kenya was busy dismantling the restrictive interpretations of waqf by reverting to the classical Hanafi position, other countries, where there is a Muslim majority, in contrast were indulging in attempts to bring waqf property back on to the commercial market and prevent further waqf from being created. Thus, in Egypt, an Act of 1946 provided that a waqf khayri may be either perpetual or temporary at the option of the waqif. More important, the *perpetual* waqf dhurri was abolished, although a waqif could still establish a waqf dhurri so long as it was restricted to two generations or to a period not exceeding sixty years from the date of the waqif's death. In addition, the waqif was given the power to revoke the waqf

---

[30] 1946 33 AIR Bom 342. See before.
[31] *Mohammad Sabir v. Tahir Ali*, 1957 AIR All 94.
[32] 1958 EA LR 623.

either wholly or in part, in addition to the right to alter conditions of the waqf. In 1952 the next step was taken, in the context of more general land reform, to abolish waqf dhurri completely. In Egypt today, only waqf khayri is permitted. In the Lebanon in 1947, the Egyptian law of 1946 was followed. After two generations, the waqf dhurri property reverts to the waqif or to his heirs. Moveable property and shares of stock are made the possible subject of waqf. In Syria in 1949, the creation of further waqf dhurri was prohibited, and existing waqf dhurri property was liquidated. *All* waqf ownership was expropriated in Tunisia in 1957. Major reforms in the administration of waqf property have been introduced in many Muslim countries, in particular in Libya, Algeria and Kuwait.

In Pakistan and Bangladesh, waqf is now made subject to limitation of upper limits of land holdings. More important, in Pakistan, changes were made in West Pakistan by the 1959 West Pakistan Land Reform Regulations. This regulation provided that all agricultural land included in a waqf dhurri should forthwith, if the waqif were alive, vested in him. If the waqif were dead, the waqf would be divided between the heirs, and others, nominated by the government. Since 1959, therefore, it has been impossible in Pakistan to make agricultural land the subject of a waqf dhurri. The waqf khayri is now controlled by a central administration of waqfs under the West Pakistan Waqf Properties Ordinance (1959).

In India, however, the waqf dhurri is still a powerful force so long as it complies with the 1913 Act. It is true that the waqf legislation previously referred to, together with the constant attempts by the courts to restrict the family waqf by making the waqf subject to tax laws and the like, places important restraints on the impact of waqf property on the economic life in India.[33] Nonetheless it is often used as a legal device (a hiyal) to overcome the particular rules of succession; it is indeed for this reason that attempts in India to reform the waqf dhurri have failed.

---

[33] See for instance *Fazlul Rabbi v. State of West Bengal* AIR 1965 S.C. 1722.

10. Conflict of Laws

10.1 Introduction

This chapter is concerned with the problems of conflicting legal systems. Sometimes, problems arise when a court has to decide whether to apply the Muslim law or possibly some other legal system which may be appropriate to the case. Courts on the subcontinent are used to dealing with conflicts, for instance, between Muslim law and Hindu law. We refer to these conflict issues as "interpersonal conflict of laws". Sometimes, the conflict is between the personal law, that is Muslim law, and the law of some other country, possibly the law applied in England. We refer to these problems as "international conflict of laws". Again, judges in the subcontinent come across these issues. Increasingly, judges in England also have had to examine these issues in the context of the large influx of Muslims from India, Pakistan, Bangladesh and elsewhere. Their marriages and their divorces in particular have been the subject of judicial hearings.

It is necessary at the outset to say a few words by way of introduction to these questions. "International conflict of laws" has a long history. The "international conflict of laws" or private international law developed as a separate branch of legal science in the eleventh and twelfth centuries with the advent of feudalism in northern Europe and of the Italian city states south of the Alps. The modern notion of state sovereignty, stemming from the Reformation in Europe and the disintegration of the universality of the Church, gave an added impetus to the development of legal norms to organise and position sovereign municipal legal systems. Rules were developed to control the application by the judiciary within the municipal system of alien systems of law.

"Interpersonal conflict of laws" has an even older pedigree, and was known to the ancient Greeks and to the Romans. As a separate branch of legal science, it survived the fundamental changes in society of the early middle ages. What is a personal law? One answer is to say that it is a law which links an individual with a particular legal regime, be it race, religion, tribe, nationality, domicile or residence. The legal regimes, therefore, are racial, religious, tribal, or in the case of nationality, domicile and residence, those of the laws of a sovereign nation state. We can be even more precise and say that conflicts within the laws of the first three groups can be classified as interpersonal conflict of laws within one class. In contrast, conflicts between the law of the first class (race, religion or tribe) and the laws of the second class (that is nationality, domicile or residence) can be classified as interpersonal conflict of laws between two classes. Such distinctions however need not concern us in a book of this kind.[1] It needs to be emphasised however that the second category contains problems of interpersonal conflict of laws. Thus, despite the apparent territorial connection, we are not concerned with international conflict of laws proper, but with interpersonal conflict of laws. To use another expression, the interpersonal conflict of laws between two classes are nonetheless "internally mixed" questions as opposed to "internationally mixed" questions.

Problems of interpersonal conflict of laws between two classes have already been considered in this book in Chapter 2.[2] Problems of interpersonal conflict of laws within one class have arisen in connection with the discussion of the rules of apostasy and conversion and the effects of these rules on a pre-existing marriage. These matters have also been mentioned briefly in Chapter 2, but they perhaps require further consideration at this stage, with particular attention again on the subcontinent.

10.2 Interpersonal Conflicts within One Class

The issue arises on the subcontinent because the operation of a personal system of law creates a situation where advantage can sometimes be taken of a more sympathetic legal solution by one rather than another personal law. In particular, there may be a temptation for an unhappily married spouse to change his or her religious persuasion and thus invoke certain procedures for bringing the union to an end which may not have been available if the *status quo* had been maintained. Although the discussion is confined to cases involving Muslims, it is as well to remember that interpersonal conflict situations of a similar kind arise whenever two persons to a marriage allege that they are governed by different personal laws. It is as well to point out at the outset of the discussion that the problems are avoided in India if there has been a marriage which is solemnised under the terms of the Special Marriage Act or there has been a marriage in religious form which is subsequently registered under the Act.

---

[1] See D.Pearl *Interpersonal Conflict of Laws in India, Pakistan and Bangladesh.* London and Bombay, 1981.

[2] See before.

Conflict of Laws

10.2.1 Traditional Law: Apostasy

The Shari'a views apostacy from Islam as a treasonable offence punishable by death in the case of the male and imprisonment in the case of the female.[3] The male-apostate is permitted a three-day clemency. During this period he is given every opportunity to return to Islam. The interesting questions for us relate to the effect apostacy has on an existing marriage. All four Sunni schools, together with the Shi'i sects, are agreed that an apostasy by either spouse brings the marriage to an end. There are differences relating to the dower. The Hanafi law, as applied on the subcontinent, draws a distinction between a marriage which has been consummated and a marriage which has not been consummated. In the latter case, the wife is entitled only to half her dower, and if she herself apostasises, the marriage not being consummated, she is not entitled to any dower at all. In contrast, if the marriage has been consummated, then the apostacy does not affect the dower obligation. Indeed, the wife is entitled to a full dower in this situation even if she is the apostate.[4]

One important Indian jurist took a different view to the consensus which acknowledged the termination of a Muslim marriage when either of the parties became an apostate regardless of the circumstances. Ameer Ali argued for the continued validity of a marriage in one situation of apostacy. It was his view that if the wife converted to one of the revealed religions then the marriage celebrated in Muslim form would not be affected. He said:

> The jurists of Balkh and Samarkand...have laid down that when a woman abjurs Islam for a scriptural or revealed religion like Judaism or Christianity,*her renunciation of the faith does not dissolve the marriage*. Their arguments in support of their contention are ... two-fold. In the first place, they say that as a marriage between a Moslem and a Scripturalist woman (kitabia) is lawful under the Mussulman law the adoption of a revealed religion by a Moslem woman cannot affect the *status* of marriage. In the second place, they contend that when the circumstances of the age are such that a woman abandoning Islam can neither be imprisoned nor constrained to re-enter the fold of the Faith, to hold that abjuration of the Islamic Faith dissolves the marriage-tie would further the very object for which she apostasises – *viz* to

---

[3] Qur'an Sura III 80, Sura IV 90, Sura V 59, Sura XVI 108. See S.M.Zwemer, *The Law of Apostacy in Islam*. London, 1924.

[4] *Md Ebrahim v. Ma Ma* AIR 1939 Rangoon 28; *Sarwar Yar Khan v. Jawahar Devi* 1964 1 Andh WR 60. The decision was taken somewhat reluctantly in the second case.

Conflict of Laws

"release herself of the burden of marriage".[5]
Ameer Ali agreed with this view. The Indian courts however rejected his argument. In *Amin Beg v. Saman*[6] Stanley CJ said:

> We find ourselves unable to disregard the authorities in support of the view taken by the courts below and depart from the course of decision hitherto prevailing. However weighty be the view expressed by Mr Ameer Ali we do not think that we should be justified in doing so.[7]

The law was changed, however, with regard to female apostasies by Section 4 of the Dissolution of Muslim Marriages Act 1939 (Act VIII of 1939).

> The renunciation of Islam by a married Muslim woman or her conversion to a faith other than Islam shall not by itself operate to dissolve her marriage:

> Provided that after such renunciation, or conversion, the woman shall be entitled to obtain a decree for the dissolution of her marriage on any grounds mentioned in s.2:

> Provided further that the provisions of this section shall not apply to a woman converted to Islam from some other faith who re-embraces her former faith.

It will be apparent that the traditional law will still be relevant when a wife, originally converted to Islam, reverts to her former faith. Section 4 is law in India, Pakistan and Bangladesh. The traditional law, of course, is also still relevant when the husband renounces Islam.

A case from Pakistan which illustrates the operation of the law is *Zainab Bibi v. Bilquis Bibi*.[8] The case concerned a succession dispute. The respondent alleged that Zainab Bibi was not the widow of the deceased because she had been married to a person called Allahdawaya, and that this marriage had not been dissolved. The appellant, Zainab Bibi, admitted that she had indeed been

---

[5] S.Ameer Ali *Mohammedan Law* (Lahore ed. 1976) p. 443.
[6] 1911 ILR 33 All 90.
[7] 1911 ILR 33 All 90 at 92,93. See also *[Mst] Resham Bibi v. Khuda Bakhsh* 1938 ILR 19 Lah 277; *Abdul Ghani v. Azizul Huq* 1912 39 Cal 409.
[8] 1981 PLD SC 56.

married to this man but that in 1924 she had become a Christian and that therefore her marriage was automatically dissolved by operation of the law. She had subsequently re-embraced Islam and married the deceased, a Muslim. The Supreme Court held that her apostacy did indeed dissolve the earlier marriage. Thus the appellant succeeded to the property of the deceased, together with her children by the deceased, as the lawful heirs under Muslim law.

In the classical systems of Islamic law, the apostate from Islam loses his or her right to inherit on a intestacy of a Muslim relative. This rule was abandoned in India, as a whole, as early as 1850 when the Caste Disabilities Removal Act (Act XXI of 1850) was passed. Section 1 reads:

> So much of any law or usage now in force within the territories subject to the government of the East India Company as inflicts on any person forfeiture of rights or property or may be held in any way to impair or affect any right of inheritance, by reason of his or her renouncing, or having been excluded from the communion of any religion or being deprived of caste, shall cease to be enforced as law in the Courts of the East India Company, and in the Courts established by Royal Charter within the said territories.[9]

In Pakistan, as we have already had occasion to remark, this section has been repealed by a 1963 amendment. The Islamic law applies with all its force in Pakistan, and non-Muslim heirs, including those who have left Islam for some other faith, are excluded from any rights to participate in the division of the estate of their Muslim relatives.

10.2.2 Traditional Law: Conversion

The Muslim law regarding conversion to Islam as understood in India can be stated by the following propositions. First, if it is the husband alone who converts to Islam, then if the wife is a Kitabiyya (a Christian or a Jew), any existing marriage continues and is recognised by the Muslim law as a valid marriage. Secondly, if the wife is a polytheist, as Muslim law is not the law of the land, the marriage is dissolved without the intervention of any judicial

---

[9] Act XXI of 1850 extended the principles of section 9 Regulation VII of 1832 of the Bengal Code throughout the territories subject to the Government of the East India Company.

body after the lapse of a period of three months.[10] Thirdly, if the wife converts to Islam then the same rules are applied except that no allowance is made for the continued validity of the marriage in a case where the husband is either a Jew or a Christian. These rules of substantive Muslim law, at any rate as understood in India and Pakistan, have been the focus of a number of cases decided by the courts in the subcontinent.

Where a non-Muslim converts to Islam, a complete change occurs in his personal status with regard to inheritance, for according to Muslim law, the non-Muslim relations will not be entitled to his estate on his death.[11] This situation of course must be read subject to the Special Marriage Act (1954 as amended) so far as India is concerned.

10.2.3 Case Law and Statutes: Apostacy

A common situation in India before 1939 was for a Muslim woman to convert to Hinduism and then rely on her own personal law before her conversion when seeking a declaration from the court that the marriage celebrated in Muslim form had been *ipso facto* dissolved. Quite often, the husband would attempt to pre-empt such an application, by himself applying to court for an order for restitution of conjugal rights. Amongst the arguments heard from the husband would be that, according to Hindu law (which now governed the status of the wife), the marriage would not be dissolved. In such a situation the court was faced with an important conflict of laws problem; namely to apply the law of the celebration of the marriage (Muslim law), or the personal laws of the parties at the time of the marriage (Muslim law), or the personal laws of the applicant or of the defendant at the time of the suit (Hindu law or Muslim law). Before 1939, there was no statute dealing directly with the problem and the court was forced to look to general statutory and executive directives. The Dissolution of Muslim Marriages Act (1939) which was enacted at first for what were known as "Part A States" directs, as we have seen, that irrespective of the claim before the court, the conversion of a Muslim wife to another religion (so long as it is not a reversion to a previously held faith) or her renunciation of Islam does not affect the status of

---

[10] In Islamic political theory, if the conversion takes place in an Islamic state (dar al-Islam) and the other spouse is also resident there, then the Muslim qadi offers Islam to the polytheistic partner. After a threefold refusal, the judge separates the parties.

[11] See *Mitar Sen Singh v. Maqbul Hasan Khan* 1930 57 LR IA 313; *K.P.Chandrasekharappa v. Govt of Mysore* AIR 1955 Mys 26; *Farooq Leivers v. Adelaide Bridget Mary* 1958 PLD (WP) Lah 431; *Nur Ali v. Malka Sultana* 1961 PLD Lah 431.

Conflict of Laws

the existing marriage. Indeed, the wife is permitted to petition for divorce on any of the grounds laid down in Section 2 of the Act. The husband, presumably, can divorce his wife by talaq.[12] In this one situation, namely that of an apostacy from Islam by the wife, the Dissolution of Muslim Marriages Act lays down an interpersonal conflict of law rule to the effect that on an apostasy by the wife, the law governing a dispute to the marriage is Muslim law. The act does not specify, however, whether this law is to be applied as the *lex celebrationis* or as the *lex personae* of the parties at the time of the marriage. Having ascertained the statutory choice of law rule from the Dissolution of Muslim Marriages Act, the judge then applies the substantive laws of Muslim law including the reforms of the law contained in the Act.[13]

10.2.4 Case Law and Statutes: Conversion

The two decisions of interest which deal with this question are *Robaba Khanum v. Khodadad Boman Irani* and *Rakeya Bibi v. Anil Kumar Mukherji*.[14] These and other cases dealing with conversion are discussed in Chapter 2,[15] but it would be appropriate to consider in this context the case of *Syed Faiz Ali Shah v. Ghulam Abbas Shah*[16] which produced a different result to the cases discussed earlier.

Baqar Shah had married two wives – Said Begum and Madad Bi. Said Begum was a Muslim and Madad Bi was a Hindu who had embraced Islam before her marriage to Baqar Shah. At the time of Madad Bi's marriage with Baqar Shah, she was married by Hindu law to a man who was still alive. After Baqar Shah's death, litigation commenced between his two sons from his two wives over the property left by him. The plaintiffs, the sons of Baqar Shah by Madad Bi, could only inherit if they could show that they were the

---

[12] *Jatoi v. Jatoi* 1967 PLD SC 580.

[13] A Divisional Bench of the Andhra High Court has held that Section 4 of the Dissolution of Muslim Marriages Act has *no* retrospective effect. (*Sarwar Yar Khan v. Jawahar Devi* 1964 1 Andh WR 60). The preamble to the Act, however, suggests that this case is wrong. It states that Section 4 was created in order to "remove doubts as to the effect of the renunciation of Islam by a married Muslim woman on her marriage tie". See also *Rashid Bibi v. Tufail Muhammad* 1941 AIR Lah 292; *Rabian Bibi v. Ghulam Ali* 1941 AIR Lah 292; *Zainab Bibi v. Bilquis Bibi* 1981 PLD SC 56; See also *Fazal Begum v. Hakim Ali* 1941 AIR Lah 22 to the contrary.

[14] ILR 1948 Bom 233; ILR 1948 2 Cal 119. See also the case of *Noor Jehan Begum v. Eugene Tiscenko* 1942 ILR 2 Cal 165.

[15] See before.

[16] 1952 PLD AJK 32.

Conflict of Laws

legitimate sons of Baqar Shah. The judge applied the personal law of the children, Muslim law, to determine their legitimacy, and it is therefore distinguishable from the other cases under discussion. The judge commented *obiter* that the Muslim law relating to conversion and the effect of the conversion on an existing marriage, if directly in issue, would have been recognised by the court.

10.3 International Conflict of Laws

Problems of International Conflict of Laws are often posed in courts that are faced with questions of the recognition of a divorce or a marriage or in the case of inheritance disputes. These questions are, to a large extent, outside the scope of the book but it is nonetheless necessary to make one or two observations. An interesting case which illustrates the problem is *Yusuf Abbas v. Ismat Mustafa*.[17]

Table 58
Yusuf Abbas v. Ismat Mustafa

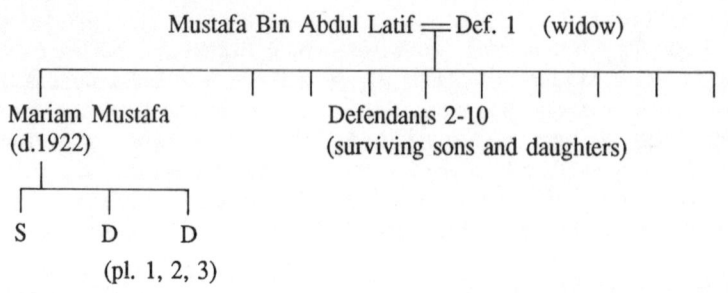

```
              Mustafa Bin Abdul Latif == Def. 1  (widow)
         ┌─────────────┬──┬──┬──┬──┬──┬──┬──┬──┐
   Mariam Mustafa              Defendants 2-10
   (d.1922)                    (surviving sons and daughters)
   ┌────┬────┐
   S    D    D
        (pl. 1, 2, 3)
```

The case arose out of a claim by the plaintiffs for shares in the assets of Mustafa Bin Abdul Latif under the provisions of the Muslim Family Laws Ordinance 1961.[18] The defendants contested the plaintiffs' action because they

---

[17] 1968 PLD Karach 480.

[18] As we know, Section 4 of the Ordinance substantially amends Muslim law in Pakistan by providing the orphaned grandchild with a share of the grandfather's estate equivalent to the share the parent would have received if alive. The section reads as follows: "In the event of the death of any son or daughter of the propositus before the opening of succession, the children of such son or daughter, if any, living at the time the succession opens, shall per stirpes receive a share equivalent to the share which such son or daughter, as the case may be, would have received if alive."

denied that the plaintiffs were heirs of Mustafa Bin Abdul Latif, and, in the alternative, they contended that even if the plaintiffs were heirs of the deceased, then the Ordinance was not applicable to property the subject of the dispute.

The deceased died in 1964 seized of both moveable and immoveable property situated both in Pakistan and in the Gulf. At the time of his death, he was a national of and domiciled in Pakistan. On the preliminary point of jurisdiction, Noorul Arfin J held that the Court had jurisdiction under Section 20 of the Civil Procedure Code (1908) to entertain an action with respect to properties situated outside Pakistan. The Judge then went on to consider the principles which should apply to the succession of the deceased's estate situated within the foreign territory. He held that Muslim law, the personal law of the propositus, does not recognise any principle of scission between moveables and immoveables for the purposes of succession. He then went on to make the following proposition:

> [I]f a Muslim dies domiciled in England, the courts in this country [i.e. Pakistan] will apply, not *lex domicilii* but his personal law, that is Islamic law as administered in this country, to succession to his moveables in Pakistan. Even the will with regard to these moveables, though valid in English law, will be recognised by the courts of this country only so far as it is consistent with Islamic law.[19]

This suggestion, representing as it does the concept of the universality of Islamic law to the Muslims wherever they may be,[20] raises important issues for the English lawyer in relation to the immigrant community of that country. There seems no doubt, however, that for Pakistan both the moveable and the immoveable property of a Muslim deceased devolves on the heirs in accordance with the Muslim personal law of the deceased and no regard is paid either to the law of his domicile or to the *lex situs*. Questions of construction arising out of the will or the intestacy may also be governed by the personal law.

Section 1(2) of the Muslim Family Laws Ordinance lays down that the provisions of the Ordinance "extend to the whole of Pakistan, and applies to

---

[19] 1968 PLD Karachi 480 at p. 502.

[20] See S.Ameer Ali *Mohammedan Law* (Lahore ed. 1976) at p 180: "Mussulman law generally is a personal law; that is, its incidents remain attached to the individual Mussulman whatever the domicile, so long as [he] continues even outwardly faithful to the Islamic faith."
"A Musulman", says the Kifaya, "is absolutely subject to the laws of Islam, whatever the domicile", cited by Noorul Arfin J at p 502.

all Muslim citizens, wherever they may be". Noorul Arfin J laid emphasis on the phrase "wherever they may be":

> If a Muslim citizen of Pakistan dies domiciled in a foreign country, the law of his domicile cannot, by the force of the words used in s.1(2) and s.4 of the Ordinance, be applied to his estate in Pakistan. On the same principle, if a Muslim citizen dies domiciled in Pakistan and leaves property, both immoveables and moveables, in foreign jurisdiction, the succession to his estate will be according to the rule of Islamic law as modified by s.4 of the Ordinance. The Courts in Pakistan, in matters of succession to the estate of a Muslim citizen, can apply only his personal law, irrespective of the rules of the lex domicilii or situs.[21]

In the result, the Judge held that the plaintiffs had a cause of action in the suit and that the defendants were liable to render account to the plaintiffs for the latter's share in the estate of Mustafa Bin Abdul Latif. As the deceased was held to be domiciled in Pakistan at the time of his death the Judge's comments are *obiter*. Nevertheless, the only limitation which the Judge was prepared to accept in a case where the deceased was not so domiciled in Pakistan was the effectiveness of the judgment of the Pakistan court.

10.3.1 The Talaq

Yusuf Abbas has echoes in the position in Pakistan of the capacity of a Pakistan Muslim to invoke the procedure of the 1961 Ordinance with respect to talaq. The leading case in this context is *Jatoi v. Jatoi*.[22] In May 1959, a marriage was solemnised in a register office in London between a Christian girl, Marina, domiciled in Spain and Nuruddin Jatoi, a Muslim Bar student domiciled in Pakistan. The marriage was not a happy one and within the year the husband returned to Pakistan. The wife and their newly born son remained in London. In March 1961 Jatoi married a second wife, a Swedish girl, who had converted to Islam. The marriage ceremony was celebrated in a mosque in Karachi in Muslim form. Meanwhile, Marina applied to the Magistrates' Court in London for maintenance under the Matrimonial Proceedings (Magistrates' Courts) Act (1960).[23] Marina obtained a maintenance order which was then registered in Pakistan and confirmed by the Karachi District

---

[21] 1968 PLD Karachi 480 at p. 503.

[22] 1967 PLD SC 580.

[23] This Act has now been replaced by the Domestic Proceedings (Magistrates Courts) Act 1978.

Magistrates Court.[24] The husband failed to remit any maintenance to the wife. In 1965, she travelled to Karachi with the intention of seeking enforcement. Whilst she was in the city, Jatoi repudiated his wife by talaq, and sent a copy of the talaq to the chairman of his local Union Council as required by the Muslim Family Laws Ordinance.[25] After the requisite 90 days, Mr Jatoi applied to the District Court for rescission of the English maintenance order on the ground that he was no longer married to Marina. As we know, according to Muslim law the husband is not obliged to maintain an ex-wife beyond a three month period (known as the 'idda period) after the talaq has become irrevocable. The District Court refused to rescind the registration of the order, but on appeal to the High Court of West Pakistan the ruling of the lower court was reversed. Marina appealed to the Supreme Court of Pakistan. Her appeal was rejected by the majority (Yaqub Ali J dissenting). The majority took the view that the talaq was effective to dissolve the marriage between Marina and Jatoi. Pakistan law was applied as the *lex domicilii:*

> Under the rules of Private International law, the *lex loci celebrationis* as such has nothing to do with the question of divorce which is a matter solely for the law that happens to be the *lex domicilii* of the parties, at the time of the suit. This may well be different from the law that governed the solemnisation of the marriage.[26]

Faced with an internal conflict between the Muslim law (the personal law of the husband) and the provisions of the Indian Divorce Act (1869) (the marriage was celebrated under the British Marriage Act, and the wife was at all times a Christian), the majority chose to apply the Muslim law. There is no provision in the Divorce Act (1869) or the Christian Marriage Act (1872), say the majority which "in express terms, prevents a Muslim husband of a Christian woman, from having resort to his own personal law for the purpose of the dissolution of marriage." S.A.Rahman J said:[27]

> If a Muslim husband is married to a Christian woman *in a form recognised by Muslim law,* or to a non-citizen Muslim woman, there is no reason why the provisions of s.7 of this Ordinance would not apply.

---

[24] Maintenance Orders (Facilities for Enforcement) Act 1920. The Maintenance Orders Enforcement Act (1921) is in force in Pakistan.

[25] See before.

[26] *Jatoi v. Jatoi* 1967 PLD SC 580 per S.A.Rahman J at p. 599. See also the English cases; *Har Shefi v. Har Shefi* [1953] 2 All ER 373; *Qureshi v. Qureshi* [1972] Fam 173.

[27] at p. 592.

The majority took the view that the Jatoi marriage which was celebrated in a London register office would be recognised in Muslim law because the declaration and the acceptance by the couple at one and the same meeting in the presence of witnesses complied with the minimum formalities under Hanafi Muslim law.

Yaqub Ali J, dissenting, interpreted the relevant statutes in a positive way. He rejected the argument accepted by the majority that section 2 of the Divorce Act 1869 is an enabling Act. Section 2 reads:

> Nothing hereinafter contained shall authorize any court to grant any relief under this Act except where the petitioner or the respondent professes the Christian religion.[28]

The dissenting Judge stated:

> The language has therefore to be construed in the sense that if one of the parties to the marriage professed the Christian faith the marriage can be dissolved only by a decree of the court under the Act and not otherwise. A contrary view would lead to anomalous results such as, if a Muslim husband petitions to court under the Divorce Act for dissolution of his marriage with a Christian wife, he shall have to prove to the satisfaction of the court that she has been guilty of adultery and shall also be obliged to pay her alimony *pendente lite* and costs of the suit as well as permanent alimony on obtaining a decree for dissolution. On the contrary if the Muslim law applies he can avoid all these obligations by pronouncing talaq and bringing to an end the marriage by his unilateral act. No husband would, therefore, ever make resort to a court for dissolution of marriage.[29]

The dissenting Judge also rejected the argument advanced by the majority that

---

[28] This is the amended version of the Act. As originally enacted, the Divorce Act gave the court jurisdiction only where the petitioner professed the Christian religion. The words "or respondent" were added by Section 2 of Act XXX of 1927.
In Bangladesh, Ordinance XVIII of 1969 has altered the position so far as that territory is concerned. A proviso added to Section 2 of the Divorce Act states: "Provided that nothing in this paragraph shall be deemed to authorise any Court to grant relief under this Act where the petitioner or the respondent is a Muslim."

[29] *Jatoi v. Jatoi* 1967 PLD SC 580 at p. 592.

Conflict of Laws

as there are no specific ceremonies or rites for solemnising a marriage under Muslim law, therefore the register office marriage in England can necessarily be equated with a Muslim ceremony. In the Judge's opinion, the Christian and the Muslim marriage are essentially different types of status, one a voluntary union for life dissolvable only by a judicial decree, and the other a potentially polygamous marriage dissolvable on the unilateral declaration of the husband.

One could argue that the distinction suggested by Yaqub Ali J confuses the concept of a status of marriage with the incidents of that status. The judge may have been on stonger ground if he had simply recognised that an English civil ceremony of marriage possessed attributes within it of a Muslim marriage valid by Muslim law; but that so long as the wife retained her personal law, and so long as she had not married in an outwardly Muslim ceremony, then her vested rights must be protected by the Divorce Act 1969.

Another question can be posed. Supposing Marina had petitioned for a divorce in Pakistan. Presumably, the courts would have assumed jurisdiction under Section 2 of the Divorce Act 1869 rather than the Dissolution of Muslim Marriages Act 1939. Marina was not a "woman married *under* Muslim law".[30] It is slightly inequitable to permit the husband the choice between Muslim law and the Divorce Act, when the wife is denied this choice. The majority decision can only be explained in terms of the public policy of an Islamic state.

The earlier cases, all cited in *Jatoi v. Jatoi*, support the dissenting judgment.[31]

The facts of the first of these cases, *(John Jiban) Chandra Datta v. Abinash Chandra Sen* were as follows. An Indian Christian (Dukhiram) married a Christian girl (Sudakshina) under the Indian Christian Marriage Act. Subsequently, Dukhiram converted to Islam and contracted a second marriage in a mosque with a Muslim woman (Alfatanessa). The Court had to decide whether the second marriage was valid, but in the course of the judgment, Mr Justice Henderson said:

---

[30] The majority state that a register office marriage is *recognised* by Muslim law as a Muslim marriage. Even so, there would appear to be a difference, even by the majority argument, between a marriage *under* Muslim law and a marriage *recognised* by Muslim law as a Muslim marriage. See S.A.Rahman J at p. 602.

[31] *(John Jiban) Chandra Datta v. Abinash Chandra Sen* ILR [1939] 2 Cal 12; *Farooq Leivers v. Adelaide Bridget Mary* 1958 PLD (WP) Lah 431; *Syed Ali Nawaz Gardezi v. Lt.Col.Muhammad Yusuf* 1963 PLD SC 51. See also *Keolapati v. Harnam Singh* 1937 ILR 12 Luck 568; *Budansa Rowther v. Fatma Bi* 1914 26 Mad L.J. 260; *Sainapatti v. Sainapatti* AIR 1932 Lah 116.

219

It might be difficult to say whether Dukhiram could have divorced Sudakshina by talaq.[32]

In *Farooq Leivers v. Adelaide Bridget Mary*,[33] the husband and wife were Christians who had married according to Christian rites. Many years later the husband embraced Islam, asked his wife to join him in his new faith, and on her refusal, purported to divorce his wife by talaq. The suit arose out of an application to the court by the husband seeking a declaration that he was no longer married to his Christian wife. Mr Justice Changez, in the Lahore High Court, refused to grant the husband the declaration for which he sought. The judge said:

> The position that emerges is that on the one hand under the Muslim law, a Christian husband, on his conversion to Islam, is authorised to give Talaq to his Christian wife by pronouncing the formula of Talaq, but on the other hand, the Courts in Pakistan cannot recognise such a Talaq in view of the provisions of the Divorce Act of 1869 and other existing laws.[34]

In view of this conflict, the judge applied the Punjab Laws Act (1872) Section 6 which enabled him to solve the conflict according to the principles of justice, equity and good conscience.[35] According to the application of this principle, the talaq could not be recognised in the Pakistan courts. Mr Justice Yaqub Ali in *Jatoi*, of course, held that he was bound by the substantive law itself which created a statutory choice of law rule, as it were, in Section 2 of the Divorce Act.

In the Pakistan Supreme Court decision, *Syed Ali Nawaz Gardezi v. Lt. Col. Muhammad Yusuf*,[36] Mr Justice Rahman stated that the Christian wife had been fully aware of the position that the marriage celebrated in an English register office could not be dissolved by the Muslim husband's pronouncement of talaq unless she herself converted to Islam.

Reference may also be made to the Ceylonese case *Attorney General for*

---

[32] *(John Jiban) Chandra Datta v. Abinash Chandra Sen* ILR [1939] 2 Cal 12 at p.16.
[33] 1958 PLD (WP) Lah 431.
[34] at p. 447.
[35] See before Chapter 2.
[36] 1963 PLD SC 51. See before.

Conflict of Laws

Ceylon v. Reid[37] where counsel for the appellant-husband admitted that:

> a person who has embraced Islam [cannot] unilaterally succeed in divorcing the former wife by going through the procedures which are recognised in Muslim marriages.

If both parties to a Christian marriage convert to Islam, there is no objection to applying the Muslim law of divorce, and indeed Section 2 of the Divorce Act is couched in such terms that the Divorce Act is no longer available to either of the parties. Section 7 of the Act, however, as amended by Section 2 of the Act of 1912, provides the court with jurisdiction if the facts upon which the claim to relief is founded occurred at a time when both parties were Christians. Otherwise, the non-application of the Divorce Act is recognised by the case *Khambatta v. Khambatta*.[38]

The position in India is affected by the Foreign Marriages Act 1969. A recent decision from Bombay,*Abdul Rahim Undre v. Padma Abdur Rahim Undre*[39] illustrates the problems which are associated with the Act. The Act applies to all marriages solemnised outside India when one of the parties to the marriage is an Indian citizen. If the marriage is registered or solemnised under the Act, then the marriage can only be dissolved under its terms; *i.e.*, on judicial application.[40] If the marriage is not solemnised or registered under the terms of the Act, then the provision on dissolution does not apply. However, section 18(4) is a particularly cryptic provision:

> Nothing contained in subsection (1) shall authorise any court to grant any relief under this Act in relation to any marriage in any foreign country not solemnized under it, if the grant of relief in respect of such marriage (whether on any of the grounds specified in the Special Marriage Act 1954 or otherwise) is provided for under any other law for the time being in force.

It was this provision which arose for interpretation in the *Undre* litigation. The facts were as follows. The parties, both Indian citizens, married in the UK in a register office in 1966. The plaintiff-husband was a Muslim whereas his

---

[37] [1965] AC 720 at p. 728. See also *Abdoolie Drammeh v. Joyce Drammeh* 1970 Journal of African Law p. 150; *P.P. v. White* 1940 MLJ 170; *Re Soo Hai San and Wong Sue Foong* 1961 MLJ 221.

[38] 1935 ILR 59 Bom 278.

[39] AIR 1982 Bom 32.

[40] Section 18(1).

wife was a Hindu. The court in the subsequent proceedings found as a fact that at the time of the marriage both parties were domiciled in India. The parties returned to India in 1969. The husband, in his evidence, stated that the wife converted to Islam on 29 December 1969, and that a subseqent nikah ceremony was performed. Relations between the two then deteriorated, and the husband's allegation was that on 20 April 1978 he divorced his wife by talaq. After the talaq divorce, the husband attempted to restrain the wife from entering the apartment where they had once lived together as man and wife. Indeed, he brought proceedings for a permanent injunction, together with an application for a declaration that the lady was no longer his wife. He argued also that *even* on the assumption that she had not embraced Islam and had remained a Hindu, nonetheless the Muslim personal law was applicable to their relationship, and thus he was entitled to divorce his wife by talaq.

The defendant-wife denied that any conversion had taken place, and she also denied the facts relating to the nikah ceremony. Indeed, she even put in issue the talaq pronouncement itself.

At first instance, the trial judge decided that the law which governed the parties to this marriage was the Special Marriage Act read with the Foreign Marriages Act. On the contested facts relating to the conversion, the nikah, and the talaq, the trial judge decided in favour of the defendant-wife. Both suits were dismissed and the husband appealed. The appeal was dismissed by Mody J and a further appeal was taken by way of Letters Patent to a two bench court.

This appellate court decided, first, that the marriage solemnnised in 1966 in England was a valid marriage recognised as such by Indian law, notwithstanding that the wife was a Hindu and the husband was a Muslim at that time. Secondly, they then went on to consider the question whether the effect of section 18(4) of the Foreign Marriages Act was to exclude from the operation of that Act marriages where the husband was of the Muslim faith. The court rejected this view.

> The Shariat Act or the Shariat Act read with Muslim personal law cannot be said to be the law in force contemplated by s. 18(4) of the Foreign Marriages Act.

The court decided therefore that the courts below had been correct in concluding that the marriage in this case was governed by the Foreign Marriages Act, and could be dissolved only under its terms.

As to the questions of fact, the court upheld the courts below. There was no evidence to sustain the contention that the defendant had converted to Islam or that a nikah had been performed. But even if the facts had been otherwise and the court had decided that the wife had actually converted to Islam and that a religious ceremony of marriage had been performed, the court would still have held that the Special Marriage Act 1954 would have been the applicable legislation governing its dissolution. One doubts whether the court in those circumstances would have followed *Khambatta v. Khambatta*.[41] Although the court did not consider *Khambatta v. Khambatta*, it is implicit in the judgment that *Khambatta* is not relevant in the context of a foreign marriage in civil form.

The decision has been subjected to certain criticism. For instance, Neeru Sehgal writes:

> Parties who are Indian may be in some Western country for a short or temporary period. Their *lex domicilii*...must be their personal law and when they come back to India and go through a religious ceremony it should be taken as a manifestation of their intention to be governed by their personal law. In such a case, the first civil ceremony should not be allowed to govern the nature of the marriage for ever, as they had no choice but to undergo that form of marriage. It would be patently unfair to impose upon them a form of marriage in respect of which they had no choice and to prevent them from changing its nature by undergoing a subsequent religious ceremony.[42]

10.4 English Statutes and Cases

The purpose of this section is to comment on the English law relating to the recognition of talaq divorces. English cases are of course important for the Muslim communities who live there, but they also have not an unimportant influence on the development of the law in this area on the subcontinent. For instance, the enactment of legislation in 1973 resulted in the Pakistan government withdrawing facilities for Pakistan citizens resident in England to give notice of their pronouncement of talaq to the Head of Chancery of the Pakistan mission in London.

10.4.1 The UK Legislation

The relevant legislation is common to the entire UK. We shall however refer to England exclusively. Two Acts require consideration; namely, the

---

[41] 1935 ILR 59 Bom 278.
[42] N.Shehgal, (1982) vol. II Islam and Comparative Law Quarterly pp. 307 ff.

Conflict of Laws

Recognition of Divorces and Legal Separations Act 1971 and the Domicile and Matrimonial Proceedings Act 1973. The 1971 Act introduced what has been termed a "jurisdictional code" which states that a divorce shall be recognised in the UK if it has been obtained by means of "judicial or other proceedings" outside the British Isles in a country where either spouse is a national, where either spouse is habitually resident, or where either spouse is domiciled within the meaning of that term in the foreign law. The divorce must also be effective in the country where it was obtained. In addition to this "jurisdictional code", the old common law rules were retained. Section 6 of the 1971 Act (as amended) saved the old common law rules, so that a divorce obtained "abroad" will be recognised if it is obtained in the country of common domicile, or in the country of domicile of one party if recognised in the country of domicile of the other, or in a third country when recognised in the country of common domicile, (or if they have separate domiciles, recognised in both domiciles). Section 8 of the 1971 Act enables a court to withhold recognition to a foreign divorce when, *inter alia*, it considers recognition would manifestly be contrary to public policy.

The 1973 Act has a provision in Section 16 which deals with the recognition of nonjudicial divorces, and is therefore particularly relevant to the law on talaq.

> No proceeding in the United Kingdom, the Channel Islands or the Isle of Man shall be regarded as validly dissolving a marriage unless instituted in the courts of law of one of those countries.

There is a further important provision in Section 16(2). Notwithstanding what we have said about the survival of the common law grounds for recognition in Section 6 of the 1971 Act, a nonjudicial divorce obtained "abroad" (other than such a divorce where recognition would be required by the "jurisdictional code"), shall not be regarded as validly dissolving the marriage if *both* parties have throughout the period of one year immediately preceding the institution of the proceeding been habitually resident in the UK. It follows that if only one of the parties has been so habitually resident or indeed neither of them, then the validity of such a nonjudicial divorce depends on the law of the domicile of both parties.

It is with this background to the legislation that we can now go on to consider the case law in this area.

10.4.2 The Cases

The issues arise in many different contexts. They have come before the courts when a respondent files a defence to a divorce petition on the ground that the marriage has already been effectively terminated. From time to time, the superintendent-registrar of marriages refuses to grant permission for a marriage because he forms the opinion that an earlier marriage is still in existence. Immigration officers and social security personnel sometimes have to consider these issues.

The leading case is *Quazi v. Quazi*,[43] a decision of the House of Lords. The *ratio* of this case is that a talaq pronounced in Pakistan and fulfilling the procedural requirements of the Muslim Family Laws Ordinance 1961 comes within the requirements of the 1971 Act and is capable of recognition in the UK. Lord Diplock said:

> It is rightly conceded on behalf of the wife that the divorce by talaq which was obtained in Pakistan followed on acts which though not judicial do fall within the description 'other proceedings' officially recognised in that country.

The English court has drawn a distinction between the Pakistan talaq on the one hand, and the so-called "bare talaq" on the other hand. This distinction was first made by Wood J at first instance in *Quazi v. Quazi*. In the case of the "bare talaq" where there is no official intervention at all to the traditional form of unilateral and extrajudicial pronouncement, Wood J felt that the "jurisdictional code" does not apply because this code only applies to "judicial or other proceedings", and that a "bare talaq" cannot constitute *a proceedings*. Such divorces therefore were to be recognised only under Section 6 of the 1971 (the common law provisions) based on the validity of the divorce in the domiciliary law of both parties. If either party is domiciled in England, no such talaq will be valid there.

This view was followed by the Court of Appeal in *Chaudhary v. Chaudhary*.[44] In this case, the husband was a national of Pakistan originating from the territory of Kashmir. The parties were married in Kashmir and lived there until 1963 when the husband went to the UK leaving behind him his wife and children. The husband settled in England, established a relationship with another woman, and went through a register office marriage with this other woman in 1967. In 1969, they solemnised a religious marriage in Beirut,

---

[43] [1980] AC 744.
[44] [1985] 2 WLR 350.

Lebanon. The husband purported to divorce his wife on two occasions. First, he made an oral pronouncement of talaq at a mosque in London. Secondly, he pronounced a talaq divorce in Kashmir when he went there in 1978. The marriage at the register office was declared void by a High Court judge in proceedings in 1980.

In 1979, the first wife, who had arrived in the UK in 1976, filed a petition for divorce based on the fact of the husband's adultery with the other woman. The husband then presented a petition for a declaration that the marriage had been lawfully dissolved prior to the petition filed by the wife, either by the talaq pronounced in England or by the second talaq pronounced in Kashmir. The issues surrounding the talaq pronounced in England, which Wood J at first instance did not recognise, will be discussed later. So far as the second talaq was concerned, Wood J held that this talaq was a "bare talaq" because the Ordinance does not apply to the Kashmir territory, and that it could not be regarded as "judicial or other proceedings" within the meaning of the 1971 Act. As the "jurisdictional code" does not apply to the "bare talaq", Wood J went on to consider whether the talaq could be recognised under the provisions of Section 6 of the 1971 Act. This section is wider in scope than the "jurisdictional code" because there are none of the requirements of "judicial or other proceedings" or effectiveness in the country where the divorce was obtained. However, the talaq can only be valid by Section 6 if it is valid by the law of the parties domiciles. Wood J decided that at the relevant date, the husband had acquired a domicile of choice in England. He was also satisfied that the wife had acquired a domicile of choice in England. As no English domiciliary can pronounce or be a recipient to a nonjudicial divorce under the *common law*, the provisions of Section 6 had no application. Wood J refused the declaration sought by the husband and granted the wife a decree nisi of divorce on the wife's petition based on the husband's adultery with the other woman.

The husband appealed on the ground that the talaq pronounced in Kashmir in 1978 should be recognised as valid under the provisions of the "jurisdictional code" of the 1971 Act. The appeal was dismissed. Cumming Bruce LJ said:

> But neither respect for the divine origin of the procedure nor respect for the long enduring tradition which over the centuries had rendered the bare talaq effective as terminating marriage by the law of Muslim countries necessarily or sensibly should convert the procedure into a "proceeding" within the intent of section 2 of the Act of 1971. So I conclude that...a divorce obtained by a bare talaq would be construed as

not 'obtained by means of judicial or other proceedings' within the intendment of section 2 of that Act.

10.4.3 Talaq Pronounced in England

Prior to the 1971 legislation, in *Qureshi v. Qureshi*,[45] Simon P held that a talaq obtained by a husband who was domiciled in Pakistan should be recognised by the English courts even though the talaq was pronounced in England. The 1971 Act did not deal with this issue, concerned as it was with "overseas" divorces. The 1973 Act was enacted in this context to reverse the implications of *Qureshi v. Qureshi*. The courts have stated that s 16(1)[46] excludes both "bare talaqs" and "procedural talaqs". This is why the first talaq pronounced in the *Chaudhary* case could not be recognised. Oliver LJ said in *Chaudhary v. Chaudhary*.

> The obvious intention of section 16 was to deny by statute the recognition accorded by the decision in *Qureshi v. Qureshi* to informal divorces effected in this country. The *Qureshi* case was, it is true, not a case of a bare talaq, but it cannot reasonably be supposed that the legislature intended to exclude from the operation of the section and thus to permit the continued recognition of even less formal divorces obtained here...[47]

10.4.3.1 Transnational talaq

What of a talaq pronouncement in England, with communication to a chairman of a union council in Pakistan? This problem first arose in *R v. Registrar General Ex Parte Minhas*.[48] Mr. Minhas, a Pakistan national living on his own in Lancashire and now an English domiciliary, was anxious to divorce the wife he had left behind in Pakistan and remarry another fellow countrywoman. He decided to divorce his wife by talaq. He pronounced a triple talaq in England and then sent a notice of the talaq both to the chairman of the union council where his wife lived in Pakistan and also to his wife. Interestingly, he then travelled to Pakistan and actually attended a meeting of the arbitration council which had been summoned by the chairman. The attempt at reconciliation proved unsuccessful. He returned to England, and

---

[45] [1972] Fam 173.
[46] cited before.
[47] [1985] 2 WLR 350 at p. 369.
[48] [1977] QB 1.

sought a licence to marry from the superintendent registrar of marriages in his home district. This official was not satisfied that Mr. Minhas was free to marry, and he therefore sent the papers to the Registrar General. The Registrar General determined that Mr. Minhas was still married. Mr. Minhas therefore sought an order of *mandamus* against the Registrar directing him to perform his duty under the law. The Divisional Court refused to grant the application, for it held that the divorce was obtained in England and therefore it fell outside the ambit of the 1971 Act. The mandatory provisions of the Pakistan law; the pronouncement of the talaq, and the sending of notices of the talaq to the chairman and to the wife, all these took place in England. The activities which took place in Pakistan, as we know,[49] were not mandatory. Mr. Minhas had gone to the trouble of travelling to Pakistan. If he had divorced his wife by talaq in Pakistan, the position would have been entirely different.

The issue arose again in the immigration context in three cases, one of which ended up in the House of Lords;*R v. Secretary of State for the Home Department, ex parte Ghulam Fatima*.[50] In this case, and the others, the applicants, Pakistani women, sought leave to enter the UK as fiancees of their sponsors who were UK residents of Pakistan nationality. In each case there had been previous marriages to Pakistani women which the sponsors had purported to dissolve by pronouncing a talaq in England, making statutory declarations before solicitors in England that they had done so, and then sending copies of these documents to Pakistan both to their wives and to the appropriate local officials. The response of the immigration officers was to find that they could not be satisfied that the marriages had been effectively dissolved according to English law. The officials could not be satisfied that the intended marriages between the applicants and the sponsors could take place within a reasonable time, and accordingly refused entry. The applicants sought review of these decisions. One lady, Ghulam Fatima fought her case unsuccessfully right up to the House of Lords.[51] The House of Lords had no hesitation in upholding the decision of the Court of Appeal. Lord Ackner referred to Section 16(1) of the 1973 Act and said:

---

[49] See before.

[50] [1986] 2 WLR 693.

[51] The other ladies ended their appeals at earlier stages of the judicial process; in one case in the Divisional Court (*R v. Immigration Appeal Tribunal ,ex parte Secretary of State for the Home Department* [1984] 2 WLR 36), and in the other case in the Court of Appeal (*R v. Secretary of State for the Home Department ex parte Shafeena Bi.* [1984] 3 WLR 659).

it is thus clearly the policy of the legislature to deny recognition to divorces obtained by persons within the jurisdiction, and therefore subject to the laws of the United Kingdom, by any proceedings other than in a United Kingdom court. It would seem contrary to that policy to encourage the obtaining of divorces essentially by post by Pakistani nationals resident in this country by means of the talaq procedure.[52]

It is apparent that the case law produces two anomalies. First, the wealthy Pakistan national can travel to that country and pronounce a talaq there and, given the relaxed nature of the Pakistan rules relating to notice to the appropriate chairman[53] he can comply easily with Pakistan law. There is a discretion to refuse recognition inherent in Section 8 of the 1971 Act[54] but subject to this provision, this talaq will be recognised in England. This is what Mr. Minhas should have done in his situation. Secondly, the Indian national or the Kashmiri Muslim will not be able to secure recognition of his "bare talaq" even when pronounced in India or Kashmir unless both parties are still domiciled in that country, or at least domiciled in countries the law of which recognises the effectiveness of termination by such means.

One may ask if there is any way for a person to divorce his wife by the traditional Muslim form without the expense of going back to the country of his nationality. Three possibilities suggest themselves. First, to pronounce the talaq over the telephone to his wife in Pakistan. Secondly, to delegate the right to someone in Pakistan. Thirdly, to pronounce the talaq in another more convenient Muslim country. As to the first suggestion, the divorce is still of course a talaq divorce pronounced in England. In classical law, a talaq need not be communicated to his wife; thus the fact that the wife hears or does not hear of the pronouncement in Pakistan is of little consequence. The husband might be able to avoid the expense of going to the subcontinent by delegating his right of talaq to someone else either absolutely or conditional on the occurrence of a particular event.[55] Courts on the subcontinent are reluctant to infer delegation, but so long as this essentially evidential hurdle was overcome, it could be argued that the divorce subsequently pronounced was obtained in Pakistan and is therefore an overseas divorce and capable of recognition under the jurisdictional code of the 1971 Act. Against this view, it could be argued

---

[52] [1986] 2 WLR 693 at p.698.
[53] See before.
[54] See later.
[55] See before.

that the delegation was created in the UK, and that this in effect is an essential step to the pronouncement of this divorce. Also the discretionary provisions which enable an overseas divorce not to be recognised may be particularly relevant in this context.[56]

We turn now to the third situation. The divorce is pronounced in a country other than UK, the country of nationality, habitual residence or domicile within the meaning of that term in the foreign law of one of those parties. The "jurisdictional code" does not apply. The common law rules as saved by Section 6 of the 1971 Act does apply. So also does another important provision, namely Section 16(2) of the 1973 Act. Let us take as an example, a Pakistan national who divorces his wife in Kuwait by the talaq form of divorce. He informs the chairman of an appropriate union council in Pakistan that he has done this, and he also sends a copy of this notice to his wife. The legal position would appear to be as follows. If both husband and wife are habitually resident in the UK for more than one year prior to the pronouncement of the talaq, then that talaq will not be recognised. The situation will be different however if both arrived in the UK within one year of the pronouncement or one of them arrived in the UK within the year. In this case, the talaq could be recognised if it is valid in the country of domicile of both parties. If they are both domiciled in Pakistan and, assuming that the husband complied with Pakistan law, then such a "transnational Kuwait/Pakistan talaq" is capable of recognition in the English courts. If, in contrast, either party is domiciled in England, then the talaq cannot be recognised.

10.4.3.2 *Exemptions from Recognition*

Section 8(2) of the 1971 Act states:

> the validity of a divorce or legal separation obtained outside the British Isles may be refused if, and only if –
> (a) it was obtained by one spouse –
> (i) without such steps having been taken for giving notice of the proceedings to the other spouse as, having regard to the nature of the proceedings and all the circumstances, should reasonably have been taken; or
> (ii) without the other spouse having been given (for any reason other than lack of notice) such opportunity to take part in the proceedings as,

---

[56] See later.

having regard to the matters aforesaid, he should reasonably have been given; or

(b) its recognition would manifestly be contary to public policy.

Case law has suggested that paragraphs (a)(i) and (a)(ii) are of little importance in the context of the "bare talaq" and of only limited significance in the case of the Pakistan procedural talaq. As Bush J said in the case of a "bare talaq" in *Zaal v. Zaal*:[57]

> So far as para. (a)(i) is concerned...there does not seem much point in giving notice that the husband is about to undertake a unilateral act in which the wife can play no part and have no standing for objection. So far as para. (a)(ii) is concerned what part in the proceedings could the wife be expected to play when the law applicable to this talaq permits a unilateral decision?

More important is the common law provision, now contained in Section 8(2)(b) of the 1971 Act. The case law suggests that the courts will exercise their discretion in this area sparingly.[58] However, if either party is domiciled in England, recognition may well be refused. Oliver LJ stated the following in *Chaudhary v. Chaudhary*.[59]

> [It] must plainly be contrary to the policy of the law in a case where both parties to a marriage are domiciled in this country to permit one of them, whilst continuing his English domicile, to avoid the incidents of his domiciliary law and to deprive the other party to the marriage of her rights under that law by the simple process of taking advantage of his financial ability to travel to a country whose laws appear temporarily to be more favourable to him. This, as it seems to me, is precisely the sort of situation which the legislature must have had in mind in enacting the provisions of section 8(2)(b).

The English court might invoke this residual rule of public policy to refuse recognition to a talaq pronounced for instance in Pakistan by a Pakistan national domiciled in England where his wife is a non-Muslim and where the marriage was solemnised under the provisions of the English marriage legislation.

---

[57] (1983) 4 FLR 284 at p. 288.
[58] *Qureshi v. Qureshi* [1972] Fam 173; *Quazi v. Quazi* [1980] AC 744.
[59] [1985] 2 WLR 350 at p. 371.

10.4.3.3 Financial Relief after overseas divorce

Many, although not all of the cases considered in the previous pages arose because of the attempt by the husband to prevent the wife from seeking financial relief in England. The enactment of Part III of the Matrimonial and Family Proceedings Act 1984 has removed certain of the juridical advantages for a husband because the wife can now, with leave, seek ancillary relief from an English court from which she seeks recognition of an overseas divorce. The first point to make about the provision is that it applies to divorces etc which are obtained by means of judicial or other proceedings. Thus, on the authority of *Chaudhary v. Chaudhary*[60] a "bare talaq" which is recognised under Section 6 of the 1971 Act but which is not a divorce obtained by judicial or other proceedings cannot therefore be the basis upon which an application for financial relief can be made. Secondly, a person seeking relief *must* apply for the leave of the High Court or certain designated County Courts to make the application. The procedure, in effect a "filter mechanism", is likely to be a difficult hurdle to overcome. Assuming the hurdle is overcome, the court must be satisfied that it has jurisdiction to hear the case. Having accepted jurisdiction, and having granted leave, the court must then exercise its powers by taking account of nine particular matters contained in the Act so as to decide whether an order would be appropriate.[61]

This provision may well have taken some of the steam out of contested litigation in England on the recognition of the talaq. However, it will still be necessary to consider the issues in the immigration context, and for social security and taxation purposes. It is also important of course for the superintendent registrar to be certain that an applicant is free to marry. There may be evidence of an existing marriage allegedly dissolved by a talaq.

10.4.4 Conclusion

The Muslim population of the UK is usually estimated as approaching some 2 million, of which a large proportion must be of subcontinent ancestry, either born there, or whose parents were born there or in East Africa. The issues discussed in this section have been before the English courts on many occasions, and we have seen how the law has been developed both by legislation and by the case law. Sometimes, rather sadly, an English court will achieve a result which is different from the law applied on the subcontinent. What is the situation when an Englush court refuses to recognise a divorce

---

[60] [1985] 2 WLR 350.
[61] See Section 16(2).

pronounced in a nonjudicial manner in England? The divorce is valid by say Pakistan law assuming its effectiveness there because the appropriate notice has been given. If the wife remarried in Pakistan, as she would be able so to do, and then applied for an entry certificate to the UK to join her *second* husband who is settled in UK, and, if she succeeded to apply for social security benefits on her husband's insurance record, what would be the legal position? One solution would be for the English courts to decide that the validity of the new marriage depended upon the validity of the divorce. As the divorce cannot be recognised because of Section 16 of the 1973 Act, she would not be able to enter the country for settlement purposes because the marriage is not valid. However, such a solution does ignore the rule of the conflict of laws that capacity to marry depends upon the domicile of the parties at the time of the marriage. If we say that both the wife and second husband were domiciled in Pakistan at the time of the second marriage then, as Pakistan law recognises the talaq, she is a single woman in accordance with that law and free to remarry. There is no English case directly in point, although the views expressed in *R v. Secretary of State for the Home Department ex parte Ghulam Fatima*[62] suggest that the court in England would be not unduly worried by the fact that nonrecognition of the talaq divorce would lead to a limping marriage situation. The policy of the law inherent in Section 16 of the 1973 Act is paramount, and this policy when in conflict with the mischief of limping marriages must be given greater weight. Thus the second marriage in the example above would not be recognised by English courts, and neither entry clearance for settlement nor social security benefits on the second man's insurance record would be available. A marriage which is perfectly valid by the law of Pakistan would be treated as void by English law. Ultimately, such an international conflict of laws situation is resolved by applying the policy considerations of the law of the forum. Such divergencies are not perhaps surprising, but for the many Muslims settled in the UK with family connections back on the subcontinent, non recognition in England of a status which is recognised back on the subcontinent can cause hardship on occasion.

---

[62] [1986] 2 WLR 693.

11. Conclusion

In this concluding chapter, we look at the reforms which have taken place in the Islamic world in the last one hundred years, and we consider in brief the development of the call for the Islamicisation of the law which is heard increasingly today. We consider first the reforms of the Ottoman Empire.

11.1 The Ottoman Reforms

It is in the context of the background discussed in Chapter 1 that the attempts to redefine, to restate and to codify the Shari'a must be viewed. The first major redefinition occurred in the Ottoman Empire in the nineteenth century. These reforms, known as the Tanzimat reforms, inspired in large part by political motives, introduced into the Ottoman law a Commercial Code (1850), a Penal Code (1858), a Code of Commercial Procedure (1879), a Code of Civil Procedure (1880), and a Code of Maritime Commerce. In form, all the Ottoman Codes followed the European model of attempting a comprehensive codification. There was, however, some attempt to integrate certain principles of Shari'a criminal law. Thus article I of the Ottoman Penal Code reads, in part: "These provisions cannot however in any case injure the rights of the individual consecrated by the Shari'a."[1] In this way, the Code retained the rights of the victim's family to blood money (diya) in the case of homicide.

With few exceptions, the first Ottoman reforms put the Shari'a on one side. In contrast, the Majalla (Civil Code) of 1876 codified the rules of contract and tort of the Hanafi branch of the Sunni law. The Majalla, although European in form, is clearly Islamic in content. After the establishment of secular courts, it became inevitable that the Islamic law of obligations required a restatement, not least so as to make the law more easily accessible both to litigants and lawyers alike. The lawyers of the latter part of the nineteenth century were not trained in the intricacies of the Shari'a. Although not seen as exclusive, the Majalla acquired a position of supreme authority from an early period. Like an European code, the Majalla is subdivided into books, chapters and articles. It deals with contracts, with some torts, but it does not cover non-contractual obligations, family law or real property. However, it does contain some procedural rules. The Majalla is highly significant, first because it represents

---

[1] The translation is the one used in H.J.Liebesny, *The Law of the Near and Middle East (Readings and Materials)*,Albany 1975.

Conclusion

the earliest example of an official promulgation of large parts of the Shari'a by the authority of the state, and second, because within its specific articles there are certain principles derived not from the consensus of Hanafi law, but rather from divergent opinions of the Hanafi law. It represents, therefore, the first tentative example of the re-emergence of the "search" (the ijtihad) which Islamic jurisprudence had substantially brought to an end so many centuries before.

A similar development to the Majalla in the Middle East can be seen in India. Indian courts, from the early part of the nineteenth century have tended to treat two texts both as authentic and exclusive; namely, the *Fatawa Alamgiri* and the *Hadeya* of Marghinani. The former text is a compilation of excerpts from Hanafi sources prepared in 1663 under the authority of the Emperor Aurangzeb. The Hadeya was a school textbook compiled in the latter part of the twelfth century, translated into English from a Persian version.[2]

In contrast with the Majalla, reforms in the family law area have been based upon *ad hoc* expediency to solve particular problems. Thus, in 1915, the Ottoman rulers, by Imperial edicts, enacted legislation to improve the status of Muslim wives and provide them with certain, albeit limited, rights to petition for divorce. These rights did not exist in the dominant Hanafi law; thus the authorities based the reforms on Hanbali (and also Maliki) law and on the minority or "weaker" Hanafi doctrine. An eclectic choice was thus made – although admittedly for a limited purpose.

11.2 Twentieth Century Reforms and the Codes

These early reforms of family law in the Ottoman Empire provide the key to the legislative activity in the Muslim world in recent years. Only in Turkey has the government abolished entirely the Shari'a and replaced it with codes of European inspiration.[3] The two major trends, both in the areas regulated by Islamic law and in those areas already subjected to secularisation, has been: first, an increased eclecticism in the selection of the sources, and second, the synthesis of Islamic and Western legal ideas. This latter development is particularly apparent in the field of contract.

---

[2] See before ch. 2.

[3] The Civil Code and the Code of Obligation (1926) are based on Swiss models. In contrast, the Criminal Code (1926) is based upon the Italian Penal Code, the Code of Criminal Procedure (1929) is based upon the German Code, and the Code of Civil Procedure (1927) is based upon the Code in the Swiss canton of Neuchatel.

Conclusion

Perhaps the foremost advocate of these two trends has been the Egyptian, Dr Abd al-Sanhuri. Dr Sanhuri approached the issues in a pragmatic way, for he formed the view that the Islamic system could not be reintroduced, in particular in relation to matters relating to land law and commercial law, without prior adaptation to the needs of a modern civilisation. He was primarily responsible for the drafting of the Egyptian Civil Code (1948), the Iraqi Code (1951), the Libyan Code (1953), and the Kuwaiti Codes and Commercial Law (1960/1).[4] The Syrian and Libyan Codes state:

Article 1(2).

In the absence of an applicable legal provision the judge shall decide in accordance with the principles of the Islamic Shari'a, and in the absence of these, in accordance with custom. In the absence of custom, the Judge will apply the principles of natural law and the rules of equity.

Moreover, the Introduction to the Syrian Code makes it clear that Article 1(2) does not limit derivation to the authoritative view of any one school. The entire corpus of relevant Shari'a principles is available to the Judge.[5] Major theoretical problems abound in the interpretation of these provisions, and similar provisions in other Middle Eastern codes. For instance, to which works should the judge turn? Should the judge be looking for principles (which will be difficult to find) or should he be looking for solutions? If the judge is looking for solutions, he will, of course, find himself faced with several contradictory solutions even within one school of law. An Egyptian commentator, Professor Chafik Chehata, has suggested that the Egyptian judge should be looking, not for solutions, but rather for "the spirit which has inspired the various solutions found there".[6]

11.3 Early Family Law Reforms

In the field of family law, the legislator, faced with the need to reform an area of the law seen to be at the heart of the Shari'a, has been able to justify the reforms as being wholly within the context of Islamic jurisprudence. Some

---

[4] The Civil and Commercial Code of 1961 was amended in 1980 by a new Code.

[5] See J.N.D.Anderson, "The Shari'a and Civil Law", (1954) vol. 30, The Islamic Quarterly, pp. 30-32. see also J.N.D.Anderson,*Law Reform in the Muslim World* (London, 1976) pp. 86 ff.

[6] The Egyptian and Iraqi Codes have significant differences in phrasing. Recourse to the Shari'a in Egypt and Iraq is to be made only after recourse to custom. See Chafik Chehata, "Les survivances Musulmanes dans la codification du Droit Civil Egyptian", (1965) Revue Intenationale de Droit Compare, p. 852.

Conclusion

expedients which have been used have been of a procedural variety; namely, the right of the ruler to confine and define the jurisdiction of his courts. This expedient was used in Egypt in 1931 to restrict the solemnisation of child marriages by precluding the court from hearing any claim of marriage whatever if the husband had not reached the age of 18 and the bride the age of 16 at the time of the litigation. Furthermore, the court could not hear any *disputed* claim of marriage unless that marriage contract had been registered. Earlier, in 1923, it had been made a criminal offence for a registrar to register a marriage in a case where the bride was not above 16 and the bridegroom above 18.

Eclecticism (takhayyur), first seen in the Majalla, has become the notable basis for the reform in the family law field.[7] At first, the concept of takhayyur was limited to the adoption of variant opinions within the particular school, or to the introduction of the dominant doctrine of another Sunni school. Later, justification for reform was based on any opinion of any jurist regardless of his school. Occasionally the doctrine of one school (or jurist) is combined with another. This concept, known as talfiq or "piecing together" permits reforms which are seen as socially desirable, yet at the same time ensures that there is no departure from the essence of Islam. In fact, of course, an entirely new principle has been created.

11.4 Later Reforms

Before 1946, the principle of taqlid (imitation) was formally followed, notwithstanding these innovations. The authority of medieval legal manuals was paramount; it was seen that these manuals contained the Fiqh, the authoritative presentation of the corpus of Islamic law as it had been created by the ijma' (the consensus). But at the same time, however, the principle of taqlid was beginning to be challenged, and scholars in the Muslim world propounded the view that the right to ijtihad (search by independent deduction) could be invoked by modern legislators.[8] This view gained considerable acceptance in the Muslim world by the end of the 1970s. Many of the reforms

---

[7] For examples see J.N.D.Anderson,*Law Reform in The Muslim World*. (London, 1976) pp. 48 ff.

[8] See for example Muhammad Iqbal, *The Reconstruction of Religious Thought in Islam* (reprinted Lahore, 1968). He said: "The claim of the present generation of Muslim liberals to re-interpret the foundational legal principles, in the light of their own experience and the altered conditions of modern life is, in my opinion perfectly justified...each generation, guided but unhampered by the work of its predecessors, should be permitted to solve its own problems."

237

Conclusion

were based on the right to exercise ijtihad, although it is also true that a spirit of "secular radicalism" influenced the changes in countries such as Somalia and the South Yemen.

It will be recalled that after Shafi'i's death in 820 AD, there developed a process of interaction between the schools of law when concepts of one school were accepted by another school. Similarly, modern Muslim legislators went through an almost identical period of growth. Indeed, as in the ninth century, when the work of Shafi'i tended to attract the schools together, so today the reformist movement has drawn the schools closer together in the search for solutions to particular problems within the Islamic framework. With an increased tendency towards codification and restatement, this trend will inevitably continue to play a dominant role in the Muslim world in the last decade of the twentieth century.

11.5 Islamicisation

But there is another equally fascinating development in the Muslim world. Taking a broad view of the reforms over the last 100 years, it can be seen that there have hitherto been four distinct periods of reform: first, the nineteenth-century reforms in the Ottoman Empire; second, the early sporadic reforms in family law prior to the second world war, usually, although not always, based on the doctrine of siyasa shar'iyya; third, the reforms based on talfiq; and finally, the acceptance that some reforms can be introduced purely for social or economic reasons without recourse to juristic arguments. Those reforms based on social need only are rare, and at least on the surface juristic arguments have been adduced. Thus even Tunisia has found it necessary to justify in juristic terms the changes which have been introduced. The abolition of polygamy in Tunisia is justified by a reinterpretation of Sura 4 verse 3 in the Qur'an. In that verse, the doctrine of justice is equated not only with nafaqa, but also with love and affection. Only the Prophet can treat two wives equally in this way; thus in today's conditions there is an irrebuttable presumption that a Muslim cannot fulfil the requirements laid down in the Qur'an. Thus polygamy is prohibited.

The question which must be asked at the end of the 1980s is whether the Muslim leaders have actually gone too far in the direction of reform and whether we are not witnessing a reintroduction of Shari'a principles long discarded.

Conclusion

11.5.1 Pakistan

Pakistan illustrates a fascinating case study of this development. In 1978, the Government of Pakistan introduced Shariat Benches attached to each of the Provincial High Courts. These new courts were subsequently remodelled as a Federal Shariat Court by a new Article 203C of the Constitution. The Court consists of not more than eight Muslim members. Article 203C(3) states that the Chairman shall be a person who is or has been or is qualified to be a Judge of the Supreme Court, and a member shall be a person who is or has been or is qualified to be a Judge of the High Court.

The powers, jurisdiction and functions of the Court are contained in Article 203(D) and are worthy of citation in full: *Powers, jurisdiction and functions of the Court*.

(1) The Court may, on the petition of a citizen of Pakistan or the Federal Government or a Provincial Government, examine and decide the question whether or not any law or provision of law is repugnant to the Injunctions of Islam as laid down in the Holy Quran and the Sunnah of the Holy Prophet, hereinafter referred to as the Injunctions of Islam.

(2) If the Court decides that any law or provision of the law is repugnant to the Injunctions of Islam, it shall set out in its decision –

   (i) the reason for its holding that opinion; and

   (ii) the extent to which such a law or provision is so repugnant; and specify the day on which the decision shall take effect.

(3) If any law or provision of law is held by the Court to be repugnant to the Injunctions of Islam –

   (i) the President in the case of a law with respect to a matter in the Federal Legislative List or the Concurrent Legislative List, or the Governor in the case of a law with respect to a matter not enumerated in either of those Lists, shall take steps to amend the law so as to bring such law or provision into conformity with the Injunctions of Islam; and

   (ii) such law or provision shall, to the extent to which it is held to be repugnant, cease to have effect on the day on which the decision of the Court takes effect.

It is important to mention, that "law" for the purposes of this Article includes any custom or usage having the force of law but does not include the Constitution, Muslim personal law, or any law relating to the procedure of any

Conclusion

court or tribunal. Two cases illustrate the limitations of the Constitutional mechanisms. The first case to be considered is *B.Z.Kaikus v. President of Pakistan*.[9] In this case, brought by a celebrated former Judge of the Pakistan Supreme Court, the Supreme Court had to consider the relationship between the judiciary on the one hand and the executive and legislature on the other hand in the context of the process of Islamicisation. The petitioner sought both a declaration and an injunction. He argued that the Muslims of Pakistan:

> being bound only by the divine law, ie the Sharia, the Sharia is the only law in this State, the status of the so-called remaining laws including the Constitution being only that of orders whose validity depends on their acceptance as Allah's will by the judicial ulama or the judiciary, and that any order or so-called law including the Constitution which is in conflict with any part of the Holy Qur'an and Sunnah...including the directions relating to justice and righteousness is null and void.

The Supreme Court refused to grant either of the reliefs sought. The Court took the view that the process of Islamicisation was the task of the Government, and that the Courts had no jurisdiction to interfere except to the limited extent laid down in the Constitution itself. The majority judgment was expressed as follows:

> [T]he point which we want to emphasise is that the job...is of a legislative and political character to be performed by the State by enacting the necessary laws for islamicization of the existing laws or even to promulgate new laws on that pattern but within the hemisphere of the Holy Qur'an and Sunnah.

The second case of interest is *Federation of Pakistan v. Farishta*.[10] In this case, the petitioner sought a declaration that Section 4 of the Muslim Family Laws Ordinance 1961 was un-Islamic and therefore void by virtue of Article 203 of the Constitution. It will be recalled that this section introduced a system of representation into the law of inheritance to benefit the orphaned grandchild of the deceased when that person is in competition with a closer survivor, such as a son or a brother of the deceased. The Government relied on section 203 itself which, in its view, excluded the court's jurisdiction from a review of the 1961 Ordinance. The Supreme Court accepted this argument, stating that the expression "Muslim Personal Law" was sufficiently wide to cover the special statutory laws applicable to the Muslim citizens of Pakistan; thus the

---

[9] 1980 PLD SC 160.
[10] 1981 PLD SC 120.

Conclusion

Ordinance and in particular Section 4 was immune from scrutiny.

These two cases illustrate the limitations of the Constitutional provisions designed to reintroduce Islamic law. As Keith Hodkinson has said:[11]

> *Farishta* reduces the potential role of the judiciary in Islamicisation by excluding from its scrutiny almost all the controversial legislation in matters of family and succession law.

Thus it has been left to the executive to realise the Islamicisation of the inherited laws. Four important Ordinances on criminal law were introduced in 1979; those relating to zina, qazf, drinking and theft. We deal with the first of these, as zina of course has repercussions in the family law field.

Ordinance VII of 1979 introduces the offence of zina. This is defined as:

> A man and a woman are said to commit "zina" if they wilfully have sexual intercourse without being validly married to each other.

If the person convicted of zina is someone who at some stage was married and who had marital sexual relations (muhsan), then that person is liable to the hadd penalty. Hadd is defined in section 5(2)(a) of the Ordinance as stoning to death at a public place. If he or she is not a muhsan, then the punishment is whipping numbering 100 stripes. Similar punishments are prescribed in the case of zina-bil-jabr (rape).

The standard of proof required for the draconian hadd penalty is very high indeed. It is laid down in Section 8:

> Proof of zina or zina-bil-jabr, liable to hadd shall be in one of the following forms, namely:
>
> (a) the accused makes before a court of competent jurisdiction a confession of the admission of the offence, or
>
> (b) at least 4 Muslim adult male witnesses, about whom the court is satisfied, having regard to the requirement of tazkiyah al-shuhood, that they are truthful witnesses and abstain from major sins (kabair), give evidence as eye-witnesses of the act of penetration necessary for the offence.

Tazkiyah al-shuhood refers to the mode of inquiry which the court would adopt to satisfy itself as to the credibility of a witness. If proof in either of these two forms as laid down in Section 8 is not available then the accused may nonetheless be punished according to the doctrine of ta'zir or discretionary punishment. By Section 8(2), in the case of zina, he or she shall in these circumstances be punished with rigorous imprisonment for a term which may extend to 10 years and with whipping numbering 30 stripes, and in

---

[11] 1981 vol. 40, Cambridge Law Journal p. 248.

Conclusion

the case of zina-bil-jabr, he shall be punished with imprisonment which may extend to 25 years and with whipping numbering 30 stripes.

The Zina Ordinance has received much international publicity. Less well known is the Offence of Qazf (Enforcement of Hadd) Ordinance 1979. Section 3 of this Ordinance defines qazf as follows:

> Whoever by words either spoken or intended to be read, or by signs or by visible representations, makes or publishes an imputation of zina concerning any person intending to harm, or knowing or having reason to believe that such imputation will harm, the reputation, or hurt the feelings, of such person, is said, except in cases hereinafter excepted, to commit qazf.

The two exceptions are, first, to impute truth which "public good requires to be made or published", and, second, to make an allegation of zina in good faith to any of those who have lawful authority over that person. The exception does not protect a complainant who makes an accusation of zina in court but who fails to produce four witnesses in support. The exception also does not protect a witness who gives false evidence of zina, or a complainant who makes false accusations of zina. This important provision is surely designed to keep allegations of zina to a minimum, for if the allegations turn out not to be proved, he or she may find himself or herself in considerable difficulties. The punishment for qazf liable to hadd, under Section 7 of this Ordinance, is whipping numbering 80 stripes. In addition, after a person has been convicted for the offence of qazf liable to hadd, his evidence shall not be admissible in any court of law.

There are many cases which have now been decided under the provisions of the Zina Ordinance. *Noor Khan v. Haq Nawaz*[12] has already been discussed in the context of Section 7 of the Muslim Family Laws Ordinance 1961.[13] Probably the most important litigation in this area is *Hazoor Bakhsh v. Federation of Pakistan; Chaudry v. Islamic Republic of Pakistan.*[14] The question before the court was whether stoning to death (rajm) as prescribed in Section 5(2)(a) and Section 6(3)(a) is hadd or obligatory under the injunctions of Islam. Sura 24 verse 2 of the Qur'an states:

---

[12] 1982 PLD FSC 265.
[13] See before.
[14] 1982 PLD FSC 145; 1983 PLD FSC 255.

Conclusion

> The woman and the man guilty of adultery or
> fornication, flog each of them, with a hundred
> stripes; let not compassion move you, in their
> case, in a matter, prescribed by Allah, if ye
> believe in Allah...and let a party of the
> believers witness the punishment.

The Qur'anic verse does not specify rajm; yet there are a number of hadith which specify this draconian punishment when zina is committed by a married person. The most important of the hadith is the tradition of Obada bin Samit. He reported that the Prophet said:

> Fornication of a virgin with a virgin – 100
> stripes and exile for a year, and one married with
> another married – 100 stripes and stoning to
> death.

When the case first came before the Federal Shariat Court, two judges, Salahuddin Ahmed J and Aftab Hussain J in particular, go through in detail the four cases during the lifetime of the Prophet in which it was reported that rajm was imposed as a punishment for zina. Salahuddin Ahmed J suggested that rajm was not imposed on the basis of the injunctions in the Qur'an but rather in accordance with the then customs of the Arabs. It was therefore an imposition of a ta'zir penalty. This Judge stated categorically that the hadith cannot override the definite and clear injunction in the Qur'an. Thus it was clear that the provisions on rajm in the Ordinance were repugnant to the provisions of Islam, for the only penalty which could be imposed on a person guilty of zina, whether married or unmarried, is 100 stripes to be inflicted in public. The Ordinance must accordingly be brought into conformity with the injunctions of Islam. Agher Ali Hyder J in agreeing with Salahuddin Ahmed J said that it was not possible, as he put it, to "tag on" the punishment of hadd a further punishment by way of ta'zir. Aftab Hussain J said that the consensus view of the hadith of Obada bin Samit was that this hadith had been abrogated by the Quranic verse Sura 24 verse 2. Zakrullah Lodhi J also agreed with this view. Aftab Hussain J disagreed with his brother judges on one issue; it was his view that stoning can be added to the provisions of ta'zir. Karimullah Dullahi J in a dissenting judgment disagreed entirely with the majority view. On a majority, however, the court held that the provisions were contrary to the injunctions of Islam and ordered that the necessary amendments be made.

Conclusion

No such amendment was introduced by the Government. The Government filed an appeal against the judgment before the Supreme Court which stayed the operation of the orders. A "power of review" was then added to the powers of the Federal Shariat Court by a President's Order. In the review hearing, Aftab Hussain CJ notes the point that Muslim personal law is excluded from examination by the court as a result of Article 203(B) of the Constitution. Thus the earlier Court lacked jurisdiction in the matter. The other judgments add little to the fact that the original decision was *ultra vires* the Constitution. Thus the order that the necessary amendments be made to the law was withdrawn.

11.6 Conclusion

We have concentrated in the previous section on the trends in Pakistan. What of the rest of the Muslim world? The revolution in Iran swept away all the reforms of the Shah in the family law field. Changes in Egypt have been held by the Court there to be unconstitutional. Similar shifts are noticeable from Turkey to Malaysia. There are those who believe that the reforms in the family laws described in this book have undermined the basic values of the Muslim way of life. Yet there are others who consider that the restrictions on the husband's unilateral right to repudiate his wife, and the restrictions on polygamy, and such other changes as those described, in no way militate against the basic tenets of Islam. Nonetheless, reforms which outwardly improve the legal status of the woman in society, such as those in Somalia in relation to the rights of inheritance of the female which are now exactly equal to the male of equal degree removed from the propositus, these reforms may all be subjected to the current attempts to repeal legislation which is supposedly Western inspired.

Writing in 1976, Sir Norman Anderson commented on the possibility of a revival of orthodoxy and fervour, although he doubted whether this would be more than a temporary phase, at least in so far as the law is concerned. Indeed, he seemed inclined to think that there may be an upsurge in secular radicalism along the lines of the reforms in Somalia (and also South Yemen).[15] As in the first edition of this book published in 1979, it is no part of the brief to speculate on the future. But the changes in Pakistan discussed in the last few pages have brought about a radical change in the legal framework for the Muslim community in that country. Further attempts can be expected to remove the Muslim Family Law Ordinance 1961 from the Statute book. As a

---

[15] J.N.D.Anderson *Law Reform in the Muslim World.* (London,1976).

Conclusion

social experiment, these changes are impressive. Indeed, they are as impressive as the reforms for instance introduced by Attaturk in Turkey in the opposite direction so many years ago. It may well be that Pakistan Islamicisation will provide the inspiration for other Muslim countries over the next twenty years rather than Tunisian ijtihad or Somalian secular radicalism. The debate however has really only just begun, and the conflicting tensions apparent in the Muslim legal world will be resolved by the Muslim communities themselves drawing upon their remarkable legal traditions and history.[16]

---

[16] So far as the non-family law area is concerned, there is already a trend in the Muslim world to introduce new Codes which are far more Islamic in their content than their predecessors. A good example of this trend is the Law of Civil Transactions of the UAE enacted in 1986.

Appendix I

TABLE OF CASES

1.1 Jurisdictions outside South Asia.

Abdoolie Drammeh v. Joyce Drammeh 1970 JAL 150. 223
Abdulla bin Said bin Hassan v. Halima binti Said bin Hassan 1957 EA LR 688. 204
Attorney General for Ceylon v. Reid [1965] AC 720. 220
Chaudhary v. Chaudhary [1985] 2 WLR 350. 120, 225ff, 231
Fatima binti Mohamed v. Mohamed bin Salim 1952 AC 1. 204
Har Shefi v. Har Shefi [1953] 2 All ER 373. 217
Mahbub v. Mahbub 1964 108 Sol Jo 337. 102
Malik v. Secretary of State for the Home Dept [1972] Imm AR 37.
Nasreen Akhtar v. Secretary of State for the Home Department (2166) (1981) (unreported). 42
Parveen Choudry v. M.Hanif Choudry 159 N.J.Sup. 566. 117
P.P. v. White 1940 MLJ 170. 221
Quazi v. Quazi [1980] AC 744. 103, 116, 119, 129, 225, 231
Qureshi v. Qureshi [1972] Fam 173. 103, 217, 227, 231
R v. Immigration Appeal Tribunal, ex parte Secretary of State for the Home Department [1984] 2 WLR 36. 120, 228
R. v. Registrar General of Births, Deaths and Marriages, ex parte Minhas [1977] 1 QB 1. 227
R v. Secretary of State for the Home Department, ex parte Ghulam Fatima [1986] 2 WLR 693. 228ff
R v. Secretary of State for the Home Department, ex parte Shafeena Bi [1984] 3 WLR 659. 228ff
Rafiq v. Secretary of State for the Home Dept [1972] Imm AR 167.
Re Soo Hai San & Wong Sue Foong 1961 MLJ 221. 221
Shahnaz v. Rizwan [1965] 1 QB 390. 61
Sheikha v. Halima 1958 EA LR 623. 205
Syed Abdullah Shatiri v. Sharifa Salman 1959 25 MLJ 137. 44
Tohur Ali v. Entry Clearance Officer, Dacca [1985] Imm AR 33. 92
Viswalingham v. Viswalingham [1979] 1 FLR 15. 30
Zaal v. Zaal (1983) 4 FLR 284. 231

Appendix I

1.2 India, Pakistan, Bangladesh.

Abdool Futteh v. Zabunnessa 1881 ILR 6 Cal 631. 70
Abdool Kadir v. Salima 1886 ILR 8 All 149. 60
Abdool Razack v. Aga Mahomed Jaffer Bindaneem 1893/4 21 LR IA 56. 51ff
Abdul Fazal v. S.Sayeeda Khatun 1963 PLD Dacca 343. 201
Abdul Ghani v. Azizul Huq 1912 ILR 39 Cal 409. 210
Abdul Ghani v.Taleh Bibi 1962 PLD (WP) Lah 531. 38ff, 87ff
Abdul Hafiz Beg v. Sahebbi 1975 AIR Bom 165. 147, 148
Abdul Khader v. Azeeza Bee 1944 AIR Mad 227. 103
Abdul Karim Adenwalla v. Rahimabai 1946 33 AIR Bom 342. 200, 205
Abdul Mannan v. Safuran Nessa 1970 SCMR 845. 112
Abdul Rahim Undre v. Padma Abdur Rahim Undre 1982 AIR Bom 32. 221
Abdul Rahimin v. Aminabai 1935 ILR 59 Bom 426. 44
Abdulla v. R.Khatoon 1967 PLD Dacca 47. 42
Aboobacker Haji v. Mamu Koya 1971 KLT 663. 135
[K] Abubukkur v. V.Marakkar 1970 AIR Ker 277. 44
Abul Fata Mahomed Ishak v. Russomoy Dhur Chowdhry 1894/5 22 LR IA 76. 28, 198ff
Adnan Afzal v. Sher Afzal 1969 PLD SC 187. 70
Advocate-General v. Richmond 1845 Perry's Oriental Cases 566. 22
Ahmad Ali v. Sabha Khatun Bibi 1952 PLD Dacca 385. 70
Ahmed G.H.Ariff v. Wealth Tax Commissioner 1971 AIR SC 1691. 203
Ahmed Kasim Molla v. Khatun Bibi 1932 ILR 59 Cal 833. 103
Aizunnissa Khatoon v. Karimunnissa Khatoon 1895 ILR 23 Cal 130. 55
Akhlaq Ahmad v. Kishwar Sultana 1983 PLD SC 169. 125
Akhtar Hussain v. Collector, Lahore 1977 PLD Lah 1173. 119
Amanullah Khan v. Eidat Shah 1981 [NLR] 164. 112
Amar Ilahi v. Rashida Akhtar 1955 PLD Lah 413. 96
Amin Beg v. Saman 1911 ILR 33 All 90. 210
Anis Begum v. Muhammad Istafa Wali Khan 1933 ILR 55 All 743.
Asha Bibi v. Nabissa Sahib 1957 AIR Mad 583. 201
Ashidbhai v. Abdullah 1906 ILR 31 Bom 271. 193
Asma Bibi v. Abdul Samad Khan 1910 ILR 32 All 167. 62
Asmat Begum v. Hussain Jan 1956 PLD (WP) Pesh 5. 147
Atia Waris v. Sultan Ahmad Khan 1959 PLD (WP) Lah 205. 93
Ayesha Bibi v. Bireshwar Ghosh Mazumdar (Unreported). 1929 33 Cal WN 179. 33

Appendix I

Ayesha Bibi v. Subodh Chandra Chakrabarty 1945 ILR 2 Cal 405. 32, 33
Aziz Khan v. Muhammad Zarif 1982 PLD FSC 156. 114
Bachun v. Hamid Husain (1871) 14 Moo I.A. 377. 66
Bai Tahera v. Ali Husain 1979 AIR SC 362. 72ff
Bakshi v. Bashir Ahmed 1970 PLD Lah 386. 42
Balqis Fatima v. Najm-ul-Ikram Qureshi 1959 PLD Lah 566. 124
Bazayet Hossein v. Dooli Chund 1877/8 5 LR IA 211. 141
Beguman v. Saroo 1964 PLD (WP) Lah 451. 170
Behram Khan v. Akhtar Begum 1952 PLD Lah 548. 44
Bikani Mia v. Shuk Lal Poddar 1893 ILR 20 Cal 116. 199
Bilquis Fatima v. Noor Muhammad 1978 PLD Lah 1109. 125
Budansa Rowther v. Fatma Bi 1914 26 Madras LJ 260. 33, 50, 219
Buffatan v. Sh. Abdul Salim 1950 AIR Cal 304. 120
(J.J.) Chandra Datta v. Abinash Chandra Sen 1939 ILR 2 Cal 12. 219
Chelimutnessa v. Surrendra 1924 (Unreported). 33
Chuhar v. Ghulam Fatima 1984 PLD Lah 235. 112
Daulan v. Dosa 1956 PLD (WP) Lah 712. 45
Eidun Nisa Begum v. Member, Board of Revenue 1973 PLD Pesh 1. 188
Emperor v. Maha Ram 1918 ILR 40 All 393. 95
Fahmida Begum v. Habib Ahmad 1968 PLD Lah 1112. 96
Fahmida Bibi v. Mukhtar Ahmad 1972 PLD Lah 694. 112, 118
Farooq Leivers v. Adelaide Bridget Mary 1958 PLD (WP) Lah 431. 32, 212, 219ff
Fateh Muhammad v. Chairman, Union Committee Ward 14/15, Lahore 1975 PLD Lah 951. 82
Fauzia Hussain v. Khadim Hussain 1985 PLD Lah 166. 82
Fazal Begum v. Hakim Ali 1941 AIR Lah 22. 213
Fazlul Rabbi v. State of West Bengal 1965 AIR SC 1722. 206
Federation of Pakistan v. Farishta 1981 PLD SC 120. 183, 240
Fuzlunbi v. K.Khader Vali 1980 AIR SC 1730. 72ff
Ghulam Bhik v. Hussain Begum 1957 PLD (WP) Lah 998. 88
Ghulam Fatima v. Abdul Quyyum 1981 PLD SC 460. 112
Ghulam Fatima v. Sheikh Muhammad Bashir 1958 PLD (WP) Lah 596.
Ghulam Kubra Bibi v. Mohammad Shafi 1940 AIR Pesh 2. 41
Ghulam Mohammad v. Ghulam Husain AIR 1932 PC 81. 145
Ghulam Mohy-ud-Din Khan v. Khizar Hussain 1929 ILR 10 Lah 470. 86
Ghulam Sakina v. Umar Bakhsh 1964 PLD SC 456. 127
Ghulam Shabbir v. Mst. Nur Begum 1977 PLD SC 75. 202ff
Grace Abdul Hadi Haqani v. Abdul Hadi Haqani 1961 PLD (WP) Kar 296. 94

Appendix I

Habib v. The State 1980 PLD Lah 791. 42
Habibur Rahman Chowdhury v. Altaf Ali Chowdhury 1920/21 48 LR IA 114. 91
Hajiran Bibi v. Abdul Khaliq 1981 PLD Lah 761. 70
Hakim Zadi v. Nawaz Ali 1972 PLD Kar 540. 125
Hamid Ali v. Imtiazan 1872 ILR 2 All 71. 102
Hamida Begum v. Murad Begum 1975 PLD SC 624. 38, 39
Hamira Bibi v. Zubaida Bibi 1915/16 43 LR IA 294. 60
Harbai v. Usman 1963 PLD Kar 868. 97
Hazoor Bakhsh v. Federation of Pakistan; Chaudry v. Islamic Republic of Pakistan 1983 PLD FSC 255. 243
Hussain v. Rahim Khan 1954 AIR Mysore 24. 66
Imambandi v. Mutsaddi 1917/18 45 LR IA 73. 97
Inamal Islam v. Hussain Bano 1976 PLD Lah 1466. 116, 129
Iqbal Mai v. Falak Sher 1986 PLD SC 228. 185
Ismail Ahmed Peebadi v. Momin Bibi 1941 AIR PC 11. 86
Ittachialil Meethal Moosa v. Pachiparambath Meethal Fathima and Pathumma 1983 KLJ 610. 135
Ismail Haj Arat v. Umar Abdulla 1942 ILR Bom 441. 201
Itwari v. Asghari 1960 AIR All 684. 83, 136
Jafri Begam v. Amir Muhammad Khan 1885 ILR 7 All 822. 193ff
Jahan Khan v. Feroze 1951 PLD Lah 433. 147
Janudul Haque v. Zubair Haider 1981 AIR Patna 345. 65
Jan Mohammad v. Karam Chand AIR 1953 SC 2981. 141
Jatoi v. Jatoi 1967 PLD SC 580. 32, 212, 216ff
Jiauddin Ahmed v. Anwara Begum (unreported). [1978]. 120
[B.Z.] Kaikus v. President of Pakistan 1980 PLD SC 160. 240
Kamal Khan v. Zainab 1983 PLD Lah 546. 184ff
Kammu v. Ethiyumma 1967 Kerela Law Times 913. 44
Kapore Chand v. Kidar Nissa Begum 1953 AIR SC 413. 66
Karimanissa Bibi v. Hamedulla 1925/6 30 Cal WN 129. 147
Kasim Husain v. Sharif-un-Nissa 1883 ILR 5 All 285. 192
Keolapati v. Harnam Singh 1937 ILR 12 Luck 568. 219
Khambatta v. Khambatta 1935 ILR 59 Bom 278. 221, 223
Khoja and Memons Case 1847 Perry's Oriental Cases 110. 34
Khurshid Bibi v. Muhammad Amin 1967 PLD SC 97. 123ff
K.P.Chandrasekharappa v. Government of Mysore 1955 AIR Mysore 26. 169, 212
Kunhambi v. Kalanthar 1915 ILR 38 Mad 1052. 35
Kunhi Moyin v. Pathumma 1976 KLT 87. 71

Appendix I

M.Zikria Khan v. Aftab Ali Khan 1985 PLD Lah 319. 119, 120, 121
Madapathi v. Susheda 1978 Andh LT 7. 71
In the matter of Mahin Bibi 1874 13 Bengal LR 160. 95
Maina Bibi v. Chaudhri Vakil Ahmad 1924/5 52 LR IA 145. 65
Maqbool Alam v. Khodaija 1966 AIR SC 1194 189
Maqbool Jan v. Arshad Hussan 1975 PLD Lah 147. 121
Masood Khan v. Chairman, Arbitration Council, Wah 1982 PLD Lah 532. 117ff
Mazhar Ali v. Budh Singh 1885 ILR 7 All 297. 39, 40
Md. Ebrahim v. Ma Ma 1939 AIR Rang 28. 209
Mitar Sen Singh v. Maqbul Hasan Khan 1930 57 LR IA 313. 170, 212
Mohammad Abdul Ghani v. Fakhr Jahan Begam 1921/2 49 LR IA 195. 188, 189
Mohammad Afzal v. Din Mohammad 1946 ILR 27 Lah 300. 201
Mohammad Sabir v. Tahir Ali 1957 AIR All 94. 201, 204
[N.K.] Mohammad Sulaiman v. [N.C.] Mohammad Ismail and ors. 1966 1 SCR 937. 141, 142
Mohan v. Mohan 1943 AIR Sind 311. 52
Mohd Ahmed Khan v. Shah Bano Begum 1985 AIR SC 945. 72ff
Mohd Zaman v. Irshid Begum 1967 PLD Lah 1104. 60
Moonshee Buzul-ul Raheem v. Luteefut-oon-Nissa 1859/61 8 LR IA 379. 122
Moselle Gubbay v. Kwaja Ahmad Said 1957 PLD (WP) Kar 50. 93, 94
Muchoo v. Arzoon 1866 5 WR 235. 95
In Re Muhammad Alam Md. Ibrahim 1939 AIR Sind 311. 95
Muhammad Allahdad Khan v. Muhammad Ismail Khan 1888 ILR 10 All 289. 86, 90ff
Muhammad Amin v. Surraya Begum 1970 PLD Lah 475. 127, 136
Muhammad Azam Khan v. Akhtar-un- Nisa Begum 1957 PLD (WP) Lah 195. 119
Muhammad Azam Khan v. Hamid Shah 1946 ILR All 575. 201
Muhammad Bashir v. Ghulam Fatima 1953 PLD Lah 73. 96
Muhammad Bibi v. Raja 1962 PLD AJK 7. 44
Muhammad Faiz Ahmad Khan v. Ghulam Ahmad Khan 1880/81 ILR 3 All 490. 193
Muhammad Gulshere Khan v. Mariam Begam 1881 ILR 3 All 731. 147
Muhammad Ishaque v. Ahsan Ahmad 1975 PLD Lah 1118. 127, 130, 136
Muhammad Ismail v. Lala Sheo-mukh Rai 1913 15 Bom LR 76 (PC). 36
Muhammad Khan v. Zarina Begum 1975 PLD AJK 27. 83, 126
Muhammad Latif v. Hanifan Bibi 1980 P.Cr.J. 123 (Lahore). 112
Muhammad Mustafizur Rahman Khan v. Rina Khan 1967 PLD Dacca 652. 32

Appendix I

Muhammad Nasir Siddique v. Muhammad Salahuddin Khan 1984 CLC (Lahore) 879. 114
Muhammad Nawaz v. Mst. Faiz Eliahi 1978 PLD Lah 38. 127
Muhammad Rafiq v. Ahmad Yar 1982 PLD Lah 825. 112, 114
Muhammad Salah-ud-Din Khan v. Muhammad Nazir Siddiqui 1984 SCMR 583. 114
Muhammad Sharif v. Khuda Bakhsh 1936 AIR Lah 683. 44
Muhammadi v. Jamil-ud-din 1960 PLD (WP) Kar 663. 68
Muhammed v. Sunabii 1976 KLT 711. 71
Mumtaz Mai v. Ghulam Nabi 1969 PLD Baghdad-ul Jadid 5. 127
Muni v. Habib Khan 1956 PLD (WP) Lah 403. 65
Nasim Akhtar v. The State 1968 PLD Lah 841. 42, 57
Nasir Ahmad Khan v. Asmat Jehan Begum 1967 PLD Pesh 328. 63
Nazar Muhammad v. Shahzada Begum 1974 PLD SC 22. 169
Niaz Bibi v. Fazal Ilahi 1953 PLD Lah 442. 97
Noor Khan v. Haq Nawaz 1982 PLD FSC 265. 112, 242
Noor Jehan Begum v. Eugene Tiscenko 1942 ILR 2 Cal 165. 213
Noor Muhammad v. The State 1976 PLD Lah 516. 44, 45
Nur Ali v. Malka Sultana 1961 PLD (WP) Lah 431. 171ff, 212
Nur-ud-Din Ahmad v. Masuda Khanam 1957 PLD Dacca 242. 68
Parveen Begum v. Muhammad Ali 1981 PLD Lah 116. 126
Parveen Chaudhry v. VIth Senior Civil Judge, Ist Class, Karachi 1976 PLD Kar 416. 116, 117
Princess Aiysha Yasmien Abbasi v. Maqbool Hussain Qureshi 1979 PLD Lah 241. 128, 129
[Mst.] Qadul v. Allah Bachaya 1973 PLD BJ 48. 53
Rabian Bibi v. Ghulam Ali 1941 AIR Lah 292.213
Rahim Bibi v. Chiragh Din 1930 AIR Lah 97. 38, 86
Rahim Jan v. Muhammad 1955 PLD Lah 122. 68
Rahimuddin v. Abdul Malik Bhuyia 1968 PLD Dacca 801. 98
Rakeya Bibi v. Anil Kumar Mukherji 1948 ILR 2 Cal 119. 30ff, 213
In the matter of Ram Kumari 1891 ILR 18 Cal 264. 50
Ranee Khujooroonissa v. Mussumut Roushun Jehan 1875/76 3 LR IA 291. 189
Rashid Ahmad v. Anisa Khatun 1931 59 LR IA 21. 50
Rashid Ahmad Khan v. Nasim Ara 1968 PLD Lah 93. 70
Rashid Bibi v. Tufail Muhammad 1941 AIR Lah 292.213
Rashida Begum v. Shahab Din 1960 2 PLD Lah 1142. 93
Rashidan Bibi v. Bashir Ahmad 1983 PLD Lah 549. 125
Resham Bibi v. Khuda Bakhsh 1938 ILR 19 Lah 277. 210

Appendix I

Resham Bibi v. *Muhammed Shafi* 1967 PLD AJK 32. 83
Robaba Khanum v. *Khodadad Boman Irani* 1948 ILR Bom 223. 30, 213
Ruckhsana Parvin v. *Sheikh Mohamed Hussein* 1976 79 Bom LR 123. 71
Sadik Hussen Khan v. *Hashim Ali Khan* 1915/16 43 LR IA 212. 91
Safia Begum v. *Abdul Rajack* 1945 AIR Bom 438. 147
Sahi Bi v. *Khalid Hussain* 1973 SCMR 577. 59
Sainapatti v. *Sainapatti* 1932 AIR Lah 116. 219
[Mst.] Sakina v. *The State* 1981 PLD FSC 320. 49
Sarabai v. *Rabiabai* 1906 ILR 30 Bom 537. 103
Sardar Nawazish Ali Khan v. *Sardar Ali Raza Khan* 1948 75 LR IA 62. 191, 193
Sarwar Yar Khan v. *Jawahar Devi* 1964 1 Andh WR 60. 209, 213
Sayeeda Khanam v. *Muhammad Sami* 1952 PLD Lah 113. 123, 124
Sayeda Khatoon v. *M. Obadiah* 1944/5 49 Cal WN 745. 31, 32
Shah Bano Begum v. *Iftikhar Muhammad Khan* 1956 PLD (WP) Kar 363. 64
Shahban Mohib v. *Hemraj Raghavji* 1942 AIR Sind 14. 201, 204
Shahzada Begum v. *Sh. Abdul Hamid* 1950 PLD Lah 504. 42, 56
Shamshad Ali Shah v. *Syed Hassan Shah* 1964 PLD SC 143. 147
Shamshad Begum v. *Abdul Haque* 1977 PLD Kar 855. 126
Sher Afzal v. *Shamin Firdaus* 1980 PLD SC 228. 42, 92
Sibt Muhammad v. *Muhammad Hameed* 1926 ILR 48 All 625. 38, 86
Siddiq v. *Sharfan* 1968 PLD Lah 411. 125, 126
Siddiqui v. *Family Judge Court III, Karachi* 1980 PLD Kar 477. 61
[Abdus] Sobhan Sarkar v. *Md. Abdul Ghani* 1973 25 Dacca LR 227. 118
The State v. *Tauqir Fatima* 1964 PLD (WP) Kar 306. 112
Sufuddin v. *Sureka* 1955 AIR Assam 153. 121
Sughran Mai v. *The State* 1980 PLD Lah 386. 42, 46, 56
Sulaiman v. *Iqbal* 1981 PLD AJK 33. 97
Syed Ali Nawaz Gardezi v. *Lt. Col. Muhammad Yusuf* 1963 PLD SC 51. 104, 110, 219, 220
Syed Faiz Ali Shah v. *Ghulam Abbas Shah* 1952 PLD AJK 32.213ff
Syed Yusuf Akbar Hussaini v. *Syed Mirturza Akbar Hussaini* (1983) 1 An WR 273. 66
Tahera Begum v. *Saleem Ahmad* 1970 PLD Kar 619. 97
Tajbi v. *Mowla Khan* 1917 ILR 41 Bom 485. 55
Tajbi v. *Nattar* 1940 AIR Mad 888. 64
Thilothama v. *Kunjappan* 1983 KLT 90. 72
Valanhiyal Kunhi Avulla v. *Eengahil Peetikayil Kunhi Avulla* 1964 AIR Ker 201. 145
Waghela Rajsanji v. *Sheikh Masludin* 1886/7 14 LR IA 89. 21, 29

Appendix I

Wahidunnisa v. Shubrattun 1870/71 6 Bengal LR 54. 141
Yusuf Abbas v. Ismat Mustafa 1968 PLD Kar 480. 183, 214ff
Yusuf Rowthan v. Surramma 1970 KLT 477. 135
In Re Zainab 1986 PLD Kar 269. 168
Zainab Bibi v. Bilquis Bibi 1981 PLD SC 56. 210, 213
Zarin Qaisha v. Arbub Wali Mohd 1976 PLD Pesh 128. 61
Zeenat Bi v. Zaman Mehdi 1956 PLD (WP) Lah 760. 189
Zobair Ahmad v. Jainandam Prasad Singh 1960 AIR Patna 147. 66
Zohara Khatoon v. Mhd. Ibrahim 1981 AIR SC 1243. 72
Zohra Begum v. Latif Ahmad Manawwar 1965 PLD (WP) Lah 695. 96, 97

Appendix II

TABLE OF MAJOR STATUTES ETC.

1.1 Indian Subcontinent

* 1772 Regulation II 25ff
* 1781 Regulation VI 26
* 1793 Regulation IV 26
* 1832 Regulation VII (Bengal Code)
  s.9 95, 211
* 1850 Caste Disabilities Removal Act 27, 95, 169, 173, 211
* 1869 Divorce Act 217
  s.2 218
  s.7 221
* 1871 Bengal Civil Courts Act 29
* 1872 Special Marriage Act 52
* 1872 Special Marriage Act 52
* 1872 Punjab Laws Act 32, 35, 220
* 1872 Contract Act 28
  s.23 84
* 1872 Evidence Act 28
  s.2(i) 84
  s.107 39
  s.108 39, 40
  s.112 38, 86
* 1872 Christian Marriage Act 217
* 1875 Majority Act 143
* 1876 Oudh Laws Act 62

Appendix II

* 1882 Transfer of Property Act 28, 194
* 1882 Trust Act 28
* 1887 Bengal, Agra and Assam Civil Courts Act 29
* 1890 Guardian and Wards Act
  s.7 93
  s.17 93
* 1898 Code of Criminal Procedure
  s.488 10
* 1913 Musalman Wakf Validating Act 28, 200
  s.2(i) 202
  s.3 201, 202
  s.4 202
  s.5 202
* 1929 Child Marriage Restraint Act 43
* 1936 General Clauses Amendment Act
  s.6(A) 88, 89
* 1937 Muslim Personal Law (Shariat) Application Act 28, 36, 202
* 1938 Repealing Act 88
* 1939 Dissolution of Muslim Marriages Act 28, 40
  s.2(i) 134
  s.2(ii) 135
  s.2(iii) 135
  s.2(iv) 135
  s.2(v) 135
  s.2(vi) 135
  s.2(vii) 44ff, 127, 136
  s.2(ix) 123ff
  s.4 210

India

* 1949 Shariat Act (Madras Act XVIII) 37
* 1954 Special Marriage Act 52, 83, 169, 212

Appendix II

* 1954 Waqf Act 203
* 1957 Wealth Tax Act 203
* 1963 Kerela Act XLII 37
* 1969 Foreign Marriages Act
  s.18(1) 221
  s.18(4) 221
* 1973 Code of Criminal Procedure
  s.125 71
  s.125(3) 73, 83
  s.127(3)(b) 71
  s.127(3)(c) 72
* 1977 Sri Pratap Jammu and Kashmir Laws Consolidation Act 36
* 1978 Child Marriage Restraint (Amendment) Act 43
* 1984 Waqf (Amendment) Act 203
* 1986 Muslim Women (Protection of Rights on Divorce) Act 74, 75

Pakistan

* 1948 W. Punjab Muslim Personal Law (Shariat) Application Act 37
* 1951 Punjab Muslim Personal Law (Shariat) Application (Amendment) Act 37, 87
* 1959 West Pakistan Waqf Properties Ordinance 206
* 1961 Muslim Family Laws Ordinance
  s.1(2) 216
  s.2(b) 116
  s.4 182, 214, 240ff
  s.5 42
  s.6 81
  s.7 109ff, 217
  s.8 123ff
  s.9 70
  s.10 64
  s.12 43
  s.13 44

Appendix II

* 1962 West Pakistan Muslim Personal Law (Shariat) Application Act 37
* 1963 Caste Disabilities Removal (Amendment) Act 169, 211
* 1964 West Pakistan Family Lands Act 70
* 1973 Constitution of Islamic Republic of Pakistan
  Art.203(B) 114
  Art.203(C) 239, 244
  Art.203(D) 183, 239
  Art.227 113
* 1976 Dowry and Bridal Gifts (Restriction) Act 63
* 1979 Offence of Zina Ordinance 106, 112
  s.5(2)(a) 241
  s.6(3)(a)
  s.8(2) 241
* 1979 Offence of Qazf Ordinance
  s.3 242
  s.14(1) 105
  s.14(2) 105
  s.14(3) 105
* 1983 Muslim Personal Law (Shariat) Application Act 37

1.2 England

* 1971 Recognition of Divorces and Legal Separations Act
  ss.2-5 224
  s.6 224
  s.8 224, 230ff
* 1973 Matrimonial Causes Act
* 1973 Domicile and Matrimonial Proceedings Act
  s.16 224
* 1984 Matrimonial and Family Proceedings Act 232
* 1986 Family Law Act Preface

Appendix II

1.3 Elsewhere

* 1850 Ottoman Commercial Code 234
* 1858 Ottoman Penal Code 234
* 1876 Ottoman Majalla (The Civil Code) 234
* 1879 Ottoman Code of Commercial Procedure 234
* 1917 Ottoman Law of Family Rights 83
  Art.119 131
  Art.121 131
  Art.126 131
* 1920 Egyptian Law No. 25
  Art.4 132
* 1929 Egyptian Law No. 25
  Art.1 106
  Art.3 106
  Art.4 106
  Art.5 106
  Art.6 131
  Art.9 131
  Art.10 133
  Art.12 131
  Art.13 131
  Art.15 86
  Art.17 86
* 1946 Egyptian Law No. 71 (law of testamentary succession) 178, 179ff
* 1951 Wakf Commissioners Ordinance (East Africa)
  s.3 204
  s.4 204
* 1951 Jordanian Law of Family Rights 78, 79, 132
* 1952 Egyptian Law No. 180 (law on Waqf) 206
* 1953 Syrian law of Personal Status
  Art.17 80
  Art.92 107
  Art.117 107

Appendix II

* 1956 Tunisian Code of Personal Status
  Arts.18-33 80, 108, 137
* 1958 Moroccan Code of Personal Status 79, 80
* 1959 Iraqi law of Personal Status
  Art.4 79
  Art.5 79
  Art.6 79
* 1963 Iraqi law of Personal Status (amendment) 179
* 1964 Wakf Commissioners Act (East Africa) 205
* 1967 Iranian Family Protection Act
  Art.11 108
  Art.14 79
  Art.17 109
* 1975 Somali Law No. 23 (family law)
  Art.13 80
  Art.36 108
  Arts.42ff. 133ff
  Arts.62ff. 97
  Art.110 92
* 1975 Iranian Family Law 79
* 1975 Indonesian Family Law 80
* 1976 Jordanian Family Law 78, 79, 133
* 1979 Egyptian Law No. 44 (Family Law Reforms) 107, 133
* 1980 Kuwait Civil Code 236
* 1984 Algerian Family Law 81, 108, 133
* 1986 UAE Law of Civil Transactions 245

Appendix III

Select Bibliography

Extensive bibliographies appear in J. Schacht, *An Introduction to Islamic Law* (Oxford, 1964 reprinted 1982), K.Hodkinson, *Muslim Family Law; A Sourcebook* (Beckenham, 1984), J.L.Esposito, *Women in Muslim Family Law* (Syracuse, 1982), and J.Makdisi, 'Islamic Law Bibliography' (1986) vol.78 *American Association of Law Libraries* pp. 103 ff.

A major journal devoted to Islamic law themes is the *Islamic and Comparative Law Quarterly* published from New Delhi. The first edition was published in 1981 and the editor is Professor Tahir Mahmood.

1.1 Preparatory Reading

* Anderson, J.N.D. *Islamic Law in the Modern World*, (London, 1959).

* Anderson, J.N.D. 'The Significance of Islamic Law in the World Today', *American Journal of Comparative Law*, (1960) vol. 9 p. 187.

* Anderson, J.N.D. 'The Eclipse of the Patriarchal Family in Contemporary Islamic Law' in J.N.D. Anderson (ed.), *Family Law in Asia and Africa*, (London, 1965).

* Coulson, N.J. *Conficts and Tensions in Islamic Jurisprudence* (Chicago,1959).

* Coulson, N.J. 'Islamic Law' in J.D.M. Derrett (ed.), *An Introduction to Legal Systems*. (London, 1968) p. 54.

* Levy, R. *The Social Structure of Islam*. (Cambridge, 1957).

* Schacht, J. 'Islamic Law in Contemporary States', *American Journal of Comparative Law*, (1959) vol. 8 p. 133.

Appendix III

1.2 Introduction to Civil Law

* Nabil A.Saleh. *Unlawful Gain and Legitimate Profit in Islamic Law*, (Cambridge, 1986).
* Coulson, N.J. *Commercial Law in the Gulf States*, (London, 1984).

1.3 Textbooks on Family Law – General

* Ameer Ali, S. *Mohammedan Law* (2 vols.), vol. I, 5th edition, Raja Said Akbar Khan (ed.) (Lahore, 1976); vol II, 7th edition, Raja Said Akbar Khan (ed.) (Lahore, 1976).
* Anderson, J.N.D. *Islamic Law in Africa*, (London, 1954).
* de Bellefonds, Y.L. *Traite de droit musulman compare*, (Paris,1965).
* Chehata, C. *Droit Musulman*, (Paris, 1969).
* Fyzee, A.A.A. *Outlines of Muhammadan Law.* 4th edition, (Oxford, 1974).
* Khadduri, M.K. and Liebesny, H. *Law in the Middle East*, (Washington, 1955).
* Mahmood, T. *The Muslim Law of India*, 2nd ed., (Allahabad, 1982).
* Mulla, D.F. *Principles of Mahomedan Law*, 18th ed., (Bombay, 1976).
* Schacht, J. *An Introduction to Islamic Law*, (Oxford 1964, reprinted 1982).
* Tanzil-ur-Rahman. *A Code of Muslim Personal Law*, 2 vols. (Karachi, 1978, 1980).

1.4 Law Reform

* Anderson, J.N.D. and Coulson, N.J. 'Islamic Law in Contemporary Cultural Change', *Saeculum*, (Munich) (1967) vol. 18 p. 13.
* Anderson, J.N.D. *Law Reform in the Muslim World*, (London, 1976)
* Esposito, J.L. *Women in Muslim Family Law*, (Syracuse, 1982).

Appendix III

* Liebesny, H.J. *The Law of the Near and Middle East*, (Albany, 1975).
* Mahmood, T. *Family Law Reform in the Muslim World*, (New Delhi, 1972).

1.5 History and Jurisprudence

* Aghnides, N. *Mohammedan Theories of Finance*, (Lahore, 1961; reprinted from New York ed. 1916).
* Coulson, N.J. *A History of Islamic Law*, (Edinburgh, (1964, reprinted 1978).
* A.Rahman I. Doi. *Introduction to the Hadith*, (Sevenoaks,1981).
* Faruki, K. *Islamic Jurisprudence*, (Karachi, 1962).
* Fyzee, A.A.A. *A Modern Approach to Islam*, (Bombay, 1963).
* Goldziher, I. *Muslim Studies* 2 vols. (Albany, 1967 and 1971).
* Goldizer, I. *Introduction to Islamic Theology and Law*, (translation of German 1910 edition. Princeton, 1979).
* Mahmasani, Subhi. *Falsafat al-Tashri fi al-Islam* (The Philosophy of Jurisprudence in Islam), translated by Farhat J.Ziadeh, (Leiden, 1961).
* Makdisi, G. *The Rise of Colleges: Institutions of Learning in Islam and the West*, (Edinburgh, 1981).
* Rahim, A. *The Principles of Muhammadan Jurisprudence*, (Madras, 1911).
* Schacht, J. *The Origins of Muhammadan Jurisprudence*, (Oxford, 1967, reprinted from Oxford, 1950).

1.6 Reception of English Law in India

* Ahmad, M.B. *The Administration of Justice in Medieval India*, (Aligarh, 1941).
* Derrett, J.D.M. *Religion, Law and the State in India*, (London, 1968).

Appendix III

* Derrett, J.D.M. 'Justice, Equity and Good Conscience' in J.N.D. Anderson (ed.), *Changing Law in Developing Countries*, (London, 1963).
* Fawcett, C. *The First Century of British Justice in India*, (Oxford, 1934).
* Fyzee, A.A.A. *Cases in the Muhammadan law of India and Pakistan*, (Oxford, 1965), [see especially the Introduction].
* Mahmood, T. *Muslim Personal Law: Role of the State in the Indian SubContinent*, (Nagar, 1983).
* Rankin, C. 'Custom in the Muslim Personal Law of India', *Transactions of the Grotius Society,* (1939) vol. 25 p. 89.
* Setalvad, M.C. *The Common Law in India*, (London, 1960).
* Setalvad, M.C. *The Role of English Law in India*, (Jerusalem, 1966)

1.7 Marriage and Divorce

* Ahmed, K.N. *Muslim Law of Divorce*, (Islamabad, 1972).
* Ali, S.A. *Law of Family Courts*, (Karachi, 1975).
* Anderson, J.N.D. 'Irregular and Void Marriages in Hanafi law', *Bulletin of SOAS,* (1950) vol. XIII p. 357.
* Coulson, N.J. and Hinchcliffe, D. 'Women and Law Reform in Contemporary Islam.' in L.Beck and N.Keddie (eds) *Women in the Muslim World*, (Harvard, 1978).
* Esposito, J.L. *Women in Muslim Family Law*, (Syracuse, 1982).
* Hinchcliffe, D. 'Polygamy in Traditional and Contemporary Islamic Law', *Islam and the Modern Age*, (1970) vol. I no.3 p. 13.
* Hinchcliffe, D. 'The widow's dower debt in India', *Islam and the Modern Age,* (1973) vol. IV p. 5.
* Hussain, F. (ed.) *Muslim Women*, (London, 1984).
* Smith, D. (ed.) *South Asian Politics and Religion*, Chs. 16,19, (Princeton, 1966).

Appendix III

1.7.1 Particular Countries

Pakistan

* Coulson, N.J. 'Reform of Family Law in Pakistan', *Studia Islamica Fasc.* (1957) vol. VII.
* Esposito, J.L. 'Perspectives on Islamic Law Reform: The Case of Pakistan', (1980) vol.13 *J.I.L.P.* p. 217.
* Hinchcliffe, D. 'Divorce in Pakistan: Judicial Reform', *Journal of Islamic and Comparative Law* (1968) p. 13.
* Jahan, R. in Ruby Rohlich-Leavitt (ed.), *Women Cross-Culturally*, (The Hague, 1975).
* Pearl, D.S. 'Family law in Pakistan', *Journal of Family Law* (1969) vol.9 p. 165.

Iran

* Hinchcliffe, D. 'The Iranian Family Protection Act', *ICLQ* (1968) vol 17 p. 516.

Iraq

* Anderson, J.N.D. 'A Law of Personal Status for Iraq', *ICLQ* (1960) vol 16 p. 542.
* Anderson, J.N.D. 'Changes in the Law of Personal Status in Iraq', *ICLQ* (1963) vol 12 p. 1026.

North Africa

* Anderson, J.N.D. 'Reforms in Family Law in Morocco', *Journal of African Law'*, (1958) vol 2 p. 140.
* Anderson, J.N.D. 'The Tunisian Law of Personal Status', *ICLQ* (1958) vol 7 p. 262.

Appendix III

1.8 International and Internal Conflict of Laws

* Basu, K.K. 'Hindu-Muslim Marriages', *Indian Law Review* (1948/9) vol 2 p. 249.

* Pearl, D.S. *Interpersonal Conflict of Laws in India, Pakistan and Bangladesh*, (London and Bombay, 1981).

* Pearl, D.S. *Family Law and the Immigrant Communities*, (Bristol, 1986).

1.9 Inheritance

* Abdulaziz Mohammed Zaid. *The Islamic Law of Bequest*, (London, 1986).

* Anderson, J.N.D. 'Recent reforms in the Islamic Law of Inheritance', *ICLQ* (1965) vol 14 p. 349.

* Chowdhury, A.B.M. Sultanul Alam. 'Problems of Representation in the Muslim Law of Inheritance', *Islamic Studies* (1964) vol 3 p. 375.

* Coulson, N.J. *Succession in the Muslim Family*, (Cambridge, 1971).

* Faruki, K. 'Orphaned Grandchildren in Islamic Succession Law', *Islamic Studies* (1965) vol 4 p. 253.

1.10 Waqfs

* Anderson, J.N.D. 'Waqfs in East Africa', *Journal of African Law*, (1959) vol 3 p. 152.

* Habibullah, Syed A.M. *The Law of Wakfs*, (Calcutta, 1976).

Appendix IV

Index and Glossary

'Abbas 176
The Prophet's uncle.
Abbasid dynasty 8, 10, 16
Abu Bakr 5, 6, 161
The first Caliph after the Prophet.
Abu Dawud (as-Sijistani) 12 16, 47, 67, 68, 101, 196, 197
He was responsible for one of the six authoritative collections of Hadith of the Sunni schools.
Abu Hanifa 11
The leading jurist from Kufa. He died in 767 A.D.
Abu Laila
An early scholar from Kufa. He was also a judge. Schacht says of Abu Laila's work: 'taken as a whole [it] shows a considerable amount of technical legal thought, but is generally of a primitive kind, somewhat clumsy and untrained, and therefore shortsighted and often unfortunate in its results.' Origins p.290.
Abu Talib 176
The paternal uncle of the Prophet
Abu Yusuf 10, 16, 46, 67, 101, 196, 198,199, 201
A disciple of Abu Hanifa. He was appointed as Chief Qadi by Caliph Harun. He died in 799 AD.
acknowledgement 90ff
'adala 19
A witness must possess religious probity before his evidence can be received by the Qadi in court. 'adala refers to this quality; 'adl is a person who has this quality.
administration of an estate 138ff
adoption 1, 36, 91, 92
Afghanistan 16
Africa, Central 16
Africa, East 16
Africa, West 16

Appendix IV

agnatic inheritance 2, 148ff, 174ff
Agoronomus 7
A Byzantine market inspector.
Ahl al-Hadith 11
Those who give priority to the Traditions of the Prophet over the usage in the community.
Ahl al-Kitab 7
Those who follow one of the revealed religions, namely Judaism or Christianity.
Ahl al-ra'y 11
Those who accept the right of the jurist to solve a particular problem based on his own independent reasoning.
'A'isha 1
The Prophet's wife.
Akhbar 20
The Moghul Emperor.
Algeria 16, 81, 133
'Ali 5, 6, 7, 17, 176
The fourth Caliph.
Ameer Ali, Syed 51, 209, 210, 215
Anderson, J.N.D. 47, 135, 178, 203, 236, 237, 244
Anglo-Hindu law 24
apostacy 95, 169, 209ff, 212
Arabia 2, 4, 16, 77, 148
Arabs 148, 243
arbitration council 70, 82, 109ff
'ariyya 189, 191
A transfer by way of intervivos gift of the usus (income) of property.
'asaba 148ff
Agnatic relatives.
'asaba bi ghayriha 157
The daughter of the deceased, when she inherits with the son.
'asaba bi nafsihi 157
The son of the deceased, when he inherits with the daughter.
Assam 36
Aurangzeb 20, 235
The Moghul Emperor who ordered the collection of opinions and precepts of law known as the Fatawa Alamgiri.

Appendix IV

'awl 168
The method by which a distribution of property to heirs adding up to more than is available from the estate can be reduced by a process of proportionate reduction.
'ayn 189
The corpus (substance) of property.

Balkan countries 16
Bangladesh *passim*
al-Baqir, Muhamad 17
An early Shi'i Imam.
Basra 9
Basu K.K. 33
batil 14, 46ff
A void transaction.
bay' 14
The contract of sale.
Bengal 36
Bombay 21ff
Buddhists 51, 52
Bukhari 12
al-Bukhari died in 870 AD. He compiled one of the six authoritative collections of hadith of the Sunni schools.
Byzantium, Byzantine 6, 19

Cairo 16
Calcutta 24
Ceylon 16
Charles II 21
Chehata, C. 236
Christians, Christianity 7, 51, 52
consummation, definition of 50
consummation, failure to consummate 130
conversion to Islam 211ff
Coulson, N.J. 3, 5, 12, 13, 18, 107, 138
custody of children 92ff

Appendix IV

cyprès 202
The method by which the income from Waqf can be transferred to a similar charitable purpose, if the purpose specified in the waqfnama has disappeared or does not exist.
Cyprus 16

Damascus 9
Dar al-Islam 30, 212
The land of Islam governed by Islamic law.
Dar al-harb 7
The land of war.
darar 131
cruelty or harm.
Dawad ibn Khalaf 16
The founder of the Zahiri school. This school was literalist in its interpretation of the law. He died in 883 AD.
Derrett, J.D.M. 23, 24
Dhimma 7
An obligation.
Dhimmi 6, 7
A person who is protected by the Muslim state.
distant kindred 11, 149, 168
divorce *passim*
Diwani, Dewan 25, 26
diya 234
Financial compensation (blood money) which can be paid by relatives of a convicted person to the relatives of the victim as satisfaction.
dower 3, 10, 47, 60ff
dower, proper 47, 60
The sum of money worked out as the appropriate amount to be paid by the husband to the wife in a case where the sum is not specified.
dowry 63

East India Company 21ff
Egypt 16, 55
Eritrea 16

Appendix IV

evidence, rules of 86ff

fasid 46ff
irregular.
Faruki, K. 178
faskh 130ff
A judicial rescission of a marriage.
Fatawa Alamgiri 21, 235
The collection of excerpts from Hanafi texts prepared in 1663 AD under the authority of the Emperor Aurangzeb.
fiqh 13, 237
jurisprudence.
fuduli 98
A meddler. Someone who interferes in the administration and transfer of property belonging to another.
Fyzee, A.A.A. 76

Goldhizer, I. 4, 12
Greeks 7, 207
Gulf States 16

hadana 92ff
Care and control of children.
hadd, hudud 19, 59, 61
The specified fixed penalty laid down for illicit sexual relations, slanderous allegations of unchastity, theft in certain cases, wine-drinking, armed robbery and apostacy. Pakistan has introduced the penalties in the first five instances by Ordinances IV,VI,VII, and VIII of 1979.
Hadeya 21, 235
A school text book compiled in the latter part of the twelfth century and translated into English from a Persian version.
Hadith 4, 5, 9, 10, 13
Report of a precedent established by the Prophet, or his immediate followers. The 'Traditions of the Prophet.'

Appendix IV

Haj 202
Pilgrimage to Mecca.
Hanafi school, law 16, *passim*
Hanbali school, law 16, 49, 81, 83, 143
Harbi 7
A person who is a polytheist and against whom the Muslim is at war.
hasan 14
to make good.
Hebrews 7
hiba 189
Intervivos gift of the corpus (substance) of the property.
hiba bi'l-iwad 193, 194
An intervivos gift with a return.
hiba-i-muddat 76
A gift of the period of time still remaining in the mut'a marriage.
hiba bi-sharti'l-iwad 194
A gift made with a stipulation for a return.
Himariyya Case 5, 6, 165
A decision of 'Umar permitting full brothers (the agnatic heirs) to share equally with the uterine brothers (the Qur'anic heirs).
Hinchcliffe, D. 65, 77, 125
Hindu law 173, 207
Hindus, Hinduism 7, 51, 52
hire 15
hisba 7
Safeguarding the standards of religious morality.
hiyal 193, 206
legal fictions
however low so ever 150
A phrased used to describe lineal descendants of a particular line; son, son's son, son's son's son, etc., and son's daughter, son's son's daughter, etc.

Ibrahim Nakha'i 10
Schacht refers to this man as 'a specialist in religious law'. Many Traditions are ascribed to Ibrahim Nakha'i.
'idda 3, 47, 53, 54, 69ff, 100ff, 169
The period of time following the dissolution of a marriage by divorce or by death during which the divorcee or the widow is not permitted to remarry.

ijab 41, 189
An offer.
ijma' 9, 11, 16
consensus of opinion
ijra 76
A reward paid by the husband to his wife in a mut'a marriage.
ijtihad 14, 180, 235
The exercise of human reasoning to search for the rule of Shari'a.
ikrah 64, 121
duress.
ila' 104, 105
A variant form of repudiation
Imam, Imamate 17
India *passim*
Indonesia 16
international conflict of laws 207, 214ff
interpersonal conflict of laws 207
interpersonal conflict of laws between two classes 208
interpersonal conflict of laws within one class 207, 208ff
Iqbal, Muhammad 237
iqrar 90ff
The doctrine of acknowledgement. It is used in the context of the acknowledgement by a man that he is the father of his child.
Iran 16
Iraq 16
Iraqis 10, 15
Isma'il 17
The founder of the Isma'ili school of Shi'i Islam.
Isma'ilis 17
isnad 4, 5, 11, 12, 13
The chain of authority for a hadith.
Israel 16, 78, 131
istihsan 14
The exercise of discretion (Ra'y) because of the appropriateness of the decision.
istislah 14, 15
The exercise of discretion (Ra'y) because of the public interest.
Ithna 'Asharis 17, 146

Appendix IV

iwad 188, 193
Goods or payment made from A to B in return for goods transferred by B to A.

Ja'afar al-Sadiq 17
A leading Shi'i Imam.
Jaina 52
jam' 54, 55
unlawful conjunction of two partners making a marriage void (batil).
Jammu and Kashmir 36
Jewish law 7
Jews. Judaism 7, 52
jizya 6, 7
A poll tax.
Jordan 16
Judicial Committee of the Privy Council 21
'justice, equity and good conscience' 23, 25, 26, 29ff
'justice and right' 24ff, 29ff

kafa'a 55
Social and economic equality necessary between spouses.
Kenya 203ff
khalwat 49, 54
A period of privacy as between members of the opposite sex.
kharaj 6, 7
The land tax.
khiyar 44ff, 55, 122, 145
An option.
khiyar al-bulugh 44ff, 55
The option of puberty.
Khojas 34
'*A small caste in Western India who appear to have originally come from Sind or Kutch and who, by their own traditions, which are probably correct, were converted to Hinduism about 400 years ago.*' cf. Perry C.J. in the Khoja and Memons Case 1847 Perry's Oriental Cases p. 110.

Appendix IV

khul' 121ff
A consensual divorce, the wife usually providing compensation to the husband in return for her release from the marriage.
Kitabiyya 29ff, 50, 211
girl who follows one of the revealed religions; namely Judaism or Christianity.
Kufa 7, 9, 10, 11, 14, 55
Kutch 34
Kuwait 181, 236

Lebanon 131
legitimate, legitimacy 38ff
li'an 86ff, 105
A method by which the husband may repudiate paternity of a child born to his wife.
Libya 16, 106
Liebesny, H.J. 234

Madras 24, 35, 37
Magians 7, 51
mahr 3, 10, 60ff
The dower.
mahr al-mithl 60, 64
The 'proper dower'.
mahr, deferred 63ff
mahr, prompt 63ff
mahr, specified 61ff
maintenance 68ff
Ibn Maja 12
Abu Abdi'illah Muhammed Ibn Maja was responsible for one of the six authoritative collections of hadith of the Sunni schools.
Majalla 234ff
The Ottoman Civil Code 1876.
Malaysia 16, 51
Malik Ibn-Anas 11, 134
He was the foremost Medinan scholar. He died in 796 AD.

Appendix IV

Malik's rule 165
This name is given to a rule of succession law which is developed from the Himariyya decision regarding the distribution of the estate when the deceased is survived by a paternal grandfather as well as by uterine and full brothers.
Maliki school, law 16, 43, 49, 55, 61ff, 69, 125, 131, 166
Manfa'a 191
Usufruct (income) of property.
Mappillas 35
marad al-mawt 138, 146ff, 170
death sickness
marriage *passim*
marriage guardian 43ff
marriage, batil 46ff
Void marriage.
marriage, fasid 46ff
irregular marriage.
marriage, sahih 46ff
valid marriage.
marriage stipulations 81ff
maslihat al mashru'a 79
lawful interest.
Ibn Mas'ud 10
A companion of the Prophet. Many hadith are ascribed to him. Schacht argues that many of the legal traditions ascribed to Ibn Mas'ud are not genuine.
Maulvis 26
Experts in Muslim law appointed to advise the courts in British India.
Mayor's Court 25
Mazalim 18
Jurisdiction exercised by the executive branch of Government to investigate complaints.
Mecca 9
Medina 7, 9, 10, 11
Memons 34
There are two groups of Memons; the Halai Memons from Bombay who are governed by Hanafi law, and the Cutchi Memons (a former Hindu community) who also follow the Hanafi school of Sunni law.
Minbariyya case 6
A decision of 'Ali given from the pulpit concerning the procedure for reducing shares allotted by the Qur'an when they add up to more than unity.

Appendix IV

Mofussil 25
The area of India outside the three Presidency Towns of Bombay, Calcutta, and Madras.
Moghul dynasty 20
Morocco 16
Mu'awiya 17
The founder of the Umayyad dynasty in 661 AD.
mubah 91
Activities towards which Islam is indifferent.
mudda'a 'allayhi 18
The defendant.
mudda'i 18
The plaintiff.
Musa al-Kazim 17
A Shi'i Imam of the Ithna 'Ashari sect.
musahara 48
Prohibited to intermarry because of a relationship by affinity.
Muhammas b. Qazim 20
The Muslim conqueror of Sind.
mubara'a 127
A consensual divorce where both parties desire a separation.
Muhtasib 7
An Umayyad official responsible for market affairs and for safeguarding the standards of religious morality (hisba).
Mujtahid 14
A person who exercises ijtihad (the search for the meaning of the Shari'a).
Mullah 41
A Muslim religious leader.
Muqallid 14
A person who is bound to observe the principles of taqlid (imitation).
musha' 193
Property which is jointly owned by two or more persons.
Muslim Ibnu'l-Hajjaj 12
The author of one of the six authoritative collections of hadith of the Sunni schools.
Musta'min 7
A foreigner who is granted protection whilst he remains on the territory of the Muslim state.

Appendix IV

mut'a marriage 76
A marriage contracted for a specified time period. Such a marriage is not recognised as a valid marriage amongst the Sunni communities.
mut'a (a present) 65
A small present granted in certain circumstances by husbands to their divorced wives.
mutawali 195ff
The manager of waqf property.

nafaqa 68ff
'maintenance and support.' The husband is under a legal duty to provide nafaqa to his wife (or wives).
nasab 47, 48
Blood relations.
nashiza, nashuz 59ff, 70
A 'disobedient wife.' If the wife is disobedient, then the husband no longer is under a legal duty to provide her with nafaqa.
Nasa'i 12
He was responsible for one of the six authoritative collections of hadith of the sunni schools.
nass 16
The text of the Qur'an.
Nigeria 16
nikah 41ff, *passim*
The Muslim marriage.
nikahnama 62
The marriage contract.

Ottoman Empire 16

Piae Causae 194
A religious trust in Byzantine law.
Pakistan *passim*

Appendix IV

Panchayats 23
Caste courts.
Pandits 26
Experts in Hindu law appointed to advise the courts in British India.
Parsees, Pasi 30, 52
Persia 6, 19
Personality of laws 7
Philippines 16
pledge 140
polygamy 1, 77ff, 236
polytheist 211
Portugal, Portuguese law 21
Presidency Towns 25
Calcutta, Madras, and Bombay.
puberty 42
Punjab 35
purdah, pardahnashin 143
The seclusion of a woman. A woman who observes the system of strict seclusion is called, on the subcontinent, a pardahnashin.

qabda 190
The delivery of possession to the donee. Qabda is a necessary part of a valid donation.
qabul 41, 188
Acceptance.
qadhf 1, 6, 242
A slanderous allegation of illicit sexual intercourse.
Qadi, Qadis' courts 7, 8, 10, 14, 18ff
qiyas 10, 12, 13
Reasoning based on analogical deduction.
Qur'an *passim*
The translations in this book are taken from Abdullah Yusaf Ali (first edition, Lahore 1934). Sura refers to the Chapters which are invariably called after some key word appearing in the text.

Appendix IV

```
Sura II v. 180    144, 149, 180
Sura II v. 215    188, 194
Sura II v. 221    51
Sura II v. 229    124, 125
Sura II v. 241    107
Sura III v. 80    209
Sura III vv. 104, 110    7
Sura IV v. 3    3, 77, 238
Sura IV vv. 7-14    2, 150, 156
Sura IV v. 19    3
Sura IV v. 23    54
Sura IV v. 24    76
Sura IV v. 34    68
Sura IV v. 35    131, 134
Sura IV v. 37    108
Sura IV v. 90    209
Sura V v. 59    209
Sura XVI v. 108    209
Sura XVII v. 32    58
Sura XXII v. 17    7
Sura XXIV v. 2-3    59, 243
Sura XXIV v. 4    1, 6
Sura XXXIII v. 37    1, 91
```

Qur'anic heirs 150ff
Qur'aysh 55
The tribe of the Prophet.

rada'a 49
Marriage prohibition based on the foster-mother (milk) relationship.
radd 167
Return. The distribution of the remainder of an estate to the Qur'anic heirs in proportion to their interest. The surviving spouse only benefits in the absence of other heirs.
Rahman, Fazlur 77
Rajasthan 36
rajih 100
Preferable.
Rankin, C. 34

Appendix IV

ra'y 7, 9, 10, 12, 13
Juristic reasoning.
Restitution of conjugal rights 59, 60, 67
riba 261
Speculative profit, which would be limited in a narrow definition to usury in its most blatant form, but which would be wide enough to cover fixed or floating interest in a more expansive definition.
Roman law 7, 23

Sa'ad's case 3
This case is the basis of the relationship and the priority as between the Qur'anic and the Agnatic heirs.
sabab 55
Prohibition of a marriage because of a cause other than consanguinity.
sadakah 192
A donation to charity.
Sahib ar-radd 18
An official who heard cases which were not dealt with by the Qadi primarily because the rules of evidence would in all probability prevent a conviction. He often dealt with criminal matters, although his jurisdiction was not exclusively in this field. There was also another official, the wali al-jara'im, who exercised jurisdiction in criminal matters as a representative of the executive.
sahih 46ff
valid.
St. John, Dr. 23
Sale 15
salih 15
In the general interest.
al-Sanhuri, Dr. 236
Saudi Arabia 7, 16
Schacht, J. 1, 4, 5, 8, 9, 12, 13
Shafi'i school, law 16, 30, 43, 49, 51, 97
Shafi'i 11-13, 15, 55, 238
'The colossus of Islamic legal history.' Coulson, History p. 55.
shahada 18
Oral evidence.
Shari'a (Shariat) *passim*

Appendix IV

Muhammad ash-Shaybani 46, 67, 195
He died in 804 AD. Coulson refers to him as the 'true founder of Hanafi law.' History p. 51.
Shi'i law 17ff, 51, 75ff, 104ff, 145ff, 174ff
shubha 46, 47, 56ff
Semblance of a valid marriage.
shurut 19, 56, 57
Formularies. Also used to express Conditions.
shurut al-in'iqad 56, 57
Conditions as to form.
shurut al-luzum 56, 57
Conditions as to the binding nature.
shurut al-madaidh 56, 57
Conditions as to effect.
shurut al-sihha 56, 57
Conditions as to essence.
shurut al-sijill 56, 57
Conditions as to registration.
Sikh 52
Sind 20, 34
Singapore 16
siyasa shar'iyya 19, 238
The right of the Executive branch of the Government to 'complete the Sharia' by regulations of an administrative kind.
slaves 11
Somalia 16
succession, intestate 148ff
succession, testate 148ff
Sudan 16
as-suma't 62, 63
A private agreement for the payment of a small sum by way of dower, even though there is a publicly acclaimed agreement for a larger sum.
Sunna 4, 5, 9, 10, 13, *passim*
In its classical form, Sunna refers to the practice of the Prophet.
Sunni law, Sunni Muslims *passim*
Syria 16

Appendix IV

tafwid at-talaq (talaq i-tafwid) 120
Delegated talaq.
tahdid 46, 121
A threat.
takhayyur 237
An eclectic choice from divergent juristic opinions.
talaq 3, 50, 100ff
The unilateral pronouncement of divorce by the husband.
talaq al-bid'a 101
A disapproved form of talaq.
talaq kubra 101
A talaq pronounced for the third time.
talaq sughra 101
A talaq pronounced once only.
talaq as-sunnah 100
The approved form of talaq.
talaq as-sunnah (ahsan) 100
The most approved form of talaq.
talaq as-sunnah (hasan) 101
The next most approved form of talaq.
talfiq 237
'Piecing together' bits and pieces from different sources. Talfiq represents takhayyur (the eclectic choice) at its most extreme.
ta'liq at-talaq 120
A suspended talaq; to take effect only upon the occurrence of a particular happening in the future.
Tanzimat Reforms 234
The Ottoman reforms of the nineteenth century.
taqlid 10, 14, 237
Imitation.
ta'sib 155, 160
The system known as 'agnatisation' by which, in certain circumstances in the law of inheritance, a Qur'anic heir inherits agnatically.
ta'zir 19, 242
Discretionary punishments.
Tirmidhi 12
He was responsible for one of the six authoritative collections of hadith of the Sunni schools.
tuhr 100
The period of a woman's cycle when she is free from her menstrual flow.

Tunisia 16, 78
Turkey 16, 78, 235

UAE 245
UK 223
'Ulema 7
Religious leaders.
'Umar 5, 6, 76, 156, 165
The second Caliph.
'Umariyyatan 156
The decision of 'Umar relating to the distribution of the estate when the mother, the father and the spouse relict are in competition.
Umayyad dynasty 6, 7, 8, 9, 12, 17, 104
Umma 3, 13, 16
The community of Islam.
United Provinces 36
usul al-fiqh 13, 237
The sources of law.
'Uthman 5
The third caliph.

vakil 41
An agent or attorney.

al-walad l'il-firash 85ff
Legitimacy by birth.
wali 44, 55, 97ff
The guardian.
waqf, wakf 74, 75, 193ff
A charitable settlement. The usufruct is used for a charitable purpose and the property becomes inalienable.
waqf dhurri 194
A family waqf.

waqf khayri 194
An immediate charitable waqf.
waqif 194
The settlor of the waqf.
waqfnama 197
The waqf document.
Warren Hastings 25
wet nurse 15
wilayat al-ijbar, jabr 98
The guardian over the person.
wills, bequests 143ff

Zahiri school 16
Zayd 1
The adopted son of the Prophet.
Zayd (son of Zayn al-Abidin) 17
One of the sons of the fourth Shi'i Imam, Zayn al Abidin. Some followed Zayd as the new Imam and he became the founder of the Zaydi sect.
Zaydis 17
Zayn al-Abidin 17
The fourth Shi'i Imam.
zihar 104, 105
An impious declaration.
zina 46, 59, 105, 241
Illicit sexual relations.
Zoroastrians 51
Zwemer, S.M. 209